LEE'S
TERRIBLE
SWIFT SWORD

LEE'S TERRIBLE SWIFT SWORD

From Antietam to Chancellorsville
An Eyewitness History

RICHARD WHEELER

HarperPerennial
A Division of HarperCollinsPublishers

HarperCollins books may be purchased for educational, business, or sales promotional use. For information please write: Special Markets Department, HarperCollins Publishers, Inc., 10 East 53rd Street, New York, NY 10022.

First HarperPerennial edition published 1993.

Designed by Irving Perkins Associates

The Library of Congress has catalogued the hardcover edition as follows:

Wheeler, Richard.
    Lee's terrible swift sword : from Antietam to Chancellorsville : an eyewitness history / Richard Wheeler.—1st ed.
        p.   cm.
    Sequel to: Sword over Richmond.
    Includes bibliographical references (p.   ) and index.
    ISBN 0-06-016650-9
    1. United States—History—Civil War, 1861–1865—Campaigns. 2. Antietam, Battle of, 1862.   3. Fredericksburg (Va.), Battle of, 1862.   4. Chancellorsville (Va.), Battle of, 1863.   5. Lee, Robert E. (Robert Edward), 1807–1870.   I. Title.
E470.2.W47   1992
973.7'3—dc20   91-58378

ISBN 0-06-092244-3 (pbk.)

93 94 95 96 97 PS/CW 10 9 8 7 6 5 3 2 1

To my editor, Buz Wyeth,
who conceived the idea

Contents

vii

List of Illustrations

List of Maps

Preface

LEE'S TERRIBLE SWIFT SWORD continues my series of Civil War histories presented as largely as possible in the words of participants and observers, with the emphasis on the human side of events. This book is a sequel to *Sword Over Richmond*.

The period involved is of special significance in that it set the stage for Robert E. Lee's invasion of Pennsylvania and the climactic Battle of Gettysburg. Lee's first penetration of the North was thwarted at Antietam; then, through his wins at Fredericksburg and Chancellorsville, he gained the confidence and the strategic justification he needed to make a second try. The period was also that which saw President Abraham Lincoln issue both the preliminary draft and the final draft of his Emancipation Proclamation.

Although the book is intended for the general reader rather than for the Civil War scholar, it does not shy from the scholar's perusal, for it is offered as a veracious study. The technical statements have been checked against the official records, and the personal episodes have been analyzed for credibility. Although most of the book's ellipses indicate the employment of condensation, some were used to eliminate details that appeared to be faulty. Where necessary clarification has been provided, it has been enclosed in brackets.

Some of the quotations presented here were extracted from the Civil War's better-known eyewitness records, but many others come from materials that have never achieved more than transient notice. Sources of the individual quotes are not given, for I was reluctant to clutter the narrative with numbers that the general reader would be apt to find more annoying than useful. A good portion of the quotes can be readily traced through the bibliography.

The illustrations were taken from *Battles and Leaders of the Civil War, Frank Leslie's Illustrated History of the Civil War, Harper's Pictorial History of the Great Rebellion,* and other publications of the postwar years. Many of the illustrations are adaptations of sketches or photographs made while the book's events were in progress.

LEE'S
TERRIBLE
SWIFT SWORD

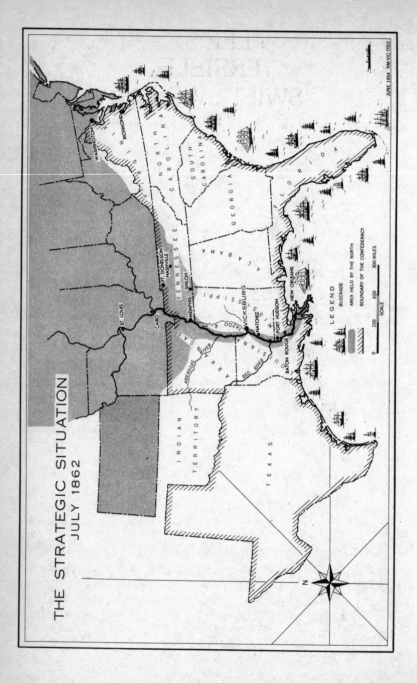

THE STRATEGIC SITUATION
JULY 1862

LEGEND

BLOCKADE
AREA HELD BY THE NORTH
BOUNDARY OF THE CONFEDERACY

SCALE
0   100   200   300 MILES

JUNE 1954 NM-VIC-7002

1

Prelude on the Peninsula

IT WAS July 1862. The Union's Peninsula Campaign against Richmond, conducted at a high cost in lives and treasure, had failed. Consternation was sweeping the North. President Abraham Lincoln, upon whom a major part of the responsibility rested, said later: "I was as nearly inconsolable as I could be and live."

There had seemed good reason to believe that the venture would succeed and that the South might even be brought to terms without further fighting. The Union's Army of the Potomac, organized at Washington after the disgraceful retreat of Lincoln's provisional forces from the Bull Run battlefield at Manassas, Virginia, in July 1861, was a superior fighting machine, one with great potential.

The army's creator was thirty-five-year-old General George B. McClellan, a West Point honor graduate, a veteran of the Mexican War brevetted for gallantry, and, during a four-year sojourn in civilian life just prior to the Civil War, a railroad executive. McClellan was not only an expert on military and railway affairs but was also a student of ancient and modern languages, literature, history, philosophy, art, and archaeology.

Five feet nine inches tall, the general was sturdily built, measuring forty-five inches around the chest. He moved with an attractive buoyancy, and he had a genial, magnetic manner. The idol of his new army, he kept morale high by seeing that the men were well-fed and well-accoutered, and by making them feel that they ranked with the finest soldiers ever mobilized. They called him "Little Mac" with the deepest devotion, and they broke into frenzied cheers whenever he came in sight.

Abraham Lincoln

McClellan's rise as a Civil War figure occurred in a singular way. Three weeks after the war began at Fort Sumter, and two-and-a-half months before First Bull Run, he was ordered by Washington to set up a Department of the Ohio, with his headquarters at Cincinnati. After assembling a command of twenty thousand men, he undertook to drive the Confederate forces, some five thousand in number, from western Virginia (soon to become the state of West Virginia), where most of the citizens were Unionist. In an engagement at Rich Mountain the Confederates were quickly bested, and the bloodshed was minimal.

As the war was still in its infancy, the newspapers were eager for battles to write about and heroes to glorify, and much was made of McClellan's small success. "It stands before us," said Kentucky's *Louisville Journal*, a Unionist paper, "perfect and entire, wanting nothing. . . . There is something extremely satisfactory in contemplating what might be called a piece of finished military workmanship by a master hand." The *New York Times* enthused as follows: "We feel very proud of our wise and brave young Major General. There is a future before him . . . which he will make illustrious."

Some of the papers went so far as to call McClellan "The Young Napoleon."

And so it followed that, in the wake of the Bull Run debacle, with confusion reigning in Washington, McClellan was the man who was called upon to put things in order. And, to his eternal credit, he did this nobly, not only creating his fine army but also integrating and bolstering the city's defenses. Unfortunately, his subsequent performance in battle was another matter.

McClellan could have been a first-rate field commander, for, along with his consummate knowledge of strategy and tactics, he had the absolute trust of his troops. Unfortunately, he was wholly without a spirit of daring. It was true that while he was preparing an advance on the foe he issued bold pronouncements about his intentions, but as soon as he made contact he began to fear defeat and became almost paralyzingly cautious. He invariably overestimated the enemy's numbers, partly because of a poor intelligence system and partly because it was his nature to do so. Reciprocating the love of his men, he agonized over risking their lives, committing them unreservedly only when he had to, such as when he was attacked and on the defensive.

But perhaps McClellan's gravest shortcoming was that, behind his compassion and his charm, he had an ego of such proportions

George B. McClellan

as to put him out of touch with reality. Every decision he made, whatever its outcome, was precisely the right one; each fight he won, whatever its degree of importance, was a military master-piece; and his defeats were always the fault of others, notably his superiors in Washington, who never sent him enough reinforce-ments. He grew impatient with these superiors, President Lincoln included, for not deferring to his every wish. Didn't they realize that by creating the Army of the Potomac and ensuring the capi-tal's safety he had singlehandedly saved the nation?

McClellan considered Lincoln an irresolute leader of inferior intellect, but, at least in the beginning, was willing to be generous about it. He said in a letter to his wife (née Ellen Marcy, now bearing the lyrical name of Ellen McClellan): "The President is honest and means well." McClellan was condescendingly amused by Lincoln's humble deportment, his passion for relating anecdotes, and his amateur interest in things military; and the general once said to a fellow officer, "Isn't he a rare bird?"

Lincoln was well aware of how he impressed McClellan, but the knowledge did not disturb him. "I will hold McClellan's horse," he said, "if he will only bring us success." And until the failure of the Peninsula Campaign, Lincoln had placed a heavy reliance upon McClellan. Appreciative of what he had done as a mobilizer, the President had hoped to see the general develop into a real "Young Napoleon."

McClellan had planned and prepared his Peninsula Campaign with great thoroughness, consuming so much time that he frus-trated both the Administration and the Northern public. But when he finally moved (in March 1862), he did so with skill. Aided by the United States Navy, he floated his hundred thousand men down the Potomac and Chesapeake and massed them in the environs of Union-held Fort Monroe, at the tip of that part of Virginia which lay between the York and the James and was known as the Peninsula. He had made an auspicious beginning.

But McClellan's northwesterly march toward Richmond soon bogged down (at Yorktown) before a thin line of Confederates. The defenders were surprised when the huge army drew up, for they expected to be overrun. In McClellan's eyes the Yorktown defenses were formidable, and, deciding they could be taken only by siege, he had some big guns brought down from Washington. A disturbed Lincoln wired him a protest at the delay, but McClellan was un-moved. He wrote Ellen: "The President very coolly telegraphed me yesterday that he thought I had better break the enemy's lines at

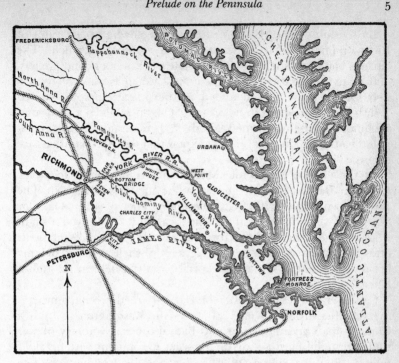

Richmond and the Peninsula

once! I was much tempted to reply that he had better come and do it himself."

The Confederate defense of Yorktown, and, indeed, the defense of Richmond itself, was placed in the hands of short, slender, and dapper General Joseph E. Johnston, son of a Revolutionary War officer whose sword he carried, and grand-nephew of orator Patrick Henry, proclaimer of the battle cry "Give me liberty or give me death!"

At Yorktown Johnston was able to mass an army only about one-half the size of McClellan's. When, at the end of April, Johnston saw that McClellan was preparing to assault, he abandoned the York-town defenses and began falling back toward Richmond, where reinforcements were assembling.

McClellan called his walkover at Yorktown a great victory, and he pursued Johnston, forcing him to turn and do battle at Williams-burg before continuing his retreat. To McClellan, Williamsburg was another spectacular success. "Every hour," he informed Ellen, "its importance proves to be greater."

By the middle of May Johnston was deploying at the gates of Richmond, and McClellan was making a counterdeployment. The citizens had been stirred to a high state of excitement and anxiety, and many now gathered up their most valuable possessions and fled. One of those who remained, a government employee named Judith McGuire, wrote in her diary: "The hospitals in and around Richmond are being cleaned, aired, etc., preparatory to the anticipated battles. Oh, it is sickening to know that these preparations are necessary!"

At the end of May, while McClellan was preparing to attack Johnston, the Confederate general made an attack of his own. The Federals withstood it (the battle becoming known as Fair Oaks, or Seven Pines), and Johnston became a casualty. "I received a slight wound in the right shoulder from a musket shot, and a few moments after was unhorsed by a heavy fragment of shell which struck my breast. Those around had me borne from the field in an ambulance."

Confederate President Jefferson Davis—a reedily built, temperamental Mississippian who had served in Washington as both a Congressman and a Senator and had also been secretary of war under Franklin Pierce—was on the scene in company with his chief military advisor, General Robert E. Lee; and the president gave Lee the command.

Son of the American Revolution's famed "Light-Horse" Harry Lee, Robert E. Lee was at the time fifty-five years of age. Possessing a fine face and figure, he bore himself with a manly grace, and he was almost knightly in his ways, though he wasn't without a temper. He'd had a career of more than thirty years in the Federal military service, and, as one of the foremost soldiers of the land, had been offered command of the Union forces at the war's beginning. "I declined the offer ... stating as candidly and as courteously as I could that, though opposed to secession and deprecating war, I could take no part in an invasion of the Southern states."

In spite of his name as a soldier, Lee was not automatically qualified for high command. His reputation was based on first-rate service as an engineer in the Mexican War, a well-run superintendency of West Point, conscientious cavalry service on the Texas frontier, and the adroit leadership of a team formed to suppress John Brown, the antislavery insurrectionist. Lee had never led a large force in the field.

McClellan, of course, worked so long at renewing his state of readiness after his fight with Johnston that Lee was given plenty of

Robert E. Lee

time to get a good grip on things. In mid-June the Confederate general sent his enterprising cavalry leader, twenty-nine-year-old James Ewell Brown "Jeb" Stuart, on a reconnaissance that carried him entirely around the Union army, and McClellan was made to look foolish. A Richmond newsman reported that he "had got his rear well-spanked."

At the end of June, with McClellan still hesitating, Lee assumed the offensive. He had been reinforced both by recruits and by experienced troops drawn from other defensive areas in the East, notably by the army of General Thomas Jonathan "Stonewall" Jackson, down from Virginia's Shenandoah Valley after completing a

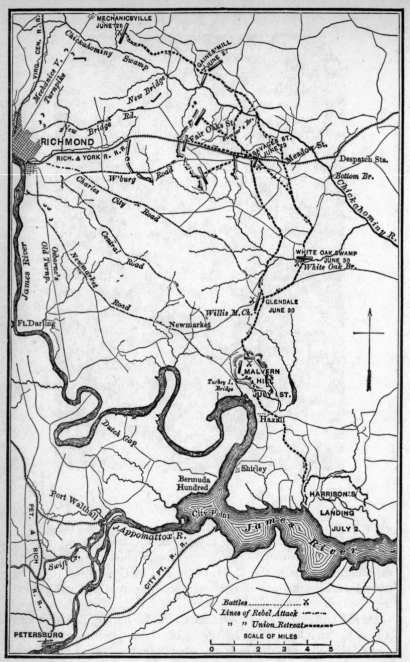

Battlefields of the Seven Days

highly successful campaign against the Federals there. Even with all of his reinforcements, however, Lee had only about ninety thousand men, whereas McClellan's original hundred thousand had been considerably swelled by reinforcements provided by Lincoln.

Grossly overestimating Lee's numbers, McClellan lost his nerve and retired before the onset, pausing only to fight delaying actions—which, it must be conceded, were skilfully conducted. They were bloody enough, these battles of the "Seven Days," which came to be called Mechanicsville (or Beaver Dam Creek, or Ellerson's Mill), Gaines' Mill (or First Cold Harbor, or the Chickahominy), Savage's Station, Glendale (or Frayser's Farm, or White Oak Swamp), and Malvern Hill.

In his haste to reach safer territory, McClellan abandoned many of his dead and wounded to the Confederates. Believing that he had been holding off at least 200,000 men, the general was almost in panic by the time his battered army arrived at Harrison's Landing on the James. There, covered by a fleet of Union warships with heavy guns, he was able to regroup and establish a camp. General Lee, who had taken his own share of battering and hadn't the strength to assail the Union combination, withdrew to his Richmond defenses.

President Jefferson Davis congratulated the army for "skillfully and heroically" preserving the South's "just cause." The people of the city flocked to the churches to give thanks for their delivery. The dark side was that the campaign as a whole had cost the Confederates some 28,000 in killed, wounded, captured, or missing, with the dead coming to about 4,650. A little girl who visited one of the cemeteries exclaimed, "Why, the soldiers' graves are as thick as potato hills!"

Richmond itself had contributed a host of men to the fighting. According to one of the citizens, Sarah "Sallie" Putnam: "There was scarcely a family that had not someone of its numbers in the field. . . . Every house was a house of mourning or a private hospital. The clouds were lifted, and the skies brightened on our political prospects, but death held a carnival in our city."

The consequences of McClellan's failure to defeat Lee and occupy Richmond (his attempt costing him some 23,000 casualties, of which about three thousand were fatalities) were momentous. Gone were all of Washington's hopes for a speedy end to hostilities and the reestablishment of the Union as it had been, with the states' rights issue and the slavery problem back in the hands of Congress. Presi-

Jefferson Davis

dent Lincoln decided he had no choice now but to launch a war aimed at subjugating the South.

He would have to ignore the wishes of the Peace Democrats, who were soft on slavery; and, a Republican himself, he would have to ally himself with his party's abolitionist wing and issue an emancipation proclamation. "I felt that we had reached the end of our rope on the plan of operations we had been pursuing; that we had about played our last card, and must change our tactics or lose the game!" An emancipation proclamation would give the Union effort a new impetus, at the same time tending to discourage foreign intervention in favor of the South, whose cotton was a coveted trade item. Interventionists would appear to be coming in not just to protect their cotton market but also to perpetuate slavery.

The rise of Robert E. Lee, of course, also had a profound effect on events. One of the effects was rather curious: For all practical purposes, the war in the East was about to become a contest between Lee the military man and Lincoln the statesman. Lee had begun to make himself the heart and soul of the Confederacy's eastern effort, and he would only improve upon his aptness for utilizing the limited soldiery and material resources available to him, while it would be Lincoln's task to find among his generals one with enough skill and combativeness to destroy Lee's power.

Lincoln and Lee, though strikingly different in background, appearance, and style, were similar in intellect, both possessing a strong will, a deep wisdom, an abiding common sense, a keen understanding of human nature, and a talent for diplomacy that enabled them to deal successfully with all kinds of people in all kinds of situations. As foes they were an excellent match.

General McClellan, true to his nature, was not in the least humiliated by his rout from Richmond. He termed it a change of base that had saved his army from disaster at the hands of a greatly superior foe, a maneuver made necessary by Washington's failure to send him the kind of reserves he had requested. "The movement," he informed Ellen, "has been a magnificent one."

The majority of the troops cheered their Little Mac as lustily as ever, deeply grateful that he had saved them not only from Lee's hordes but also from the bungling of their own government. Among the more intelligent and thoughtful men, however, there were those who began to wonder about McClellan. They knew that the South was far less populous than the North. Where had Lee gotten all of those troops?

McClellan sent word to Washington that he had every intention of making a second advance upon Richmond but that he needed 100,000 reinforcements! President Lincoln voyaged to Harrison's Landing to try to decide whether McClellan should be reasonably reinforced and allowed to renew his campaign or should be withdrawn from the Peninsula and directed to operate against Richmond from the north. The latter move could be made in cooperation with a new army numbering about fifty thousand that Lincoln had put together under John Pope, a big man with a confident manner who had achieved some successes in the West. These were modest, it was true, but they seemed to indicate that Pope was a born fighter.

No firm decisions were made during Lincoln's visit with McClellan, but the President got something of a surprise when his defeated general handed him a carefully composed letter of advice concerning his presidential duties. Included were the following statements:

"The time has come when the Government must determine upon a civil and military policy covering the whole ground of our national trouble. The responsibility of determining, declaring, and supporting such civil and military policy and of directing the whole course of national affairs in regard to the rebellion must now be assumed and exercised by you, or our cause will be lost. . . . The rebellion has assumed the character of war: as such it should be regarded; and it should be conducted upon the highest principles known to Christian civilization.

"It should not be at all a war upon population, but against armed forces and political organizations.... All private property taken [from the enemy] for military use should be paid or receipted for; pillage and waste should be treated as high crimes; all unnecessary trespass sternly prohibited, and offensive demeanor by the military towards citizens promptly rebuked.... Military power should not be allowed to interfere with the relations of servitude.... A declaration of radical views, especially upon slavery, will rapidly disintegrate our present armies."

McClellan did not believe that Northern soldiers would be willing to fight a war based upon the abolition of slavery. In the general's view, nothing ought to be attempted beyond the destruction of the South's armies and political establishments. With these goals achieved, he reasoned, the South would have no choice but to begin talking again. Actually, this was largely the policy under which the war had been launched, a policy invalidated by McClellan's own failure.

Lincoln read the general's dissertation without comment, thanked him for it, and put it in his pocket, soon afterward returning to Washington. Two weeks later, on July 22, the President held a cabinet meeting at which he announced his intention of issuing an emancipation proclamation. The gist of the paper he read to the little assemblage was that he intended to put the following provisions into effect on January 1, 1863: the slave regions under acquiescence to the Union at that time would be allowed to choose either immediate or gradual emancipation, with the owners being compensated by the government, while the slaves in the regions in rebellion would become unreservedly free.

Although the cabinet members voiced apprehensions regarding the uncertainties of such a move, the majority agreed that it had become a military and political necessity. Secretary of State William Seward, however, suggested that a public announcement of the measure be delayed until a Union victory had been achieved. He felt that to make the announcement now, with the military picture dismal, would be a mistake.

"His idea," Lincoln explained later, "was that it would be considered our last *shriek*, on the retreat.... The wisdom of the view of the Secretary of State struck me with very great force. It was an aspect of the case that, in all my thought upon the subject, I had entirely overlooked. The result was that I put the draft of the proclamation aside ... waiting for a victory."

The victory, Lincoln concluded, wasn't likely to be won by Mc-

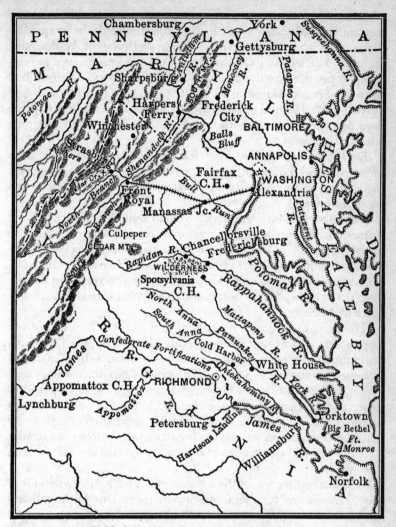

Field of operations in Virginia and Maryland

Clellan on the Peninsula. Since it did not appear to be strategically sound to keep the armies of McClellan and Pope in different places (especially since there was at least a possibility that Lee had the strength that McClellan insisted he had), McClellan was ordered, early in August, to start embarking his troops for the trip back up the Chesapeake and Potomac to a position south of Washington. The general protested vigorously, but he moved to obey.

Robert E. Lee was not long in reacting. As soon as he could be certain that McClellan was leaving the Peninsula he went after Pope, who was in northern Virginia, southwest of Washington. Some of McClellan's units made it up the Potomac in time to reinforce Pope, but Lee defeated the combined forces at Second Bull Run (or Second Manassas), fought on August 29 and 30. Pope's retreat to Washington was a particular humiliation for him, since he had preceded his march to battle with a great deal of bragging about his prowess.

For Lincoln, of course, the defeat was another severe blow, both militarily and politically. For a second time, Washington itself seemed to be in danger, and throughout the North dismay was again rampant.

McClellan had little to do with Second Bull Run. He fretted and fumed as his units were detached to Pope, uncertain of where he stood in the chain of command. Had Pope been successful, McClellan would have been ousted. But now it was Pope who went. McClellan's organizational skills were needed to revitalize the defeated and disheartened troops and to put Washington in a suitable state of defense.

The general, however, was not at first reinstated to his former command. "At this time," he explains, "the task imposed upon me was limited to the dispositions necessary to resist a direct attack of the enemy upon the capital. . . . The various garrisons were at once strengthened and put in order, and the troops were disposed to cover all the approaches to the city, and so as to be readily thrown upon threatened points. New defenses were thrown up where deemed necessary. A few days only had elapsed before comparative security was felt with regard to our ability to resist any attack upon the city."

With the completion of the fortifications, McClellan invited President Lincoln and his cabinet to inspect them. One of the military members of the party was McClellan's chief of engineers, General J. G. Barnard, who never forgot his moments in the President's company.

"The inspection commenced at Arlington, to the southwest of Washington, and in front of the enemy. We followed the line of the works southerly and recrossed the Potomac to the easterly side of the river, and continued along the line easterly of Washington and into the heaviest of all the fortifications on the northerly side of Washington. When we reached this point the President asked General McClellan to explain the necessity of so strong a fortification between Washington and the North.

"General McClellan replied, 'Why, Mr. President, according to military science it is our duty to guard against every possible or supposable contingency that may arise. For example, if under any circumstances, however fortuitous, the enemy, by any chance or freak, should, in a last resort, get in behind Washington in his efforts to capture the city, why, there the fort is to defend it.'

" 'Yes, that's so, General,' said the President. 'The precaution is doubtless a wise one, and I'm glad to get so clear an explanation, for it reminds me of an interesting question once discussed for several weeks in our Lyceum, or Moot Court, at Springfield, Illinois, soon after I began reading law.'

" 'Ah!' says General McClellan. 'What question was that, Mr. President?'

" 'The question,' Mr. Lincoln replied, 'was: "Why does a man have breasts?" '

"And he added that after many evenings' debate the question was submitted to the presiding judge, who wisely decided 'that if under any circumstances, however fortuitous, or by any chance or freak, no matter of what nature or by what cause, a man should have a baby, there would be the breasts to nurse it.' "

2

Lee Invades Maryland

Only three months had passed since Robert E. Lee had assumed Joseph Johnston's command, and in that time Lee had forced the transference of a superior foe from the gates of Richmond to the defenses of Washington, defeating and driving in an auxiliary army as well. And he continued to hold the initiative.

The quality of Lee's leadership was now fully appreciated by his troops, who were learning to love him as well. As explained by Edward A. Pollard, one of the wartime editors of the *Richmond Examiner*, who became the Confederacy's best-known historian:

"A great element of General Lee's popularity in his army was his exceeding, almost paternal care for his men. It is a remarkable circumstance that he never harangued his troops on a battlefield. He employed but little of rhetoric, and was innocent of theatrical machinery in maintaining the resolution and spirit of his army.

"He was never a conspicuous figure in the field of battle. His habit was to consult the plan of battle thoroughly, assign to each corps commander his precise work, and leave the active conduct of the field to his lieutenant-generals, unless in some case of critical emergency. . . .

"It is indeed remarkable that with such little display of his person, and with a habit bordering on taciturnity, General Lee should have obtained such control over the affections of men whom he tried not only by constant battle but by tests of hardship, privation, and suffering . . . such as [have] not been applied to any army of modern times.

"But his intercourse with his army was peculiar. He mingled with the troops on every proper occasion; he spoke a few simple words here and there to the wounded and distressed soldier; and his kindliness of manner was so unaffected that it at once gained the confidence and touched the heart. He had a rare gift, which many persons copy or affect but which can never be perfectly possessed unless by a great man and a true gentleman: a voice whose tones of politeness never varied, whether uttered to the highest or lowest in rank.

"His men not only felt a supreme confidence in his judgment as a commander, but they were conscious everywhere of his sympathy with their sufferings and his attention to their wants; and they therefore accepted every sacrifice and trial as inevitable necessity imposed upon them by a paternal hand."

The Confederate army was now composed (albeit loosely) of two wings, the one under James Longstreet, the other under Stonewall

Confederate types of 1862

Jackson, and was supported by Jeb Stuart's cavalry. All three of these ranking subordinates were possessed of exceptional military talent, and two were men of special color. Only James Longstreet—though imposing in appearance, with his height of six feet two inches, his broad shoulders, and his penetrating blue eyes—had a personality of ordinary persuasion. Jackson and Stuart stirred a fascination akin to that of Lee, with Jackson displaying many interesting peculiarities and Stuart being attractively flamboyant and irrepressibly high-humored.

Jackson, the older of the two, was in his thirty-ninth year. A West Point graduate of ordinary merit, he served with the United States Army during the Mexican War and won two brevets. Unhappy with his ensuing peacetime duties, he soon resigned his commission to become professor of natural philosophy and instructor of artillery at the Virginia Military Institute at Lexington. Many of his off-hours were spent in religious study, for he was a Christian of extraordinary devotion. In church, however, he often dozed.

Overly concerned with his health, Jackson experimented with diet and exercise regimens. He had some odd ideas about his body, at one time convinced that his arms and legs were mismatched pairs; that, for example, his right arm was overly supplied with blood. To stimulate his system, he took a cold bath every morning, even during the height of winter; and he was often seen sucking on a lemon, his palliative for indigestion.

Jackson married twice during his years at the institute. Both his wives were daughters of clergymen. His first wife died while delivering a lifeless child. The second wife was Mary Anna Morrison, of North Carolina. He was eager for children, and Mary Anna soon bore him a daughter. "The child," she explains, "lived only a few weeks, and its loss was a great, very great sorrow to him. But here, as always, religion subdued every murmur. Great as was his love for children, his spirit of submission was greater, and even in this bitter disappointment he bowed uncomplainingly to his Father's will."

Still teaching at the institute at the outbreak of the Civil War, Jackson was at once called into the Confederate service. As commander of a brigade at First Bull Run, he stood "like a stone wall," and this marked the beginning of one of history's most notable military careers, one made all the more remarkable because it occupied a span of less than two years.

"Jackson," says John Esten Cooke, a popular Virginia author who served through the war in various Confederate staff positions and

Stonewall Jackson

who wrote a biography of the general, "became the idol of his troops and the country. Wherever he moved among the camps he was met by cheers; and so unvarying was this reception of him that a distant yell would often draw from his men the exclamation, 'That's Jackson or a rabbit!,' the sight of the soldier or the appearance of a hare [which meant extra food for the men who ran it down] being alone adequate to arouse this tremendous excitement. . . .

"No general was ever so beloved by the good and pious of the land. Old ladies received him wherever he went with a species of enthusiasm, and I think he preferred their society and that of clergymen to any other. In such society his kindly nature seemed to expand, and his countenance was charming. . . . The hard intellect [which made him a stern disciplinarian] was resting. . . . I have seen him look serene and perfectly happy conversing with a venerable lady upon their relative religious experiences. Children were also great favorites with him, and he seldom failed to make them love him. . . .

"Jackson had little humor. He was not sour or gloomy, nor did he look grimly upon 'fun' as something which a good Presbyterian should avoid. . . . But he had *no ear* for humor, as some persons have none for music. A joke was a mysterious affair to him. . . . Even this

Confederates trying to add to a meager menu.

thick coating of 'matter-of-fact' was occasionally pierced, however. At Port Republic [during his famous Valley Campaign] a soldier said to his companion, 'I wish these Yankees were in hell,' whereupon the other replied, 'I don't, for if they were Old Jack would be within half a mile of them, with the Stonewall Brigade in front!' When this was told to Jackson, he is said to have burst out into hearty laughter. . . . But such enjoyment of fun was rare with him. . . .

"Of wit, properly speaking, he had little. But at times his brief, wise, matter-of-fact sentences became epigrammatic. Dr. Hunter McGuire, his medical director, once gave him some whiskey when he was wet and fatigued. Jackson made a wry face in swallowing it, and Dr. McGuire asked if it was not good whiskey. 'Oh, yes,' replied Jackson, 'I like liquor, the taste and effect—*that's why I don't drink it.*' . . .

"Jackson was an apparently commonplace person, and his bearing neither striking, graceful, nor impressive. He rode ungracefully, walked with an awkward stride, and wanted ease of manner. He never lost a certain shyness in company . . . but . . . he made a most agreeable impression by his delightful natural courtesy. . . .

"The eccentricities of the individual were undoubtedly a strong element of his popularity. The dress, habits, bearing of the man all made his soldiers adore him. . . . Jackson's appearance and manners . . . were such as conciliate a familiar, humorous liking. His dingy old coat, than which scarce a private's in his command was more faded; his dilapidated and discolored cap; the absence of decorations and all show in his dress; his odd ways; his kindly, simple manner; his habit of sitting down and eating with his men; his indifference whether his bed were in a comfortable headquarter tent on a camp couch, or in a fence corner with no shelter from the rain but his cloak; his abstemiousness, fairness, honesty, simplicity; his never-failing regard for the comfort and the feelings of the private soldier; his oddities, eccentricities, and originalities—all were an unfailing provocative to liking, and endeared him to his men. Troops are charmed when there is anything in the personal character of a great leader to 'make fun of.' Admiration of his genius then becomes enthusiasm for his person. Jackson had aroused this enthusiasm in his men—and it was a weapon with which he struck hard.

"One of the most curious peculiarities of Jackson was the strange fashion he had of raising his right hand aloft and then letting it fall suddenly to his side. It is impossible, perhaps, to determine the meaning of this singular gesture. It is said that he had some physical ailment which he thus relieved [he may have been trying to drain the "surplus blood" from his "heavy arm"]; others believed that at such moments he was praying. Either may be the fact. Certain it is that he often held his hand, sometimes both hands, thus aloft in battle, and that his lips were then seen to move, evidently in prayer. Not once, but many times, has the singular spectacle been presented of [Jackson] sitting on his horse silently as his column moved before him—his hands raised to heaven, his eyes closed, his lips moving in prayer. . . .

"There are those who said that all this indicated a partial species of insanity—that Jackson's mind was not sound. . . . The present writer can only say that Jackson appeared to him to be an eminently rational, judicious, and sensible person in conversation. . . . If Jackson was crazy, it is a pity he did not bite somebody and inoculate them with a small amount of his insanity as a soldier."

Jeb Stuart had none of Jackson's mystery. He was exactly what he appeared to be: an able and adventurous leader who loved the limelight, and a faithfully married man with a friendly eye for all of womankind.

Fortunately for history, one of Stuart's memorialists was an associate with a special gift for observation and delineation. This was Heros von Borcke, a member of Stuart's staff, a Prussian aristocrat who had come to America to fight for the South. Von Borcke himself was a personality. In the words of a Southern woman who knew him:

"Major Von Borcke was a man of noble presence, standing over six feet without his shoes, and of size corresponding to his height. He was remarkably handsome, of a pure German type of beauty, and his manners combined a courtly ease and elegance with much dignity, which only contact with the best society could give. He was quite the rage with the girls, and his attractions were enhanced by his speaking English very brokenly. That made him altogether charming."

Von Borcke met Stuart for the first time during the fighting on the Peninsula, finding him to be "a stoutly built man, rather above the middle height, of a most frank and winning expression, the lower part of his fine face covered with a thick brown beard which flowed over his breast. His eye was quick and piercing, of a light blue in repose but changing to a darker tinge under high excitement. His whole person seemed instinct with vitality, his movements were alert, his observation keen and rapid, and altogether he was to me the model of a dashing cavalry leader.

"Before the breaking out of hostilities between the North and South he had served in the First United States Cavalry . . . against the Indians of the Far West, and was severely wounded in an encounter with the Cheyennes . . . in July, 1857. In that wild life of the prairie, now chasing the buffalo, now pursuing the treacherous savage, Stuart had passed nearly all his waking hours in the saddle, and thus became one of the most fearless and dexterous horsemen in America, and he had acquired a love of adventure which made activity a necessity of his being.

"He delighted in the neighing of the charger and the clangour of the bugle, and he had . . . [a] weakness for the vanities of the military parade. He betrayed this latter quality in his jaunty uniform, which consisted of a small grey jacket, trousers of the same stuff, and over them high military boots, a yellow silk sash, and a grey slouch hat surmounted by a sweeping black ostrich plume. Thus attired, sitting gracefully on his fine horse, he did not fail to attract the notice and admiration of all who saw him ride along."

In a very short time Stuart and Von Borcke were fast friends, and the Prussian found himself sharing all of his commander's zeal for

Jeb Stuart

the Confederate cause. Von Borcke says of the situation in early September, 1862:

"General Lee had now decided not to attack the enemy in their strong fortifications around Alexandria [south of Washington], but boldly to carry the war into the enemy's territory, or at least into the fertile plains of Maryland. Many advantages, it was hoped, might be secured by this policy. For a considerable period he would be able there to subsist his army.... The confident belief was also entertained that our army would be increased by 20,000 to 25,000 recruits [men of Maryland with Confederate sympathies], who were supposed to be only awaiting the opportunity of taking up arms against the Federal Government. Being so reinforced, our commander-in-chief doubted not that he might easily strike a blow against Baltimore, or even Washington, or transfer the theater of military operations across the border into the rich agricultural region of Pennsylvania.

"On the morning of the 5th September there was again presented through the Confederate camps a scene of bustling activity. Every regiment was preparing for the march, officers were riding to and fro, and the long artillery trains were moving off along the turnpike, their rumbling noise combining with the rattle of the drums and the roll of the bugles to wake the echoes for miles around. Our direction was *northward*, and as we rode onward towards the little town of Leesburg . . . many a youthful hero looked forward to his triumphant entry into the Federal capital, or to a joyous reception at the hands of the fair women of Baltimore, whose irrepressible sympathies had been always with the South.

"After a [lengthy] march . . . the column reached Leesburg, and the streets of the village were at once so compactly filled with troops, artillery, and wagon trains that General Stuart determined to make a detour with his cavalry, which had been halted about a mile distant, in preference to proceeding through the place. It was necessary, however, for the General to repair for final instructions to the headquarters of General Lee in the town, and in this ride he was accompanied by his staff.

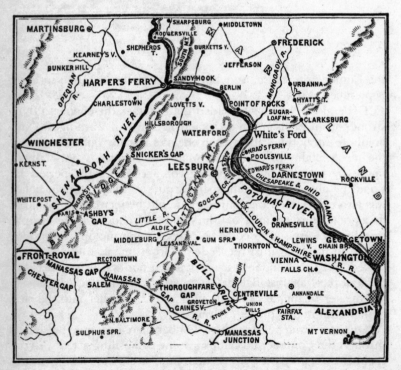

Field of operations between Washington and Sharpsburg

"Leesburg . . . is a town or village of about four thousand inhabitants, some four miles from the Potomac River, and, as might be readily supposed from its proximity to the border [between the North and the South], was alternately in the possession of the Yankees and the Confederates, having undergone a change of masters several times during the war. General Lee's headquarters was set up in the commodious dwelling of a prominent citizen. Jackson and Longstreet had both already arrived there, and our great commander was soon engaged in a council of war with his lieutenants. . . .

"About two o'clock in the afternoon we received orders to move on, and, after a dusty and very much impeded march of two hours, winding through infantry columns and compelled frequently to halt, we reached the Potomac at White's Ford, where the cavalry were to cross. The banks of this noble river, which is of great width at this point, rise to the height of about sixty feet above the bed of the stream and are overshadowed by gigantic trees of primeval growth. . . . At White's Ford the Potomac is divided into two streams by a sandy strip of island in the middle. . . .

"It was indeed a magnificent sight as the long column of many thousand horsemen stretched across this beautiful Potomac. The evening sun slanted upon its clear placid waters and burnished them with gold, while the arms of the [riders] glittered and blazed in its radiance. There were few moments, perhaps, from the beginning to the close of the war, of excitement more intense, of exhilaration more delightful, than when we ascended the opposite bank to the . . . thrilling music of 'Maryland, my Maryland.' "

The crossing of the infantry is thus described by D. Augustus Dickert, a sergeant from South Carolina: "Men sang and cheered, hats filled the air, flags waved, and shouts from fifty thousand throats reverberated up and down the banks of the river, to be echoed back from the mountains and die away among the hills and highlands of Maryland."

Since the crossing was a three-day affair, the fifty thousand voices were not raised in simultaneous chorus. Troops were pushing into Maryland while others were still approaching the river. An unidentified private gives this picture of the entry into Maryland: "The country people lined the roads, gazing in open-eyed wonder upon the long lines of infantry that filled the roads for miles, and as far as the eye could reach was the glitter of the swaying points of the bayonets. These were the first Ragged Rebels they had ever seen,

Confederates on the march

and though they did not act either as friends or foes, still they gave liberally, and every haversack was full that day at least. No houses were entered, no damage was done, and the farmers in the vicinity must have drawn a long breath as they saw how safe their property was in the very midst of the army."

The citizens of Maryland were divided in their loyalties. Southern sympathizers were plentiful, but many of these people hesitated to make open demonstrations in favor of Lee's army lest it be forced to retreat and thus leave them and their property subject to reprisal at the hands of the state's Unionists. Other citizens, however, were not so cautious. A Confederate officer, William Miller Owen of the Washington Artillery of New Orleans, tells of something that happened during an extended break in the march:

"The young ladies are wild to see General Lee, and we agree to find him for them; so . . . a caravan is made up of all the old family carriages in the country, and filled with pretty girls, and we escort them to where 'Uncle Robert' is resting. He is immediately surrounded and kissed and hugged, until the old gentleman gets very red in the face and cries for mercy. We young ones look on, and only wish they would distribute those favors a little more 'permiscus,' so to speak. But the fair ones, though coy, are very agreeable, and we each forthwith select one whose colors we shall wear until we reach the next town. But all pleasures have an end, and the bugle sounds 'Forward,' and away we march."

As added by another Confederate officer, Henry Kyd Douglas, a member of Stonewall Jackson's staff: "Before we had been in Maryland many hours, one enthusiastic citizen presented Jackson with a gigantic gray mare. She was a little heavy and awkward for a war horse, but as the general's 'Little Sorrel' had a few days before been temporarily stolen, the present was a timely one, and he was not disposed to 'look a gift horse in the mouth.' Yet the present proved almost a Trojan horse to him, for the next morning when he mounted his new steed and touched her with his spur the ... undisciplined beast reared straight into the air, and, standing erect for a moment, threw herself backward, horse and rider rolling upon the ground. The general was stunned and severely bruised, and lay upon the ground for some time before he could be removed. He was then placed in an ambulance, where he rode during the day's march."

It was now Saturday, September 6, and Jackson's column, in Lee's van, soon reached Frederick, a town of about fifteen thousand people. One of the Southern newspaper correspondents traveling with the army was "Personne" of the *Charleston Mercury*, and he reported: "As Jackson's army marched through, the houses were mostly closed, and from between the window blinds the citizens could be seen anxiously peering, as if they expected to see a crowd of bugaboos intent upon nothing but rapine and slaughter. A few of the residences were open, however, and in those ladies and gentlemen were waving their handkerchiefs and displaying the Confederate flag."

These were the moments that provided the setting for Yankee poet John Greenleaf Whittier's fanciful composition "Barbara Frietchie." Mrs. Frietchie, a Frederick Unionist in her mid-nineties, is supposed to have become so upset because no Union flags were flying that she affixed a staff-mounted flag outside her attic window. As Whittier would have it:

> Up the street came the Rebel tread,
> Stonewall Jackson riding ahead.
> Under his slouch hat left and right
> He glanced: the old flag met his sight.
> "Halt!"—the dust-brown ranks stood fast;
> "Fire!"—out blazed the rifle blast.
> It shivered the window, pane and sash;
> It rent the banner with seam and gash.

> *Quick as it fell from the broken staff*
> *Dame Barbara snatched the silken scarf;*
> *She leaned far out on the window-sill*
> *And shook it forth with a royal will.*
> *"Shoot, if you must, this old gray head,*
> *But spare your country's flag," she said.*
> *A shade of sadness, a blush of shame*
> *Over the face of the leader came;*
> *The nobler nature within him stirred*
> *To life at the woman's deed and word:*
> *"Who touches a hair of yon gray head*
> *Dies like a dog! March on!" he said.*

Stonewall Jackson was actually riding in his ambulance at this time. Says Henry Kyd Douglas: "Nothing like the scene so graphically described by the poet ever happened. Mr. Whittier must have been misinformed as to the incident."

Whittier says in his defense: "The poem 'Barbara Frietchie' was written in good faith. The story was no invention of mine. It came to me from sources which I regarded as entirely reliable; it had been published in newspapers and had gained public credence in Washington and Maryland before my poem was written. I had no reason to doubt its accuracy then, and I am still constrained to believe that it had foundation in fact."

A period historian who investigated the story concluded: "The flag-waving act was done ... by Mrs. Mary S. Quantrell, another Frederick woman; but Jackson took no notice of it, and as Mrs. Quantrell was not fortunate enough to find a poet to celebrate her deed, she never became famous."

Returning to newsman Personne's account of the march through the town: "From ... the residence of a Mr. Ross, a lawyer of high standing, his family were distributing to the soldiers as they passed eatables and clothing to such as seemed most needy. Afterwards the family invited many officers to the house, where they were handsomely entertained with wines, cigars, and other luxuries. Mr. Ross himself has been confined in Fortress McHenry for the bold stand he took at an early hour in favor of the South.

"As soon as the troops were encamped, many were permitted to enter the town, and in a short time it was thronged. Confederate money was taken ... by all who opened their stores, and for the first time during the campaign we enjoyed the privilege of purchasing at 'peace prices' the articles we most required. Coffee could be had in abundance at twenty-five cents per pound, sugar at eleven and twelve cents, salt fifty cents a sack, boots five and seven dollars a pair, shoes three dollars, flannel forty cents a yard, and everything else in proportion. Lager beer, ice cream, dates, confections, preserves, all found ready sale, and were liberally dispensed and disposed of."

Again in the words of Henry Kyd Douglas, of Jackson's staff: "Generals Lee, Longstreet, Jackson, and for a time Jeb Stuart had their headquarters near one another in Best's Grove. Hither in crowds came the good people of Frederick, especially the ladies, as to a fair. General Jackson, still suffering from his hurt, kept to his tent, busying himself with maps and official papers, and declined to see visitors. Once, however, when he had been called to General Lee's tent, two young girls waylaid him, paralyzed him with smiles and embraces and questions, and then jumped into their carriage and drove off rapidly, leaving him there, cap in hand, bowing, blushing, and speechless. But once safe in his tent he was seen no more. . . ."

Heros von Borcke, of Jeb Stuart's staff, had occasion to ride alone through Frederick that day. "Every officer who wore a plume in his hat was immediately taken for Jackson or Stuart. All averments to the contrary, all remonstrances with the crowd, were utterly useless. The public would have it their own way. So it happened that I was very soon followed by a wild mob of people of all ages, from the old greybeard to the smallest boy, all insisting that I was Jackson and venting their admiration in loud cheers and huzzas. Ladies rushed out of their houses with bouquets. In vain did I declare that I was

Confederate treasury note

not Jackson. This disclaimer, they said, was prompted by the well-known modesty of the great hero and afforded them the surest means of recognizing him. The complication grew worse and worse every minute.

"To escape these annoying ovations I dismounted at last at a hotel, but here I was little better off. . . . The proprietor of the establishment being a German, many of Germania's sons were there assembled, immersed in beer and smoking like so many furnaces. I am quite sure that most of them were very decided Yankee sympathizers, but as a grey uniform was right among them, and many others were not far off, they talked the hottest secession, and nearly floored me with their questions. One who had seen Jackson's columns on the march affirmed they numbered not a man less than 300,000. Another was only in doubt as to the day and hour when we should victoriously enter Washington, Baltimore, Philadelphia, and New York. All were sure that thirty thousand Marylanders were ready to follow in the next few days our invincible army. . . .

"I was exceedingly glad to break away from all this."

There was a Union military hospital in Frederick, and the Confederates took it over for their own use. Says the Union surgeon who had been running the place: "They were the filthiest set of men and officers I ever saw, with clothing that was ragged and had not been cleaned for weeks. They could be smelt all over the entire enclosure. . . . The brigade in the [hospital] grounds obtained some flour speedily and commenced cooking rations. . . . Their brigades were small, and horses and men all but starved. . . .

"*Evening.* . . . The streets were filled with soldiers who had been drinking freely, though, to their credit, when they commenced drinking they speedily became dead drunk and were then harmless. Did any one of them attempt to create a disturbance, a guard would slip up to him and say something to him, and the [offender] would immediately cease his brawling and go quietly to the guardhouse."

Newsman Personne wrote as follows on Sunday, September 7: "We are now encamped around the town. Martial law has been proclaimed, a provost marshal appointed, and a strong guard of our men patrols the streets to preserve order. . . . The sentiment of the people . . . is apparently about equally divided. . . . There are three or four churches in the town, and today they are filled with our officers and men attending divine service."

According to Henry Kyd Douglas, Stonewall Jackson waited until evening to do his worshipping. "There being no service in the Presbyterian Church, he went to the German Reformed. As usual he fell asleep, but this time more soundly than was his wont. His head sunk upon his breast, his cap dropped from his hands to the floor. The prayers of the congregation did not disturb him, and only the choir and the deep-toned organ awakened him. Afterward I learned that the minister was credited with much loyalty and courage because he had prayed for the President of the United States in the very presence of Stonewall Jackson. Well, the general didn't hear the prayer."

By this time Jeb Stuart's cavalry brigades were occupying a line of outposts southeast of Frederick, their job to provide a screen between the town and the approaches from Washington. Stuart himself, with Wade Hampton's brigade, was at the village of Urbana. Stuart, von Borcke, and several other officers had spent Sunday afternoon visiting at the home of a man of secessionist loyalties. Von Borcke relates:

"There were several very charming and pretty young ladies staying at Mr. C.'s house, and among them one from New York, a relation of the family on a visit to Urbana, whom General Stuart, from her warm outspoken Confederate sympathies, jokingly called the New York Rebel. In the agreeable conversation of these ladies, in mirth and song, the afternoon . . . passed lightly and rapidly away; and then came night, queenly and beautiful, with a round moon whose beams, penetrating the windows, suggested to our debonnaire commander a promenade [i.e., a walk out of doors], which he at once proposed. . . .

"Leaving to our fair friends the choice of their partners, we were guided by them to a large building crowning the summit of a gentle hill on the edge of the village. . . . This building had been occupied before the breaking out of the war as an academy, but was now entirely deserted . . . and our footsteps echoed loudly as we walked through its wide, empty halls, once so noisy with human voices. Each storey . . . had its ample verandah running round it, and from the highest of these we had a magnificent view of the village and the surrounding country.

"The night was calm, the dark blue firmament was besprinkled with myriads of stars, and the moon poured over the landscape a misty bluish light that made it all look unreal. . . . We were indulging in the dreamy sentiment natural to the hour when the gay voice of Stuart broke in—'Major, what a capital place for us to give a ball in honor of our arrival in Maryland! Don't you think we could manage it?' To this there was a unanimous response in the affirmative, which was especially hearty on the part of the ladies. . . .

"I [agreed] to make all necessary arrangements for the illumination and decoration of the hall, the issuing the cards of invitation, etc., leaving to Stuart the matter of the music, which he gladly consented to provide. . . . We determined on our way home, to the great joy of our fair companions, that the ball should come off on the following evening."

3

Time Out for a Ball

I N WASHINGTON, Lee's withdrawal from the Alexandria front was viewed with relief coupled with uncertainty. The capital was apparently safe for the moment, but what were Lee's intentions? It was quickly learned by cavalry reconnaissance that he was heading for the Potomac, and this seemed to indicate that he planned to invade the North. Did he mean to come down upon Washington's western flank?

Lincoln reacted by restoring McClellan to full command of the Army of the Potomac. The President would have much preferred to give the job to an abler fighter, but none was available. He had no Robert E. Lee or Stonewall Jackson. He did have a Ulysses S. Grant and a William T. Sherman, but these commanders were presently honing their skills in the war's western theater, figures of promise but not of assured greatness.

McClellan's task was an obvious one. While his cavalry corps kept in touch with the Confederates and tried to determine their intent, he must assemble the Army of the Potomac in such a way as to cover both the capital and Baltimore, and he must assume a line of march by which he remained between the Confederates and these cities. "Again," McClellan informed his wife, "I have been called upon to save the country."

The various units of the Army of the Potomac began converging in the Rockville area, north of Washington, during the same weekend that Lee occupied Frederick. As recounted by George T. Stevens, surgeon of the 77th Regiment New York Volunteers, which had been helping to hold the lines southwest of the city: "It was on the evening of the 6th [Saturday] that orders were issued to move. It was but short work to pack up our limited supply of clothing, cooking utensils, and the few other articles which constituted our store of worldly goods, and prepare to march. We left Alexandria, and, proceeding toward Washington, passed Fort Albany and crossed the Long Bridge, the moon and stars shining with a brilliancy seldom equalled, rendering the night march a pleasant one.

"As the steady tramp of the soldiers upon the pavements was heard by the citizens of Washington, they crowded upon the walks, eager to get a glance, even by moonlight, of the veterans who had passed through such untold hardships. Many were the questions regarding our destination, but we could only answer, 'We are going to meet the rebels.' Passing through Georgetown, we reached the little village of Tenallytown, where, weary from the short but rapid march, we spent the remainder of the night in sleep."

As added by Francis W. Palfrey, an officer in the 20th Massachusetts Infantry: "Washington and its environs presented singular sights in the early days of September, 1862. The luxury and refinements of peace contrasted sharply with the privations and squalor of war. There are few prettier suburban drives than those in the neighborhood of Washington, and no weather is more delightful than that of late summer, when a cooler air comes with the shortening days. . . . Well-appointed carriages rolled along those charming drives, bearing fair women in cool and fresh costumes, and by their side the ragged, dusty, sunburnt regiments from the Peninsula trudged along."

By Sunday afternoon nearly all of the army's units had reached the prescribed rendezvous area. McClellan, still in Washington, took a few moments to write to Ellen: "I leave in a couple of hours to take command of the army in the field. I shall go to Rockville tonight and start out after the rebels tomorrow. I shall have nearly 100,000 men, old and new. . . ."

The army was composed of three wings, the right under Ambrose E. Burnside, the center under Edwin V. Sumner, and the left under William B. Franklin. Burnside and Franklin, both in their late thirties, were typical of their generation of military commanders, having graduated from West Point and served as junior officers in the Mexican War. Sumner was sixty-five years old, had begun his military career in 1819, and had seen many years of service on the Western frontier before being sent to Mexico, where he was brevetted colonel. He was military governor of New Mexico from 1851 to 1853.

Alfred Pleasonton

The army's cavalry commander was thirty-eight-year-old Alfred Pleasonton, a small, trim-figured West Pointer who, like the three infantry commanders, was a veteran campaigner.

While McClellan completed his preparations, the Confederates continued their comfortable occupation of Frederick. Well aware of McClellan's propensity for caution, Lee made his plans with a deliberateness he would not have employed if his adversary had been a leader of more dispatch.

On Monday, September 8, Confederate newsman Personne wrote: "Frederick today presents a busy scene, more like that of a Fourth of July festival than a gathering of armed invaders. A majority of the stores are closed to general admission because of the crowds eager to press and buy, but a little diplomacy secures an entrance at the back door, or past the sentinel wisely stationed to protect the proprietor from the rush of anxious customers. Prices are going up rapidly. . . . Bitter complaints are uttered against those who refuse Confederate money. . . .

"The people are beginning to recover from their surprise at our sudden appearance, and to realize the magnitude of our preparations to advance through and relieve Maryland from her thraldom. Some are moody, and evidently hate us heartily, but we are more than compensated by the warm welcome of others. . . . Only a few minutes ago I met a lady who . . . introduced me to a large room in her house where there were fourteen ladies, young and old, busy as bees making shirts, drawers, and other clothing for the soldiers. . . . Judging probably from my rags that I too was in a destitute condition, she benevolently desired to take me in hand and replenish my entity throughout, but of course I declined. . . .

"Though thousands of soldiers are now roaming through the town, there has not been a solitary instance of misdemeanor. I have heard no shouting, no clamor of any kind. . . . All who visit the city are required to have passes, and the only persons arrested are those who are here without leave. . . .

"The only outrage, if outrage it can be called, was committed by the citizen Secessionists, who entered the office of the *Frederick Examiner*, a Black Republican newspaper of the darkest dye, and tore it to pieces, the editor himself fleeing on the first symptoms of our advance.

"We pay for everything as we go, the farmers being compensated for all damage by the burning of [fence] rails, use of forage, or destruction of crops. . . .

"Altogether, our movement has been thus far marked by the most gratifying success. Every detail has been successfully carried out, the troops are in good health and full of enthusiasm, the commissariat is improving, and we wait for nothing more anxiously than the order to resume our march onward."

Conditions were not as auspicious as the newsman claimed. During his march in Virginia before crossing the Potomac, Lee lost thousands of men through straggling. A great many of these had been worn down by their previous campaigning and simply could not keep up. To worsen matters, Maryland was not providing Lee the enlistments he had anticipated. Only a relatively few men were signing up. That Monday, September 8, he published an address by which he hoped to clarify his position and gain the kind of support he needed.

"To the People of Maryland: It is right that you should know the purpose that has brought the army under my command within the limits of your State, so far as that purpose concerns yourselves. The people of the Confederate States have long watched, with the deepest sympathy, the wrongs and outrages that have been inflicted upon the citizens of a commonwealth allied to the States of the South by the strongest social, political, and commercial ties. They have seen, with profound indignation, their sister State deprived of every right and reduced to the condition of a conquered province. . . .

A Confederate straggler

"Believing that the people of Maryland possessed a spirit too lofty to submit to such a government, the people of the South have long wished to aid you in throwing off this foreign yoke. . . . In obedience to this wish our army has come among you and is prepared to assist you with the power of its arms in regaining the rights of which you have been despoiled. . . . It is for you to decide your destiny, freely and without constraint. This army will respect your choice, whatever it may be; and while the Southern people will rejoice to welcome you to your natural position among them, they will only welcome you when you come of your own free will."

The day the petition was published was a sober and thoughtful one for the Confederate leaders in Frederick, but it was an altogether different kind of day for Jeb Stuart and Wade Hampton at Urbana. As explained by Heros von Borcke: "There was a great stir of preparation at headquarters on the morning of the 8th. Invitations to the ball were sent out to all the families in Urbana and its neighborhood and to the officers of Hampton's brigade. The large halls of the academy were aired and swept, and festooned with roses and decorated with battle flags borrowed from the different regiments."

It must not be supposed that the military situation in Stuart's area of responsibility was wholly secure and peaceful. Alfred Pleasonton's Yankee troopers from Washington, pursuing their reconnaissance duties, were prowling the country in front of Stuart's line of outposts, and there was contact that day about twenty miles south of his Urbana headquarters. The incident began when two regiments of Confederate troopers led by Colonel Thomas T. Munford made a probe toward Poolesville. As related in the journal of George M. Neese, a gunner in Roger Chew's battery of Confederate horse artillery:

"When we got to within one mile of Poolesville we spied the first Yanks that we saw since our arrival in the United States [i.e., in Maryland]. They were cavalry, and showed fight right away. We went in battery on a hill in the edge of a woods about a mile from the town and fired some six or eight rounds at them, when they drew up their cavalry in columns with drawn sabers ready for a charge on our pieces, but we threw a shell which anchored dangerously near them, broke their ranks and scattered them rearward.

"They brought up a battery then and opened a well-directed fire on us, and eventually drove us from our position. Their battery was about a mile and a half from us, and every shell after the first two fell and exploded right in the midst of us. I believe that the confounded Yankees can shoot better in the United States than they can when they come to Dixieland. They did better shooting with their artillery today than any I have seen since I have been in the service.

"For a while we seemed to be in a dangerous locality, for while the battery in our front was pouring in some good warm work, some two or three regiments of Yankee cavalry closed in on us in our rear. Heaven only knows where they came from or how they got so completely in our rear, and on the very road we came over, and which was the only way of escape for us if there was to be any getting-out business in the game. Our situation was critical indeed, for the Yankees in our front were advancing rapidly and getting very bold, and those in our rear charging and closing in on us. . . .

"At this juncture of affairs, Colonel Munford . . . became unduly excited, and as he galloped past us he shouted, 'Cut loose from your pieces!' But the calm and gallant Chew, whose judgment could not be dethroned by a little danger or excitement, quietly unheeded Colonel Munford's hasty advice or suggestion, and told us to stick to our guns.

"Just then a regular fusillade of pistols and carbines opened all around us, with some of our cavalry with drawn sabers rushing first one way, then another, not knowing whom to fight first, the ones in our front or the flankers in our rear. Fortunately, and just in time, the grand old 7th Regiment of cavalry charged with drawn sabers . . . and repulsed the enemy in our rear, and we slipped through the meshes of the dangerous web that the Yanks were weaving around us, and brought all our pieces out safely.

"Even then we were not on the dead-sure side of safety yet, as the Yanks that were in our front at first attempted to flank and cut us off from the Urbana road, but the Twelfth Virginia Cavalry stubbornly held them at bay until we got past the cutting-off place and were once more where we felt the gratifying virtue of an open and unobstructed rear.

"After we wriggled out of the most hazardous and eventful situation the battery was ever in, we fell back a mile and went in position on the road, but the Yanks did not pursue us. After we . . . found that the Yanks had settled down for the day—and I know *we* had enough for one dose—we fell back ten miles and bivouacked . . . at the southern base of Sugar Loaf Mountain.

"Our cavalry lost very few men today, considering the close and mixed-up encounter that we were all in. I saw some of the shells from the Yankee battery explode right in the ranks of our cavalry, but it seems they did very little harm, and our side sustained very little damage all through.

"If today's proceedings is an average specimen of the treatment the dear Yanks intend to give us in these dear United States, I think the best thing we can do is to go back to Dixie right away."

The encounter at Poolesville had no effect upon the preparations for Jeb Stuart's ball at Urbana. Returning to the account by Heros von Borcke:

"At seven in the evening all was complete, and already the broad avenue [leading to the academy] was filled with our fair guests, proceeding to the scene of festivity according to their social rank and fortune—some on foot, others in simple light 'rockaways,' others again in stately family coaches driven by fat Negro coachmen who sat upon the box with great dignity.

"Very soon the sound of distant bugles announced the coming of the band of the 18th Mississippi Infantry—the colonel and staff of the regiment, who had been invited as an act of courtesy, leading the way, and the band playing in excellent style the well-known air of 'Dixie.'

"Amid the loud applause of the numerous invited and uninvited guests, we now made our grand *entrée* into the large hall, which was brilliantly lighted with tallow candles. As master of the ceremonies, it was my office to arrange the order of the different dances, and I had decided upon a polka as the best for an animated beginning. I had selected the New York Rebel as the queen of the festival, and had expected to open the ball with her as my partner, and my surprise was great indeed when my fair friend gracefully eluded my extended arms, and, with some confusion, explained that she did not join in round dances, thus making me uncomfortably acquainted for the first time with the fact that in America, and especially in the South, young ladies rarely waltz [i.e., engage in paired dances] except with brothers or first cousins, and indulge only in reels and *contredanses* with strangers.

"Not to be baffled, however, I at once ordered the time of the music to be changed, and had soon forgotten my disappointment as to the polka in a very lively quadrille. Louder and louder sounded the instruments, quicker and quicker moved the dancers; and the whole crowded room, with its many exceedingly pretty women and its martial figures of officers in their best uniforms, presented a most striking spectacle of gaiety and enjoyment.

"Suddenly enters an orderly covered with dust, and reports in a loud voice to General Stuart that the enemy have surprised and driven in our pickets, and are attacking our camp in force, while at the same moment the sound of shots in rapid succession is distinctly borne to us. . . .

"The excitement which followed this announcement I cannot undertake to describe. The music crashed into a *concordia discors*. The officers rushed to their weapons and called for their horses. Panic-stricken fathers and mothers endeavored in a frantic way to collect around them their bewildered children, while the young ladies ran to and fro in most [evident] despair.

"General Stuart maintained his accustomed coolness and composure. Our horses were immediately saddled, and in less than five minutes we were in rapid gallop to the front. Upon arriving there we found, as is usually the case in such sudden alarms, that things were by no means so desperate as they had been represented.

"Colonel [L. S.] Baker, with the splendid 1st North Carolina regiment, had arrested the bold forward movement of the Yankees. Pelham, with his guns in favorable position, was soon pouring a rapid fire upon their columns. [This was John Pelham, the popular "boy major," whose artillery feats were becoming legendary.] The other regiments of the command were speedily in the saddle. The line of battle having been formed, Stuart gave the order for a general attack, and with great rage and fury we precipitated ourselves upon the foe, who paid with . . . killed and wounded and a considerable number of prisoners for their unmannerly interruption of our social amusement. They were pursued in their headlong flight for several miles by the 1st North Carolina, until, a little past midnight, they got quite out of reach, and all was quiet again.

"It was about one o'clock in the morning when we got back to the academy, where we found a great many of our fair guests still assembled, awaiting with breathless anxiety the result of the conflict. As the musicians had never dispersed, General Stuart ordered them again to strike up; many of our pretty fugitives were brought back by young officers who eagerly volunteered for that commendable purpose; and, as everybody was determined that the Yankees should not boast of having completely broken up our party, the dancing was resumed in less than half an hour, and kept up till the first glimmer of dawn.

"At this time the ambulances laden with the [Confederate] wounded of last night's engagement were slowly approaching the academy as the only building at Urbana that was at all suited to the purposes of a hospital. Of course the music was immediately stopped and the dancing ceased, and our lovely partners in the quadrille at once became 'ministering angels' to the sufferers.

"Captain [William W.] Blackford and I went down with our New York Rebel to an ambulance in which there was a poor fellow fearfully wounded by a ball in the shoulder. His uniform jacket was quite saturated with blood, and the tender white hands of our charming friend had just become fairly employed in the compassionate office of stanching the wound and cooling the inflammation with applications of cold water when her strength broke down and she fainted away.

"When after a few minutes she had recovered, we did our best to persuade her to go home; but with a courage equalling that of [a] warrior on the field of battle, she replied, 'I must first do my duty.' This she did bravely and tenderly, until the wounded man, greatly relieved by her ministrations, expressed his gratitude with tears streaming from his eyes, and begged her now to take care of herself.

"Blackford and I accompanied the noble creature to the house of Mr. C., and left her with the highest admiration for her tenderness and fortitude.

"The sun was high in the heavens when we rose from our camp pallets the following day."

4

McClellan Starts in Pursuit

IT WAS NOW Tuesday, September 9. McClellan's Army of the Potomac was on the move in the direction of Frederick, albeit slowly. McClellan was still largely in the dark as to Lee's plans. Jeb Stuart's troopers were doing a good job of disrupting Alfred Pleasonton's reconnaissance work. About the only reports McClellan received that he felt he could accept as helping to clarify matters were those indicating that Lee (as usual) had him heavily outnumbered!

Also limiting McClellan's pace were admonitions from the general-in-chief of the Union armies, Henry W. Halleck, who was sitting in Washington fretting that Lee, with McClellan moving away from the city, might suddenly fall back across the Potomac and again become a threat from the south. (Halleck, incidentally, was despised by McClellan, as was Halleck's superior, Secretary of War Edwin M. Stanton. These men were always "interfering" in McClellan's plans. The truth was that neither trusted his generalship.)

Early on that Tuesday, McClellan wrote his wife: "I hope to learn this morning something definite as to the movements of secesh, to be enabled to regulate my own. I hardly expect to equal the genius of Mr. Pope, but I hope to waste fewer lives and to accomplish something more than lame defeat. I have ordered a general advance of a few miles today, which will bring us on the line of the Seneca [Creek], and near enough to secesh to find out what he is doing, and take measures accordingly. I shall follow him wherever he goes and do my best to beat him. . . . The fact is that commanding such an army as this, picked up after a defeat, is no very easy thing."

It was helpful to him, however, that most of the men still idolized

Edwin M. Stanton

him. Says a volunteer from Boston named George Kimball: "Whenever General McClellan appeared among his troops . . . it was the signal for the most spontaneous and enthusiastic cheering I ever listened to or participated in. Men threw their caps high in the air, and danced and frolicked like schoolboys, so glad were they to get their old commander back again."

Among those who were not glad about this development was French-born P. Regis de Trobriand, a naturalized American presently serving as commander of a regiment of New York volunteers, a contemplative man who understood the tragedy of McClellan's performance at the gates of Richmond. The colonel recapitulates: "We had started out [for the Peninsula] in the spring, gay, smart, well-provided with everything. The drums beat, the bugles sounded; the flag, with its folds of immaculate silk, glistened in the sunshine. And we [had returned] before the autumn, sad, weary, covered with mud, with uniforms in rags. Now the drummers carried their cracked drums on their backs, the buglers were bent over and silent; the flag—riddled by balls, torn by shrapnel, discolored by the rain—hung sadly upon the staff. . . .

"Where were the red pantaloons? Where were the Zouave jackets? And, above all, those who had worn them, and whom we looked in vain along the ranks to find—what had become of them? Killed at Williamsburg, killed at Fair Oaks, killed at Glendale, killed at Malvern Hill; wounded or sick in the hospitals; prisoners at Richmond; deserters, we knew not where."

The destination of the present march was something of a mystery, but all were aware that another crisis was pending. In the words of Samuel Fiske, a New England clergyman who, while serving as a volunteer, sent regular reports (under the pseudonym Dunn Browne) to a Massachusetts newspaper, the *Springfield Republican*: "It is a tremendously big thing of which we are a part at this present time. . . . We move on up the country, through woods and vales, on roads and on byways, in three long parallel anaconda lines, no one of which is ever all visible at once, which seem absolutely interminable, and of whose numbers we . . . can scarcely form an idea; and when we double up and crowd together at night for a bivouac, we cover the whole face of the country round about like a cloud of locusts, as thick and as destructive.

"Acres and acres of soldiers, but not an acre of corn or potatoes or fruit, or anything else eatable [left] within a circle of miles, I suppose—and that, too, though we have been here only a night. A crop of soldiers kills out any other crop in the quickest possible time. Our orders against plundering [usually called "foraging"] are very strict, too, and guards generally placed over property. It seems to be impossible to keep an army from destroying everything through which it passes. The orders are strict enough; but a strict enforcement of the great principle of obedience seems to be utterly repugnant to the spirit of our citizen soldiers. I am sorry to acknowledge it, and yet more sorry to see and believe, that our soldiers very generally are . . . a set of lawless plunderers."

There were, of course, men with conscience enough to pay for the goods they took; and in other cases foodstuffs were handed out freely by their owners, zealous Unionists who regarded the soldiers as heroes of the cause. Some of the outright raids were made in a punitive manner. As explained by the New York surgeon, George Stevens: "Our . . . brigade . . . was quartered on the plantation of a noted secessionist who, on our approach, had suddenly decamped, leaving at our disposal a very large orchard whose trees were loaded with delicious fruit, and his poultry yard well-stocked with choice fowls. Our boys were not slow to appropriate to their own use these luxuries."

Some personal experiences of the earliest days of the march are

related by a sergeant from Pennsylvania named A. F. Hill: "We . . .
bivouacked for the night in a beautiful clover field near the residence of a wealthy gentleman. It was here that I had a striking
illustration of the effect shoulder-straps [worn by officers] are wont
to produce on the fair, especially when contrasted with the humble
apparel of a common soldier like myself. Jim, my messmate, was
unwell. He had refused to remain in Washington at a hospital,
insisting on accompanying us through our Maryland campaign. We
had just halted on the evening in question, when, perceiving that he
looked wan, I asked him how he felt.

" 'Oh, I can get along,' he answered evasively.

" 'Jim,' said I, 'you are not well enough to march. I advise you to—'

" 'No,' he interrupted, 'I never was in a hospital, and I never will
enter one. I consider it suicide.'

" 'I cannot but acknowledge that I am of the same opinion, when
I come to think about it, Jim. Have you anything you feel like
eating?'

" 'No; I—'

" 'Would you relish some milk?'

" 'I think so.'

McClellan's troops with Maryland women.

" 'Then I will go to that house and get some, if they have any.'

"And I threw down my effects, took my canteen, and walked to the residence of the wealthy gentleman before alluded to.

"Two young ladies of from eighteen to twenty years were seated on the front piazza. They were tastily dressed, and the moment I looked upon them I perceived that they were handsome. A second glance convinced me that *they* knew that before *I* did. Howbeit, I had nothing to do with their beauty, and I bowed, said 'good evening,' told them that I had a sick comrade, and that 'if they would be kind enough,' and all that sort of thing, I would be glad to be able to procure some milk for him.

"A sly wink [of amused tolerance] was exchanged by the bewitching pair. They didn't suppose that I observed it, but I did. At that moment the mother made her appearance at the door, and one of the maidens apprised her of the object of 'that soldier's' errand. The old lady took my canteen and entered the house, while I stood upon the steps awaiting her return, feeling just as awkward as possible— for any man will feel awkward when he knows that his general appearance is being criticised by two saucy-looking angels.

"Now, the lady of the house had but disappeared with my canteen when the father came up the path and ascended the steps of the piazza accompanied by an officer, a major. The officer was *not* a fine-looking fellow, but he wore two rows of bright buttons on his blue cloth coat, and, on each shoulder, a great broad gold shoulder-strap about the size of a spade.

" 'Daughters,' said the Marylander, 'let me introduce you to Major— a— eh—'

" 'Smith!' whispered the major, coming to his relief.

" 'Smith! Yes, Major Smith! My daughters, Major.'

"The two lasses arose, executed scientific curtsies, smiled, and said, 'Major Smith' in the most killing manner.

" 'A beautiful evening,' remarked Major Smith.

" 'Splendid!' exclaimed Miss Mary, the elder.

" 'Lovely!' agreed Miss Louisa Catharine, the younger.

" 'You have a beautiful place here,' remarked Major Smith, taking a seat which was offered him.

" 'Do you think so?' said both ladies, somewhat pleased.

" 'Indeed I do! And I think that—I *observe* that there is a great resemblance between the— the—; in fact, the people seem well-suited to the place.'

"The ladies were still more pleased, for they saw in this a compliment to them. They blushed and said, 'Oh, no!' although it was evident that they thought, 'Oh, yes!'

"Meanwhile, I was standing there unnoticed, waiting for that milk, ruminating on the weakness of human nature and mentally making promiscuous calculations as to the relative value of brass and lead, of swords and rifles, of blue cloth and kersey [coarse wool]. At last, to my great relief, the kind lady of the house reappeared with my canteen filled with milk. I asked her how much I should pay for it, but she wouldn't take any pay for it; and I thanked her, bade her good evening, and departed.

"A deep sigh of relief escaped me as I passed through the gate and found myself once more in the clover field.

"Next morning we arose, prepared our breakfast, dispatched it, and felt ready to move. But the morning began to wear away. Near twelve o'clock we moved on; but not by the pike; we took a byroad to the left and marched over some of the most beautiful country I ever saw. Many beautiful orchards full of ripe tempting fruit met our eyes as we marched along. To leave the ranks and attack any of the orchards was a thing strictly forbidden, and consequently unsafe.

"Near evening we were passing an orchard of nice fruit when a corpulent fellow of our regiment concluded that those red apples were too tempting for human nature to bear. Looking about to make sure that he was not observed by any field or general officer, he mounted the fence at the roadside, and was soon standing beneath the nearest tree. The heavy laden branches hung low, and, grasping a limb, he gave it such an energetic shake that about a bushel and a half of apples came showering down.

"Simultaneously with the rattling of the fallen apples, a grim buzzing sound was heard in the tree above the soldier's head. A moment he stood and listened.

" 'Buz-z-z-z-z-z' greeted his ears, and a great swarm of hornets came darting at him.

"With a cry of horror, he turned him about and 'streaked it' for the fence. But too slow were his feet for the wings of the pursuing fiends. On they came— 'buz-z-z-bat!' Just as he reached the fence, *they* reached *him*; and, as he sprang over, one of the monsters settled on his nose, another over his eye, and half a dozen among his hair; while any number buzzed unwholesomely near his ear, undecided as to where to attack him.

"This was a warning to all evil-doers, and no more such attempts were made that evening.

"The sun was just sinking when we filed off into a beautiful green field, stacked arms, and bivouacked for the night. There was a house near the field, and I started for it at once to procure some milk for Jim. General [George G.] Meade was riding up a lane near the house as I approached, and, seeing a peach tree laden with fruit, he called a cavalryman—one of his orderlies, I think—and left him to watch the tree till a guard should be detailed. [Meade was at this time a division commander.] He then rode up to the house for the purpose of ascertaining what number of guards would be required to protect the premises.

"I got my canteen filled with milk and was returning to our line of stacked arms when I observed that the cavalry sentinel who had been placed on guard over the peach tree was busily engaged in helping himself to the delicious fruit, for he could reach it while sitting upon his horse. But how romantic it was that at that very moment General Meade was returning from the house and 'caught him in the act.'

" 'What are you about there?' he called out savagely.

"The guard started.

" 'Why, you thief!' exclaimed General Meade.

"The cavalryman looked confused.

George G. Meade

" 'You mercenary villain! I set you to guard that tree, and—and— you—' And Meade rode at him.

"The sentinel was terrified.

" 'I'll cut your head off!' And the general drew his sword and flourished it above his head as he reached the offender.

"The young gentleman looked awful.... General Meade, with the *back* of his sword, began to saw upon the back of the terrified offender's neck, who, feeling the cold steel . . . drew in his head . . . like a tortoise . . . and . . . seemed on the point of falling from his horse for dead.

"General Meade, thinking that he had punished the poor fellow enough, suspended operations.... The soldier heaved a sigh of relief as the sword returned to its place with a clank.

" 'Oh, you deserve killing!' said Meade.

"The soldier groaned. He feared that the general might kill him yet before he should go away.

" 'Don't you think I ought to kill you?' persisted the latter, looking savagely upon the offender from behind his spectacles.

"The soldier was silent.

" 'Say!' demanded Meade.

" 'Yes, sir,' was the faint reply.

"General Meade rode away, and I imagine I saw a slight smile play about his firm lips."

A regimental chaplain from Pittsburgh, the Reverend A. M. Stewart, found the conduct of the Union soldiers in Maryland a matter for philosophical study. He recorded his thoughts in a letter he sent to the editor of a Pennsylvania newspaper: "Did you ever find yourself in a quandary as to the right adjustment of moral questions which have arisen for solution? Causes in which morals and physic, reason and appetite, judgment and inclination, did not seem fully to harmonize? Well, here is a case in hand—one of no ordinary interest, and, at present, widely extended in its application. As your correspondent finds himself beclouded in the matter, you and your readers will much oblige him by giving it a careful attention, accompanied with a just solution.

"During the past six months our regiment has been almost entirely confined to strong, coarse army grub—hard crackers, salt pork and beef, with coffee, and occasionally rice, beans, and fresh beef. In consequence of such a diet so long continued, when the Peninsula was abandoned scurvy had become quite common. After long, wearying, and almost bewildering marches, we were at length halted . . . in Montgomery County, Maryland. The neighborhood abounded in apple, pear, and peach orchards; fruit plenty, ripe, and tempting the hungry longing appetite—also with cornfields affording roasting ears in unmeasured quantities.

"Owing to their past diet and long want of such things, the appetite of our soldiers had become so intense as to appear almost uncontrollable. These, moreover, were the very things needed to give proper tone to the system by driving away scorbutic affections. . . . Our boys have been in possession of no money for long months; scarcely a copper among a hundred. . . . Nor has the quartermaster the authority to purchase and distribute [the produce] as rations, on the credit of the Government. If taken without pay, their families, as the owners . . . declare, will be left in want and to suffer, at least during the present season.

"It must be taken in account that almost every family in this half-loyal state is as good a Unionist as anybody else *so long as their domains are in possession of our troops.*

"With respect to the moral of taking the fruits and vegetables without pay . . . my own inability to act as an unbiased umpire has already been hinted. Scenes and interlocutories like the following have not been infrequent of late. It may be prefaced that the young men of our regiment are in every possible way kind and obliging to their chaplain. One of them, brave and generous from a dozen bloody battlefields, lately visited my humble bunk, and, after the due military salutation, says, 'Doctor . . . will you accept half a dozen beautiful ripe peaches?' at the same time producing the delicious-looking and fragrant-smelling fruit.

" 'O, what beautiful peaches! Why, where, and how did you obtain them?'

"With a peculiarly knowing look and tone, as the peaches are laid beside me he replies, 'Ask no questions, Doctor, for conscience' sake.'

"Another comes with the salutation, 'Doctor, will you accept these two roasting ears? They are very good, and nicely cooked.'

" 'Roasting ears, my dear young friend, are great favorites with me.'

"And still another— 'Doctor, here is a big boiled potato. . . . See how it laughs through a dozen cracks in its bursted skin.'

" 'Much obliged; very fond of a good potato.'

"Though personally I have pulled no roasting ears, shaken no apple tree, plucked no peaches, nor turned up a single potato hill, yet will the inferences be irresistible—these things have been taken and eaten, the owners uncompensated. And in our camp there may be no impartial judge of the right or wrong in the matter."

It was only during these days of McClellan's march through Maryland that the people of the other Union states began to grow acutely aware of the threat posed by Lee's army. Especially vulnerable was the neighboring state of Pennsylvania. According to John S. C. Abbott, a Northern historian who wrote the story of the war even while its events were in progress: "In the southern counties . . . the greatest excitement and alarm prevailed. The farmers collected their wives, children, and cattle, and sent them for safety into the northern counties, while they remained to defend their homesteads and to repel the invaders. Far and near, stores were closed, alarm bells were rung, mass-meetings gathered, and, after a few words of consultation, the men organized immediately for drill. . . . Governor [Andrew G.] Curtin . . . issued a proclamation calling upon every able-bodied man in the state to be ready for immediate service."

These turbulent conditions in Pennsylvania were investigated by one of the Union's most diligent and most popular news correspon-

Union newsman
Charles Carleton Coffin,
with notebook and telescope

dents, Charles Carleton Coffin, of the *Boston Journal*. "Taking the train from Philadelphia, I went to Harrisburg, Lancaster, and York. . . . Everywhere the people were arming. All the able-bodied men were drilling. All labor was at a standstill. The fires of the foundries went out. The farmers left their uncut grain in the field. Men worth millions of dollars were in the ranks as privates. Members of Congress, professors of colleges with their classes, ironmasters with their workmen, ministers and the able-bodied men of their congregations, were hastening to the rendezvous. The State Capitol grounds were swarming with men receiving arms and ammunition. It was a glorious exhibition of patriotism; yet I could but think that they would offer a feeble resistance in the open field to well-drilled troops."

5

A Change of Guard in Frederick

B Y THIS TIME Lee was beginning to move in Maryland. He was obliged to pursue his campaign with little more than his original army, since his appeal for help from the state had fallen largely on deaf ears. It is a curious fact that even the men who journeyed to Frederick to sign up found themselves reluctant to do so when they arrived. This is explained by another period historian, Evert A. Duyckinck:

"A gentleman of Maryland who passed four days in Frederick during the rebel rule answered a series of questions which, with his replies, were published in the *Baltimore American*. He was asked whether the rebels obtained many recruits in Frederick, to which he answered, 'Not many in Frederick, but there were about five hundred came in from Baltimore, Anne Arundel, Montgomery, and Carroll Counties, and some from Baltimore City. After seeing the character of the army and the life which the men led, many of them refused to join, and were [for] getting home again. When leaving myself, I met six young men from Carroll County, and [accompanied] them to Westminster. They acknowledged they had been to Frederick to join the army, but after *seeing and smelling it* had concluded to return home. They begged me not to give their names.'

"Question: 'What did they mean by smelling it?'

"Answer: 'They meant exactly what they said. I have never seen a mass of such filthy, strong-smelling men. Three of them in a room would make it unbearable, and when marching in column along the street the smell from them was most offensive. There are some of the better class of men among them, but the great mass are men of lowest caste, and although under strict discipline, the filth that pervades them is most remarkable. Their sympathizers at Frederick have been greatly disappointed in the character of the army, and most of them are now as anxious for them to disappear as they were for them to come. They have no uniforms, but are well-armed and equipped, and have become so inured to hardships that they care but little for any of the comforts of civilization.'

"Question: 'What was the appearance of the rebel soldiers?'

"Answer: 'They were the roughest set of creatures I ever saw, their features, hair, and clothing matted with dirt and filth; and the scratching they kept up gave warrant of vermin in abundance. . . .'

"It was observed, however, in spite of their ragged and filthy appearance, that these half-fed, barefooted soldiers of the rebellion, accustomed to hard fare and privations, were robust and healthy—while of their warlike spirit they had given too many proofs on various battlefields to leave that any longer a matter of doubt."

Lee planned to invade Pennsylvania, but first he had to attend to a problem in his rear. There was a Federal garrison at Harpers Ferry, some twenty miles southwest of Frederick, where Virginia's Shenandoah River, flowing from the south, entered the Potomac.

Maryland Heights   Loudoun Heights

Bolivar Heights

Harpers Ferry in 1862

Federals at a Harpers Ferry sutler's store

(This region was at the time still a part of Virginia. The state of West Virginia was not yet officially established.) The Federals at Harpers Ferry controlled the mouth of the Shenandoah Valley, and Lee had to have this corridor as his route of communications with the Southern states. He had expected the Federals to abandon Harpers when he crossed the Potomac and cut them off from Washington, but they had stood fast.

Now, counting heavily upon McClellan's known timidity, Lee took a venturesome step. He ordered his army divided into four segments. Three were to march so as to surround and capture Harpers Ferry while the fourth probed northwestward to Hagerstown, which lay near the Pennsylvania border. Stonewall Jackson was to be in overall command of the Harpers Ferry mission, and Lee was relying upon Jackson to finish it quickly so that the army could be reunited not only to press its march northward but also to be ready for a contest with McClellan. With Harpers Ferry reduced and McClellan defeated, the North would be at Lee's mercy.

But Jackson's assignment was far from an easy one. While two segments of his special command took relatively direct routes to

Harpers Ferry (the one to mount Maryland Heights, the other to Loudoun Heights), he himself was to lead the third segment on a long roundabout march, heading initially northwest along the same route as the troops bound for Hagerstown. (See map, the Antietam Campaign, below.) Jackson was to recross the Potomac in such a way as to enable him to move first against Martinsburg, northwest of Harpers Ferry, where about 2,500 Federals were stationed. This capture achieved, he was to mount Bolivar Heights, just west of Harpers, and establish contact with his command's other two segments for the garrison's reduction. Jackson, of course, was confident he could manage the whole operation with the required dispatch.

During Lee's departure from Frederick on September 10, with Jackson leading, the city was the scene of another great parade of troops, wagons, and artillery batteries. In the words of a Union woman who watched: "Their coming was unheralded by any pomp and pageant whatever. . . . No brilliant staff, no glittering cortege dashed through the streets. . . . I asked myself in amazement, were these . . . the men who had coped and encountered successfully, and driven back again and again, our splendid legions? . . . I felt humiliated at the thought that this horde of ragamuffins could set our grand army of the Union at defiance. Why, it seemed as if a single

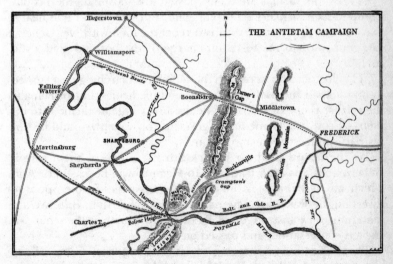

Zones of combat after Lee moved westward from Frederick: Catoctin Mountain, South Mountain, Harpers Ferry, and Sharpsburg. Jackson's special march is shown in its entirety.

regiment of our gallant boys in blue could drive that dirty crew into the river without any trouble. . . .

"They behaved [like] a crowd of boys on a holiday . . . on the broad grin all the time. . . . I saw some strikingly handsome faces . . . or, rather, they would have been so if they could have had a good scrubbing. They were very polite, I must confess, and always *asked* for a drink of water, or anything else . . . never . . . coming inside of a door without an invitation. . . . I felt sorry for the poor, misguided wretches, for some of them limped along so painfully, trying hard to keep with their comrades."

Another spectator who recorded his impressions of the army's departure was the Union surgeon whose hospital had been invaded when the army arrived. "Their supply wagons were few in number and mostly empty. The men carried no knapsacks, merely a blanket—and many of them my hospital blankets, stolen from the beds—and ordinary accoutrements of cup, canteen, etc.

"During their passage I saw Lee riding in an ambulance, he having recently been injured by a fall from his horse. [Actually, the horse shied while Lee was dismounted, holding the reins, and he was thrown down upon his hands, which were painfully sprained. In one, a small bone was broken.]

". . . As the various divisions passed the hospital, they coolly dumped their sick at the hospital gate, and very soon I had nearly five hundred rebel sick, with two rebel doctors, with me. General Lee sent word to me to retain charge of the hospital, and I did so. . . .

"The doctors who were with the regiments marching past rushed in and helped themselves to liquor and medicines, but principally the spirits, as one of them said he used very little medicine with his men—it cost [the Confederate government] so much—and he, for his part, preferred whisky or brandy.

"As the troops filed up Patrick Street . . . one of them asked, 'Where does this road lead to?' To Hagerstown, he was told. 'And which way is Baltimore?' he said. Fifty-five miles in the opposite direction, he was told. 'The devil! Do you hear that, Bill? We are marching *from* instead of *to* Baltimore.' And they then had an excited conversation, and passed on."

These were men belonging to James Longstreet's wing of the army. Another such man was William Miller Owen, the artilleryman from New Orleans. "The columns were soon upon the high road towards Boonsboro [an intermediate point on the way to Hagers-

James Longstreet

town], and we were all struck with the beautiful scenery of this section of the country. As we climbed the hills, long stretches of valley extended as far as the eye could reach in the direction of the Potomac. How still and peaceful it all looked. . . .

"As we were marching today over the turnpike road the rear chest of a caisson exploded. Although against the orders of his officers, Private Alsobrook seated himself for a ride upon the caisson and smoked his pipe. Presently came the explosion, and he was hurled twenty feet into the air and fell upon the road, entirely denuded of all his clothing and burned from head to feet. Strange to say, he received no serious injuries. He had hardly been removed when the shells in the chest began to explode and caused a stampede of officers and men.

"Then Corporals Kursheedt and Ruggles, of the First Company, stepped to the front and, going deliberately up to the smoking chest, emptied their canteens of water upon the burning cotton used for packing; then, taking the shells, some already ignited, threw them into the ditch of water alongside the road, where some exploded, making an awful scatteration of mud and water, but fortunately hurting no one. The danger over, the march was resumed.

"For this gallant act these corporals quite modestly received the

Longstreet's wartime servant

warm approbation of their comrades, and no more was thought of it. But the 'Victoria' and the 'Cross of the Legion of Honor' have been pinned to a soldier's breast for acts of lesser heroism."

During this march in Maryland, according to the sergeant from South Carolina, D. Augustus Dickert, "the great horde of Negro cooks and servants that usually followed the army were allowed to roam at will over the surrounding country, just the same as down in Virginia. The Negroes foraged for their masters ... gathering chickens, butter, flour, etc. Even now, when so near the Free States, with nothing to prevent them from making their escape, the Negroes showed no disposition to take advantage of their situation and conditions. . . . Some few were lost, of course, but they were lost like many of the soldiers—captured by [Union] foraging parties or left broken down along the roadside."

Returning to the account by William Miller Owen:

"On the 11th the march was continued towards Boonsboro and Hagerstown. We find that our welcome along the road is not cordial, and the 'general rising' of 'downtrodden Maryland' will not be on hand. On the 12th we reached Hagerstown, and find the people here are more demonstrative, and we have much polite attention shown us. Many young girls approached us as we marched through the streets, and presented us with beautiful flowers. . . .

"We did some shopping at Hagerstown, devoting ourselves chiefly to the dry goods line, and bought waterproof cloth and some dress patterns to present to our lady friends in Richmond, where they were in great need of such things. I should have liked to carry a wagon-load back.

"One merchant had upon his top shelves, where they had lain for many years, about one hundred old-fashioned bell-crowned beaver hats, with long nap upon them—just the style our fathers wore, and caricaturists are wont to place upon the head of 'Brother Jonathan.' These were discovered by some funny fellow, who appeared upon the street with one upon his head. The new mode took like wildfire—as new fashions always do—and the store was soon relieved of the stock of beavers, and the streets were thronged with men with the new 'Brother Jonathan' hat. . . .

"We found excellent lager beer and cigars in Hagerstown, and the secessionists entertained us hospitably."

Twenty-five miles to the south, September 12th found Stonewall Jackson's march a day behind schedule, since the distance involved was greater than he had expected, but things were proceeding respectably. In the morning the general made a personal entry into Martinsburg, the Federal garrison of which had fled toward Harpers Ferry. Jackson checked into a hotel to do some paper work. As recalled by staff officer Henry Kyd Douglas: "A great crowd hastened to the hotel to greet him. At first he shut himself up in a room to write dispatches, but the demonstration became so persistent that he ordered the door to be opened. The crowd, chiefly ladies, rushed in and embarrassed the general with every possible outburst of affection, to which he could only reply, 'Thank you; you're very kind.'

"He gave them his autograph in books and on scraps of paper, cut a button from his coat for a little girl, and then submitted patiently to an attack by the others, who soon stripped the coat of nearly all the remaining buttons. But when they looked beseechingly at his hair, which was thin, he drew the line there, and managed to close the interview. These blandishments did not delay his movements [toward Harpers Ferry]. . . . In the afternoon he was off again."

It appears that Jackson was losing some of his men through straggling. According to Mary Bedinger Mitchell, who lived in Shepherdstown, on the Potomac River east of Martinsburg: "Suddenly, on Saturday, the 13th of September, early in the morning, we found ourselves surrounded by a hungry horde of lean and dusty tatterdemalions. . . . I did not know where they came from. . . . General Jackson [had] recrossed into Virginia at Williamsport and hastened to Harpers Ferry by the shortest roads. These would take him some four miles south of us, and our haggard apparitions were perhaps a part of his force. They were stragglers, at all events—professional, some of them, but some worn out by the incessant strain of that summer. . . . All day they crowded to the doors of our houses, with always the same drawling complaint: 'I've been a-marchin' an' a-fightin' for six weeks stiddy, and I ain't had n-a-rthin' to eat 'cept green apples an' green cawn, an' I wish you'd please to gimme a bite to eat.'

"Their looks bore out their statements, and . . . we . . . went to get what we had. They could be seen afterward asleep in every fence corner and under every tree. But after a night's rest they pulled themselves together somehow, and disappeared as suddenly as they had come. Possibly they went back to their commands, possibly they only moved on to repeat the same tale elsewhere."

With Jackson beginning to invest Harpers Ferry, and with Longstreet occupying Hagerstown, Lee's campaign seemed to be in promising shape. But the general's fortunes were about to undergo a radical change. One of the reasons for this was that when his army marched out of Frederick on the tenth, something damaging had accidentally been left behind: a copy of his order concerning the army's division. The piece of paper, as the result of some unknown officer's carelessness, had been left lying in one of the fields used as a campsite.

This ill stroke was compounded by the fact that McClellan's army, moving faster than Lee had anticipated, began arriving at Frederick on the twelfth, even while Longstreet's men were romping about Hagerstown in their beaver hats and Jackson was entertaining the ladies of Martinsburg.

"About ten o'clock," relates Frederick's Union hospital surgeon, "our pickets were announced approaching. . . . About six hundred [Confederate] cavalry were concealed in a bend in Patrick Street, awaiting their arrival. *On* our advance cavalry guard came. 'Charge!' was the order on both sides, and a short skirmish took place in the streets. . . .

"I was within fifty yards of it and saw it. What an exciting time there was then! Pistols firing, men shouting and brandishing swords, horses plunging and tearing along as if mad, and cannon roaring, with shells exploding. It did not last three minutes [before the Confederates retreated westward], and yet on each side several were killed and eight or ten wounded.... The wounded were brought to the hospital.

"From the top of a house, the sight [of the advance troops of Ambrose Burnside's wing] was magnificent, nothing but moving masses of men and gleaming bayonets visible, surging along like the flood-tide on a sandy beach.... What a change then appeared in our truly rescued city! Flags of all size, and from every conceivable place, were displayed."

It was at this time that ninety-five-year-old Barbara Frietchie became the subject of an authentic episode. As explained by a grandniece: "We were glad that the rebels had gone and that our troops came. My mother and I lived almost opposite aunt's place. She and my mother's cousin, Harriet Yoner, lived together. Mother said I should go and see aunt and tell her not to be frightened.... When I reached aunt's place, she knew as much as I did about matters, and cousin Harriet was with her. They were on the front porch, and aunt was leaning on the cane she always carried.

"When the troops marched along, aunt waved her hand, and cheer after cheer went up from the men as they saw her. Some even ran into the yard. 'God bless you, old lady,' 'Let me take you by the

Barbara Frietchie

hand,' 'May you live long, you dear old soul,' cried one after the other. . . .

"Cousin Harriet Yoner said, 'Aunt ought to have a flag to wave.' The flag was hidden in the family Bible, and cousin Harriet got it and gave it to aunt. Then she waved the flag to the men and they cheered her as they went by."

Returning to the account by the Union surgeon: "Stores were opened . . . and houses were opened, and our tired soldiers fed in truly hotel style. When Burnside rode through, the acclamations were universal, but nothing to the reception given McClellan when he entered [the next day]. Bouquets were thrown; men, women, and children rushed to [his horse], he bowing and speaking to all; girls embracing his horse's neck and kissing the animal, only because they could not reach the general."

This was September 13. At the day's dawning, Jesse L. Reno's corps of Burnside's wing, preceded by elements of Pleasonton's cavalry, had pressed a couple of miles westward from Frederick toward the Middletown pass of the Catoctin Mountain. Middletown was west of the pass, and it was here that Jeb Stuart had headquartered himself the previous evening, relying upon an artillery-supported detachment of his troopers to keep the pass covered. As related by Heros von Borcke, who spent the night with Stuart:

"The boom of artillery summoned us to the saddle at an early hour of the 13th, and we rode as rapidly as possible to the front, where Hampton with his brigade had been gallantly defending the Middletown Path since daylight against vastly superior numbers of the enemy, and had, up to that moment, successfully repelled every attack. The position was extremely favorable for defense. No other passage to the right or left led across the mountain spur, and our two batteries, posted to great advantage, played with telling effect upon the numerous guns of the enemy in the open flat below, which, not being able to get the necessary elevation, proved almost harmless to us.

"Nevertheless it was evident that our small body of men would be soon obliged to give way before the overwhelming odds of the Yankees, who, just at the time we reached the spot, were preparing for a renewal of the assault under cover of an energetic fire from five or six batteries.

"At this juncture I was ordered by General Stuart to take one of our mountain howitzers—very light guns which often did excellent service upon difficult ground and could easily be drawn by two horses—and try to find an eligible place on our extreme left from which we could open fire with it upon the dense columns of Yankee infantry. With a good deal of trouble, and after we had been obliged several times to cut our way through the thick undergrowth, I found a little plateau of perhaps fifty feet in diameter, and in a few minutes the rapid discharges of our little gun announced to General Stuart that I was at work.

"The extended view from this plateau . . . was now animated in the extreme. Frederick lay before us, distinctly seen through the clear air of the morning. The valley beneath, stretching away from the immediate base of the mountain, was literally blue with the Yankees. . . . Their long columns of infantry with a waving glitter of bayonets, their numerous bodies of cavalry with 'many a flirt and flutter' of gay flags and pennons, their imposing artillery trains with the sunlight reflected from the polished brass pieces, and their interminable lines of wagons . . . broke upon my sight.

"Directly beneath my feet the masses of the enemy were as busy as a swarm of bees. Two lines of sharpshooters were advancing in excellent style; the cavalry galloped hither and thither, seeking to get out of range of our cannon, while their numerous batteries, under the galling effect of our fire, were every moment changing position. The fire of my howitzer from a point hitherto regarded as inaccessible, plunging at this short range . . . into the compact ranks of the enemy, greatly augmented the commotion. Several batteries at once opened upon us, but so far overshot their mark that at every fire my cannoneers threw their kepis into the air with loud yells of derision.

"Meanwhile I had sent an orderly to General Stuart, reporting the state of affairs and expressing my opinion that the time had come for our retreat. The general soon arrived upon the spot and gave orders for the withdrawal of the mountain howitzer; but, as he had not seen the lines of the advancing infantry skirmishers, who had already disappeared in the thick underwood below us, he did not share in my opinion as to the danger of our situation.

"The firing of small arms now became louder and louder on our right, and seemed to proceed from a point even a little to the rear of the place we occupied. Annoyed at my continued remonstrances, Stuart at last said, 'Major, I am quite sure those shots come from our own men, who are firing at far too great a range. Ride over there at once and order them to reserve their ammunition until they can see the whites of the Yankees' eyes.'

"I knew very well that it was rushing into a wasp's nest, but orders were to be obeyed; and, making my way as quickly as the nature of the ground would admit, I proceeded to the scene of action, giving my orders [for a cease fire] in a loud voice as I heard several men breaking down the tangled thicket near at hand.

"In a moment the bushes before me parted, and a Yankee, as blue as ever I saw one, emerged from them. At the same instant a bullet tore the bark from a tree behind me at a very few inches from my head, and several other [bluecoats] made their appearance; and I had just time to turn my horse and gallop back to General Stuart, who now fully credited my report and made off with me as fast as our chargers could carry us over the rocky surface of the mountain.

"The Yankees . . . now advanced their whole line at a run—and with loud cries of encouragement—towards an open space over which we must ride, and where a shower of bullets fell around us, fortunately without touching a rider or a horse.

"The order for our general retreat [from the mountain] was now given, and executed at a quick trot. I expected every moment to hear the roar of the Yankee artillery, which from the heights behind us must have inflicted very serious loss upon our column; but General Hampton, with admirable foresight, had so well barricaded the roads that we were out of range before they had gained our former position. . . .

"Near Middletown we took up a new position."

The Confederates were driven from this position as well, and they took refuge in the next set of heights to the west, those of South Mountain. This left McClellan in full control of the long north-south valley between the two ridges. He knew that Lee's army was behind the South Mountain chain, but he did not know how its units were disposed.

It was at this time—and the development seemed almost magical—that McClellan came into possession of Lee's lost order. As explained by Silas Colgrove, commander of the 27th Indiana Volunteers, a regiment of the Twelfth Army Corps that reached Frederick that day about noon:

"We stacked arms on the same ground that had been occupied by General D. H. Hill's division. . . . Within a very few minutes after halting, the order was brought to me by First Sergeant John M. Bloss and Private B. W. Mitchell, of Company F . . . who stated that it was found by Private Mitchell near where they had stacked arms. When I received the order it was wrapped around three cigars, and

Private Mitchell stated that it was in that condition when found by him.

"General A. S. Williams was in command of our division. I immediately took the order to his headquarters and delivered it to Colonel S. E. Pittman, General Williams's adjutant-general.

"The order was signed by Colonel [R. H.] Chilton, General Lee's [assistant] adjutant-general, and the signature was at once recognized by Colonel Pittman, who had served with Colonel Chilton [in the U.S. Army] at Detroit, Michigan, before the war, and was acquainted with his handwriting. It was at once taken to General McClellan's headquarters by Colonel Pittman.

"It was a general order giving directions for the movement of General Lee's entire army, designating the route and objective point of each corps."

McClellan soon decided that the order was authentic. Waving it above his head, he exclaimed, "Here is a paper with which if I cannot whip Bobbie Lee, I will be willing to go home!"

6

Thunder Over South Mountain

S ELDOM IN military history has a commander been handed so
great an advantage. Possession of the lost order even mini-
mized McClellan's fears about the "superior numbers" he was facing. Right now Lee's strength, whatever it might be, was not a
critical matter. His army was divided. It might be attacked in detail.
And Harpers Ferry could be relieved. But McClellan had scarcely
been given his remarkable opportunity before he began to fritter it
away. He decided to wait till the following day to force the South
Mountain passes, whereas he should have begun moving at once.
That evening the passes were not manned for major resistance.

Lee had not expected to fight McClellan at South Mountain, but
had planned to draw him farther from his base of supplies at
Washington, perhaps into Pennsylvania, before turning for the
showdown. Now, with his army divided and McClellan almost upon
him, Lee was about to lose the initiative, with a defense of the South
Mountain passes becoming vital to his army's very survival.

In the northern zone, west of Middletown, there were two passes,
close together: Turner's Gap and Fox's Gap. In the south, about five
miles from the upper passes and west of Burkittsville, was another
pair of passes: Crampton's Gap and Brownsville Gap. That night
Lee ordered all of his available forces to cover the four passes.

It happened that the division under Stonewall Jackson's brother-
in-law, the fearless, Yankee-hating South Carolinian D. H. Hill, was
acting as Longstreet's rear guard on his way to Hagerstown and was
still at Boonsboro, not far from the western mouths of Turner's and
Fox's; and Hill needed only to swing his five thousand men around,

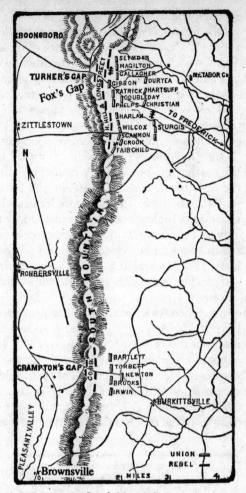

South Mountain

march them over the mountain, and deploy them on the eastern slopes so as to cover the roads of entrance. Longstreet was ordered by Lee to reverse his march and join Hill, but Hagerstown was too far away for Longstreet to be of immediate service.

To defend Crampton's Gap and Brownsville Gap in the south, Lee looked to one of Stonewall Jackson's segments at Harpers Ferry (which place was now under siege, invested on three sides). Lafayette McLaws was in command of two divisions on the Maryland

bank of the Potomac (on Maryland Heights), his artillery aimed at
Harpers across the water. The general's position was less than ten
miles southwest of the Crampton's Gap–Brownsville Gap area, and
he was in easy union with it by means of a corridor called Pleasant
Valley. With the enemy known to be spreading from Frederick,
McLaws was concerned about this route to his rear, and he had
already assigned two brigades to guard the passes.

At all four of the passes the Confederate lines were thin, but the
ground was generally well-suited to defensive operations.

McClellan assigned Ambrose Burnside's wing of his army to
march upon the northern passes, while William Franklin's wing was
sent toward the ones in the south. On the bright, autumn-tinged
morning of Sunday, September 14, the Confederates who occupied
some of the mountain's higher positions were awed by the sight of
many thousands of Federals making their approach on the roads
across Middletown Valley. "The marching columns," says Confederate General D. H. Hill, "extended back far as eye could see. . . . It
was a grand and glorious spectacle, and it was impossible to look at
it without admiration."

The columns stretched back through the Catoctin passes and into
the streets of Frederick. Among those who marched through the
city that morning was the Pennsylvania sergeant, A. F. Hill, and his
mind was on something other than combat. "At almost every door
stood some bewitching creature with a pail of clear, cold, sparkling
water; while others stood with glasses in their hands inviting us to
drink. They talked pleasantly with us, and manifested every indication of preferring us to the rebels. I can't for the life of me tell what

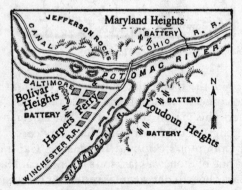

Harpers Ferry under siege

made me so thirsty that morning; for I must have stopped a dozen times for a drink. . . .

"As we progressed, the sound of artillery began to be heard in front."

There was something of unusual note about the artillery fire that resounded over the region that morning. It came not only from the contested mountain but also from Harpers Ferry, to the south. At Shepherdstown, west of both places, the Confederate woman, Mary Bedinger Mitchell, found the situation confusing: "We were expecting the bombardment of Harpers Ferry, and knew that Jackson was before it. . . . Our interest there was so intense that we sat watching the bellowing and smoking heights for a long time before we became aware that the same phenomena were to be noticed in the north. From our windows both points could be observed, and we could not tell which to watch more keenly."

The day was not to be one of decision at Harpers Ferry. The beleaguered Federals would manage to hold out, although, according to an unidentified Northern newsman who was on the scene, "shot and shell flew in every direction, and the soldiers and citizens were compelled to seek refuge behind rocks, in houses, and elsewhere."

South Mountain was the zone of immediacy, with Turner's Gap and Fox's Gap, in the north, seeing the hardest fighting, the front expanding to a width of three miles.

As summed up by Union officer Francis Palfrey, then commanding the 20th Massachusetts Infantry: "So much of the Battle of South Mountain as was fought at Turner's Gap [and Fox's] hardly admits of a precise description. It lasted a long time . . . and a good many troops were used first and last, but the ground was so peculiar and so little known to our commanders, that much precious time and many gallant efforts were almost wasted. . . . There were frequent charges and counter-charges, and many attempts, more or less successful, to turn the flanks of the opposing forces."

In the early afternoon, General McClellan, on horseback, stationed himself on the Middletown Road, a mile or two from the thunder-racked, smoke-patched mountain. He became an inspiration to the troops still coming out of Frederick on their way to the front. In the words of George Kimball, the soldier from Boston: "As each organization passed the general, the men became apparently forgetful of everything but their love for him. They cheered and cheered again, until they became so hoarse they could cheer no longer. It seemed as if an intermission had been declared in order that a reception might be tendered to the general-in-chief.

"A great crowd continually surged around him, and the most extravagant demonstrations were indulged in. Hundreds even hugged his horse's legs and caressed his head and mane. While the troops were thus surging by, the general continually pointed with his finger to the gap in the mountain through which our path lay. It was like a great scene in a play, with the roar of the guns for an accompaniment."

As the result of McClellan's habitual caution, it wasn't till well into the afternoon that the battle was fully developed. On the Confederate side, the first of Longstreet's units from Hagerstown came panting up the west side of the mountain around three o'clock. One of the men in the fore was the Reverend George G. Smith, who recounts:

"A year before, I had been the pastor of a charming little church in a beautiful valley in upper Georgia. I was just married, and ought to have been content to have staid at home, but in my veins was the blood of those who had fought in the Revolution, and when I saw my parishioners going to the front I went too, as the chaplain of the Phillips Legion. We had fifteen companies—nine of infantry, five of cavalry, and one of artillery—commanded by Colonel William Phillips. . . .

"Somehow I got the name of the 'fighting chaplain,' and, candidly, I did not like it. . . . I went to the army as a chaplain, and as a chaplain I did my work; and yet that day I got a bullet through my neck. . . .

"My regiment . . . was behind a stone fence on the right of the Boonsboro and Frederick pike. . . . A battery of [our] light artillery was firing overhead, and we lay quietly looking toward the south. Suddenly the order came to change front. We were now to face towards the west. The turnpike was narrow, and the enemy were upon us. The change of position called for a change from line of battle to column, and then from column into line. My own regiment did beautifully, and for a moment we looked to the woods, expecting the Federals to charge upon us, but instead we were ordered . . . to charge into the woods.

"As we entered the woods I saw a poor fellow fall and heard him say, 'Lord Jesus, receive my spirit.' I went to him and said, 'My friend, that's a good prayer; I hope you feel it.' He answered, 'Stranger, I am not afraid to die; I made my peace with God over thirty years ago.'

". . . [Soon afterward] I saw . . . that the Federals were east, south, and west of us. The firing was now fierce . . . and the regiment [began] retreating in a broken and confused manner. One of the boys, Gus Tomlinson, in tears, said, 'Parson, we've been whipped; the regiment is retreating.'

" 'And none too soon either,' said I, 'for we are surrounded on all sides but one.'

"Just then I felt a strange dizziness, and fell, my arm dropping lifeless by my side. . . . Blood was gurgling from my throat. The dear boys rushed to me, laid me on a blanket, and bore me off the field. I thought I was mortally wounded; so did they. 'Yes, parson,' said they, 'it's all up with you.' The ball had entered my neck, and, ranging downward, came out near my spine, paralyzing my arm.

"How does a man feel under such circumstances? Well, one thing I felt, and that was that it's a good thing in such an hour to have faith in Christ and love toward all men. . . .

"As we came out, [John B.] Hood's division went in."

Hood restored Confederate fortunes on that part of the field. But, nearly everywhere, the Federals kept coming. Sergeant A. F. Hill (who had drunk so much water in Frederick that morning) fought on the Union right as a member of Meade's division of Joseph Hooker's corps.

"About four o'clock we began to advance. We toiled up the steep ascent in front of us, when we discovered that a valley lay yet between us and the main ascent of South Mountain. While passing through a cornfield upon the hill, the enemy's artillery . . . opened upon us with solid shot. Down the hill we [continued]—across the small valley—up the steep ascent of the mountain. A few hundred yards from the base of the mountain was a stone fence. . . . When within fifty yards of the stone fence, a murderous fire of musketry was opened upon us by the rebels who lay concealed behind it, and swarms of bullets whistled about our ears.

"With a wild shout we dashed forward—almost upward—while volley after volley was poured upon us; but we heeded it not; we rushed madly on. The rebels, intimidated by our voices and taken aback by our recklessness and disregard of their bullets, began to give way. We reached the stone fence and sprang over. The rebels reformed among the rocks [of the mountainside] and fought with remarkable obstinacy. . . .

"We pressed the rebels closely. They stood awhile, loading and firing, but at last began to waver. Directly in front of the right of our regiment they gave way; and several companies from the right—

ours among them—pressed forward, becoming detached from the regiment. We soon found ourselves thirty or forty paces ahead of the regiment, having gained the flank of the 17th South Carolina. We were within twenty or thirty steps of them, directly on their left, and they did not see us. . . . We mowed them down. Poor fellows! I almost pitied them to see them sink down by dozens at every discharge. I [took] deliberate aim at a tall South Carolinian who was standing with his side to me, loading his gun. I fired, and he fell into a crevice between two rocks.

"Step by step we drove the rebels up the steep side of the mountain. By moving a little to the left I reached the spot where I had seen the rebel fall. . . . He arose to a sitting position, and I was convinced he was not dead yet. I inquired whether he was wounded, and he very mournfully nodded assent. The blood was flowing from a wound in the neck. He also pointed to a wound in the arm. The same bullet had made both wounds; for, at the time I fired, he was in the act of ramming a bullet home, his arm extended vertically.

"He arose to his feet, and I was pleased to find him able to walk. I informed him that, in the nature of things, he was a prisoner; and I sent him to the rear."

Among the numerous other Confederates who were captured late in the day was Captain Robert E. Park, who had led forty men of Colonel B. B. Gayle's 12th Alabama Regiment on a daring advance down the mountain but had at length been obliged to draw back before superior numbers. Captain Park relates: "I had lost only four men wounded up to this time, but six or eight more became demoralized and, despite my commands, entreaties, and threats, left me and hastily fled to the rear. With the brave squad which remained, we retreated slowly, firing as rapidly as we could load, and doing fatal work with every step. . . .

"The sun was rapidly setting. Corporal Myers, of Mobile, at my request aimed at and shot an exposed officer, receiving himself a terrible wound as he did so. I raised him tenderly, gave him water, and reluctantly was about to abandon him to his fate when a dozen muskets were pointed at me and I was ordered to surrender. . . . The Federals had got in my rear, and at the same time had closed upon me in front. If I had not stopped with Myers I might have escaped capture. . . . I was mortified and humiliated by the necessity of yielding myself a prisoner. Certain death was the only alternative.

"The enemy pushed forward after my capture, and came upon

Federals advancing at Turner's Gap

Colonel Gayle and the rear support. Colonel Gayle was ordered to surrender, but, drawing his pistol and firing it in their faces, he exclaimed, 'We are flanked, boys, but let's die in our tracks!' and continued to fire until he was literally riddled by bullets.

"I was accompanied to the rear by three Federal soldiers, and could but notice, as I walked down the mountain, the great execution done by my little squad as shown by the dead and wounded lying all along the route."

The last hours of daylight found the Unionists gaining the advantage, though not decisively. They were unable to do more than to secure a firm grip on the easterly hillsides and loosen the enemy's grip on the summit.

As the action continued, Union Colonel Harrison S. Fairchild's brigade of New Yorkers marched into it for the first time that day. Their participation is described by David L. Thompson, a member of the 9th New York Volunteers: "The brigade was ordered ... to support a regular battery posted at the top of a steep slope, with a cornfield on the left, and, twenty yards or so in front, a thin wood. We formed behind the battery and a little down the slope—the 89th on the left, the 9th next, then the 103d. We had been in position but a few minutes when a stir in front advised us of something unusual afoot, and the next moment the Confederates burst out of the woods and made a dash at the battery.

"We had just obeyed a hastily given order to lie down when the bullets whistled over our heads and fell far down the slope behind us. Then [our] guns opened at short range, full-shotted with grape and canister. The force of the charge was easily broken. . . . It was in this charge that I first heard the 'rebel yell.' Not the deep-breasted Northern cheer, given in unison and after a struggle to signify an advantage gained, but a high shrill yelp uttered without concert and kept up continually when the fighting was approaching a climax as an incentive to further effort.

"This charge ended the contest for the day on that part of the line. Pickets were set well forward in the woods, and we remained some time in position, waiting. . . . Before the sunlight faded I walked over the narrow field. All around lay the Confederate dead—undersized men mostly, from the coast district of North Carolina, with sallow hatchet faces, and clad in 'butternut,' a color running all the way from a deep, coffee brown up to the whitish brown of ordinary dust. As I looked down on the poor pinched faces, worn with marching and scant fare, all enmity died out.

Confederate dead at Fox's Gap

There was no 'secession' in those rigid forms, nor in those fixed eyes staring blankly at the sky . . . .

"Some of our men primed their muskets afresh with the finer powder from the cartridge boxes of the dead. With this exception, each remained untouched as he had fallen. Darkness came on rapidly. . . . As little could be done at that hour in the way of burial, we unrolled the blankets of the dead, spread them over the bodies, and then sat down in line, munching a little on our . . . rations . . . and listening to the firing, which was kept up on the right, persistently.

"By 9 o'clock this ceased entirely."

By this time the fighting at the lower passes, five miles away, had also ended. This action, which had centered upon Crampton's Gap, was a relatively small-scale affair that had resulted in a clear-cut decision—which was inevitable, since the Confederates were overwhelmingly outnumbered. Among the defenders was George Neese, the gunner in Chew's battery of the horse artillery; and Neese recorded in his journal:

"Crampton's Gap is really neither gorge nor gap, only a little notch in the crest of South Mountain; and nearly all the fighting today in trying to defend it was done on the eastern face of the mountain. It is marvelous how a few hundred of our men held in check nearly all day two divisions of Yankees, besides their artillery and cavalry; and I will venture the assertion that, as usual, correspondents of the Northern newspapers will say that a little band of heroic Union patriots gallantly cleared out Crampton's Gap, that was defended by an overwhelming force of Rebels strongly posted all over the mountain and standing so thick that they had to crawl over each other to get away."

The Confederate force was very nearly as thin as Neese claimed. It was made up of Thomas Munford's brigade of cavalry, three or four regiments of infantry, and a sparse array of artillery. All of the guns were on the heights, but there was a line of riflemen in a lower position behind a stone wall.

Neese gives this description of the battle's beginning: "At about ten o'clock we saw the first of the Yankee host, about three miles away, approaching our gap cautiously and slowly. As they drew nearer, the whole country seemed to be full of bluecoats. . . . What would, or could, our little force . . . do with such a mighty host that was advancing on us with flying banners? As they came nearer to the mountain they threw out a heavy skirmish line of infantry on both sides of the road, and were still advancing very slowly when their skirmish line came to within about a mile of our position, so we opened on it with our rifled guns. Our line of fire was right over the village of Burkittsville, and completely checked their skirmishers about half a mile [beyond] Burkittsville.

"The yanks now brought up a battery and opened fire on us, but they were about two miles off, and all their shell fell short. I fired at them in return, but in so doing I disabled my gun. The mountain where we were in battery was a little steep, and my gun is a vicious little recoiler, and the recoil space of our position was too sloping, rough, and limited for a free kick, consequently with the second shot that I fired—with a two-mile range—at the Yankees, my piece snapped a couple of bolts of its mounting, entirely disabling it for the day.

"After my gun was damaged, there was nothing for me to do but leave the field of action, but before I left I stood for a while and

Federal artillery under fire at South Mountain.

gazed at the magnificent splendor of the martial array that was slowly and steadily moving toward us across the plain below like a living panorama, the sheen of the glittering side-arms and thousands of bright, shiny musket barrels looking like a silver-spangled sea rippling and flashing in the light of a midday sun. . . .

"To observe the caution with which the Yankees, with their vast superior numbers, approached the mountain, it put one very much in mind of a lion, king of the forest, making exceedingly careful preparations to spring on a plucky little mouse."

The comparison was an apt one. There was soon a delay in the action while the Union wing commander, William Franklin, pondered the situation. He was worried about trying to carry the pass with no reinforcements behind him. The afternoon was well advanced before the bluecoats resumed their movement in earnest, their wide front rolling toward Burkittsville and the slopes beyond it.

The Confederates employed their meager power in a formidable manner. According to the New York surgeon, George Stevens, whose unit was a part of the attack:

"The mountains . . . belched forth fire and smoke. . . . The air was filled with the howling of shells which flew over our heads and ploughed the earth at our feet. At the same time, the line of battle behind the stone wall opened upon us a fierce fire of musketry. . . . The corps pressed forward at double-quick, over the ploughed grounds and through the cornfields, halting for a few moments at the village.

"The citizens, regardless of the shells which were crashing through their houses, welcomed us heartily, bringing water to fill the canteens and supplying us liberally from the scanty store [of food] left them by the marauding rebels. Patriotic ladies cheered the Union boys. . . .

"After a few minutes, in which our soldiers took breath, the advance was once more sounded, and again we pushed on in face of a murderous fire, at the same time pouring into the face of the foe a storm of leaden hail. [Henry W.] Slocum's division of the Sixth Corps advanced on the right of the turnpike, while [William F.] Smith's division pushed directly forward on the road and on the left of it. . . . Having driven the enemy from point to point, Slocum's troops . . . succeeded in seizing the pass, while our Second Division [Smith's] pressed up the wooded sides of the mountain, charging a battery at the left of the pass and capturing [one] of its guns."

By this time, with the day near its close, the Confederate defenders had been joined by some additional regiments that had been rushed through Pleasant Valley from Lafayette McLaws's command on Maryland Heights at Harpers Ferry. But nothing was gained by their arrival. Union narrator George Stevens continues:

"The Confederates fled precipitately down the west side of the mountain, and our flags were waved in triumph from the heights.... As we advanced [to the summit] ... great care was required ... to avoid treading upon the lifeless remains which lay thickly upon the ground.... A continual procession of rebel wounded and prisoners lined the roadsides, while knapsacks, guns, canteens, and haversacks were scattered in great profusion.

"The rebel force made its way into Pleasant Valley, leaving in our hands their dead and wounded, three stand of colors, [one piece] of artillery, and many prisoners."

Confederate General McLaws himself was now on the way through Pleasant Valley from Maryland Heights. Riding ahead of him were Jeb Stuart and Heros von Borcke, who had spent the afternoon at the heights and had become as concerned as McLaws over the ominous sounds from Crampton's Gap. The troopers hadn't gone far before they encountered a mass of Confederates from Crampton's pouring southward in the valley, their intent to get back to Maryland Heights and the protection of the parent units from which they had been detached.

Von Borcke relates: "Hundreds of soldiers, many of them wounded, were arriving in disorderly array from the fight, while guns and caissons, huddled together with wagons and ambulances moving towards the rear, blocked up the road. We at once posted a strong guard [presumably made up of men chosen from among the more stalwart refugees] along the road, with orders to arrest every man who was not too badly hurt to renew the conflict; and, taking the artillery with us, continued our ride. After about an hour's progress we reached the spot where General [Howell Cobb], an ex-politician and agriculturist who had commanded the troops at Crampton's Gap, was vainly endeavoring to rally the remainder of his brigade.

"The poor general was in a state of the saddest excitement and disgust at the conduct of his men. As soon as he recognized us in the dusk of the evening, he cried out in heartbroken accents of alarm and despair, 'Dismount, gentlemen; dismount if your lives are dear to you! The enemy is within fifty yards of us; I am expecting their attack every moment! Oh, my dear Stuart, that I should live to experience such a disaster! What can be done? What can save us?'

"General Stuart did his best to comfort and encourage his disconsolate friend, assisted him in rallying his scattered troops, and quickly placed in position all the artillery. Then, turning to me, he said, 'Major, I don't believe the Yankees are so near at hand, but we must be certain about it. Take two couriers with you and find out at once where the enemy is.'

"My general was very fond of sending me on these ticklish expeditions, and much as I appreciated the honor thus paid me, I did not feel greatly obliged to him on this particular occasion as I rode forward into the darkness, feeling that I should run a narrow chance of being shot by our own men on my return—if, indeed, I escaped the bullets of the Yankees.

"Cautiously I proceeded, fifty yards, a hundred, two hundred yards—everything quiet; not a trace of the enemy. At last, after a ride of more than a mile, I discovered the long lines of the Federal campfires, where Messieurs the Yankees had halted and were busily employed in cooking supper. And, at sixty yards' distance I could see in the road a cavalry picket, clearly defined against the glare of the fires—horse and trooper—who seemed to have no idea of our approach.

"Leaving the hostile sentry undisturbed, we rode quietly back to our lines, where the generals awaited my return with the greatest interest and anxiety. In the meantime General McLaws had arrived [from Maryland Heights] with reinforcements. Our line of battle was formed, and several batteries, in favorable positions, were ready for action. As it was evident, however, that the enemy did not intend making any further forward movement until the next day, General Stuart and I soon galloped back [through Pleasant Valley] to our cavalry, with whom we bivouacked during the remaining hours of the night."

In the scattered battle zones, hundreds of men spent the chilly September night attending to the wounded. The Confederates turned their ambulances toward the west, their destination the Potomac crossing at Shepherdstown. Typical of the activities on the eastern side of the mountain were those at Crampton's Gap, described as follows in the diary of Thomas T. Ellis, a Union army surgeon:

"The road leading to the gap was filled with long and winding lines of ambulances, going and returning. As fast as the men could be placed in the ambulances, they were removed to the principal private houses in Burkittsville, and their wounds dressed. . . . The inhabitants of Burkittsville opened their houses with alacrity for the reception of the wounded and offered the kindest attentions to the sufferers.

"The surgeons were busy all night, and the most painful operations were submitted to. . . . As soon as [the patients] are able to bear removal they will be sent to Frederick, where arrangements are made for the reception of one thousand. . . .

"The rebel wounded were nearly all taken to the Baptist Church in Burkittsville, which has been converted into a temporary hospital, where they receive the same attention as our men, at which they express their surprise and gratitude."

Those wounded Confederates who could not be brought in that night (limited facilities were to blame) did not have an easy time of it. Lieutenant Wilson Hopkins, of the Union Ambulance Corps, tells of some who had to be left:

"We . . . placed them in a group near the top of the mountain, gave them food and water, built fires to warm them; and I directed two Confederates, found hiding behind the rocks and uninjured, to remain with their wounded comrades, attend to their wants, and keep the fires burning. At sunrise the next morning I went with my stretcher-bearers to the camp I had made for the wounded Confederates, and found the fires burned out, six of the forty dead, and learned that the two men I had placed in charge of them with directions to keep the fires burning had, soon after I left them the night before, abandoned their charge and rejoined the Confederate army encamped in the valley beyond. We carried the survivors to the hospital, leaving a detail to bury the dead."

The day of fighting at the South Mountain passes had been costlier to Lee than to McClellan. Lee lost upwards of 2,800 in killed, wounded, captured, and missing, while McClellan lost about 2,300. Death claimed a valuable general officer on each side. McClellan lost corps commander Jesse Reno, while Lee lost a young brigade commander named Samuel Garland, who was thus eulogized by Confederate General D. H. Hill: "I never knew a truer, better, braver man. Had he lived, his talents, pluck, energy, and purity of character must have put him in the front rank of his profession, whether in civil or military life."

Among the wounded on the Union side was a thirty-nine-year-old colonel named Rutherford B. Hayes, commander of the 23rd Ohio Volunteers. (This regiment happened to be harboring another future president, nineteen-year-old William McKinley, then a supply sergeant, who remained unhurt. McKinley was destined to die by gunfire, but not for another thirty-nine years.)

For General Lee, the evening hours following the Battle of South Mountain were filled with anxiety. The two wings of his army should have been reunited by this time. The capture of Harpers Ferry was taking too long. Lee seemed to have no choice now but to abandon his campaign and reassemble his army in Virginia. At 8 P.M. he sent word to Harpers Ferry that the siege be lifted. Jackson, already on the Virginia side of the Potomac, must turn his efforts to covering the crossing of Longstreet's wing.

Then came word from Jackson that Harpers seemed about to fall, and Lee at once reconsidered. If Harpers could be taken early the next day, there might still be time for Jackson to return to Maryland for a reunion with Longstreet before McClellan could mass for another attack. A defensive position could be established at Sharpsburg, a half-dozen miles west of South Mountain. There the army could fight with its back to the Potomac, and, if compelled to retreat, could cross by fording near Shepherdstown. On the other hand, a victory at Sharpsburg would put the whole campaign back on track. At 11:15 P.M. Lee countermanded his earlier order. The attack on Harpers was to be continued. Longstreet enacted his part in the plan by making a night march from South Mountain to Sharpsburg.

If Lee at first believed that his campaign had been concluded at South Mountain, so did McClellan. The happy general sent glowing wires to Washington, saying he had learned that Lee had admitted publicly to losing fifteen thousand men and to having been "shockingly whipped." There were those at the capital who, recalling that McClellan had sent similar reports from the Peninsula, were dubious about the finality of his success, but Abraham Lincoln wired back: "God bless you and all with you. Destroy the rebel army if possible."

On Monday morning, September 15, even while Stonewall Jackson was completing his conquest of Harpers Ferry, McClellan wrote his wife: "We yesterday gained a glorious and complete victory. Every moment adds to its importance. I am pushing everything after them with the greatest rapidity, and expect to gain great results. I thank God most humbly for His great mercy. How glad I am for my country that it is delivered from immediate peril! I am about starting with the pursuit and must close this. . . . If I can believe one-tenth of what is reported, God has seldom given an army a greater victory than this."

7

Movements Toward a Showdown

T HE FIGHTING at Harpers Ferry, which included musketry exchanges as well as artillery duels, had produced a great deal of noise but wasn't excessively harmful to the combatants. By daybreak on Monday the casualties were probably less than two hundred on each side.

Under cover of night, the Confederates had intensified the situation by strengthening their artillery encirclement. Their morning bombardment was intended as a prelude to an infantry assault from Bolivar Heights, west of the town. One of the bombardment's casualties was the Federal commander himself, Colonel Dixon S. Miles, who was fatally struck just after he had decided to surrender, and while he was lamenting to an aide about McClellan's failure to save the situation.

Now, according to the unidentified Northern newsman quoted earlier, "white flags were run up in every direction and a flag of truce was sent to inquire on what conditions a surrender would be accepted. General A. P. Hill [not to be confused with D. H. Hill, who was with Longstreet at Sharpsburg] sent back word that it must be unconditional. Further parleying resulted in our obtaining the following liberal conditions, which were accepted: The officers were to be allowed to go out [on parole] with their side arms and private effects, the rank and file with everything save arms and equipments.

"As soon as the terms of surrender were completed, Generals A. P. Hill and Jackson rode into the town. . . . Old Stonewall . . . was dressed in the coarsest kind of homespun, seedy and dirty at that . . . and in his general appearance was in no respect to be

Ambrose P. Hill

distinguished from the mongrel, barefooted crew who follow his fortunes."

Henry Kyd Douglas, of Jackson's staff, was surprised by the way the general's presence was received. "The curiosity in the Union army to see him was so great that the soldiers lined the sides of the road. Many of them uncovered as he passed, and he invariably returned the salute. One man had an echo of response all about him when he said aloud, 'Boys, he's not much for looks, but if we'd had him we wouldn't have been caught in this trap!'"

Another episode of the moment is given by a Union regimental commander from Vermont, Colonel George J. Stannard: "General Jackson halted his horse in front of the 9th Vermont, and, taking off his hat, solemnly said, 'Boys, don't feel bad. You could not help it. It was just as God willed it.'

"One of Jackson's staff asked whether I had anything [alcoholic] to drink. I handed him my flask, and the young Confederate captain poured out a horn and arrogantly said, 'Colonel, here is to the health of the Southern Confederacy.'

"I answered, 'To ask and accept a courtesy of a prisoner and then insult him is act that an honorable soldier would scorn.'

"Jackson turned on his staff officer and gave him a severe scolding, saying the repetition of such an insult to a prisoner would cost him his place. Then, turning to me, General Jackson apologized for the conduct of his officer, saying that it was an exceptional act of

Jackson in the field, drawn from life.

insolence on the part of a young and reckless man. And, bowing gravely, the famous Confederate captain rode away."

Jackson's capture of Harpers Ferry was somewhat marred by the fact that 1,300 Union cavalrymen who had been a part of the garrison had, the previous night, managed to slip through his lines and make good their escape. But Jackson's haul was impressive enough: 11,500 men; some seventy pieces of artillery; 13,000 small arms; a large store of ammunition; a good deal of food (much of it eaten on the spot!); items of clothing; many tents, wagons, horses and mules, plus machinery and other equipment from the town's machine shops. There were Confederate soldiers who believed that these spoils were enough to make Lee's Maryland campaign a success even if the army had to retreat.

That morning there was a formal surrender ceremony on a

plateau west of town, and Confederate trooper Heros von Borcke
was on hand to watch. "The entire garrison . . . was drawn up in
imposing lines, presenting, with their well-kept equipments, their
new uniforms and beautiful banners, a striking contrast to Jackson's
gaunt and ragged soldiers, who formed opposite to them. . . . To the
long roll of the drums, the two armies came to 'present arms,' and
then the Federal troops laid down their standards and weapons,
which were at once taken possession of by our men. . . .

"General Jackson appeared quite satisfied with his success, but
when I congratulated him upon it, he said, 'Ah, this is all very well,
Major, but we have yet much hard work before us.' And indeed we
had."

At Shepherdstown, Mary Bedinger Mitchell had seen the smoke
and heard the sounds of the final fighting at Harpers, but she was
unaware of what it meant. Even the news of the Confederate defeat
at South Mountain the previous day had not yet reached the Virginia town. It was even while Mary was wondering about the outcome at Harpers that she learned what had happened at South
Mountain.

"We were sitting about in disconsolate fashion, distracted by the
contradictory rumors, [when] our Negro cook rushed into the room
with eyes shining and face working with excitement. She had been

Confederates exchanging rags for U.S. Army clothing.

down in 'de ten-acre lot to pick a few years ob cawn,' and she had seen a long train of wagons coming up from the ford [across the Potomac], and 'dey is full ob wounded men, and de blood runnin' outen dem dat deep,' measuring on her outstretched arm to the shoulder.

"This horrible picture sent us flying to town, where we found the streets already crowded, the people all astir, and the foremost wagons, of what seemed an endless line, discharging their piteous burdens. The scene speedily became ghastly. . . . There were no preparations, no accommodations. The men could not be left in the street . . . on the brick pavements. . . .

"The first thing was to find roofs to cover them. Men ran for keys and opened the shops, long empty, and the unused rooms. Other people got brooms and stirred up the dust of ages. Then swarms of children began to appear with bundles of hay and straw, taken from anybody's stable. These were hastily disposed in heaps and covered with blankets—the soldiers' own, or blankets begged or borrowed. On these improvised beds the sufferers were placed, and the next question was how properly to dress their wounds. No surgeons were to be seen. A few men, detailed as nurses, had come, but they were incompetent. . . .

"Our women set bravely to work and washed away the blood or stanched it as well as they could, where the jolting of the long rough ride had disarranged the hasty binding done upon the battlefield. But what did they know of wounds beyond a cut finger or a boil? Yet they bandaged and bathed with a devotion that went far to make up for their inexperience. Then there was the hunt for bandages. Every housekeeper ransacked her stores and brought forth things new and old. I saw one girl, in despair for a strip of cloth, look about helplessly, and then rip off the hem of her white petticoat.

"The doctors came up, by and by, or I suppose they did, for some amputating was done—rough surgery, you may be sure. The women helped, holding the instruments and the basins, and trying to soothe or strengthen. They stood to their work nobly. . . .

"One girl who had been working very hard helping the men on the sidewalks and dressing wounds afterward in a close, hot room, told me that at one time the sights and smells—these last were fearful—so overcame her that she could only stagger to the staircase, where she hung, half conscious, over the banister, saying to herself, 'Oh, I hope if I faint someone will kick me into a corner and let me lie there!' She did not faint, but went back to her work in a few moments; and through the whole of what followed was one of the most indefatigable and useful. She was one of many. Even children did their part."

At this time Generals McClellan and Lee, not yet aware of the outcome at Harpers Ferry, were proceeding with their immediate affairs, which had begun to center upon the village of Sharpsburg.

The narrative is assumed by another Northern newsman, William Swinton of the *New York Times*, who followed the fortunes of the Army of the Potomac from its creation and became its chief historian, at the same time making himself an authority on Lee's Army of Northern Virginia. Swinton had a talent for objective analysis. Here he sets the stage for the looming showdown:

"Descending the western slope of the South Mountain, one suddenly emerges into a lovely valley, spreading out in many graceful undulations and picturesque forms of field and forest, to the Potomac. This stream, turning sharply to the north at Harpers Ferry, forms the western limit of the valley, whose breadth from the mountain to the river may be from eight to twelve miles. But before reaching the Potomac, at a distance of six or eight miles from the passes of the South Mountain, one comes upon the stream Antietam, which, flowing from the north in drowsy, winding course, empties into the Potomac a few miles above Harpers Ferry. As this brook makes with the Potomac an acute angle, and the Potomac forms a reentrant angle on itself, there is thus left between the two streams an enclosed space of two or three miles broad and twice or thrice that length. [See map of the Antietam Campaign, page 57.]

"From the western margin of the Antietam the ground rises in a slope of woods and cultivated fields to a bold crest, and then falls back in rough outlines of rock and scaur to the Potomac. The town of Sharpsburg nestles just behind the ridge, above which the steeples of its churches are visible from the east side of the Antietam; and in the rear of Sharpsburg is the Shepherdstown ford of the Potomac.

"It was upon this coign of vantage, his back towards the Potomac, his front covered by the Antietam, that Lee, on the morning of the 15th of September, drew up his force, or rather what of his force was with him—to wit: the divisions of Longstreet and [D. H.] Hill that during the night had been compelled to abandon the defense of the South Mountain passes. Jackson and McLaws and [John G.] Walker were still at Harpers Ferry ... from which Lee had yet no reports. In taking post behind the Antietam, therefore, Lee was in

position either to repass the Potomac by the Shepherdstown ford, if
he should be pressed too hard by McClellan, or to stand and receive
battle if the conclusion of operations at Harpers should set Jackson
and his companions free to unite with him at Sharpsburg.

"While there anxiously awaiting the turn of events, Lee, during
the forenoon of the 15th, received from Jackson tidings of the
surrender of Harpers Ferry—tidings which he says 'reanimated the
courage of the troops.' Forthwith he instructed his lieutenant to
march with all haste by way of Shepherdstown ford and join him at
Sharpsburg. His arrival was hardly to be looked for that day, but it
was certain next morning; and in the interim Lee judged he could
readily hold McClellan in check. . . .

"[Lee] was no longer offensive but defensive. Strategically, he was
already foiled. Why, then, did he resolve still to remain in Maryland? The answer is obvious. To have recrossed the Potomac without a battle would have weakened him morally, investing the whole
enterprise with the aspect of an aimless and quixotic adventure.
Besides, he believed himself to be able to worst his antagonist in a
trial of strength, for he was elated by many successes, and he
counted much on the supposed demoralization of the Army of the
Potomac [after the defeats of the Peninsula and Second Bull Run].
In taking his stand, therefore, in that southwestern corner of Maryland, he challenged combat that must in its very nature be decisive.
If beaten, he would be compelled to seek safety in flight across the
Potomac; if victorious, Washington and Baltimore would lie open
to him.

"While Lee, awaiting anxiously the arrival of Jackson, occupied
his mind with these grave speculations, the [head of] the Union
army, which, on the morning of the 15th, had defiled from the
South Mountain and moved in long shining columns athwart the
valley, reached the heights on the east side of the Antietam, across
which, defined on the rim of the opposite crest, the hostile infantry
and artillery were plainly visible.

"Unhappily, if McClellan, as [he] averred, had designed to assail
Lee immediately on meeting, and thus take advantage of the yet-
divided condition of the Confederate force, he lost the opportunity.
In spite of his efforts to launch forward the army in rapid pursuit,
much time had been lost. Burnside delayed several hours beyond
his appointed time of starting in the morning. There was considerable confusion and cross purpose in the marches. And when, well
on in the afternoon, McClellan [himself] reached the Antietam, no
more than two divisions . . . had yet come up; so that, by the time a

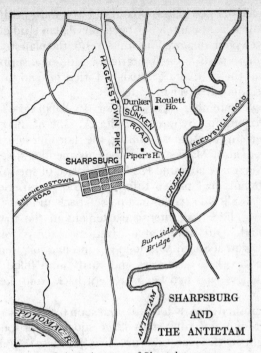

Orientation map of Sharpsburg area

sufficient force was in hand to authorize his seizing the offensive,
the day had passed by, and with it the opportunity to take Lee in his
sin."

McClellan was doubtless very glad to have an excuse not to attack
on the fifteenth. Lee's defiant stand with only a part of his army, the
units deployed on a wide front, banners aloft and guns in battery,
baffled the Young Napoleon. Hadn't reports indicated that Lee had
been totally beaten, his casualties woeful, at South Mountain?
Wasn't he supposed to be in headlong retreat? McClellan had expected the van of his own army to come upon Lee's rear guard
splashing across the Potomac as the general made an ignominious
return to Virginia. What was happening here? Whatever it was, one
thing was certain: it would have to be addressed with the strictest
caution!

By the next morning McClellan had sixty thousand men on the
field, with more approaching. Lee had no more than eighteen
thousand. But McClellan's telescope, as it swept the Confederate
front, magnified these modest numbers into a formidable mass. An

attack would have to be made, of course, but it must be thoroughly prepared. Much of the day went by as McClellan studied the terrain, devised a plan, deployed his units to suit the plan, fretted over not having more units to deploy, ordered additional supplies to be brought from the rear, and graciously doffed his cap to the men, who cheered him wherever he rode.

On this day, September 16, reserves for McClellan were still on the way from Washington by way of Frederick. One of the regiments that marched through the city during the morning hours was the newly formed 20th Maine, and among its members was Private Theodore Gerrish, who found Frederick a place of special interest.

"Its inhabitants had passed through a strange experience that week, as the two hostile armies had passed back and forth through its streets. . . . There was intense excitement in the town as we passed through. Our troops had driven the enemy from his intrenched position at South Mountain . . . and had followed him . . . to Antietam Creek. The houses and yards were filled with the wounded soldiers who had been brought back from the field of battle.

"We were pushed rapidly forward, and soon began to see signs of the [South Mountain] conflict. A large squad of prisoners were being brought to the rear—the first live 'Johnnies' our regiment ever saw. They were tall, lank, slouchy-looking fellows clad in dirty gray uniforms.

"We soon came to where the earth had been torn up by exploding shells. Buildings were riddled through and through with shot, and trees were torn and twisted by flying missiles. We marched over the field and up the hillside where our troops had fought. Every house and barn was filled with the wounded. Fresh mounds on the hillsides told where our dead had been buried.

"Surgeons with sleeves rolled to their shoulders were busily at work around the rough tables they had hastily constructed. Legs and arms were being amputated by dozens, and the poor groaning victims upon the tables were objects of pity. Squads of men were at work caring for the wounded and burying the amputated limbs. It all looked cruel and bloody to us who were unused to such scenes.

"I climbed the stone wall and rude breastwork where the enemy had made their final stand, and from which our men had driven them. There had not been time to bury the rebel dead. They lay as they had fallen, in groups of half-a-dozen each and single bodies scattered here and there, all through the scattering oak growth that crowned the crest of the hill. They were of all ages, and looked grim and ghastly. Old men with silvered hair, strong men in the prime of manhood, beardless boys whose smooth, youthful, upturned faces looked strangely innocent, although sealed in a bloody death.

"With a hushed voice and careful tread I passed over them, wondering if the time would come in the varying fortunes of war when the enemy would thus pass over the bodies of our own regiment, lying lifeless and cold upon some bloody field.

"Ominous sounds were coming from the front."

Through the early hours of the day, these sounds were chiefly those of artillery exchanges across the Antietam. It was at this time that the village of Sharpsburg began to suffer, for it was close behind Lee's lines. In one of the houses used as a headquarters—the residence of a physician—was Heros von Borcke, newly arrived from Harpers Ferry, who explains:

"General Stuart started on the morning of the 16th . . . with a part of his cavalry on a reconnaissance up the Potomac, leaving me with ten of our couriers at headquarters, with orders to receive and open all reports and dispatches addressed to him, and to forward any important information to Generals Lee, Jackson [then approaching from Harpers Ferry], and Longstreet.

"Sharpsburg is a pretty little village of perhaps two thousand inhabitants. It presented, during these memorable September days, a busy scene of military life. Wagon trains blockaded its streets, artillery rattled over its pavements, orderlies were riding up and down at full speed. The house of Dr. G., one of the largest in the place, was situated just opposite the principal church and was still occupied by his hospitable family, who awaited with an indifference peculiarly American the momentous events that were so close upon them.

"About 11 A.M. the enemy began to throw shells into the town, which, being aimed at the church steeple [apparently because it was one of the only objects in the town clearly visible to the gunners], fell all around their dwelling in such perilous proximity that I felt it my duty to order the ladies into the cellar as the safest place of refuge. This order they obeyed, but, impelled by feminine curiosity, they were running upstairs every five minutes to witness the effect of the cannonade. (I had frequent occasion during the war to observe how much stronger is curiosity with women than the fear of danger.)

"Accordingly, while the fire was every moment growing hotter, it was not long before the whole of Dr. G.'s family were again assembled in the room I occupied. All at once, while they were looking out of the windows at some wounded men carried by, a shell fell with a terrific crash through the top of the building, and sent them in precipitate flight to the security of the vaults.

"About noon the bombardment became really appalling, and the explosion of the innumerable projectiles stunned the ear. Still deeming it obligatory on me to remain at my post, I was seated on the sofa, engaged in writing in my journal, when a shell, piercing the wall of the room a few feet above my head, covered me with the debris, and, exploding, scattered the furniture in every direction. At the same moment another missile, entering the upper part of the house and passing directly through, burst in the courtyard, killing one of our horses and rendering the others frantic with terror.

"Regarding further exposure of my own life and the lives of my couriers as now unnecessary, I gave orders for our immediate departure. But it was not easy, amid the blinding dust and smoke out of doors, to find my horse, nor, after I had found him, to get into the saddle, so furiously did he rear and plunge, as if fully conscious of the danger of his situation.

"In the street there was the greatest confusion. Dead and wounded men and horses lay about in every direction, in the midst of wagons and ambulances overturned in the hurry and anxiety of [many soldiers and civilians] to get out of the village, where cannonballs whizzed incessantly through the air, and pieces of bursting shells, splinters of wood, and scattered fragments of brick were whirled about in the dense cloud of powder smoke that enveloped all things.

"After an exciting ride of a quarter of an hour ... I gained an eminence beyond the town, and was happy to find that my followers, one and all, had, like myself, escaped death. . . . My horse had been the only sufferer. A piece of shell had struck him in the right hind leg, and he went lame and bleeding."

Confederate officer William Miller Owen of the Washington Artillery was riding through Sharpsburg at this time looking for General Longstreet, wanting to ask him a question about the employment of the battalion's guns. An attempt had been made to duel with the long-range guns of the Yankees, but the shots had fallen short. Owen wasn't able to find Longstreet, but he did obtain an answer to his question.

"I met General Lee on foot, leading his horse by the bridle. It was during the artillery firing, and the shells of the enemy were falling in close proximity to him, but he seemed perfectly unconscious of danger. He directed us to keep the artillery ammunition for the enemy's infantry only."

Other Confederate guns already had some of the Yankee infantry units under fire. Says the colonel from Massachusetts, Francis Palfrey, whose regiment was stationed behind a ridge east of the Antietam: "Occasionally we would go to the crest of the ridge to see what we could see. There was plenty to see, but unfortunately that was not all of it. The Confederate batteries were wide awake, and their practice was extremely good, and projectiles flew over the crest so thickly that mere curiosity was not sufficient to keep anyone there long."

As for General Lee, at the time William Miller Owen encountered him in Sharpsburg he was on his way to his headquarters tent west of the town, where he was shortly visited by some people he was very glad to see. One of them was General John Walker, who recounts:

"A little past the hour of noon . . . General Stonewall Jackson and myself reached General Lee's headquarters. . . .

"The thought of General Lee's perilous situation, with the Potomac River in his rear, confronting, with his small force, McClellan's vast army, had haunted me through the long hours of the night's march, and I expected to find General Lee anxious and careworn.

"Anxious enough, no doubt, he was; but there was nothing in his look or manner to indicate it. On the contrary, he was calm, dignified, and even cheerful. If he had had a well-equipped army of a hundred thousand veterans at his back, he could not have appeared more composed and confident. . . . He simply expressed his satisfaction with the result of our operations at Harpers Ferry, and with our timely arrival at Sharpsburg—adding that, with our reinforcement, he felt confident of being able to hold his ground until the arrival of the divisions of R. H. Anderson, McLaws, and A. P. Hill, which were still behind."

Lee placed Jackson north of Longstreet, or on the army's left. (See map of the Battle of Antietam, page 96.) The Confederate line formed a four-mile arc with the convex side toward the Federals, which gave Lee some vital leverage against the two-to-one odds he was facing. He would be able to shift troops from place to place on relatively short interior lines, reinforcing hard-pressed spots as it became necessary.

Returning to the account by Northern newsman William Swinton: "Lee stood on the defensive. In order, therefore, to assume the offensive it was necessary for McClellan to pass the Antietam. That

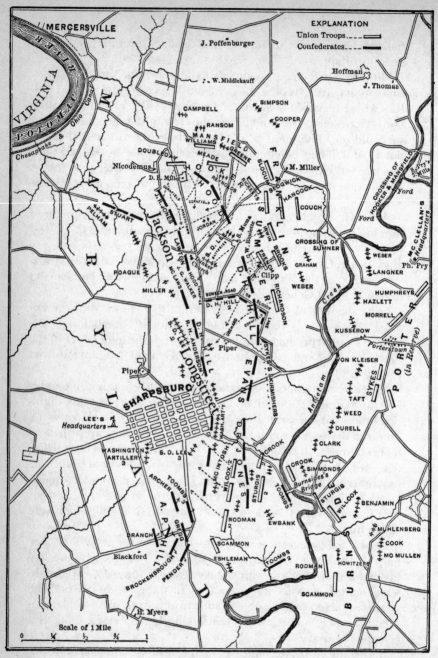

The Battle of Antietam

stream is in this vicinity crossed by several stone bridges. . . . It has a few fords, but they are difficult. The [southernmost] of these bridges, which was opposite the Union left, under Burnside, was found to be covered by marksmen protected by rifle trenches. The [next bridge northward], opposite the Union center, under [Fitz John] Porter, was unobstructed save by the fire of the hostile batteries on the crest. The . . . upper bridge, beyond the Union right, was entirely unguarded, and a ford hard by was also available.

"The plan formed by McClellan was to cross at the upper bridge, assail the enemy's left with the corps of Hooker and [Joseph] Mansfield, supported by Sumner's, and, if necessary, by Franklin's. And, as soon as matters should look favorably there, to move the corps of General Burnside across the lower bridge against Lee's extreme right. . . . Finally, whenever either of these flank movements should be successful, to advance the center with all the forces then disposable.

"The execution of the plan was begun on the afternoon of the 16th, when Hooker's corps was ordered to cross the Antietam by the upper bridge and ford."

McClellan had chosen Hooker to lead this important northwesterly movement (see map, page 96) because the men of his corps had performed well as a part of Burnside's command at South Mountain. (It is one of the sadder facts of military life that troops who excel in difficult and dangerous situations are subjected to repeated exposure to such situations, whereas mediocre troops are given easier, safer work.)

Hooker was in his late forties, a West Point graduate, and a veteran of the Mexican War. He was a tall man of smart appearance, a keen mentality, and aggressive energy. He had a reckless tongue, however, and his fondness for strong drink did nothing to restrain it. Hooker was sometimes insubordinate, and he intrigued without compunction to further his own advancement. His personal performance at South Mountain had not been as vital to the victory as he had reported to McClellan. At the outset, in fact, Burnside had to prod him into action. Usually, however, Hooker measured up to his sobriquet of "Fighting Joe." He was a likely choice to launch McClellan's offensive.

Hooker's march that afternoon is described as it was experienced by the Pennsylvania sergeant, A. F. Hill, of George Meade's division, who was at first uncertain of the measure's aim.

"We marched out the road, crossed Antietam Creek, marched

Flanking column crossing the Antietam.

three-quarters of a mile, and halted for half an hour. All was
still. . . . We moved on half a mile further, then marched into a field
on our left, where we formed close column of divisions. Then we
advanced across several fields, our course nearly westward. Having
gained the crest of a gentle slope, the head of the column wheeled
to the left. I imagined the whole movement to be one intended to
gain the flank of the enemy. . . .

"When our column turned to the left I observed that a general
who did not belong to our division was directing the movements. As
at one time he chanced to ride very near our regiment, I discovered,
to my gratification, that it was McClellan! And it led me to believe
that the movement in progress was one of no little importance.
Noble Little Mac! How his very presence cheered us! The very
mention of his name was sufficient to inspire us with a ready desire
to meet the enemy; for when McClellan was with us we knew that all
would be well.

"We were now marching toward a wood that skirted the field on
the south side. On our right and on our left were cornfields. When
within two hundred yards of the wood, a rebel battery opened upon
us from a slight elevation beyond, and shot and shell began to fly
about us in a way at once lively and disagreeable. [The Federal
movement had come upon the defensive zone occupied by Hood's

division of Jackson's wing.] We instantly deployed into line, while a [Union] battery took position in the cornfield on our right, another on our left, and a third, well supported [by infantry], went forward and took position in the wood.

"They opened vigorously upon the rebels, when several additional rebel batteries joined in. Evening was now approaching.

"We advanced to the margin of the wood and formed line of battle. A rebel battery far to the right opened a flank fire. The [artillery exchange] was terrible. Amid the storms of iron hail, General McClellan rode up to the battery in the cornfield on our right and directed it to change its position in order that it might play upon the rebel battery on our flank to greater advantage.

" 'Lie down!' Such was the command that passed along the lines shortly after, and I took a seat upon a stump that was near where I stood, for I thought I should be as safe in a sitting posture as in a horizontal one. Most of the boys stretched themselves upon the ground to avoid the missiles which were now being copiously rained about us. Just as I sat down, a large ragged fragment of a shell whizzed savagely past the top of my head and struck the ground a few paces in rear with a fierce *splat*. It must have struck my head had I been a moment later in sitting down.

" 'Whew!' exclaimed [a private known as] Juggie, with an oath—

McClellan riding a line of battle.

he was a profane young man. 'What if that had hit you!' Juggie had lain down near the stump.

" 'I suppose it would have killed me,' I replied. 'But what if it had hit *you* with that great oath in your mouth? I tell you, Juggie, a man is mighty apt to get hit for swearing. You had better quit it.'

"Whiz! bang! went a shell at that moment, bursting into fragments ten or fifteen feet above our heads.

" 'Je— Oh, I forgot!' exclaimed Juggie. He had come very near swearing again. . . .

"The cannonading continued with great fury. Meantime, the musketry had opened on our left, with some fierceness.

"At half-past nine the firing ceased. All became quiet."

Hooker was now in position to strike the blow with which McClellan planned to start the battle in the morning. Mansfield's corps marched the same route and bivouacked a distance behind Hooker. All of this was very well, except that the skirmishing initiated by Hooker served to warn Lee what McClellan was up to. Jackson's wing would be quite ready to meet the attack.

McClellan's other maneuvering was all done east of the Antietam and was less obvious to the Confederates. Says Union soldier David Thompson of the 9th New York:

"Our corps—the Ninth under Burnside—was on the extreme left [i.e., in the south], opposite the stone bridge. Our brigade stole into position about half-past 10 o'clock on the night of the 16th. No lights were permitted, and all conversation was carried on in whispers. As the regiment was moving past the 103d New York to get to its place, there occurred . . . one of those unaccountable panics . . . by which each man . . . for the moment . . . surrenders to an utterly causeless fear.

"When everything was at its darkest and stealthiest, one of the 103d stumbled over the regimental dog and . . . staggered against a stack of muskets and knocked them over. The giving way of the two or three men upon whom they fell was communicated to others . . . till two regiments were in confusion.

"In a few seconds order was restored, and we went to our place in the line—a field of thin corn sloping toward the creek, where we sat down on the plowed ground and watched for a while the dull glare on the sky of the Confederate campfires behind the hills. We were hungry, of course, but, as no fires were allowed, we could only mix our ground coffee and sugar in our hands and eat them dry."

The night was growing misty. According to Confederate General

James Longstreet: "A light rain began to fall. . . . The troops along either line were near enough to hear voices from the other side, and several spats occurred during the night between the pickets, increasing in one instance to the exchange of many shots. But for the most part there was silence or only the soft, smothered sound of the summer rain over all that field on which was to break in the morning the storm of lead and iron."

8

The Bloodiest Day Begins

B Y THE DAWN of September 17, the rain had reverted to a light
overcast. Though well-dampened, the terrain was not soggy.
The air was mild.

The story of this fateful day, "the bloodiest of the war," is begun
by a Southerner, John B. Gordon, a tall, straight-backed, stentorian-
voiced Georgian who, at age thirty, was emerging as one of the war's
great commanders even though he'd had no prewar military train-
ing. Right now he was a colonel in charge of the 6th Alabama
Infantry, a unit he'd helped to raise. Gordon relates:

"As these vast American armies, the one clad in blue and the other
in gray, stood contemplating each other from the adjacent hills,
flaunting their defiant banners, they presented an array of martial
splendor that was not equalled, perhaps, on any other field. It was
in marked contrast with other battlegrounds. On the open plain,
where stood these hostile hosts in long lines, listening in silence for
the signal summoning them to battle, there were no breastworks, no
abatis, no intervening woodlands [except for modest patches], nor
abrupt hills, nor hiding places, nor impassable streams. The space
over which the assaulting columns were to march, and on which was
soon to occur the tremendous struggle, consisted of smooth and
gentle undulations and a narrow valley covered with green grass
and growing corn.

"From the position assigned me near the center of Lee's lines,
both armies and the entire field were in view. The scene was not only
magnificent to look upon, but the realization of what it meant was
deeply impressive. . . .

"On the elevated points beyond the narrow valley the Union
batteries were rolled into position, and the Confederate heavy guns

unlimbered to answer them. For one or more seconds, and before the first sounds reached us, we saw the great volumes of white smoke rolling from the mouths of McClellan's artillery. The next second brought the roar of the heavy discharges and the loud explosions of hostile shells in the midst of our lines, inaugurating the great battle. The Confederate batteries promptly responded; and while the artillery of both armies thundered, McClellan's compact columns of infantry fell upon the left of Lee's lines with the crushing weight of a landslide."

Stonewall Jackson had mustered three divisions, about 7,500 men, to meet the onslaught of Hooker's corps, which numbered about 8,500 men, also in three divisions. Hooker advanced directly southward, hoping to break through the Confederate line (a rough east-west formation) and establish himself on a plateau near a small, whitewashed brick building—the church of a group of Dunkers (or Dunkards)—that stood about a mile from his starting point. With the seizure of this spot, Lee's army would be ripe for destruction.

Meade's division of Pennsylvanians played a strong part in Hooker's attack, and the regiment to which Sergeant A. F. Hill belonged was assigned to one of the hottest spots.

"I examined my cartridge box, and found it all right; it contained

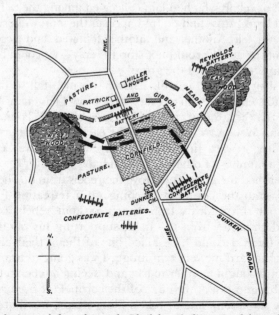

Hooker's attack from the north. Black bars indicate Confederate lines.

forty rounds. I examined my cap box, and found *it* all right; it contained about half a pint of caps. . . .

"We soon found ourselves . . . moving directly toward a large cornfield [from that day on to be spelled with a capital *C*]. Just in front of us, near the cornfield, there was a slight depression, on reaching which we hurriedly deployed into line. A battery took position upon a slight elevation behind us and opened upon the rebels who occupied the cornfield. The rebel infantry suddenly opened upon us from the cornfield. The fight had commenced in earnest.

"Presently Colonel [Albert L.] Magilton, who sat calmly upon his horse near us, ordered our regiment to a small grove [the "East Woods"] two hundred paces to our left, where a regiment of rebels were amusing themselves by picking off our artillerymen. We moved by the left flank, and I had an opportunity to look around. I saw General Meade sitting quietly upon his horse by the battery. He was calmly surveying the prospect in front through his spectacles, while the rebel bullets were spattering the ground at his horse's feet, and many, no doubt, singing about his ears. The brave Magilton, too, still sat tranquilly upon his horse in the very face of death.

"As we neared the grove—it was at the corner of the field—a regiment of rebels who had lain concealed among the tall corn [on our right flank] arose and poured upon us the most withering volley we had ever felt. Another and another followed, and a continuous rattle rent the air. We could not stop to reply—we could but hurry on [in our attack toward the grove].

"The slaughter was fearful. I never saw men fall so fast. I was obliged to step over them at every step. I saw Lieutenant Moth fall senseless to the ground, stunned by a spent ball. Poor Page fell dead. John Woodward, too, fell to the earth, a bullet buried in his brain. Putty Stewart, Jim Hasson, John Swearer, Dave Cease, Juggie, and a number of others fell wounded.

"We reached the grove and drove the rebels from it. They retired obliquely into the cornfield, keeping up a retreating fire. I observed, not thirty yards from me, two stout rebels assisting a wounded comrade from the field, supporting his fainting form between them. I could have killed one of them; their backs were presented toward me very temptingly. I was going to fire, but . . . I could not. I sought another mark; and, seeing a rebel in the act of loading his gun just at the edge of the cornfield, I fired at him.

"I now saw a long line of rebels filing from a wood at the right and rear of the cornfield [the "West Woods"] and coming upon the scene. They hurriedly marched by [their] right flank, which brought them toward those already in the cornfield. As we had driven the rebels entirely from the wood [to the east], we opened fire upon the yet far-off reinforcements. But they changed their course slightly by an oblique movement and came to the aid of the rebel lines two hundred paces to our right.

"Lieutenant Moth having been wounded and assisted from the field by Sergeant Anawalt, and Lieutenant Cue having remained [in the rear] sick, I suddenly, for the first time, found myself in command of Company D—and in battle, too. I saw, however, that our boys did not stand in need of much commanding just then; they were doing very well—selecting their own positions and firing at any rebels who presented the most tempting mark.

"In order to gain a better view of the field, I stepped forward to the crest of a slight elevation and stood by a small oak tree which I hoped would shield me from observation—it was too small to afford protection. From this point I had an excellent view of the rebel lines in the cornfield. I could distinctly see their colors. I saw that they were not aware of the position of our regiment—they were looking to the front—and it occurred to me that it would be a beautiful thing, in a military point of view, for us to open a flank fire upon them.

"I turned and called to our boys, beckoning at the same time, and they joined me. Will Hoffman and Charley Brawley stood beside me. At the same moment Haman Jeffries glided by us and took his position by a tree still farther toward the front. As he did so, a spent ball struck him on the ankle, and he fell; but he immediately sprang up, stood by his tree, and proceeded to retaliate [by firing] with great deliberation.

" 'Boys,' said I to Will and Charley, 'do you see those rebels?'

" 'Is that their line?'

" 'Yes.'

" 'So close as that?'

" 'Yes—don't you see their flag? And look. See how they are peppering away at our fellows on the right! Fire away, boys! Who will be the first to bring down that flag?'

"Without further ado, we went to work. I aimed every shot at the point over which the flag waved. At every fire I looked eagerly to see it fall.

"I had fired a dozen rounds at the rebel flag when I suddenly became conscious of a most singular and unpleasant feeling in my left leg. I was in the act of ramming down a ball at the time, and I would have finished, but my left foot, of its own accord, raised from the ground, a benumbing sensation ran through my leg, and I felt the hot blood streaming down my thigh. The truth flashed upon me—*I was wounded.*

"I could not yet tell where the ball had struck me, but, on looking down, I perceived, by a small round hole in my pantaloons, that I was shot in the thigh about three inches below the hip joint. It was plain that the bone was broken. The contracting of the muscles had shortened the limb and raised the foot from the ground.

" 'Boys, I—I—I'm shot!' I said. . . .

" 'Where?' [Brawley and Hoffman] asked in a breath.

" 'Here.' And I pointed to the perforation which the bullet had made.

"They took hold of my arms.

" 'Let me fire this charge yet,' I said.

"I endeavored to ram the ball home, but I grew weak and faint, my head became dizzy, and a mist obscured my eyesight.

" 'Boys, I—I—can't make it,' I said; and I leaned my rifle against the small tree by which we stood.

" 'We must carry him away, Brawley,' said Hoffman . . . and they supported me between them.

" 'Wait a moment,' I said—I felt my strength fast leaving me—and I threw off my haversack, canteen, and knapsack. The cartridge box remained. I hesitated; I thought of some stamped envelopes which I carried therein. Would I throw it off and lose them? Yes. Perhaps I should never need them. And off it went. While ridding myself of these encumbrances, I had been standing on my right leg. 'Now, boys.'

"Supporting my whole weight between them, my brave comrades moved slowly toward the rear. My left leg hung powerless, my foot dragged upon the ground, and I felt the shattered pieces of bone grinding together. The pain . . . was so acute that I grew deathly sick; everything faded from my sight, and sense left me.

"But I soon awoke. Where was I? I could not at once recall my scattered senses. The rattle of musketry and the roar of artillery sounded familiarly in my ear, and I soon remembered what had happened. My comrades had laid me down and were standing anxiously over me. They feared that I was dead. When I opened my eyes they were much relieved, and I was asked, 'How do you feel? Are you in much pain?'

" 'No—not—m—oh! oh!'

" 'Let us place him on this blanket,' suggested Charley as he picked up a blanket that lay near.

" 'Yes, we can carry him better on that, and—here, let us get those two fellows to help.'

"They called to two men who had just carried a wounded comrade from the field and were returning to the fight. They assisted, and I was soon laid on the blanket. Then, each seizing a corner of the blanket, they moved slowly toward the rear. The pain caused by every motion was terrible. I had never experienced anything worthy of being compared with it.

"As yet we were scarcely fifty·paces from our line of battle, and many a bullet flying over the heads of our boys followed us, striking the ground . . . about us, plainly manifesting that they had no respect for a wounded man.

"I was carried directly through the strip of woods near which we had lain on the previous evening and during the night. Just in the rear of this wood stood a number of ambulances ready to convey wounded men from the field. I was placed in one—*a one-horse one*. Another sufferer was placed beside me, and the jumping, jostling, springing, shaking, quaking vehicle moved off.

"I opened conversation with my companion in misery. 'Where—are—you . . . wounded?' I asked as the ambulance went plunging along.

" 'In the side—oh!' he exclaimed as it gave a sudden leap. Then he asked, 'Where are you wo—oh!'

" 'In the . . . leg—thigh. . . .'

" 'Partners,' interrupted the driver at that moment, 'we are about to go over a little rough place now, but we'll soon be over it. . . . It's only a little cornfield.'

"The ambulance now began to go over the ridges of the cornfield, and it made such a succession of starts, and knocked me about so alarmingly that I really wondered that the wounded limb stayed on at all. My companion groaned in agony.

"At last the vehicle came to a standstill, and we were lifted out and laid down in front of a barn. Many wounded were lying in and around the barn. Someone very near me uttered a deep, agonizing, heartfelt groan; and, turning my head in that direction, I beheld Juggie lying prostrate upon the ground—pale as death, and his clothes sprinkled here and there with blood. 'Juggie, is that you?' I asked.

" 'Oh, yes!'

" 'Where are you wounded?'

" 'Through and through. . . .' And he pointed to a bullet hole in his right side. [This type of wound was almost invariably fatal, but we are not told how long Juggie suffered, nor whether his final utterances included any swearing.]

"A youthful surgeon was passing at that moment, and I requested him to look at my wound. 'In one moment,' said he, passing into the barn.

"After a lapse of a hundred times 'one moment,' he returned, made a slight examination of my wound, and said . . . 'The bone is all smashed, and—'

" 'And what?'

" 'Why, I expect that leg will have to come off.'

" 'What!'

" 'I'm afraid that—here's the bullet that struck you,' and he produced that interesting article, having taken it from my drawers, where it had lodged after passing through my thigh. It was much bruised [from its contact with the bone], but I could make out that it was an ounce minie ball. . . .

" 'Do you really think there is any probability of amputation being necessary?' I asked.

" 'It is almost *certain*.' And he again passed into the barn.

"Oh, horror! Could it be so? Must I lose my leg? *I*? I would not—I could not reconcile myself to it. The surgeon was a young man; perhaps he didn't know.

"About this time, our boys in front began to give way. The fighting came nearer and nearer, and a shell or two came flying over the barn. It was decided to remove the wounded, if possible; and I was placed, with several others, in a two-horse ambulance. After a ride of twenty minutes the vehicle stopped, and we were lifted out and laid upon the ground near a small schoolhouse. Within this little building the work of amputation was going on. It was a kind of field hospital.

"The surgeon in charge came out after half an hour, and I asked him what he thought of my wound. He examined it, and very coolly and indifferently said, 'I'll have to take that leg off for you after a while, but I haven't time just now—there are so many cases on hand, you know.'

"I assured him that I could wait; and he left me and returned to his work."

At the front the brutal contest had continued, but a decision had not developed. Hooker's corps had charged through the cornfield and was nearing the Dunker Church when Jackson counterattacked. He had been reinforced by three of D. H. Hill's brigades, and he had a special artillery advantage: Jeb Stuart was operating fourteen guns on a commanding hill to the northwest. Hooker was driven back to the northern edge of the cornfield, where he was able to hold with the aid of his own batteries.

These suffered severely, however, both men and horses going down. One gunner, taken to the rear in agony from a wound through the middle, was told by a surgeon that he had but a few hours to live. "If that is the case," the man said, "those few hours are not worth living." And he drew his revolver and put a bullet through his brain.

A great change had come over the appearance of the cornfield. Its stalks, which had greeted the dawn in perfect array, had been shredded by blasts of canister, clipped by volleys of minie balls, and trampled by myriad pairs of feet. The tangled matting of leveled stalks was heavily strewn with corpses, both Federal and Confederate, both gold-trimmed officers and plain-coated men of the ranks. They were lying in every conceivable position and had been mutilated in every conceivable way, their bright red blood in odd contrast with the autumn-faded green. Some of these forms, like the cornstalks originally, were in well-aligned rows, having been felled in their unit formations.

A Union charge through the cornfield.

There was a new development at about 7:30 A.M. Union General Joseph Mansfield's corps, which had crossed the Antietam in Hooker's wake and had bivouacked north of his position, came marching down and attacked past his disorganized front. For a second time Stonewall Jackson was severely pressed, and for a second time his defense prevailed, though his right fell back a dangerous distance.

It was Union General George S. Greene's division that did the driving. As recalled by one of the unit's junior officers:

"Their line began to waver, and General Greene shouted 'Charge!' With a yell of triumph we started with levelled bayonets; and, terror-stricken, the rebels fled. Like hounds after the frightened deer, we pursued them ... killing, wounding, and taking prisoners almost every rod. Their colors fell. A [Union] private soldier leaped forward and tore them from the staff.

"Across the fields we pursued the foe, who ... took shelter in a heavy piece of timber [near the Dunker Church], flanked by their artillery. A battery of twelve-pound howitzers came to *our* support, and most efficient service it rendered. We formed in two lines in rear of the battery and lay behind a low ridge, sufficiently high to protect from a direct shot, but which offered no shelter from the fragments of shells bursting ... over us. These were continually striking amongst us, often grazing a cap or an arm, but doing no particular harm.

"The howitzers were doing splendidly, when suddenly we heard, 'But eight rounds left!' Twenty more rounds would silence the rebel battery, but we had them not. Soon the rebel fire was more rapid, and a yell in the distance denoted an advance of their infantry.

"Shall we retreat? No! We will hold our ground or die! On they come, yelling defiantly. . . . We look anxiously for another battery. It comes! It comes! We are safe!"

The Confederates, too, were safe, for Greene's troops advanced no farther.

The new round of fighting added thousands of casualties to the earlier toll. Numerous units on both sides were depleted almost to the point of impotence. This included Confederate General John Hood's entire division. On the Union side, corps commander Mansfield himself was among the fatalities. He had recently marked his fortieth year in the regular service.

By this time the civilians of the farms and towns scattered for miles in all directions from Sharpsburg were in a state of anxiety over the sounds that assailed their ears. Some of the people of Sharpsburg itself were still in their homes, while others had fled the town for safer spots but remained within range of the awful din. Conditions at Shepherdstown, in its position a few miles southwest of Sharpsburg on the opposite bank of the Potomac, are described by Mary Bedinger Mitchell:

"There was no sitting at the windows now and counting discharges of guns or watching the curling smoke. We went about our work [in the Confederate hospitals] with pale faces and trembling hands, yet trying to appear composed for the sake of our patients, who were much excited.

"We could hear the incessant explosions of artillery, the shrieking whistles of the shells, and the sharper, deadlier, more thrilling roll of musketry; while every now and then the echo of some charging cheer would come, borne by the wind; and as the human voice pierced that demoniacal clangor we would catch our breath and listen, and try not to sob, and turn back to the forlorn hospitals, to

J. F. K. Mansfield

the suffering ... before our eyes, while imagination fainted at thought of those other scenes hidden from us beyond the Potomac.

"On our side of the river there were noise, confusion, dust; throngs of [Confederate] stragglers; horsemen galloping about; wagons [carrying supplies called up by Lee] blocking each other, and teamsters wrangling; and a continued din of shouting, swearing, and rumbling, in the midst of which men were dying, fresh wounded arriving, surgeons amputating limbs and dressing wounds, women going in and out with bandages, lint, medicines, food."

On the battlefield, Union General Hooker, at his combative best that morning, had begun to rally his frayed forces to resume the offensive. As reported by Northern newsman George N. Smalley, on the field for the *New York Tribune*: "He rode out in front of his furthest troops on a hill to examine the ground for a battery. At the top he dismounted and went forward on foot, completed his reconnaissance, returned, and remounted. The musketry fire ... was all the while extremely hot. As he put his foot in the stirrup, a fresh volley of rifle bullets came whizzing by. The tall, soldierly figure of the general, the white horse which he rode, the elevated place where he was—all made him a most dangerously conspicuous mark. . . .

"He had not ridden five steps when he was struck in the foot by a ball. . . . He kept on his horse for a few minutes, though the wound was severe. . . . It was found that the bullet had passed completely through his foot. The surgeon who examined it on the spot could give no opinion whether bones were broken, but it was afterward ascertained that, though grazed, they were not fractured. Of course the severity of the wound made it impossible for him to keep the field."

Hooker's departure at about 9 o'clock was a serious setback for the Union effort. But there was new hope in that another fresh corps, Edwin Sumner's Second, was approaching the field from the east, having crossed the Antietam during Mansfield's attack.

Returning to Union newsman George Smalley: "As I rode over toward the left I met Sumner at the head of his column, advancing rapidly through the timber [of the East Woods]. . . . The veteran general was riding alone in the forest, far ahead of his leading brigade, his hat off, his gray hair and beard and mustache strangely contrasting with the fire in his eyes and his martial air. . . . [John] Sedgwick's division was in advance. . . . Sedgwick . . . deployed and advanced in line over the cornfield."

The bluecoats made for the West Woods, where Jackson's troops were deployed. According to Confederate newsman Personne: "It was a trying hour. The Federals saw their advantage and pressed it with vigor. Eight batteries were in full play upon us, and the din of heavy guns, whistling and bursting of shells, and the roar of musketry was almost deafening. At this juncture Lee ordered to the support of Jackson the division of General McLaws, which had been held in reserve [since arriving from Harpers Ferry earlier that morning]. And blessing never came more opportunely. Our men had fought until not only they but their ammunition was well-nigh exhausted, and discomfiture stared them in the face. But, thus encouraged, every man rallied and the fight was redoubled in its intensity. Splendidly handled, the reinforcement swept on like a wave, its blows falling thick and fast upon the audacious columns."

The attack amounted to an ambush, with the storm of fire hitting the Federals not only in the front but on the left flank and in the left-rear. Within fifteen minutes Sumner lost more than two thousand in killed and wounded, and his regiments were thrown into disorder.

"General Sedgwick," says Northern newsman Smalley, "was three times wounded, in the shoulder, leg, and wrist, but he persisted in remaining on the field. . . . His adjutant-general . . . [while] bravely rallying and trying to re-form the troops, was shot through the body, the bullet lodging in the spine, and fell from his horse. . . .

Edwin V. Sumner

General [N. J. T.] Dana was wounded. General [Oliver O.] Howard, who took command of the division after General Sedgwick was disabled, exerted himself to restore order, but it could not be done. . . . The test was too severe for volunteer troops under such a fire. . . . Sumner himself attempted to arrest the disorder, but to little purpose. . . . It was impossible to hold the position."

The Federals retreated northward, and the cornfield was lost again. Shortly the uproar abated to scattered musketry and light artillery exchanges, and the two sides began regrouping upon very nearly the same ground they'd held when the fighting opened at dawn.

Southern newsman Personne makes this assessment: "The success, though not decisive as compared with our usual results, was complete as it was possible to make it in view of the peculiar circumstances of the battle and the topography of the country. Certain it is that, after the cessation of the fight at half-past [nine], the Yankees did not renew it again at this point during the day. . . .

"It was beyond all doubt the most hotly contested field on which a battle has taken place during the war."

Confederate casualties at East Woods rim of the cornfield. Man sitting at right is a young Georgian with a shattered ankle. His father lies dead before him.

Adds Confederate staff officer John Esten Cooke: "The event had been decided by the pertinacity of the Southern troops and by the prompt movement of reinforcements by General Lee from his right and center. Posted near his center, he had surveyed at one glance the whole field of action. The design of General McClellan to direct his main assault upon the Confederate left was promptly penetrated, and the rapid concentration of the Southern forces in that quarter had, by defeating this movement, decided the result of the battle."

9

Midday at the Sunken Road

AMONG THE MORE prominent Northern newsmen who covered events at Antietam was the *Boston Journal's* Charles Carleton Coffin, but it was only at the close of the first round that he reached the scene, riding down from Hagerstown and striking the rear of the Federal line above the blood-drenched cornfield.

"It was my privilege," Coffin tells us, "to be a witness of all that took place during the remainder of the day. It was a battle fought by piecemeal, beginning on the right and continuing to the left. It was a battle in which there was little concerted action between the various corps. . . .

"I came upon a line of cannon with their muzzles pointed southwest. For the moment the brazen guns were cooling. The cannoneers were lying beside their pieces. There was a lull in the battle. A few steps brought me to Poffenberger's house. I rode through the dooryard, where the hollyhocks were opening their white and red flowers to the morning sun, at that moment making its appearance through the rifted clouds.

"A Confederate shell had exploded among the beehives nearby. The Union soldiers had gathered the honey, and the swarms were angrily buzzing in the air. Solid shot had passed through the house. The sides of the building were pockmarked by Confederate bullets. A tree nearby was scarred by cannon shot, its limbs twisted and broken. The palings had been torn from the fence, the rails thrown down, and the garden trampled. . . .

"Riding down the turnpike southward I came upon a Union soldier crouching beneath a wall.

" 'Where are you going?' he inquired.

" 'I thought I would go to the front.'

" 'The front! You have passed it. I am on the skirmish line. You had better get out of here mighty quick. The rebs are in the corn right there.'

"The advice was timely, and I turned back.... I came upon General Howard.... I had made his acquaintance early in the war. He gave me a hearty welcome, extending his left hand. He had lost his right arm at Williamsburg. Not having any pass, he kindly wrote one for me while sitting in his saddle."

On the Confederate side, General Lee was using the lull to ride along his lines, just behind the front. He was accompanied by Longstreet and D. H. Hill. Longstreet relates: "We received a report of movements of the enemy and started up the ridge to make a reconnaissance. General Lee and I dismounted, but Hill declined to do so. I said to Hill, 'If you insist on riding up there and drawing fire, give us a little interval so that we may not be in the line of the fire when they open upon you.'

"General Lee and I stood on the top of the crest with our glasses, looking at the movements of the Federals on the rear-left. After a moment I turned my glass to the right—the Federal left. As I did so I noticed a puff of white smoke from the mouth of a cannon. 'There is a shot for you,' I said to General Hill. The gunner was a mile away, and the cannon shot came whisking through the air for three or four seconds and took off the front legs of the horse that Hill sat on and let the animal down upon his stumps. The horse's head was so low and his croup [i.e., his hind end] so high that Hill was in a most ludicrous position.

"With one foot in the stirrup, he made several efforts to [swing] the other leg [back] over the croup, but failed. Finally we prevailed upon him to try the other end of the horse, and he got down."

The dauntless general was soon remounted.

While Lee was traversing the central part of his line, where Hill's brigades were now deployed along the course of a sunken road, he came upon John Gordon's regiment of Alabamians. In Gordon's words: "With that wonderful power which he possessed of divining the plans and purposes of his antagonist, General Lee had decided that the Union commander's next heavy blow would fall upon our center, and those of us who held that important position were notified of this conclusion. We were cautioned to be prepared for a determined assault and urged to hold that center at any sacrifice, as a break at that point would endanger his entire army.

"My troops held the most advanced position on this part of the field, and there was no supporting line behind us. It was evident, therefore, that my small force was to receive the first impact of the expected charge and to be subjected to the deadliest fire. To comfort General Lee and General Hill, and especially to make, if possible, my men still more resolute of purpose, I called aloud to these officers as they rode away, 'These men are going to stay here, General, till the sun goes down or victory is won.' "

It was the Union divisions of William H. French and Israel B. Richardson that were preparing to hit Lee's center. The units forded the Antietam just north of McClellan's headquarters—a country home on the eastern bank behind his right wing—and they were under his eye.

As noted by newsman Coffin, who was now with McClellan: "The general was sitting in an armchair in front of the house. His staff were about him. Their horses, saddled and bridled, were hitched to the trees and fences. Stakes had been driven in the earth in front of the house, to which were strapped the headquarters telescopes, through which a view of the operations and movements of the two armies could be obtained.

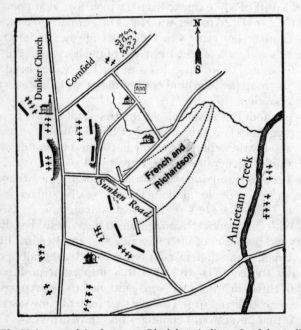

The Union attack in the center. Black bars indicate Confederate lines.

"It was a commanding situation. The panorama included fully two-thirds of the battlefield, from the woods by the Dunker Church southward to the hills below Sharpsburg. . . .

"Fitz John Porter [commander of the army's reserve] . . . was with McClellan, watching the movements of the troops across the Antietam—French's and Richardson's divisions—which were forming in the fields east of Roulette's and Mumma's houses. What a splendid sight it was!"

But the newsman's impressions of the sight were not unqualified. "As I beheld it I experienced a feeling of sadness, knowing that before sundown many of those brave men would be killed or wounded."

Coffin next looked farther westward. "Upon the crest of the hill south of the Dunker Church I could see Confederates on horseback, galloping, evidently with orders, for, a few moments later, there was [a] gleam in the sunshine from the bayonets of their troops, who were apparently getting into position to resist the threatened movement of French and Richardson."

It was French who was ready first.

Again in Coffin's words: "The hillside on the right [of the Federal formations] suddenly burst into flame. The Union batteries began a cannonade, under cover of which French advanced. The white powder clouds floated down the ravine and swept over the men. It was beautiful to see, through its rifts, the Stars and Stripes waving in the sunlight.

"From the hill beyond Mumma's house the Confederate artillery opened fire, a portion of the guns replying to the Union artillery, and another portion hurling shells upon the advancing line. A short distance from Mumma's house was a cemetery, from which came puffs of smoke from muskets fired by [Confederates] concealed behind the white marble headstones. Other sharpshooters fired from the windows.

"French's skirmishers crept along the fences and soon drove the Confederates from the cemetery and the house, which was set on fire either by the departing enemy or by a shell. The building burned rapidly.

"If there can be grandeur in a battle scene, the scenery at this moment formed a grand picture, with the cannon of both armies flaming, the buildings on fire, a dark pillar of cloud rising heavenward, ten thousand men advancing slowly across the green fields, their banners waving and bayonets gleaming."

In his position at D. H. Hill's salient at the sunken road, John

Gordon was alert to every development. "The men in blue . . . formed in my front, an assaulting column four lines deep. . . . The brave Union commander, superbly mounted, placed himself in front, while his band in rear cheered them with martial music. It was a thrilling spectacle. The entire force, I concluded, was composed of fresh troops from Washington or some camp of instruction. So far as I could see, every soldier wore white gaiters around his ankles. The banners above them had apparently never been discolored by the smoke and dust of battle. . . .

"With the precision of step and perfect alignment of a holiday parade, this magnificent array moved to the charge, every step keeping time to the tap of the deep-sounding drum. . . . Every act and movement of the Union commander . . . clearly indicated his purpose to discard bullets and depend upon bayonets. [This meant that his guns would be left unloaded, lest some of the men be tempted to stop and fire, thus disrupting the cohesion of his front.] He essayed to break through Lee's center by the crushing weight and momentum of his solid column. It was my business to prevent this; and how to do it with my single line was the tremendous problem which had to be solved, and solved quickly. . . .

"As I saw this solid mass of men moving upon me with determined step and front of steel, every conceivable plan of meeting and repelling it was rapidly considered. To oppose man against man and strength against strength was impossible, for there were four lines of blue to my one of gray. My first impulse was to open fire upon the compact mass as soon as it came within reach of my rifles, and to pour into its front an incessant hailstorm of bullets during its entire advance across the broad, open plain; but after a moment's reflection that plan was also discarded . . . because, during the few minutes required for the column to reach my line, I could not hope to kill and disable a sufficient number of the enemy to reduce his strength to an equality with mine.

"The only remaining plan was one which I had never tried, but in the efficacy of which I had the utmost faith. It was to hold my fire until the advancing Federals were almost upon my lines, and then turn loose a sheet of flame and lead into their faces. I did not believe that any troops on earth, with empty guns in their hands, could withstand so sudden a shock and withering a fire.

"The programme was fixed in my own mind; all horses were sent to the rear; and my men were at once directed to lie down. . . . They were quickly made to understand, through my aides and line officers, that the Federals were coming upon them with unloaded guns;

that not a shot would be fired at them; and that not one of our rifles was to be discharged until my voice should be heard from the center commanding 'Fire!' They were carefully instructed in the details. They were notified . . . that they were not to expect my order to fire until the Federals were so close upon us that every Confederate bullet would take effect. . . .

"In close order, with the commander still riding in front, this column of Union infantry moved majestically in the charge. In a few minutes they were within easy range of our rifles, and some of my impatient men asked permission to fire. 'Not yet,' I replied. 'Wait for the order.'

"Soon they were so close that we might have seen the eagles on their buttons, but my brave and eager boys still waited for the order. Now the front rank was within a few rods of where I stood. It would not do to wait another second, and with all my lung power I shouted 'Fire!'

"My rifles flamed and roared in the Federals' faces like a blinding blaze of lightning accompanied by the quick and deadly thunderbolt. The effect was appalling. The entire front line, with few exceptions, went down in the consuming blast. The gallant commander and his horse fell in a heap near where I stood—the horse dead, the rider unhurt. Before his rear lines could recover from the terrific shock, my exultant men were on their feet, devouring them with successive volleys.

"Even then these stubborn blue lines retreated in fairly good order. My front had been cleared; Lee's center had been saved; and yet not a drop of blood had been lost by my men. The result, however, of this first effort to penetrate the Confederate center did not satisfy the intrepid Union commander. Beyond the range of my rifles he reformed his men into three lines, and on foot led them to the second charge, still with unloaded guns.

"This advance was also repulsed; but again and again did he advance in four successive charges in the fruitless effort to break through my lines with the bayonet. Finally his troops were ordered to load. He drew up in close rank and easy range, and opened a galling fire upon my line. . . . The fire from these [two] hostile American lines at close quarters now became furious and deadly. The list of the slain was lengthened with each passing moment. . . .

"My extraordinary escapes from wounds in all the previous battles had made a deep impression upon my comrades as well as upon my own mind. So many had fallen at my side, so often had balls and shells pierced and torn my clothing, grazing my body without drawing a drop of blood, that a sort of blind faith possessed my men that I was not to be killed in battle. This belief was evidenced by their constantly repeated expressions: 'They can't hurt him.' 'He's as safe one place as another.' 'He's got a charmed life.'

"If I had allowed these expressions of my men to have any effect upon my mind, the impression was quickly dissipated when the Sharpsburg storm came and the whizzing Miniés, one after another, began to pierce my body.

"The first volley from the Union lines in my front sent a ball through the brain of the chivalric Colonel Tew of North Carolina, to whom I was talking, and another ball through the calf of my right leg. On the right and the left my men were falling . . . like trees in a hurricane. The persistent Federals, who had lost so heavily from repeated repulses, seemed now determined to kill enough Confederates to make the debits and credits of the battle's balance-sheet more nearly even. . . .

"Higher up in the same leg I was again shot; but still no bone was broken. I was able to walk along the line and give encouragement to my resolute riflemen, who were firing with the coolness and steadiness of peace soldiers in target practice.

"When later in the [morning] the third ball pierced my left arm, tearing asunder the tendons and mangling the flesh, they caught sight of the blood running down my fingers, and these devoted and big-hearted men, while still loading their guns, pleaded with me to leave them and go to the rear, pledging me that they would stay there and fight to the last. I could not consent to leave them in such a crisis. . . . I had a vigorous constitution, and this was doing me good service.

"A fourth ball ripped through my shoulder, leaving its base and a wad of clothing in its track. I could still stand and walk, although the shocks and loss of blood had left but little of my normal strength. I remembered the pledge to the commander that we would stay there till the battle ended or night came. I looked at the sun. It moved very slowly; in fact, it seemed to stand still. [The time was about noon.]

"I thought I saw some wavering in my line, near the extreme right, and Private Vickers of Alabama volunteered to carry any orders I might wish to send. I directed him to go quickly and remind the men of the pledge to General Lee, and to say to them that I was still on the field and intended to stay there. He bounded away like an Olympic racer; but he had gone less than fifty yards when he fell, instantly killed by a ball through his head. I then attempted to go myself, although I was bloody and faint, and my legs did not bear me steadily.

"I had gone but a short distance when I was shot down by a fifth ball, which struck me squarely in the face and passed out, barely missing the jugular vein. I fell forward and lay unconscious with my face in my cap; and it would seem that I might have been smothered by the blood running into my cap from this last wound but for the act of some Yankee, who, as if to save my life, had at a previous hour during the battle, shot a hole through the cap, which let the blood out.

"I was borne on a litter to the rear."

Switching to the Union side and to a lieutenant named A. H. Nickerson, who was a part of the attack at another point along the sunken road: "In this road the enemy were almost entirely hid from sight, while we stood exposed to a sweeping fire, totally un-protected. The range being so short and the fire therefore so deadly, I thought we should capture the position and not remain there and be wiped out of existence. Springing to the front . . . I called upon my men to follow me. . . . I believe that nearly the whole regiment followed; and we had gotten so near that the Confederates put up on their muskets and ramrods all the old dirty white clothes they could find, in token of surrender. . . .

"A [Confederate] reinforcing column soon came up in the corn-field back of the sunken road, and I could plainly see the Palmetto flag of South Carolina, side by side with the Georgia state colors, as the [column] deployed into line of battle and opened upon us. At this our friends (?) in the ditch pulled down their white flags and reopened their fire; and, all together, they swept the hillside where we stood very much as a stalwart mower cuts a swath in a meadow."

As his comrades began dropping all around him, Nickerson became involved with a particular Confederate. The two men emp-tied their muskets at each other, with both missing. Still in the act of reloading when the Confederate fired again, Nickerson was se-verely wounded in the right shoulder.

"On looking around, it did not seem that there was a living man left near me, till my eyes rested upon . . . a devoted friend. On duty he was Captain Richard Allen and I Lieutenant Nickerson, but when we were off duty he was 'Dick' and I 'Nick.'

". . . As I turned, still holding the half-loaded musket in my left hand and growing paler every minute from the loss of blood, he saw that I was badly hurt, and, calling out, said, 'Nick, go to the rear!' And then, as I still clung to the old musket and looked wistfully back to the spot where my duelistic enemy was safely posted, he put his command in more positive official form, and said, 'Lieutenant, go to the hospital immediately!'

"The 'hospital' on the field of battle is anywhere that the surgeons happen to be. In this case it was the barnyard of the Roulette house, and when I reached it the sight was appalling. It seemed as though nearly the whole of my regiment was there."

Another Union participant who was ordered to the rear after being wounded was Private Henry J. Savage of the 1st Delaware Infantry. "While retreating in good order but making most excellent time, [my] route led [me] through a portion of the Irish Brigade. Here [I] saw a sight that capped the climax of horror.

"A member of that brigade was aimlessly stumbling around with both eyes shot out, begging someone 'for the love of God' to put an end to his misery. A lieutenant of the 4th New York was passing by, and, seeing the poor fellow's condition and hearing his appeal, he halted before him and asked him if he really meant what he said.

" 'Oh, yes, comrade,' was the reply. 'I cannot possibly live, and my agony is unendurable.'

"Without another word the officer drew his pistol, placed it to the victim's right ear, turned away his head, and pulled the trigger. A half-wheel, a convulsive gasp, and one more unfortunate had passed over to the silent majority.

" 'It was better thus,' said the lieutenant, replacing his pistol and turning toward [me], 'for the poor fellow could—'

"Just then a solid shot took the lieutenant's head off."

With Union General Richardson's division coming into action on French's left, the issue began to go against the Confederates, their own reinforcements notwithstanding. The entire line at the sunken road—or, more correctly, the fraction still blessed with mobility—was soon in retreat across the fields to the southwest. This, of course, included the survivors of John Gordon's regiment, their movement breaking the colonel's vow to Lee.

Over at McClellan's headquarters, the commander and his aides were watching with avid interest. In the words of an aide named D. H. Strother: "Shot and shell followed [the Confederates] with vengeful rapidity, and anon our ordered lines were seen sweeping over the disputed field. . . . As the smoke and dust disappeared, I was astonished to observe our troops . . . passing over what appeared to be a long, heavy column of the enemy without paying it any attention whatever. I borrowed a glass from an officer, and

Confederate dead in the sunken road.

discovered this to be actually a column of the enemy's dead and wounded lying along a hollow road—afterward known as Bloody Lane. Among the prostrate mass I could easily distinguish the movements of those endeavoring to crawl away from the ground; hands waving as if calling for assistance, and others struggling as if in the agonies of death.

"I was standing beside General McClellan during the progress . . . of this attack. The studied calmness of his manner scarcely concealed the underlying excitement, and when it was over he exclaimed, 'By George, this is a magnificent field, and if we win this fight it will cover all our errors and misfortunes forever!' "

As for *errors*, the following assertion by Union newsman Charles Carleton Coffin tells the story: "Just here McClellan lost a great opportunity. It was the plain dictate of common sense that then was the time when Porter's . . . [reserves] should have been sent across the Antietam and thrown like a thunderbolt upon the enemy. It was so plain that the rank-and-file saw it. 'Now is the time,' was the universal comment. . . . The moment had come for dividing Lee's army . . . and crushing it back upon the Potomac in utter rout."

The reason that McClellan did not send in his reserves was that, in spite of his talk about victory, he was thinking mostly in terms of trying to ward off defeat. In his mind, Lee was all-powerful even with his center disrupted. If committed, the Union reserves might simply be swallowed up. So the grand attack went unsupported.

Confederate cavalry arresting flight of Antietam shirkers.

And the natural result was that, with both divisions badly hurt, the will to persist diminished.

On the Confederate side, however, the moment was one of gravest concern. Says D. H. Hill: "There were no troops near to hold the center except a few hundred rallied from the various brigades. The Yankees . . . had now got within a few hundred yards of the hill which commanded Sharpsburg and our rear. Affairs looked very critical."

James Longstreet, the senior commander in this zone, had by this time taken personal charge on the left flank. "We were under the crest of a hill occupying a position that ought to have been held by from four to six brigades. The only troops there were [Colonel John R.] Cooke's regiment of North Carolina Infantry [reinforced by the 3rd Arkansas], and they were without a cartridge. As I rode along the line with my staff I saw two pieces of the Washington Artillery . . . but there were not enough men to man them. The gunners had been either killed or wounded. This was a fearful situation for the Confederate center.

"I put my staff officers to the guns while I held their horses. It was easy to see that if the Federals broke through our line there, the Confederate army would be cut in two and probably destroyed, for we were already badly whipped and were only holding our ground by sheer force of desperation.

"Cooke sent me word that his ammunition was out. I replied that he must hold his position as long as he had a man left. He responded that he would show his colors as long as there was a man alive to hold them up. We loaded up our little guns with canister and sent a rattle of hail into the Federals as they came up over the crest of the hill.

"That little battery shot harder and faster, with a sort of human energy, as though it realized that it was to hold the thousands of Federals at bay or the battle was lost. So warm was the reception we gave them that they dodged back behind the crest of the hill. We sought to make them believe we had many batteries before them.

"As the Federals would come up, they would see the colors of the North Carolina regiment [and those of the 3rd Arkansas] waving placidly, and then would receive a shower of canister. We made it lively while it lasted.

"In the meantime . . . General Lee's chief of staff [Colonel R. H. Chilton] made his way to me and asked, 'Where are the troops you are holding your line with?' I pointed to my two pieces and to

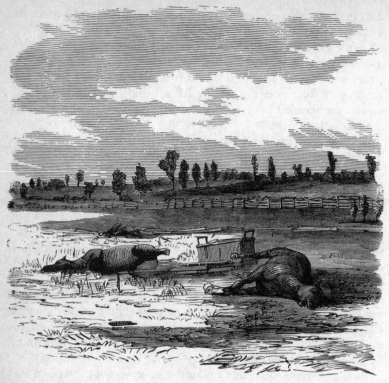

Slain artillery horses

Cooke's [reinforced] regiment, and replied, 'There they are, but that regiment hasn't a cartridge.'

"Chilton's eyes popped as though they would come out of his head. He struck spurs to his horse, and away he went to General Lee. I suppose he made some remarkable report."

Off to Longstreet's right, D. H. Hill, too, had resorted to desperate measures. "I found . . . [a] battery concealed in a cornfield and ordered it to move out and open upon the Yankee columns. . . . It moved out most gallantly, although exposed to a terrible . . . fire from the long-range Yankee artillery across the Antietam. A caisson exploded, but the battery unlimbered, and with grape and canister drove the Yankees back.

"I was now satisfied that the Yankees were so demoralized that a single regiment of fresh men could drive the whole of them in our front across the Antietam. I got up about two hundred men who said they were willing to advance to the attack if I would lead them. We met, however, with a warm reception, and the little command was broken and dispersed. . . .

"[Three North Carolina colonels] . . . had gathered up about two hundred men, and I sent them to the right to attack the Yankees in flank. They drove them back a short distance, but in turn were repulsed. These two attacks, however, had a most happy effect. The Yankees were completely deceived by their boldness. . . . They made no further attempt to pierce our center, except on a small scale."

By this time McClellan had received some reinforcements. William Franklin's corps had arrived on the field. (After its fight at Crampton's Gap, the corps had lingered in Pleasant Valley in order to guard against an enemy foray up the valley from Harpers Ferry, which would have imperiled McClellan's rear.) These new troops, however, were used only to bolster the Union right in a defensive way.

In remarkable contrast to McClellan's timidity, General Lee, despite his numerical weakness, was presently thinking in terms of trying to improve his situation by means of a counterattack, to be made by Stonewall Jackson, whose troops were at relative rest in the north after their morning fight. The plan called for Jeb Stuart to take a force of cavalry, infantry, and artillery, about five thousand

William B. Franklin

men in all, around the Union right and attack there while Jackson himself, with the rest of his wing, was striking from the front. The movement was scratched only after Stuart discovered that the Union right was bristling with well-placed guns.

The action in the center wound down at about 1 P.M. At 1:20 McClellan stated in a wire to Washington: "We are in the midst of the most terrible battle of the war—perhaps of history. Thus far it looks well, but I have great odds against me. Hurry up all the troops possible."

10

Afternoon at the Lower Bridge

IT WILL BE recalled that the Union left (its southern flank) was held by Ambrose Burnside. The general's Ninth Corps was positioned on the east bank of the Antietam at the lower bridge—thereafter to be known as Burnside Bridge. As early as 9:30 A.M., while the fight in the north was in progress, McClellan had sent word to Burnside to cross the creek and attack Lee's right.

According to McClellan's aide, D. H. Strother, the effort developed slowly. "The general [McClellan] was impatient, and frequently asked, 'What is Burnside about? Why do we not hear from him?' During the morning he sent several messengers to hasten his movements; but we only heard vaguely that he had not yet effected a crossing and could not carry the bridge."

Union newsman Charles Carleton Coffin says that Burnside's task was far from an easy one. "The banks of the [creek] at that point are steep and high. The road leading to the bridge winds down a narrow ravine. The bridge has three arches. It is 150 feet long, and the roadway twelve feet wide. The western bank is very steep. Halfway up the hill is a limestone quarry . . . [and] at the top of the hill is a stone wall which . . . afforded shelter to the Confederates. They had planted . . . artillery to sweep the bridge. . . . [Burnside's] orders directed him to carry the bridge, gain the heights beyond, and advance along their crest to Sharpsburg and reach the rear of Lee. He had less than fourteen thousand men. The task laid upon him was immeasurably greater and more difficult than that assigned to any other commander."

Hundreds of bluecoats were felled during Burnside's assaults at

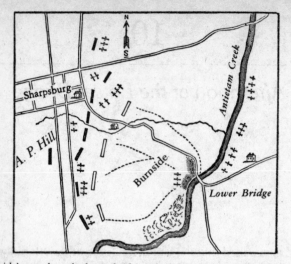

Burnside's attack at the lower bridge. Black bars indicate Confederate lines.

the bridge. The trick was finally turned by the 51st New York and the 51st Pennsylvania of Samuel D. Sturgis's division. General Sturgis relates: "They started on their mission of death full of enthusiasm, and, taking a route less exposed than the regiments which had made the effort before them, rushed at double-quick over the slope leading to the bridge and over the bridge itself with an impetuosity which the enemy could not resist; and the Stars and Stripes were planted on the opposite bank at 1 o'clock P.M. amid the most enthusiastic cheering from every part of the field from where they could be seen."

Reinforcements were soon pouring over the bridge. At the same time, units that had crossed at fords above and below the bridge were forming on the flanks. The Confederates began to fall back. These were some few hundred men belonging to D. R. Jones's division, Longstreet's corps, and their commander was Brigadier General Robert A. Toombs of Georgia. During the years before the war, Toombs, an ardent advocate of slavery, had served in both the U. S. House of Representatives and the U. S. Senate. Union news- man Coffin says that "he had boasted in Congress that the time would come when he would call the roll of his slaves on Bunker Hill, but at this moment he was retreating to the high ground near Sharpsburg."

Fortunately for Robert E. Lee, it took Burnside two hours to organize his main attack. Lee, unable to spare any worthwhile forces from his northern front, was counting upon the arrival of A. P. Hill from Harpers Ferry to save his right. Much earlier, Lee had anticipated a dire need of Hill on the field and had ordered him to come up fast. One of Hill's men was J. F. J. Caldwell, a junior officer from South Carolina, who says: "The day was hot and dusty in the extreme. All along the way we heard the boom of cannon, almost in our front. This fact, in conjunction with the rapid march, assured us that fighting was ahead of us."

The Union attack was launched at about 3 P.M. As described by Henry Kyd Douglas, of Stonewall Jackson's staff, who had come down from the north on a special mission: "General Burnside . . . moved against the hill which D. R. Jones held with his little division of 2500 men. . . . A. P. Hill was coming, but had not arrived, and it was apparent that Burnside must be stayed, if at all, with artillery. One of the sections, transferred to the right from Jackson at the request of General Lee, was of the Rockbridge Artillery, and as it galloped by, the youngest son of the general-in-chief, Robert E. Lee, Jr., a private at the guns, black with the grime and powder of a long day's fight, stopped a moment to salute his father and then rushed

The lower bridge in Federal hands

after his gun. Where else in this war was the son of a commanding general a private in the ranks?

"Going to put this section in place, I saw Burnside's heavy line move up the hill, and the earth seemed to tremble beneath their tread. It was a splendid and fearful sight, but for them to beat back Jones's feeble line was scarcely war. The artillery tore, but did not stay them. They pressed forward until Sharpsburg was uncovered and Lee's line of retreat was at their mercy.

"But then, just then, A. P. Hill, picturesque in his red battle shirt, with three of his brigades, 2,500 men who had marched that day seventeen miles from Harpers Ferry and had waded the Potomac, appeared upon the scene. Tired and footsore, the men forgot their woes in that supreme moment, and, with no breathing-time, braced themselves to meet the coming shock. They met it and stayed it. The blue line staggered and hesitated."

General Burnside, who was personally on the east bank of the Antietam, started a messenger galloping northward toward Mc-Clellan's headquarters. Among the newsmen at headquarters at this time was the *New York Tribune*'s George Smalley. "McClellan's glass for the last half hour has seldom been turned away from the left. He sees clearly enough that Burnside is pressed. . . . His face grows darker with anxious thought. Looking down into the [nearby] valley where fifteen thousand [reserve] troops are lying, he turns a half-questioning look on Fitz John Porter, who stands by his side gravely scanning the field.

"They are Porter's troops below . . . fresh and only impatient to share in this fight. But Porter slowly shakes his head; and one may believe that the same thought is passing through the minds of both generals. 'They are the only reserves of the army; they cannot be spared.'

"McClellan remounts his horse, and with Porter and a dozen officers of his staff rides away to the left in Burnside's direction. . . . Burnside's messenger rides up. His message is: 'I want troops and guns. If you do not send them, I cannot hold my position half an hour.'

"McClellan's only answer for a moment is a glance at the western sky [where the sun is dipping low]. Then he turns and speaks very slowly: 'Tell General Burnside this is the battle of the war. He must hold his ground till dark at any cost. I will send him Miller's battery. I can do nothing more. I have no infantry.'

"Then, as the messenger was riding away, he called him back. 'Tell him if he cannot hold his ground, then the *bridge,* to the last man—always the bridge! If the bridge is lost, all is lost.' "

Returning to the Confederate side and to staff officer Henry Kyd Douglas: "At the critical moment A. P. Hill was always at his strongest. Quickly advancing his battle flags, his line moved forward. Jones's troops rallied on him, and in the din of musketry and artillery . . . the Federals broke over the field. . . . Burnside was driven back to the Antietam [but remained on the Confederate side of the bridge]."

Union newsman Charles Carleton Coffin was watching the show from a high spot on the creek's eastern bank. "The daylight is dying out. . . . The battle is at this hour indecisive, but the artillery of both armies puts on new vigor as the sun goes down, as if each was saying to the other, 'We are not beaten.'

". . . I can see [northward] almost up to Poffenberger's. The [Union] batteries upon the hill in rear of his house are thundering. I can see the glimmer of the flashes and the great white cloud rising above the trees by Miller's. And there [at the northern edge of] the cornfield . . . batteries are pounding the ledges behind the church and sweeping the hillside. The woods which shade the church where Jackson [is located] are smoking like a furnace. Richardson's batteries, in front of [Lee's center] are throwing shells into the cornfield beyond Roulette's.

"The twenty-pounder Parrotts on the hill by my side open once more their iron lips. The hills all around Sharpsburg are flaming with rebel guns. The sharpshooters all along the line keep up a rattling fire. Near the town, haystacks, barns, and houses are in flames. At my left hand, Burnside's heavy guns, east of the [creek], are at work. His lighter batteries are beyond the bridge [working in his immediate defense]. His men are all along the hillside, a dark line dimly seen, covered by a bank of cloud [which their weapons are] illuminating . . . with constant flashes.

"All the country is flaming, smoking, and burning, as if the last great day, the Judgment Day of the Lord, had come.

"Gradually the thunder dies away. The flashes are fewer. The musketry ceases and silence comes on, broken only by an occasional volley and single shots, like the last drops after a shower. . . .

"[Thousands of] men who in the morning were full of life are bleeding at this hour. The sky is bright with lurid flames of burning buildings, and they need no torches who go out upon the bloody field to gather up the wounded. Thousands of bivouac fires gleam along the hillsides, as if a great city had lighted its lamps. Cannon rumble along the roads. Supply wagons come up. Long trains of ambulances go by.

"Thousands of slightly wounded work their way to the rear, dropping by the roadside or finding a bed of straw by wheat-stacks and in stables. . . . There are low wails of men in distress, and sharp shrieks from those who are under the surgeon's hands.

"While obtaining hay for my horse at a barn, I heard the soldiers singing. They were wounded but happy, for they had done their duty. They had been supplied with rations—hardtack and coffee— and were lying on their beds of straw. I listened to their song. It was about the dear old flag. . . . Then there came thoughts of home, of loved ones, of past scenes and pleasant memories, and the songs became plaintive. They sung the old song:

> "Do they miss me at home, do they miss me?
>   'Twould be an assurance most dear
> To know that this moment some loved one
>   Were saying, 'I wish he were here';
> To feel that the group at the fireside
>   Were thinking of me as I roam.
> Oh, yes, 'twould be joy beyond measure
>   To know that they miss me at home."

Among the myriad wounded who were in no mood for singing was the sergeant from Pennsylvania, A. F. Hill, whose thigh bone had been shattered by a musket ball during Hooker's attack in the north. We left Hill lying on the ground outside a small schoolhouse that was serving as a hospital. He had been told that his leg must come off.

"It was near evening when my turn came. I had lain during the whole afternoon without the schoolhouse, listening to the horrible screams which came from within, and occasionally, to kill time, gazing upon a heap of men's arms and legs which lay piled up against the side of the house. The sound of the battle could still be heard.

"But to be brief: I was carried into the schoolhouse and laid upon the operating table. 'Tell me, doctor,' I said earnestly, 'must my leg be amputated?'

"He coolly thrust his finger into the wound and felt the pieces of shattered bone. 'That bone,' said he, 'is shivered all to pieces; and if you value your life—'

A Union field hospital

" 'Can my life be saved only by—'

" 'Yes, and even then I doubt— I—' He hesitated.

" 'You think it a doubtful case, even then?'

" 'Yes.'

"I said no more. Chloroform was administered; I sank into unconsciousness; and when I awoke—it was all over."

On the Confederate side, Colonel John Gordon, five times wounded in the fight at the center and carried from the field insensible, had remained "out" all day, finally waking under the administration of stimulants.

"I found myself lying on a pile of straw at an old barn, where our badly wounded were gathered. My faithful surgeon, Dr. Weatherly, who was my devoted friend, was at my side with his fingers on my pulse. As I revived, his face was so expressive of distress that I asked him, 'What do you think of my case, Weatherly?'

"He made a manly effort to say that he was hopeful. I knew better, and said, 'You are not honest with me. You think I am going to die. But I am going to get well.'

"... Mrs. Gordon [who had followed the army in its march from Virginia] was soon with me. When it was known that the battle was on, she had at once started toward the front. The doctors were doubtful about the propriety of admitting her to my room [in a house in Sharpsburg], but I told them to let her come. I was more apprehensive of the effect of the meeting upon her nerves than upon mine. My face was black and shapeless—so swollen that one eye was entirely hidden and the other nearly so. My right leg and left arm and shoulder were bandaged and propped with pillows. I knew she would be greatly shocked. As she reached the door and looked, I saw at once that I must reassure her. Summoning all my strength, I said, 'Here is your handsome husband—been to an Irish wedding.' Her answer was a suppressed scream, whether of anguish or relief at finding me able to speak, I do not know."

Mrs. Gordon at once assumed the task of her husband's care. Later he claimed that her ministrations saved his life.

Toward the end of the day of fighting, it had been rumored on the Confederate side of the field that James Longstreet had been wounded, but the general's luck had held. He recounts: "When the battle was over and night was gathering, I started to Lee's headquarters to make my report. In going through the town I passed a house that had been set afire and was still burning. The family was in great distress, and I stopped to do what I could for them. By that I was detained until after the other officers had reached headquarters and made their reports. My delay caused some apprehension on the part of General Lee.... When I rode up and dismounted he seemed much relieved, and, coming to me very hurriedly for one of his dignified manner, threw his arms upon my shoulders and said, 'Here is my old war-horse at last!' "

Among the junior officers who entered Sharpsburg that night was Jeb Stuart's aide, Heros von Borcke, who rode in at a late hour in the company of two couriers. "It was a sad spectacle of death and destruction.... The unburied corpses of men and horses lay on every side in the streets, while helpless women and children, who had lost their homesteads, were moving about amid the smoldering ruins, seeking shelter for the night.

"The mansion of Dr. G., after having been completely riddled by shells, had been consumed. But a small summerhouse in the garden had escaped injury, and here the family found a temporary refuge. The doctor himself was quite calm and composed. He congratulated me on my escape, and said that he derived consolation from the hope that we should whip the Yankees as badly the next day as we had done already....

"For the remainder of the night I rested with my couriers in a small cow-stable, on the top of which we were fortunate enough to discover some hay for the horses.

"Several shots fired in rapid succession about daylight, very near to our little dormitory, roused us from sleep with the idea that the fighting had been renewed in the streets of the village. But, on going out of the cow-stable, I found, to my surprise and relief, that they came from some of our men who were amusing themselves with shooting the pigs and chickens which, rendered homeless . . . were wandering about in a distracted condition. . . .

"I felt obliged to rebuke a Texan, who, only a few steps from me, had just rolled over, by a capital shot, a porker galloping across the street at sixty yards distance, for his wanton disregard of the rights of property. With a look of utter astonishment he turned to me and asked, 'Major, did you have anything to eat yesterday?' and, upon my answering in the negative, said, 'Then you know what it is to be hungry. . . .' I had nothing more to say, and, mounting my horse, I rode forward to the front, where our army, in line of battle, was momentarily expecting the renewed attack of the enemy."

11

Lee Returns to Virginia

THE *Boston Journal's* Charles Carleton Coffin, astir at dawn on this eighteenth day of September, 1862, was puzzled. "The soldiers . . . were in position and lying on their arms, ready to renew the battle. . . . The cannon were silent. . . . There was no order to advance. I could hear now and then the isolated shots of the pickets. I could see that Lee had contracted his line between Dunker Church and Sharpsburg. His cannon were in position, his troops in line. Everybody knew that Franklin's corps was comparatively fresh [and Porter's unused]; that McClellan had 29,000 men who either had as yet not fired a musket or had been only slightly engaged. Why did he not attack? No one could tell."

McClellan himself explains: "After a night of anxious deliberation and a full and careful survey of the situation and condition of our army, the strength and position of the enemy, I concluded that the success of an attack on the 18th was not certain. I am aware of the fact that, under ordinary circumstances, a general is expected to risk a battle if he has a reasonable prospect of success; but at this critical juncture I should have had a narrow view of the condition of the country had I been willing to hazard another battle with less than an absolute assurance of success. At that moment—Virginia lost, Washington menaced, Maryland invaded—the national cause could afford no risks of defeat. One battle lost, and almost all would have been lost."

Says the Union army's General Jacob D. Cox (one of Burnside's corps commanders): "Could McClellan have known the desperate condition of most of Lee's brigades he would have known that his own were in much better case, badly as they had suffered. I do not doubt that most of his subordinates discouraged the resumption of the attack, for the rooted belief in Lee's preponderance of numbers had been chronic in the army during the whole year. That belief was based upon the inconceivably mistaken reports of the secret service organization, accepted at headquarters, given to the War Department at Washington as a reason for incessant demands of reinforcements, and permeating downward through the whole organization till the error was accepted as truth by officers and men, and became a factor in their morale which can hardly be overestimated."

McClellan decided to spend the eighteenth reorganizing, resupplying, and awaiting some expected reinforcements. The enemy, of course, would have to be watched sharply for signs of aggressive intent. At 8 A.M., after wiring a situation report to Washington, the general took a few moments to write to Ellen, and he included this remarkable line: "Those in whose judgment I rely tell me that I fought the battle splendidly and that it was a masterpiece of art."

Returning to Confederate narrator Heros von Borcke, who had made an early-morning ride to the front: "I found General Stuart . . . on our left flank, and at his request rode with him over the battlefield to reconnoiter the enemy's lines. It was a sickening sight. None of the corpses had yet been buried, and in Jackson's front the Federal dead lay around in great numbers, while many wounded men still remained untended in their agony in out-of-the-way spots of the woods and cornfields.

"The outposts of the two armies were separated from each other by only a few hundred yards, and frequent shots were exchanged between them whenever an enterprising fellow went forward to pick up a gun or strip a dead body upon the intermediate ground.

"After having completed our reconnaissance, and when several Yankee sharpshooters had rewarded our curiosity with the whizzing of their bullets, we proceeded towards the point where Jackson was supposed to be, and found Old Stonewall near a battery of twenty-five guns, stretched out along a fence and enjoying the luxury of a cup of coffee, quite hot, which his trusty servant had prepared from the contents of a Yankee haversack, and of which we were kindly invited to partake.

"General Lee soon arrived at the spot, and leaving these three great men to their council of war, I moved off a short distance, and, throwing myself at full length upon the soft turf, gave way to deep

Scene of a charge

reverie. I had heard much, and read much, in my own German and elsewhere, of the presentiment of approaching death, and had often speculated upon the matter. . . . This morning I was taken hold of . . . by the conviction that I should be killed before night in the coming battle. . . . I made the most mournful entry in my note-book. . . .

"Hour after hour passed away in anxiety and watching for the enemy's attack, but the perfect quietude of the morning was inter-rupted only by a flag of truce sent in by the Yankees asking permis-sion [to gather their wounded and begin the efforts] to bury their dead. This was of course granted, and the work occupied them until the afternoon, when it became evident that the battle would not be renewed, and that my misgivings for the day had been utterly idle.

"My annoyance at having indulged them was greatly mitigated when, with the evening, came my Negro, William, mounted on my beautiful little gray mule, Kitt, and, with a grin all over his black face, offered me tomatoes, apples, and roasted ears of corn, which he had promptly seized the earliest occasion of stealing from a neighboring farm.

"In the meantime our great commander-in-chief had decided to recross the Potomac [at the ford below Shepherdstown] and transfer his weakened army again to the soil of Virginia. Nothing could be accomplished by remaining longer in Maryland. Even had the battle been renewed with the most satisfactory results for our arms, General Lee had not men enough for the continued occupation of the country. . . .

"The retreat of our army was in preparation throughout the day, was commenced at night, and was executed in a masterly manner when one considers that it was conducted along a single road; that, except . . . [for the] men who were too severely wounded to bear transportation, nothing was left in the enemy's hands."

Adds Confederate General John Walker: "A little after sunrise . . . the entire Confederate army had safely recrossed the Potomac. . . . I was among the last to cross. . . . As I rode into the river I passed General Lee, sitting on his horse in the stream, watching the crossing of the wagons and artillery. Returning my greeting, he inquired as to what was still behind. There was nothing but the wagons containing my wounded, and a battery of artillery, all of which were near at hand; and I told him so.

" 'Thank God!' I heard him say as I rode on."

What happened next is told by the Shepherdstown woman, Mary Bedinger Mitchell: "General McClellan followed to the river, and, without crossing, got a battery in position on Douglas's Hill and began to shell the retreating army and, in consequence, the town. What before was confusion grew worse; the retreat became a stampede. The battery may not have done a very great deal of execution, but it made a fearful noise. It is curious how much louder guns sound when they are pointed at you than when turned the other way! And the shell, with its long-drawn screeching . . . has a way of making one's hair stand on end. . . .

"Someone suggested that yellow was the hospital color, and immediately everybody who could lay hands upon a yellow rag hoisted it. . . . The whole town *was* a hospital; there was scarcely a building that could not with truth seek protection under that plea, and the fantastic little strips were soon flaunting their ineffectual remonstrance from every roof-tree and chimney. . . .

Union burial party

"The danger was less than it seemed, for McClellan, after all, was not bombarding the town but the army, and most of the shells flew over us and exploded in the fields. But aim cannot always be sure, and enough shells fell short to convince the terrified citizens that their homes were about to be battered down over their ears. The better people kept some outward coolness . . . but the poorer classes acted as if the town were already in a blaze, and rushed from their houses with their families and household goods to make their way into the country.

"The road was thronged, the streets blocked; men were vociferating, women crying, children screaming; wagons, ambulances, guns, caissons, horsemen, footmen, all mingled—nay, even wedged and jammed together—in one struggling, shouting mass. The Negroes . . . swarmed into the fields carrying their babies, their clothes, their pots and kettles . . . and camped out of range. . . .

"There was another side to the picture that lent it an intensely painful aspect. It was the hurrying crowds of wounded . . . those maimed and bleeding fugitives! When the firing commenced, the hospitals began to empty. All who were able to pull one foot after another, or could bribe or beg comrades to carry them, left in haste.

In vain we implored them to stay; in vain we showed them the folly, the suicide of the attempt; in vain we argued, cajoled, threatened, ridiculed—pointed out that we were remaining and that there was less danger here than on the road.

"There is no sense or reason in a panic. The cannon were bellowing upon Douglas's Hill, the shells whistling and shrieking, the air full of shouts and cries. We had to scream to make ourselves heard. The men replied that the Yankees were crossing [which they really had no intention of doing at this time]; that the town was to be burned; that *we* could not be made prisoners, but *they* could; that, anyhow, they were going as far as they could walk or be carried.

"And go they did. Men with cloths about their heads went hatless in the sun; men with cloths about their feet limped shoeless on the stony road; men with arms in slings, without arms, with one leg, with bandaged sides and backs; men in ambulances, wagons, carts, wheelbarrows; men carried on stretchers or supported on the shoulder of some self-denying comrade. All who could crawl went. . . . They could not go far; they dropped off into the country houses, where they were received with . . . much kindness. . . . But their wounds had become inflamed [and] their frames were weakened by fright and overexertion. . . .

"Their places [in the hospitals] were soon taken by others, who had remained nearer the battlefield, had attempted to follow the retreat, but, having reached Shepherdstown, could go no farther. We had plenty to do, but all that day we went about with hearts bursting with rage . . . and breaking with pity and grief for the needless, needless waste of life."

The Battle of Antietam—Northern and Southern casualties combined—cost about 25,000 in killed, wounded, captured, and missing, with the balance of losses to each side nearly equal. In killed alone, however, the North lost about two thousand as compared with about fifteen hundred for the South. (These are the given figures, but the death toll was probably higher, since some of the men listed as missing might well have died.) The tragedy of at least 3,500 fatalities connected with one day's fighting was, of course, nowhere pointed up more sharply than it was on the battlefield itself. As reported by Union newsman Coffin:

"After the retreat of Lee, I rode over the ground occupied by the Rebels. . . . The dead were thickly strewn. A Rebel battery had occupied the ground around the Dunker Church. . . . At its doorstep lay a major, a captain, and eleven men, all dead. A wounded horse, unable to lie down, was standing near a dismantled cannon. Almost human was the beseeching look of the dumb beast."

The correspondent moved into a nearby field. "I came upon a Union soldier lying upon his back, the ground around stained with his blood. . . . His Bible was open upon his breast. Taking it up, I read, 'The Lord is my shepherd. . . . Yea, though I walk through the valley of the shadow of death, I will fear no evil, for Thou art with me. . . .'

"The slaughter had been terrible in the sunken road. I could have walked a long distance upon the bodies of dead Confederates. Some of them were shot dead while climbing the fence, and their bodies were hanging on the rails. One had been killed while tearing his cartridge with his teeth. He had died instantly, and the cartridge was in his hand. An officer was still grasping his sword. He had fallen while cheering his men. . . . Riding up to the turnpike a short

Confederate dead near the Dunker Church.

distance south of the Dunker Church I saw a dead Confederate hanging across the limb of a cherry tree by the roadside. He had been a sharpshooter and had taken the position to pick off Union officers, but himself had been shot. I afterward learned that several Union soldiers had seen puffs of smoke amid the foliage of the trees and had given return shots, one of which had taken effect."

A broader view of Antietam's residual panorama is given by the Union's Reverend A. M. Stewart, who sent the following account to the Pennsylvania newspaper he was furnishing with regular reports:

"For two days after the awful strife of Wednesday, the 17th, our regiment was posted in the very center of the great battlefield. A full opportunity was thus afforded me for looking over that vast Golgotha, that modern Aceldama—a real field of blood. It stretched over an extent of broken ground at least three miles in length by one and a half in breadth. Over all that wide-extended territory lay promiscuously scattered the dying and the dead, friend and foe intermingled—rifles, muskets, bayonets, scabbards, cartouch-boxes, haversacks—all manner of clothing—coats, hats, caps, shoes, blankets—stains and pools of blood—hundreds on hundreds of fine horses mutilated and torn—caissons, saddles, and harness unstinted and unnumbered.

"Scenes of carnage were here multiplied which I had nowhere seen equalled or excelled, save on some portions of Malvern Hill, on the Peninsula, where heaps of the slain were piled together.

"By Friday afternoon, all the wounded which could readily be found had been collected into extemporized hospitals—houses, barns, sheds, schoolhouses, churches, etc., or carried away altogether from the battlefield. [The army's medical corps was aided by many civilians, among them Clara Barton, later to make a name as founder of the American Red Cross Society.]

"Scarcely any extended effort had as yet been made to bury the dead, who, by this time had become black, swollen, and offensive.

"On the afternoon of Friday, while walking through a beautiful open wood in which, as seen by the uniforms of the dead, a New York regiment and the rebels had met in fierce and deadly encounter, I stopped for a moment to gaze on a group of seven or eight Union and rebel soldiers lying close together, and all seemingly still in death. One of these, a rebel as known by his dress, and in appearance about twenty-one years of age, had something about him more lifelike than the others. Interested in his appearance, I

Clara Barton

went near and discovered that he was still breathing; felt his pulse and found it regular and firm.

"Though so sadly and strangely familiar with mutilations of every possible form, with sudden deaths, as well as great tenacity of life, yet did this case excite not only my deepest curiosity but downright astonishment. Life, for days together, under such conditions, had never before been witnessed. A union of soul and body for so long, with such a wound, had not been supposed possible. A Minnie ball [properly, Minié ball, but spelled variously by the soldiers] had struck the young man on the right temple, just in the edge of the hair, and passed directly through the head, coming out on the opposite side, nearly in the same position on the left temple. A hole had been made through the head sufficiently large to have pushed the forefinger along the course of the bullet.

"The poor fellow was evidently lying in the precise position in which he fell, three days previously. A handful of brains had oozed out from the ghastly wound. I called on two men in citizen's dress who at the time were near, and a straggling soldier, for help to remove him to an old church or schoolhouse not far distant. We spread a blanket, laid him on it, and, each one taking a corner, carried him to the old, waste, lone building, all riddled with shell and ball during the late battle—pulled two benches together, took an old broom for a pillow, and laid him on the hard bed. With water from my canteen, the blood and gore were washed from his head and face. Water was poured on his parched lips and into his mouth. In a few minutes he so revived as to be able to speak faintly.

"By this time our regiment was in motion, and, lest its course and future position might be missed, I was compelled hastily to rejoin it—for in the marchings and countermarchings, the frequent changes in position of a hundred thousand men, on and near a field of battle, should one lose his regiment he might readily spend a whole half-day in fruitless efforts again to find it. That night we encamped between Sharpsburg and the Potomac. The next day, Saturday, we were ordered to Williamsport, twelve miles [up the Potomac], and our way led back across the battlefield.

"When opposite the old building, I ran aside while the column moved on, to look again after the poor young Rebel. Just as left the previous day he lay, no one seemingly having been there. He was still alive and breathing more freely. At once recognizing my voice, he answered intelligently a few brief questions. Notwithstanding an effort to refrain, as his head and face were again bathed, tears would flow down to mingle with the water. A piece of hard cracker, the only food at the time in my haversack, was broken fine, moistened with water, and put in his mouth, which he tried to eat. In reply to my question, 'Do you think of anything more I can now do for you?' his answer was, 'Nothing, dear sir.' Commending him to the care of a merciful God in a few words of prayer, I turned away and left him, with feelings of indescribable sadness.

"War—cruel, unfeeling, relentless, bloody war! I inquired not for his name, his home, nor his mother—having no desire to know them. Little doubt he would die there, unsoothed, unaided, unwept. No comforting incident, in the case, to write to his mother, if one were living; no cheerful memory for me to cherish concerning him. I asked not the name of the poor deluded young stranger who came there to die so sad, so lonely a death."

As mentioned in the foregoing account, the chaplain's regiment was on its way up the Potomac to Williamsport. The unit was part of a detachment that made this march in order to parry a demonstration by Jeb Stuart, whose purpose was to distract McClellan and enhance Lee's security. The distraction notwithstanding, McClellan ordered Fitz John Porter to muster a part of his corps and send it across the river at Shepherdstown to reconnoiter Lee's situation. Among the units picked for the mission was the 20th Maine, the regiment to which Private Theodore Gerrish belonged.

"This was to be a new experience to us. Up to this time we had not been in the advance. We had seen our comrades fight and go down in the smoke of battle, but now we were to experience that which hitherto we had only seen.

"The regiment quickly obeyed the order to 'fall in.' Then the command 'by the right flank, march' was given, and away we went. We soon reached the Potomac River, and crossed at the Shepherdstown fords. The river was wide, the water deep, the current swift; and the ledges upon which we walked were so narrow that our crossing was necessarily very slow, but we finally reached the Virginia shore.

"Not a gun had been fired, and not an enemy had been seen. Our regimental line was formed upon the bank of the river, and we began to climb the steep bluff that rose some two hundred feet above the water. Before the ascent was completed, we heard heavy firing up the river on our right, showing that those who crossed the river above us had encountered the enemy.

"With a desperate resolution to crush the rebellion, we scrambled to the top, and our line was quickly formed upon its crest. A deep forest was in our immediate front. The firing on our right had increased, and the roar of regular volleys of musketry came rolling down the river.

"Gray forms were seen flitting among the trees before us, puffs of white smoke suddenly burst out from the forest, and the uncomfortable 'zip, zip' of leaden messengers over our heads warned us that the enemy meant business. We returned the fire and sent our first greetings to the Southern Confederacy in the form of minie bullets that went singing and crackling through the forest in our front; and we made a target of every gray form we could see.

"Our regiment was about to make a charge upon them when the order came for us to get down over the bluff and recross the river as rapidly as possible. And down through the rocks and trees we ran.

"We reached the river and began to make a most masterly advance upon Maryland. The enemy followed us to the top of the bluff, and would have punished us severely as we were recrossing the river, but one of our batteries went into position on the Maryland side, threw shells over our heads, and drove the rebels back.

"Several of the regiments on our right had sustained great losses. One of them, the 118th Pennsylvania, had been almost annihilated.

"Upon reaching the Maryland shore, we took possession of the Chesapeake and Ohio Canal, and there formed the advanced line of the army.

"One very amusing incident occurred in our retreat. In Company H was a man by the name of Tommy Welch, an Irishman about forty years of age, a brave, generous-hearted fellow. He was an old bachelor, and one of those funny, neat, particular men we occasionally meet. He always looked as if he had emerged from a bandbox; and the boys used to say that he would rather sacrifice the whole Army of the Potomac than to have a spot of rust upon his rifle, or dust upon his uniform. He was always making the most laughable blunders, and was usually behind all others in obeying any command.

"When our regiment went tumbling down over the side of the bluff to reach the river, the men all got down before Tommy understood what they were doing. Then very slowly he descended, picking his path carefully among the trees and rocks, and did not reach the river until the rear of the regiment was nearly one-half of the way across.

"The officer who commanded our regiment on that day rode a magnificent horse, and, as the regiment recrossed, he sat coolly upon his horse near the Virginia shore, amidst the shots of the enemy, speaking very pleasantly to the men as they passed him. He evidently determined to be the last man of the regiment to leave the post of danger. He saw Uncle Tommy, and, although the danger was very great, he kindly waited for him. . . .

"When the latter reached the water, with great deliberation he sat down upon a rock and removed his shoes and stockings, and slowly packed them away in his blanket. Then his pant legs must be rolled up so that they would not come in contact with the water. And all the time the rebels were coming nearer and the bullets were flying more thickly.

"At last he was ready for an advance movement, but just as he reached the water the luckless pant legs slipped down over his knees; and he very quietly retraced his steps to the shore to roll them up again.

"This was too much for even the courtesy of the commanding officer, who, becoming impatient at the protracted delay, and not relishing the sound of the lead whistling over his head, cried out in a sharp voice, 'Come, come, my man; hurry up, hurry up, or we will both be shot.'

"Tommy looked up with that bewildered, serio-comic gravity of expression for which the Emerald Isle is so noted, and answered in the broadest brogue, 'The divil a bit, sur. It is no mark of a gintleman to be in a hurry.'

"The officer waited no longer, but, putting spurs to his horse, he dashed across the river, while Tommy, carrying his rifle in one hand and holding up his pant legs with the other, followed after, the bullets flying thickly around him.

"(Poor Tommy Welch—brave, blundering, and kind—was a favorite in his company; and his comrades all mourned when he was shot down in the Wilderness [in 1864]. He was there taken prisoner and carried to Andersonville prison, where he died of starvation.)"

McClellan's blunted reconnaissance ended the Antietam campaign. Lee had been found "in strong force" on the south bank of the Potomac, but there was no doubt he was retreating. Even before the reconnaissance, McClellan had reported to Washington: "I have the honor to report that Maryland is entirely freed from the presence of the enemy, who has been driven across the Potomac. No fears need now be entertained for the safety of Pennsylvania. I shall at once occupy Harpers Ferry."

To his wife, McClellan wrote: "The battle of Wednesday *was* a terrible one. . . . Our victory was complete, and the disorganized rebel army has rapidly returned to Virginia, its dreams of 'invading Pennsylvania' dissipated forever. I feel some little pride in having, with a beaten and demoralized army [a reference to Pope and Second Bull Run], defeated Lee so utterly and saved the North so completely. Well, one of these days history will, I trust, do me justice in deciding that it was not my fault that the campaign on the Peninsula was not successful. . . .

"Since I left Washington, Stanton [the Secretary of War] has . . . asserted that *I*, not Pope, lost the Battle of Manassas No. 2! [Stanton claimed that McClellan, in a pique over being eclipsed by Pope's rise to power, was deliberately slow in reinforcing him from the Peninsula—an assertion that probably wasn't true.] . . . I am tired of fighting against such disadvantages, and feel that it is now time for the country to come to my help and remove these difficulties from my path. . . .

"I feel that I have done all that can be asked in twice saving the country. If I continue in its service I have at least the right to demand a guarantee that I shall not be interfered with. I know I cannot have that assurance so long as Stanton continues in the position of Secretary of War and Halleck as general-in-chief."

These were extraordinary statements, even for McClellan. He was wrong in thinking that the entire North was now at his feet. It was true that everyone was deeply relieved that the invasion of Maryland had been frustrated, but many were disappointed that the enemy hadn't been finished for good. Abraham Lincoln, who had dared to hope that this time McClellan would take fire, was gloomy over Lee's escape. Until forced to surrender, the President knew, the Confederate chief would remain a mortal threat.

McClellan's partial victory, however, created the atmosphere Lincoln needed to announce his Emancipation Proclamation. On September 23, 1862, six days after the battle, Northern newspapers published the preliminary proclamation, which said, in part, "That on the first day of January, in the year of our Lord one thousand eight hundred and sixty-three, all persons held as slaves within any State, or designated part of a State, the people whereof shall then be in rebellion against the United States, shall be then, thenceforward, and forever free." The early announcement served not only to forewarn the South but also to give the North time to adjust to the idea.

McClellan, who was opposed to forcible emancipation, played a curious role in the proclamation's development. His failure on the Peninsula made such a measure a necessity, and his qualified success at Antietam set the stage for its introduction.

The general's belief in his ascent to Olympus was destroyed in short order. He was depressed when, on September 25, he wrote his wife: "It is very doubtful whether I shall remain in the service after the rebels have left this vicinity. The President's late proclamation, the continuation of Stanton and Halleck in office, render it almost impossible for me to retain my commission and self-respect at the same time."

McClellan had no intention of making a prompt effort to push Lee farther southward. Ellen was told on the twenty-ninth: "I think secesh has gone to Winchester. . . . If he has gone there I will be able to arrange my troops more with a view to comfort." By October 1 the general had decided that Lee might be regrouping for another advance across the Potomac, farther up: "A cloudy day. If it does not rain I think I will go to Williamsport and Hagerstown today, to see that part of the country; for there is no telling but that I might have to fight a battle there one of these days, and it is very convenient to know the ground. . . .

"I rode all over the [Antietam] battlefield again yesterday, so as to be sure that I understand it all before writing my report. I was but the more impressed with the great difficulties of the undertaking and the magnitude of the success. . . .

"I don't know where we are drifting [as a nation], but do not like the look of things. Time will show. . . . I do not yet know what are the [overall] military plans of the gigantic intellects at the head of the government."

McClellan would have been astonished had he known that history's verdict on Abraham Lincoln's intellect was to be that it was a great one. As it happened, the general's own intellect was at this time much on the mind of the President, who confided to an aide that he had begun to believe that McClellan was a little crazy.

12

Both Sides Gird Anew

THE CONFEDERATE campaign in Maryland had lasted for only two weeks. "Designed as an invasion," says Northern newsman-historian William Swinton, "it degenerated into a raid.... McClellan had come up and forced [Lee] into a corner.... Crippled at Antietam, he was fain to ... seek in Virginia the opportunity to gather up the fragments of his shattered strength....

"Both armies ... rested on their arms—the Confederates in the Shenandoah Valley in the vicinity of Winchester, and the Army of the Potomac near the scene of its late exploits, amid the picturesque hills and vales of Southwestern Maryland....

"The movement from Washington into Maryland to meet Lee's invasion was defensive in its purpose, though it assumed the character of a defensive-offensive campaign. Now that ... Lee [had been] driven across the frontier, it remained to organize on an adequate scale the means of a renewal of grand offensive operations directed at the Confederate army and towards Richmond."

McClellan was so methodical with his preparations that Lee was granted the weeks he needed to rebuild his army. "It is difficult," says J. F. J. Caldwell, the lieutenant from South Carolina, "to describe the condition of the troops at this time, so great and various was their wretchedness. They were sunburnt, gaunt, ragged, scarcely at all shod, spectres and caricatures of their former selves. Since the beginning of August they had been almost constantly on the march, they had been scorched by the sultriest sun of the year, they had been drenched with rain and the heavy dews peculiar to this latitude, they had lost much night rest, they had worn out their clothing and shoes, and received nothing but what they could pick up on the battlefield.

"They had thrown away their knapsacks and blankets in order to travel light, they had fed on half-cooked dough, often raw bacon as well as raw beef, had devoured green corn and green apples; they had contracted diarrhea and dysentery of the most malignant type, and, lastly, they were covered with vermin. They now stood an emaciated, limping, ragged, filthy mass whom no stranger to their valiant exploits could have believed capable of anything the least worthy."

Matters were not long so dismal. Better rations were provided, and there was time for rest and a greater attention to cleanliness. The turnpike southward from Winchester was soon dusty with two-way traffic. Going down in horse-drawn ambulances were the wounded and sick of the recent campaign; and coming up—on horseback, in wagons, and afoot—were men returning from furloughs or from hospital stays after recovering from wounds or ailments acquired in earlier campaigns.

Patrols scoured the countryside for the men who had straggled on the way to Sharpsburg. Out of unit pride, the patrols preferred to bring in members of rival brigades rather than their own absentees. This caused some friction. One day a patrol brought in some stragglers belonging to a rival brigade, and that brigade promptly sent out a patrol that nabbed a crowd of men from the other brigade who were not stragglers at all, but had gone to a creek to bathe and wash their clothing.

Even the army's geographical location was a factor in its revival. With autumn abroad in the Shenandoah Valley, the leaves were enriching their colors, and most of the days were deliciously bright and blue. In the words of Confederate staff officer John Esten Cooke: "The region . . . is known as the 'Garden of Virginia,' and the benign influence of their surroundings was soon seen on the faces of the troops. . . . In their camps along the banks of the picturesque little stream called the Opequan, which, rising south of Winchester, wanders through beautiful fields and forests to empty into the Potomac, the troops laughed, jested, sang rude camp ballads, and exhibited a joyous indifference to their [remaining] privations and hardships. . . ."

In a letter composed at the fireside, an unnamed soldier described the kind of humor the army enjoyed. Almost any odd occurrence, the writer said, was grist for a round of jesting. "A cavalryman comes rejoicing in immense top-boots, for which in

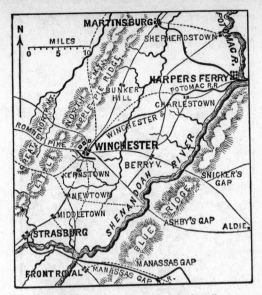

Northern regions of Shenandoah Valley

fond pride he had invested full forty dollars of pay. At once the cry from a hundred voices follows him along the line, 'Come up out o' them boots! Come out! . . . I know you're in thar; see your arms stickin' out!'

"A bumpkin rides by in an uncommonly big hat, and is frightened at the shout, 'Come down out o' that hat! Come down! 'Taint no use to say you ain't up there; I see your legs hanging out!'

"A fancy staff officer was horrified at the irreverent reception of his nicely twisted mustache, as he heard, from behind innumerable trees, 'Take them mice out o' your mouth! Take 'em out! No use to say they ain't thar; see their tails hanging out!'

"Another, sporting immense whiskers, was urged to 'come out of that bunch of har! I know you're in thar; I see your ears a-working!' "

The troops, as John Esten Cooke goes on to explain, exhibited "no want of rebound—rather, an excessive elasticity and readiness to undertake new movements. They had plainly acquired confidence in themselves—rightly regarding the event of the Battle of Sharpsburg, where they were so largely outnumbered, as highly honorable to them—and they had acquired still greater confidence in the officers who commanded them."

The attitude of the Yankees across the Potomac was considerably

Confederate foragers

different. There was a good deal of uncertainty among them. Aside from their rescue of Maryland, they'd never achieved very much. Even the Battle of Antietam, they knew, was far from a smashing triumph. Nor was there any redemption in their remaining encamped when they ought to be advancing.

A letter from the field written by New Englander Samuel Fiske (under his pseudonym Dunn Browne) included this analysis: "The soldiers ... have come to war reluctantly, from the pressure of urgent necessity and a strong sense of duty; and they want the war over within the quickest possible time.... They are not satisfied with their generals, because they have common sense enough to see that, with some few exceptions, our armies are not well-managed, nor well-provided, nor well-led into battle; that their strength, their energies, their lives are, to a very great extent, wasted...

"They go into battle aware that it is pretty much a chance whether their bravery and endurance will be of any avail, with a cheerful resolution that does them the highest honor. I glory in our common soldiers! I do not despair of the country when I see the materials that compose the army for her defense. The Government may dally. . . . Greedy contractors and corrupt officials may eat up our resources. Incompetent and traitorous commanders may waste our tremendous armies. All the more credit to the unbroken and unconquerable spirit of our people [in arms] that is carrying, and will carry, our cause through in spite of every obstacle, and at the cost of whatever sacrifice.

"Of course, I am saying this of the men in general of our armies. Some of them are poor enough material for anything, too poor to waste good powder and ball upon, utterly unworthy to fight in behalf of our glorious cause. . . . Many of them *skedaddled* from our big field of battle at Sharpsburg. The vile, obscene, blasphemous swaggerers of our regiment, the thieves and drunkards and rowdies . . . to the number of seventy-five or a hundred, were found wanting . . . and came sneaking back for days after the battle with cock-and-bull stories of being forced into hospital service and care of the wounded."

Private Theodore Gerrish of the 20th Maine takes up the narrative: "During the five weeks of inactivity in the Army of the Potomac that followed the Battle of Antietam, one of the most disastrous features of the gloomy situation was the terrible sickness of the soldiers, and this was especially true in the new regiments. The men were unused to the climate, the exposure, and the food, so that the whole experience was in direct contrast to their life at home. . . . Strong men grew weak with disease. No sanitary measures were enforced in camp. The buildings used as hospitals were but illy adapted to such a purpose, being very imperfect in ventilation, cleanliness, and general convenience. . . .

"It was a sad mission to sit by the dying in the midst of all the dirt and disorder with which they were surrounded, to gather up little trinkets to send as priceless keepsakes to distant friends, to write the last good-byes and messages of love whispered from dying lips, and to hold their thin, hollow hands as the spirit floated away from its earthen casket. Then would follow the soldier's burial, the corporal's guard with reversed arms keeping step to the mournful beat of the muffled drum. . . .

"It has been urged as a defense for this delay on the part of General McClellan that he disliked to sacrifice his men, and that a special regard for their welfare caused him to move so slowly. If this be true, it was a mistaken policy, for experience taught us that lead was a much less cruel butcher than disease, and that if soldiers must die to preserve the government, they prefer to die upon the battlefield."

A happier feature of the army's camp life is described by a private from Massachusetts named Warren Goss: "We swapped our hardtack, pork, and coffee with the people of the region for fresh meat and homemade bread, and indulged in all the luxuries of this delightful country. The corn which we gathered in the fields—ofttimes without permission—gave us hasty pudding and johnnycake. With a nail, or the point of a bayonet, we punched holes through a tin plate or the half of a canteen, thus converting them into graters, on which we rubbed the corn, on the ear, and obtained meal seemingly nicer and sweeter than that ground at a mill. It seemed to me that I never had eaten such johnnycakes as were made from this meal."

In early October, President Lincoln came by rail for a four-day visit to the camps. He conferred with McClellan (quizzing him about his inertia), went through the hospitals, made a tour of the Antietam battlefield, and attended several reviews. One of the reviews is pictured by surgeon George Stevens of the 77th New York: "The line was formed on a fine plain, and the booming of cannon announced the approach of the Commander-in-Chief of the armies of the United States. The illustrious visitor was accompanied by . . . an immense retinue. Conscious of the fatigues already endured by these veterans, the President simply passed along the line of the divisions, acknowledging the salutations which greeted him, without requiring the columns to march in review. The soldiers manifested their appreciation of the interest taken by the Chief Magistrate in their welfare by loud and repeated cheers."

An insight regarding the situation at this time is offered by Colonel Theodore B. Gates of New York, commander of a regiment known as the Ulster Guard: "There is no doubt but that the Army of the Potomac was pretty well worn out after the Battle of Antietam, but, probably much less so than the rebels were, who had done more marching and quite as much fighting. . . . The Federal army . . . was luxuriously clothed compared with its ragged adversaries. Its supplies of food and forage were abundant, while the Confederates were often suffering from want of food.

"But the systems in the two armies were entirely different—and continued to be so throughout the war. The Confederates marched and fought without regard to the question of food or clothing. If their ammunition boxes were full and their muskets bright, they considered themselves fit for duty. They moved in 'light marching order,' and were not encumbered with long trains of wagons. Their surprising marches . . . could never have been made with the *impedimenta* that loaded down the Union armies.

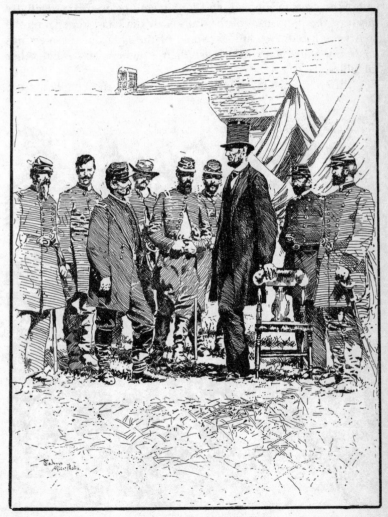

McClellan and Lincoln at Antietam

"There is no example of such vast armies as the Federal Government had in the field with such unfailing and bountiful supplies of food and clothing. If we could have adopted the Confederate system—probably a necessity in their case—we would have whipped them in half the time it took to do it our way."

That autumn the Union army was being reinforced. Recruiting officers from the various regiments were sent to the Northern towns where the units originated, and "war meetings" were arranged. By this time the patriotism of the war's early days had waned, and the men were lured by bounties. Some of the ladies at the meetings made supplementary offerings: their watches, rings, and other valuables.

A different mission from camp was given the chaplain from

Recruiting in the North in 1862

Pennsylvania, A. M. Stewart. As explained in one of his letters: "Our regiment, after nearly six months' delay, had received four months' pay. The families of the soldiers greatly needed the money. Means for transmission seemed both limited and uncertain. The letter-writer was the one fixed upon who must go to Pittsburgh, carry the various packages of money, inquire after the welfare of dwellers at home; also deliver and carry back hundreds of friendly messages. . . .

"With a large haversack filled with envelopes containing, in the aggregate, about fifteen thousand dollars, I was soon . . . within the [train] cars at Hagerstown. . . . No sooner beyond the lines of the army than all appearance of war disappeared. The farming interests of the Keystone State everywhere gave marks of unwonted thriftiness. The railroad engines puffed and snorted and screamed in a manner indicating that the track must be cleared for trains of unusual length and with more than ordinary burdens.

"In the cities, the streets were thronged with such multitudes as gave no evidence that Pennsylvania had sent a hundred and fifty thousand of her stalwart sons to the battlefield. The noisy peal of ten thousand workshops, the sound of the trowel and the hammer upon many new structures in process of erection; plethoric warehouses; stores rich to gorgeousness, and on the increase—all giving at least external evidence that this greatest war of modern times, and supported entirely from the nation's internal resources, had nevertheless brought with it universal prosperity to Pennsylvania, and also to all her Northern sisters.

"What a marvel is here! Something new under the sun! A nation, from internal resources alone, carrying on for over eighteen months the most gigantic war of modern times, [one] ever-increasing in its magnitude, yet all this while growing richer and more prosperous!

"And the *ladies*! They never looked more handsome, never appeared happier, and surely never dressed finer and more fashionably—the war notwithstanding."

The South could not boast so grand an economy. Her war machine was a limited one. She was not only less populous than the North, but was also more agricultural than industrial. Moreover, she had begun to suffer under a Union blockade of her ports. To keep her war effort waxing, a lot had to be done with a little.

Robert E. Lee's mastery of this art was now well known, and this enhanced his popularity both with his troops and with the civilian public. "While in the Shenandoah Valley," says John Esten Cooke,

". . . Lee had evidences of the position which he occupied. . . . Gray-haired men came to his camp and uttered prayers for his health and happiness as the great leader of the South. Aged ladies greeted him with faltering expressions of deep feeling and pathetic earnestness. And, wherever he went, young girls and children received him with their brightest smiles."

To the people he met casually, Lee seemed a man of uncommon imperturbability, but this aura was misleading. As explained by his youngest and most trusted aide, Colonel Walter Taylor, who knew him as well as anyone: "General Lee was naturally of a positive temperament, and of strong passions; and it is a mistake to suppose him otherwise; but he held these in complete subjection to his will and conscience. He was not one of those invariably amiable men whose temper is never ruffled; but when we consider the immense burden which rested upon him, and the numberless causes for annoyance with which he had to contend, the occasional cropping-out of temper which we, who were constantly near him, witnessed, only showed how great was his habitual self-command.

"He had a great dislike to reviewing army communications. This was so thoroughly appreciated by me that I would never present a paper for his action unless it was of decided importance, and of a nature to demand his judgment and decision. On one occasion when an audience had not been asked of him for several days, it became necessary to have one. The few papers requiring his action were submitted.

"He was not in a very pleasant mood. Something irritated him, and he manifested his ill-humor by a little nervous twist or jerk of the neck and head peculiar to himself, accompanied by some harshness of manner. This was perceived by me, and I hastily concluded that my efforts to save him annoyance were not appreciated.

"In disposing of some case of a vexatious character, matters reached a climax. He became really worried; and, forgetting what was due to my superior, I petulantly threw the paper down at my side and gave evident signs of anger. Then, in a perfectly calm and measured tone of voice, he said, 'Colonel Taylor, when I lose my temper, don't let it make *you* angry.' "

Lee was a devoted family man, and, however great the pressures of the field, he kept in close touch with affairs at home. There was a frequent exchange of letters, and the family was currently a source of agonizing concern. Again in the words of Walter Taylor: "Tidings reached General Lee, soon after his return to Virginia, of the serious illness of one of his daughters, the darling of his flock. [Her name was Annie, and she was twenty-three years old.] For several days apprehensions were entertained that the next intelligence would be of her death.

"One morning the mail was received, and the private letters were distributed [and read] as was the custom. But no one knew whether any home news had been received by the general. At the usual hour he summoned me to his presence to know if there were any matters of army routine upon which his judgment and action were desired. The papers containing a few such cases were presented to him. He reviewed and gave his orders in regard to them.

"I then left him, but for some cause returned in a few moments, and with my accustomed freedom entered his tent without announcement or ceremony, when I was startled and shocked to see him overcome with grief, an open letter in his hands. That letter contained the sad intelligence of his daughter's death. . . .

"This incident . . . illustrates one of the noblest traits of the character of that noble man. He was the father of a tenderly loved daughter . . . whose sweet presence he was to know no more in this world; but he was also charged with the command of an important and active army. . . . His army demanded his first thought and care. . . . 'Duty first' was the rule of his life. . . ."

In a letter to his wife, Mary, Lee was religiously philosophical about their loss: "I cannot express the anguish I feel at the death of our sweet Annie. . . . But God, in this as in all things, has mingled mercy with the blow in selecting that one best prepared to leave us. May you be able to join me in saying, 'His will be done!'

". . . I know how much you will grieve. . . . I wish I could give you any comfort, but beyond our hope in the great mercy of God, and the belief that He takes her at the time and place when it is best for her to go, there is none."

Lee said in a letter to a surviving daughter: "In the quiet hours of the night, when there is nothing to lighten the full weight of my grief, I feel as if I should be overwhelmed. I have always counted, if God should spare me a few days after this Civil War was ended, that I should have her with me, but . . . my hopes go out and I must be resigned."

Militarily, Lee's chief concern at this time was the reorganization of his two corps into tighter, more efficient units. This matter gave occupation also to James Longstreet and Stonewall Jackson.

For Jeb Stuart and his men, these autumn days were not without action in the field. The troopers made numerous scouts along the Potomac, and they also countered Federal probes that got them into brushes with Alfred Pleasonton's horsemen.

The indefatigable Stuart managed to combine his work in the field with a busy round of social activities involving Virginia civilians. He made his headquarters on the grounds of a charming country estate known as "The Bower," where he and his subordinate officers enjoyed gracious treatment at the hands of the owner and his family.

An episode associated with one of Stuart's field trips is described by Heros von Borcke:

"On our return through Shepherdstown, we stopped for an hour at the house of a lady, a friend of General Stuart, Mrs. L., who had lost her husband . . . at the first battle of Manassas. . . . The general's presence was no sooner known in the village than a mob of young and pretty girls collected at Mrs. L.'s house, all very much excited— to such an extent, indeed, that the general's uniform was in a few minutes entirely shorn of its buttons, taken as souvenirs; and if he had given as many locks of his hair as were asked for, our commander would soon have been totally bald. Stuart suffered all this very gracefully, with the greater resignation as every one of these patriotic young ladies gave him a kiss as tribute and reward. The latter favor was unhappily not extended to the staff officers, and it may be readily imagined that it was tantalizing for us to look on and not take part in the pleasant ceremony."

A few days later, Von Borcke was approached by Stuart "with orders to ride, upon some little matters of duty, to the camp of General Jackson. I was also honored with the pleasing mission of presenting to Old Stonewall, as a slight token of Stuart's high regard, a new and very stunning uniform coat which had just arrived from the hands of a Richmond tailor. . . . I reached the simple tent of our great general just in time for dinner. I found him in his old weather-stained coat, from which all the buttons had been clipped, long since, by the fair hands of patriotic ladies, and which, from exposure to sun and rain and powder smoke, and by reason of many rents and patches, was in a very unseemly condition.

"When I had despatched more important matters, I produced General Stuart's present, in all its magnificence of gilt buttons and sheeny facings and gold lace; and I was heartily amused at the modest confusion with which the hero of many battles regarded the fine uniform from many points of view, scarcely daring to touch it, and at the quiet way in which, at last, he folded it up carefully and deposited it in his portmanteau, saying to me, 'Give Stuart my best thanks, my dear Major. The coat is much too handsome for me, but I shall take the best care of it, and shall prize it highly as a souvenir. And now let us have some dinner.'

"But I protested energetically against this summary disposition of the matter of the coat, deeming my mission, indeed, but half-executed, and remarked that Stuart would certainly ask me how the uniform fitted its owner, and that I should, therefore, take it as a personal favor if he would put it on. To this he readily assented with a smile; and, having donned the garment, he escorted me outside the tent to the table where dinner had been served in the open air.

"The whole of [his] staff were in a perfect ecstasy at their chief's brilliant appearance, and the old Negro servant, who was bearing the roast turkey from the fire to the board, stopped in mid-career with a most bewildered expression, and gazed in wonderment at his master as if he had been transfigured before him.

"Meanwhile, the rumor of the change ran like electricity through the neighboring camps, and the soldiers came running by hundreds to the spot, desirous of seeing their beloved Stonewall in his new attire. And the first wearing of a fresh robe by Louis XIV, at whose morning toilet all the world was accustomed to assemble, never created half the sensation at Versailles that was made in the woods of Virginia by the investment of Jackson in this new regulation uniform."

During these weeks of relative inactivity, the woods and fields that held Jackson's corps assumed the air of a camp meeting grounds. As explained by Robert L. Dabney, a Virginia clergyman who spent a part of the war on Jackson's staff and became one of the general's earliest biographers: "Not only did the [regimental] chaplains now redouble their diligence in preaching and instructing the soldiers from tent to tent; but many eminent ministers availed themselves of the lull in the storm of war, and of the genial weather, to visit the camps and preach the gospel as missionaries.

"These were received by General Jackson with affectionate hospitality; and, while no military duty was neglected for a moment to make way for their ministrations, his pious ingenuity found abundant openings for them. It was now that the series of labors and the ingathering of precious souls began in the Confederate army, which . . . [became] so extraordinary a feature of its character. The most enlightened and apostolic clergymen of the country, forgetting for a time the distinctions of sect, joined in these meetings.

"Nightly, these novel and sacred scenes might be witnessed, after

Prayer in Stonewall Jackson's camp

the drill and the labors of the day were over. From the bosom of some moonlit grove a hymn was heard, raised by a few voices, the signal for the service; and, at this sound, the multitudinous noises of the camp died away, while the men were seen gathering from every side, until the group from which the hymn had arisen was swelled into a great crowd.

"The man of God then arose and began his service by the light of a solitary candle, or a fire of resinous pine wood, elevated on a rude platform. While his face and the pages of the Holy Word were illuminated thus, all else was in solemn shadow, and his eye could distinguish nothing of his audience, save the dusky outline of the multitude seated all around, in a wide circle, upon the dry leaves or the greensward. But though his eye could not mark the impress of the truth, it was drank in by eager ears; and many was the bearded cheek, which had not been blanched amidst the horrors of Sharpsburg, which was now wet with silent tears.

"At some of these meetings General Jackson was a constant worshipper, seated modestly in an unnoticed corner amidst the common soldiers, but setting the example of the most devout attention."

Perhaps the example was not always perfect. The narrator does not mention any "nodding off," but it probably occurred.

One day Jackson's camp was visited by a celebrity from nearby Martinsburg. According to James Power Smith, one of the general's staff officers: "The notable female scout, Belle Boyd, made her appearance on horseback, with the escort of a Confederate cavalryman. She was well-mounted and quite a soldierly figure, and asked to see General Jackson. But the general was averse, and . . . refused to see the young woman, of whose loyalty he was not altogether assured. She was much disappointed and went away quite angry with the aide who had denied her admission to the general's tent. Some days after this she sent a message that if ever she caught that young man in Martinsburg she would cut his ears off."

The private soldiers in Jackson's command took great pride in the times when their illustrious commander stopped, during his rounds of the camps, to pass a few words with them. One day a private went about boasting that the general had paid him very particular atten-

Belle Boyd

tion that morning. Pressed to explain, the soldier said: "He asked me what I was doing in that orchard over yonder; said he expected his men to have more respect for people's property—and told me to march right out!"

Jackson and his command were ordered by Lee to perform a special task, that of disrupting the Baltimore and Ohio Railroad on its course through the northern end of the Shenandoah Valley. The track was an important link between Washington and the West. Because of Lee's presence, the road was not now in use, but would be available for reopening as soon as he left the area. "It was determined," says clergyman Dabney, "that the enemy should be as thoroughly deprived of its use as possible. General Jackson now applied a system of his own to dismantle it. Besides burning all bridges and breaking up all culverts, he ripped the iron nails from the cross-ties . . . collected the latter into heaps two or three feet high, and, laying the bars of iron across the top, set fire to the whole.

"The heat of such log heaps in full blaze rendered the iron red hot, and the weight of the projecting ends warped and bent it into every imaginable shape. But as though this were not enough, the soldiers, seizing the great bars while heated in the middle, bent them around trees. . . . From the hamlet of Hedgesville, west of Martinsburg, to a point near Harpers Ferry, the track was thus utterly destroyed for a distance of thirty miles; and after the work was done, Jackson rode deliberately over the whole to assure himself of its completeness."

13

Stuart Visits Pennsylvania

J EB STUART and a select group of his horsemen also entered upon a special mission, a combination reconnaissance and raid into Northern territory. This was by Lee's order, and he outlined the route. Stuart was to pass west of the Army of the Potomac and circle north of its position. If expediency or necessity carried him eastward, he was to make his return to Virginia by a route skirting the foe's eastern flank. Lee's proposal offered Stuart the chance to repeat his Peninsula feat of riding entirely around the Union army.

The story of the mission is begun by Henry B. McClellan, a Confederate trooper who was not a participant but who learned the details directly from Stuart and his staff. McClellan, then a youthful captain, was a Northerner—a first cousin to the commander of the Army of the Potomac—who had chosen to fight for the South.

"For a few days before the 9th of October," McClellan recounts, "a more-than-usual stir at cavalry headquarters aroused suspicion on the part of those who were somewhat behind the scenes. On the afternoon of the 8th Stuart ordered his acting adjutant, Lieutenant R. Channing Price, to prepare all official papers which required his attention [before he could leave the area]. The evening, until eleven o'clock, was spent in the society of the ladies of 'The Bower.' Retiring to his tent, Stuart then consumed two hours in closing up the business of his office. This done, [his personal musicians] the banjo, fiddle, and bones were awakened, and a parting serenade was given to his kind friends [at the house].

"On the morning of the 9th everything was astir. Eighteen hundred cavalry were to rendezvous that day at Darkesville. Six hundred of the best-mounted and most-reliable men had been selected

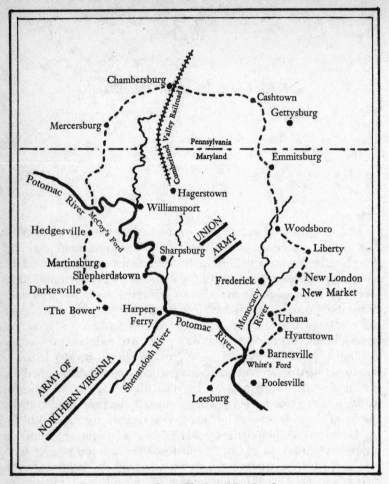

Stuart's route from "The Bower" to Leesburg.

from each of ... three brigades ... and these detachments were commanded ... by Brigadier-General Wade Hampton, Colonel W. H. F. Lee, and Colonel William E. Jones. Major John Pelham commanded the four guns which accompanied the expedition."

One of the troopers who was to be left behind was Heros von Borcke, who was presently without a sturdy mount. His set of animals had been broken down by too much hard use during recent weeks. The major says of the morning of Stuart's departure from "The Bower":

"About eight o'clock the bugle sounded to horse, and soon afterwards I, and the rest of my comrades who had been left with me behind, saw with great depression of spirits the long column disappear behind the distant hills. We determined, however, with a soldier's philosophy, to accept the situation and to forget our disappointment by indulging, as much as was compatible with the performance of duty, in rides, drives, shooting, and social visiting at 'The Bower.' "

Returning to the account by Henry McClellan: "When the troops had assembled at the [Darkesville] rendezvous, Stuart issued to them the following address:

" 'Soldiers! You are about to engage in an enterprise which, to insure success, imperatively demands at your hands coolness, decision, and bravery; implicit obedience to orders without a question or cavil; and the strictest order and sobriety on the march and in bivouac. The destination and extent of this expedition had better be kept to myself than known to you. Suffice it to say that with the hearty cooperation of officers and men I have not a doubt of its success—a success which will reflect credit in the highest degree upon your arms. The orders which are here published for your government [i.e., conduct] are absolutely necessary and must be rigidly enforced.'

"The orders which controlled the action of the troops were in substance as follows: each brigade commander was required to detail one-third of his command to seize horses and other property of citizens of the United States subject to legal capture, while the remainder of his command was held at all times in readiness for action. It was required that receipts should be given to all noncombatants for every article taken from them, in order that they might have recourse upon the Federal government for damages. Individual plundering was prohibited in the strongest manner. The arrest of public functionaries, such as magistrates, postmasters, and sheriffs was ordered, that such persons might be held as hostages for citizens of the Confederacy who had been arrested and imprisoned. The seizure of private property in the State of Maryland was prohibited.

"Every nerve of every man responded to Stuart's address. The secrecy of the movement added zest to it. Many a trooper in that company had ridden with him around McClellan's army on the [Peninsula], and all felt that they could safely follow where Stuart led the way."

The troopers were soon on the march northward to Hedgesville, located a few miles south of the Potomac, where they bivouacked for the night. Jeb Stuart assumes the narrative: "At daylight next morning . . . I crossed the Potomac at McCoy's . . . with some little opposition, capturing some two or three horses of the enemy's pickets. We were told here by citizens that a large force had been camped the night before at Clear Spring [a few miles north of McCoy's] and were supposed to be enroute to Cumberland [about fifty miles to the west].

"We proceeded northward until we had reached the turnpike leading [westward] from Hagerstown . . . known as the National Road. Here a signal station on the mountain, and most of the party, with their flags and apparatus, were surprised and captured, and also eight or ten prisoners of war, from whom, as well as from citizens, I found that the large force alluded to had crossed [my path] but an hour ahead of me toward Cumberland, and consisted of six regiments of Ohio troops and two batteries. . . . I sent back this intelligence at once to the Commanding General.

"Striking directly across the National Road, I proceeded in the direction of Mercersburg, Pennsylvania, which point was reached about twelve [noon]. I was extremely anxious to reach Hagerstown, where large supplies were stored; but was satisfied, from reliable information, that the notice the enemy had of my approach and the proximity of his forces would enable him to prevent my capturing it. I therefore turned toward Chambersburg."

Henry McClellan says that "the terms of Stuart's orders were strictly enforced. . . . Nothing whatever was disturbed on the soil of Maryland; but when once the Pennsylvania line was crossed, the seizure of horses was prosecuted with system and diligence. Six hundred men scoured the country on either side of the line of march, and, as far as scouts could extend, the country was denuded of its horses.

"With his usual courtesy toward ladies, Stuart gave orders that, whenever they might meet his column, they should be allowed to pass in their conveyances without molestation.

"So strict was the enforcement of orders that the men were not even allowed to seize provisions for themselves. They sometimes, however, obtained by strategem what they were not permitted to take by force. On the second day's march some hungry cavalrymen approached a house whose male defenders had fled, leaving the women and babies in possession. A polite request for food was met by the somewhat surly reply that there was none in the house.

Casting a wolfish glance upon the babies, a lean fellow remarked that he had never been in the habit of eating human flesh, but that he was now hungry enough for anything; and if he could get nothing else he believed he would compromise on one of the babies. It is hardly necessary to say that the mother's heart relented and a bountiful repast was soon provided."

Stuart tried to contain the news of his occupation of Mercersburg and his intentions against Chambersburg, but it leaked out. In the words of a Union officer, Colonel Alexander K. McClure (a newspaper editor in civilian life):

"I was then on duty at Harrisburg [Pennsylvania] as Assistant Adjutant General of the United States, but always spent one or two days, with Sunday, at my home in Chambersburg. When I arrived at the Chambersburg depot on one of my home visits for a brief rest I was summoned by the telegraph operator to his private office. He had just received several dispatches from Mercersburg stating that a Confederate cavalry force was then in possession of that town and was moving in the direction of Chambersburg.

"It was startling intelligence indeed, and it seemed incredible that a Confederate force would attempt to raid Chambersburg, only an hour's distance from Hagerstown, where there was a large Union force. . . .

"[Going to my own office,] I waited for an hour, and was advised of the progress of the Confederate force as it moved steadily toward Chambersburg. I telegraphed to the Union commander at Hagerstown . . . stating the facts and suggesting as a matter of precaution that a small force of infantry and artillery should be hurried to the defense of the town. In charity I will not give the name of the Union commander, who answered that the suggestion of a Confederate force entering Chambersburg was too absurd to be considered.

"Half an hour later the advancing Confederates had reached Chambersburg Turnpike and were moving directly upon us, and only ten miles distant. I then repeated an appeal to the Union commander at Hagerstown, stating the facts and urging him to send a force to intercept the enemy, as there was yet ample time to do so, but the only reply was an intimation that military commanders had no time to waste on lunatics."

The frustrated McClure felt he had no choice but to resign himself to the situation. "I quietly went to my home, took tea, and returned to my office to await events. A cold drizzling rain had been falling during the day, and, between the clouds and fog, darkness came unusually early. Some of the prominent citizens of the town had been advised of the approach of Stuart, but all agreed that it could do no good to make an alarm or to attempt defense.

"About seven o'clock in the evening there was a knock at my office door, which I promptly opened, and in came three Confederate soldiers with a dirty rag tied to a stick which they called a flag of truce. Judge [Francis M.] Kimmell and Colonel Thomas B. Kennedy were present. The Confederate officer said he had been sent in advance to demand the surrender of Chambersburg. We told him that there were no troops in the town and nobody to oppose the entrance of the insurgents. I asked who was in command of the Confederate forces, but they refused to answer. I then asked where the forces were, which they also refused to answer.

"I then asked them whether they would take us to the commanding general and give us safe-conduct back. They assured us that they would do so, and we three mounted horses and rode out on the western turnpike for nearly a mile and were there brought up before a solid column of soldiers. General Wade Hampton came to the front. . . . He said he desired to take peaceful possession of the town, and in answer to our inquiries assured us that private citizens and private property would be respected, excepting such property as might be needed for the purposes of the army.

"Remembering that I [although in civilian clothing] was a commissioned officer, I said to General Hampton, 'There are several military officers in the town in charge of hospitals, recruiting service, etc. What will be done with them?' He promptly answered, 'They will be paroled [and left unhindered], unless there are special reasons for not doing so. . . .' As we were not in a position to quibble about the terms of the surrender, and as General Hampton's proposition seemed reasonably fair, we decided to give him a town that he could [have taken] without opposition [anyway], and rode back into Chambersburg, with Hampton's command immediately following."

According to an unidentified resident: "The clattering of hoofs announced that Stuart's cavalry were taking possession of our town. In they came, without any noisy demonstration whatever. Occasionally . . . one would whisper a little loud, 'Hurrah for Southern rights!' Another would ask, 'Have you ever heard of Stuart's cavalry? This is it.' Another would ride up and ask for a drink of whisky, and offer the silver for it."

Returning to Colonel McClure: "In crossing the Center Square a short time after Hampton's force had entered, I was familiarly slapped on the shoulder, and, turning around, recognized Hugh Logan, then a captain in the Confederate army and the guide of the raid, as he had been born and grown up [in the area]. . . . I had once successfully defended him [presumably by means of newspaper writings] when charged with kidnapping. He was one of the rugged mountaineers whose fidelity is equally rugged, and he informed me that I was one of a number of citizens . . . whose names had been selected and given to General Stuart . . . to be taken as prisoners to Richmond to be held as hostages for Pope's arrest of civilians in Virginia.

"I told him that I had met Hampton, although he did not ask my name, and had his assurance that officers would be paroled, and that I was an army officer. He answered in a characteristic terse manner, 'Well, Hampton's a gentleman, and if you are taken and get to him he'll discharge you, but Jeb wants you damn bad.'

". . . I asked Logan what he thought it best that I should do, to which he answered, 'Go out to your home. We're in a hell of a hurry and you probably won't be disturbed, but if you are taken I'll put you out tomorrow night.' If I had been taken he would have fulfilled his promise, even at the peril of his life."

McClure's home was about a mile from the center of town. "When I reached there, I found that a detachment of Stuart's troops had been in advance of me and relieved me of the possession of ten fine horses [and had departed]. My house stood back from the highway some fifty yards and was largely hidden by shade trees, and I closed up the house so as to leave no lights visible, and sat on the porch awaiting [additional] visitors whom I sincerely hoped would not come.

"Shortly after midnight I heard the clatter of hoofs and the jingle of sabers. . . . Soon they arrived in front of my house. They saw corn shocks on one side of the road, a large barn and water on the other side, and a paling fence that promised a quick fire. They halted, apparently about one hundred and fifty in number, and immediately proceeded to tumble the corn shocks over to the horses and tear down the palings to start the fire.

"Seeing that their acquaintance was inevitable, I walked down to the gate and kindly said to them that if they wanted to make a fire they would find wood just a few feet from them, and showed them a short way to water. The commander of the detachment stepped up to me and very courteously inquired whether I resided there, with-

178   LEE'S TERRIBLE SWIFT SWORD

out asking my name, and said he would be greatly obliged if he and some of his officers could get a cup of coffee.

"I told them that I had plenty of coffee, but that my servants were colored and had hidden. He assured me that they were not after Negroes, whether slave or free, and that if I could find the servants and get them some coffee I could promise them absolute safety. My servants were hidden in the thicket but a little distance from the house, and I soon found some twenty Negroes, who swarmed back and speedily had hot coffee and tea for the officers of the command.

"It was evident they had no idea at whose place they were stopping, but they were thinly clad, without their overcoats and blankets in order to be in the lightest trim for rapid marching, and they were suffering from the cold rain of the entire day. They gladly accepted my invitation to come into the house and warm themselves—and they were not five minutes in the library, where the New York and Philadelphia papers lay on my table with my name on them, before they all intuitively comprehended the fact that they had asked hospitality, and were about to receive it, in the house of a man whom they were ordered to take as a prisoner to the South.

"They were all Virginians and gentlemen of unusual intelligence and culture. . . . I watched with unusual interest to see what the effect would be when they discovered in whose house they were guests. . . . They did not long leave me in doubt as to their appreciation of the peculiar condition in which they were placed. . . . It was soon evident that they had decided that, having asked and accepted hospitality, they would not permit themselves to know that they were in the house of a host whom it was their duty to arrest as a prisoner.

"We sat at tea and over our pipes and cigars until at daylight the bugle called them to the march. Every phase of the war was discussed with the utmost freedom, but no one of them spoke the name of himself or any of his fellows, and not one assumed to know my identity. . . . When the bugle sounded they arose and bade me good-bye, thanking me for my hospitality and earnestly expressing the hope that we should sometime meet again under more pleasant auspices."

The troopers moved into Chambersburg. At about 7 A.M., McClure followed. "I . . . found that the First Brigade, under General Hampton, had gone [eastward] toward Gettysburg. General Stuart sat on his horse in the center of the town, surrounded by his staff; and his command was coming in from the country in large squads,

leading their old horses and riding the new ones they had found. . . .
His demeanor to our people was that of a humane soldier. In several
instances his men commenced to take private property from stores,
but they were arrested."

Public property was treated differently. In the words of the unidentified citizen quoted earlier: "They commenced plundering the
warehouses, etc. They destroyed considerable property of some of
our forwarding and commission men. They discovered arms, ammunition, and army clothing in some of these buildings. They took
the clothing, threw their old sabers away and took new ones, exchanged pistols, and took as much ammunition as they could conve-
niently carry.

"They then set fire to the [railroad] depot, several warehouses, a
large machine shop, and burned them to the ground. The consternation this created was no little. The citizens all knew of the large
quantities of ammunition these houses contained, and much of it
was shell. The frequent explosions of these deadly missiles kept the
citizens in their houses, and thus prevented them from doing anything that might check the progress of the fire. It had rained the day
and night before, and the buildings were wet, consequently no other
buildings were destroyed, except several stables in the immediate
neighborhood of the depot and warehouses.

Fires set during the Chambersburg raid.

"After these buildings were enveloped in flames, our rebel visitors departed in the direction of Gettysburg. There was not a farmer within miles of their course that they did not visit, robbing every farmer of all his horses. The horses they took from our county, the property they destroyed and buildings they burned, we think can reasonably be estimated at two hundred and fifty thousand.

"We conversed with two or three of them upon the street, and they candidly acknowledged that Lincoln's last proclamation was more to be dreaded by them [because it might inflame the slaves to an uprising] than any other steps yet taken by our Government."

The Chambersburg raid, made north of McClellan's army in a region he should have been able to protect, was the climax of Stuart's expedition. The raid failed in only one respect. General Lee had wanted Stuart to destroy a railroad bridge north of Chambersburg in order that McClellan's influx of supplies should be inhibited, but the bridge was found to be of iron and was quite resistant to destruction.

By this time the North was in another dither. From his office in Washington, General Halleck fumed at McClellan: "Not a man should be permitted to return to Virginia." McClellan wired back: "I have given every order necessary to insure the capture or destruction of these forces, and I hope we may be able to teach them a lesson they will not soon forget."

If a lesson was taught, it was taught by Stuart. Once past McClellan's eastern flank on that Saturday, October 11, he swung southward to Emmitsburg, Maryland, and began making his way to the Potomac. His column, encumbered with twelve hundred extra horses, extended for five miles, but he managed to move rapidly over little-known roads, and the Federals failed to find him. Soon, however, they decided that he doubtless intended to recross the river in the vicinity of its junction with the Monocacy, and they prepared to meet him there.

Late Saturday night Stuart reached New Market, about twenty miles from the Potomac. Here, despite the dangers he knew were now developing, the general took time out for one of his larks. Henry McClellan explains:

"During the first Maryland campaign [i.e., the Antietam campaign], while his headquarters were at Urbana, Stuart had received many acts of kindness and courtesy at the hands of the ladies of the family of Mr. Cockey [ladies that included the visiting "New York Rebel"]. As he bade them good-bye when his cavalry fell back before

McClellan's advance, he had laughingly promised these ladies that he would call upon them again before very long.

"When he reached New Market on the night of the 11th, he, with a few of his staff and couriers, left the route of the column, rode to Urbana, aroused the family from slumber, paid his compliments to the ladies while yet on horseback, reminded them of his promise, and begged that they would accept this as the fulfilment of it. He then rode on and rejoined his column before daylight."

By this time the Union forces covering the Potomac crossings in the vicinity of the Monocacy's mouth were formidable. But when Stuart reached the area, his bold advance thwarted a coordinated response; and, maneuvering skilfully, the general managed to keep the fighting at a low key and to slip across the Potomac at White's Ford.

Henry McClellan says that "Stuart's joy at the successful termination of his expedition was unbounded. The enemy made no attempt at further pursuit, but approached the ford sufficiently near to receive a few shots from Pelham's guns, and to hear the exulting cheers with which his men greeted Stuart as he rode along their lines.

"His march from Chambersburg is one of the most remarkable on record. Within twenty-seven hours he had traversed eighty miles . . . and had forced a passage of the Potomac under the very eyes of forces which largely outnumbered his own. His only casualty was the wounding of one man. Two men, who for some reason dropped out of the line of march, were captured. . . .

Jeb Stuart's raiders fording the Potomac with stolen horses.

"Stuart himself lost two valuable animals—Lady Margrave and Skylark—which were in [the] charge of his servant Bob. The temptation of drink was too strong for Bob's constancy. He imbibed enough to make him sleepy, fell out of the line to take a nap, and awoke to find himself and his charge in the hands of the enemy."

Stuart lost three men, but he also gained a number of recruits from among Maryland's Southern sympathizers. He also brought back about thirty hostages of the type Lee wanted—a disgruntled group indeed!

After a short rest, Stuart and his troopers moved on to Leesburg, about ten miles from the ford, where they bivouacked for the night. Then they headed for their camps in the Shenandoah Valley.

"On the morning of the 13th," says Heros von Borcke, who had been awaiting the expedition's return, "General Stuart arrived again safely at 'The Bower,' heralding his approach from afar by the single bugler he had with him, whose notes were somewhat oddly mingled with the thrum of [Sam] Sweeney's banjo. Our delight in being together again was unspeakable, and was greatly enhanced by the glorious issue of the expedition. . . .

"All my comrades had mounted themselves on fresh horses, and they came back with wonderful accounts of their adventures across the border, [describing] what terror and consternation had possessed the burly Dutch farmers of Pennsylvania, and how they groaned in very agony of spirit at seeing their fine horses carried off—an act of war which had been much more rudely performed . . . by the Federal cavalry in Virginia.

"General Stuart gave me a gratifying proof that he had been thinking of me in Pennsylvania by bringing back with him an excellent bay horse which he had himself selected for my riding. . . .

"All now went merrily again at 'The Bower.' General Stuart . . . was the lightest-hearted of the whole company. On the 15th another ball was given in honor of the expedition, and the ladies of the neighborhood were brought to the festivity in vehicles captured in the enemy's country, drawn by fat Pennsylvania horses. Stuart was, of course, the hero of the occasion, and received many a pretty compliment from fair lips."

A set of golden spurs was Stuart's special gift from one woman. This inspired him to begin calling himself "Knight of the Golden Spurs." He also began signing some of his private letters "K.G.S."

14

Bugles Along the Blue Ridge

STUART'S SECOND CIRCUIT of McClellan's army left the commander looking quite as foolish as had the first. Actually, this second feat was even more embarrassing. Whereas Stuart had been on Southern soil before, this time he had violated McClellan's home territory.

The new incident put McClellan into still deeper disfavor with Abraham Lincoln, who had been hoping to hear that the Federal army, not the Confederate, had stirred itself to action.

During Stuart's ride, some of the Union infantry units that were shifted in an effort to disrupt the raider's progress found themselves in new regions to excite their interest. One of these units was the New York regiment led by Regis de Trobriand. The colonel and his men ended up encamped near Poolesville, about twenty-five miles southeast of Sharpsburg.

"It was a fine country; great woods interspersed with broad meadows and cultivated fields, in the center of which arose farmhouses of fine appearance. The opinions of the inhabitants favored the South, and more than one young man from the families around was in the Confederate army. Nevertheless, we were politely received, since we took nothing which was not paid for in ready money; and the requisitions for wood and forage were under the orders of the quartermaster's department.

"The older people were very reserved on the subject of politics. The young girls, only, gave free license to their tongues, excited by our officers, who were the more amused by this frankness as the expression was more animated, and in that the grandparents

184   LEE'S TERRIBLE SWIFT SWORD

showed themselves much disturbed by it. It was not our place, defenders of every liberty, to find fault with free speech even in the mouths of our enemies. We granted it to others as much as we asked it for ourselves. . . .

"The time passed. . . . The fine days of October, the finest weather of the pleasantest season in the United States, slipped away without any indication on the part of General McClellan of any intention to profit by them. More than a month had passed since the Battle of Antietam, and the army was immovable. It was impatient at this long inaction. The country was astonished at it. Everywhere it was asked, 'What is McClellan doing?'

"What was he doing? Nothing. What did he wish to do? Keep us in Maryland, perhaps winter there? Who knows?"

Lincoln sent McClellan a series of wires aimed at getting the army into motion. Once the President even abandoned his measured ways and resorted to sarcasm, informing the general: "I have just read your despatch about sore-tongued and fatigued horses. Will you pardon me for asking what the horses of your army have done since the Battle of Antietam that fatigues anything?"

McClellan finally bestirred himself near the end of October. His plan was to cross the Potomac east of the Blue Ridge Mountains (Lee was west of this range) and begin a southerly move that, if not quickly countered, would place him between Lee and Richmond.

Regis de Trobriand tells of the march as it was begun by the brigade to which his regiment belonged (and to the command of which he had just been elevated because the regular brigade commander had fallen sick): "We crossed the Potomac at White's Ford. . . . The troops were full of ardor and good spirits. The water was cold and the atmosphere was not warm, but the comical incidents of the passage spread good humor over all, and gave rise to a great deal of laughter. Moreover, we stopped [and went into bivouac] near the ford, and the campfires quickly dried the shoes and wet trousers. The baggage reached us the next day.

"My headquarters were on a rich farm, whose owner, Alfred Belt, an old Whig, had become a secessionist with all his family. The good man grumbled from morning until night about the soldiers, who, however, respected his barnyard and paid large prices for the milk, bread, and cakes which his daughter sold them. But he took to heart the loss of his fences, which, in the evening, made magnificent fires. He could not refrain from going continually, with a mournful air, to the windows to see them blaze up. Then he would return to the

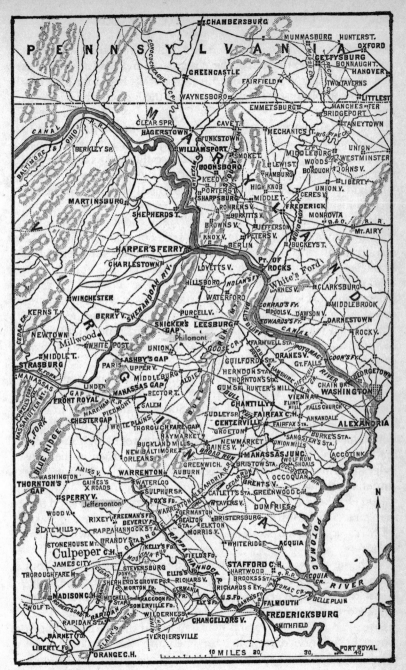

Field of operations between Sharpsburg and Fredericksburg

chimney corner and seat himself in his old armchair, to curse the
war, deplore the extinction of the Whig party, and demonstrate to us
that Henry Clay [a solon from Virginia with a talent for effecting
political compromises] would have saved the Union if he had been
living.

"He had, under various pretexts, asked of me the permission to
send some of his people beyond the line of our pickets, which I had
refused, knowing him to be a man who would send exact information as to the strength and position of the division. Several women
who had come to see him had been [turned] back. . . . So the old
secessionist had but a very mild regard for me.

"He had in the woods a valuable colt, on account of which he was
very much troubled, not being able to send out to look for him. The
second night, one of the advanced sentinels heard a movement of
branches in the thicket, and a step as of someone approaching
cautiously. 'Halt! Who goes there?' cried the sentinel. No reply.
Then a shadow was seen a short distance away. 'Who goes there?'
called our man for the second time, taking aim. And, as the shadow
approached without reply, he fired. The guard ran up and found
the unfortunate colt dying, a victim to [its] ignorance of the usages
of war.

"Imagine the feelings of the old man, Belt, on hearing this news
in the morning. He would have been glad to have persuaded me
that the Government of the United States ought to pay him the
value of the animal. But I succeeded in convincing him that he
would have to resign himself to pass the account of the colt to
the balance against the horses that his grandson, then in the Confederate army, must have carried away in Maryland during his
Antietam excursion. So that we parted poor friends.

"On October 31, we took the road to Leesburg. We supposed that
the whole army must have crossed the Potomac. It was a mistake.
With his accustomed slowness, McClellan took five days for that
operation."

With the rearward troops that crossed the river was the 20th
Maine, which, as mentioned before, was new to the army. The fledg-
ling soldiers were eager to learn the ways of the march, and they were
quickly drawn to the practice of stealing edibles, or foraging.

"We . . . did not understand it as well as did those who had been
longer in the service," says Private Theodore Gerrish, "but we applied ourselves closely to the work. . . . While marching through
Loudoun Valley, our regiment encamped one night at a small village

called Snickersville, and the following day we remained in camp. A small squad of us sallied forth in the afternoon, without permission, 'to seek whom we might devour.'

"Some few miles from camp, in an out-building on a large plantation, we found a very large hive of bees which appeared to be well-filled with honey. Now honey and hardtack together make a most desirable diet, and we knew that we had found a prize; but, as I have already intimated, foraging was new business to us, and we were a little timid, and consequently concluded that the better way for us to pursue was to return to camp and then come out after dark and secure it. We returned to camp highly elated at the prospect of securing the coveted prize. Of course our comrades were to know nothing about it.

"We held a small council of war and arranged our plans. Late in the evening we passed through the guard unnoticed by the sentinels, and quickly tramped over fences and across fields until we reached the plantation, and to our joy found the hive of honey as we had left it in the afternoon. It was a huge old-fashioned affair, some four feet in height by two and a half square. It was so heavy that it required our united strength to carry it.

"We soon found that 'the way of the transgressor is hard.' We had just passed from the building to the open yard when a smothered exclamation from Joe, which was halfway between an oath and a yell, attracted our attention. We hurriedly dropped the hive, and Joe began to make the most lively antics around the yard. We soon learned the cause. There was a small opening in the side of the hive, through which the bees had been accustomed to pass in and out. Joe had, unfortunately, placed his hand near this opening. The occupants of the hive had been aroused by their removal, and a large cluster of them had passed up under his sleeve and intrenched themselves upon his arm. It was the first wound that he had received in the war of the rebellion. 'Confound them!' muttered Joe, 'I will fix them.' And, taking off his overcoat—a new one that he had just drawn—he proceeded to wrap it around the hive in such a manner that the opening was covered. We then lifted our burden and tugged away.

"We passed out beyond the barn and reached a narrow lane enclosed on either side by a very high fence, when to our horror we heard a party of men approaching. 'Here they are,' cried one, leaping upon the fence. 'Surrender! Surrender!' cried the newcomers [now seen to be Union soldiers]. 'The provost guard!' we all exclaimed together. Now if there is a thing in the world that a new soldier is afraid of, it is the provost guard. . . .

"We dropped the hive, overcoat and all, and sprang over the high fence and ran, our pursuers crying out that if we did not stop they would fire. At a break-neck rate we went across the broad field. A deep, wide ditch was in our way. With a most desperate leap we cleared this obstacle and rushed on to our camp.

"When we arrived there we lay down together to talk over our narrow escape. We were highly elated to think that we had eluded the grasp of the much-dreaded provost guard. If we had made a charge upon the enemy and covered ourselves with honor, we would not have felt better than at that time. We were so much excited that we could not sleep.

"In about an hour we heard a commotion in the street of the adjoining company. Some men seemed to be carrying a heavy burden, while others were convulsed with laughter. . . . We listened. They were talking. Their whole company seemed to be gathered around them. As we listened, we became disgusted. They had got our honey. They had overheard us in the afternoon as we made our plans. A squad of them had followed to make us believe they were the provost guard, and they had succeeded.

"We endeavored to induce Joe to ask them about his coat, but he declared that he would freeze to death like a man before he would take such a step."

In Lee's army, affairs were not static. The commander soon learned that McClellan was on the move. Leaving Stonewall Jackson and his Second Corps in position near Winchester (pending the full development of McClellan's maneuver), Lee dispatched Longstreet and his First Corps southward through the Valley, his march corresponding with McClellan's on the other side of the Blue Ridge Mountains. The columns were in contact through gaps in the range. Jeb Stuart's troopers, indeed, were on McClellan's side, in his front and on his right flank, and there was a good deal of fighting between Stuart and Alfred Pleasonton, whose units, strong in themselves, were backed by infantry.

Heros von Borcke tells of a brush that occurred on October 31: "At the hour of sunrise . . . our column, animated by the hope of again meeting the enemy, was in motion along the road leading to the little town of Union, about midway between Upperville and Leesburg, near which latter place we were quite sure of encountering them. We reached Union at noon, where we came to a halt, sending out in various directions scouts and patrols, who speedily reported that the main body of the Federal cavalry were at Aldie, where they were feeding their horses, having arrived there since morning, but that a squadron of them was three miles nearer to us at a farm known as Pothouse.

"Towards this squadron we started immediately, and, moving upon byroads, arrived within a few hundred yards of them before they had any idea of our approach. Their earliest warning of danger was the wild Confederate yell with which our advance-guard dashed upon them in the charge. They belonged to the 3rd Indiana Cavalry, a regiment which we had often met in battle, and which always fought with great steadiness and courage.

"I could not resist joining in the attack upon our old enemies, and was soon in the midst of the fight. This lasted, however, only a few minutes. After a short but gallant resistance, the Federal lines were broken, a great part of the men were cut down or taken prisoners, and the rest of them driven into rapid flight, pursued closely by the Confederates.

"Captain [William D.] Farley and myself, being the foremost of the pursuers, had a very exciting chase of the captain commanding the Federal squadron, who, at every demand that we made for his surrender, only spurred his horse into a more furious gallop, occasionally turning to fire at us with his revolver. But each moment I got nearer and nearer to him; the long strides of my charger at last brought me to his side; and I was just raising myself in the saddle to put an end to the chase with a single stroke of my saber, when, at the crack of Farley's pistol, the fugitive, shot through the back, tumbled from his horse in the dust.

"Yet a little further Farley and myself continued in pursuit of the flying Federals, and then returned to rejoin General Stuart. While slowly retracing my steps, I discovered the unfortunate captain, lying against the fence on the roadside, apparently in great agony, and, evidently enough, in a most uncomfortable [posture]. Desirous of doing all that I could to alleviate his misery, I alighted from my horse and raised the poor fellow into an easier recumbent position, despatching at the same time one of my couriers to our staff surgeon, Dr. [Talcott] Eliason, with the request that he would come to me as speedily as possible.

"The wounded officer seemed to me in a state of delirium, calling out, as he did, to every passing horseman, that the rebels who had killed him were about to rob him also, and scattering his personal effects—his watch, money, etc.—in the road, so that I had some difficulty in saving them for him. One of our orderlies who had galloped up begged me to give him the captain's canteen, it being a very large and handsome one. This of course I refused, the more decidedly as the poor fellow had been crying out continually for drink, and, resting upon my arm, had already nearly exhausted the canteen of its contents.

"In a few minutes Dr. Eliason came up, and, having examined the wound, said to me, 'Major, this man is mortally wounded, but what you have taken for delirium is nothing more than a very deep state of intoxication, which had commenced before the shot was received.' I did not at once fully credit this medical opinion, and my surprise was therefore great when, taking a smell of the canteen, which I had supposed to contain water, I found that it had been filled with strong apple brandy, which the unfortunate man had snatched at in his dying moments.

"When the next morning I sent his effects to the temporary field-hospital, to which he had been conveyed overnight, I received the report that he had died before daybreak, still heavily intoxicated. Fortunately we were enabled to find out his address, and had the satisfaction of sending his valuables to his family in Indiana."

It was now November 1, and the day saw another cavalry clash. A part of the fight was witnessed by Union newsman Charles Carleton Coffin. That morning he was still on the Maryland bank of the Potomac at the village of Berlin (later renamed Brunswick), where a pontoon bridge had been laid, when he heard artillery fire rumbling from the distant front.

"I mounted my horse, crossed the river, and rode rapidly southward past the moving column [of infantry]. I noticed many of the soldiers had their pets, one a little dog which he had picked up on the way. As I passed a Pennsylvania regiment I noticed a gray-bearded soldier who had a young puppy, its eyes not yet open. A little boy in a Connecticut regiment had a little kitten on his shoulder.

"I passed through the little village of Purcellville and came upon the 10th and 11th New Hampshire regiments. . . . A little farther on I came upon the 21st Massachusetts. It had seen service under Burnside in North Carolina [during a seaborne expedition conducted early in 1862], and had dwindled to about two hundred. It was but a shadow of its former self.

"Riding on, I came upon Gen. Pleasonton's [cavalry] near the village of Philomont. . . . It was past noon when I reached the field.

In the foreground the artillery was sending shells across the field upon Stuart's line. Shells from Stuart's guns were screaming through the air. Under the white battle cloud in the distance I could see the Confederates. A well-directed shot from one of the Union guns struck a Confederate caisson, and the battle cloud suddenly assumed larger proportions.

"Up to this time I had not seen a cavalry charge. . . . Imagine, if you can, a body of horses in column, not in line [i.e., not abreast]. A column is concentrated energy. Those in front are stimulated by those behind, and those behind are eager to emulate those in advance. You hear the word of command, 'Draw Saber! Charge!' You hear the bugle and are thrilled by its notes. The column breaks into a trot. The hoofs of the horses are like the distant rumbling of thunder. The trot becomes a gallop, and louder than the trampling hoofs is the yelling of five hundred men. It is not a hurrah, but a prolonged yell. The horses seem to catch the enthusiasm of the men.

"A dust cloud rises. Sabers flash and gleam in the sunlight. Cannon flame. Horses and riders go down, but the column goes on. The Confederate cannoneers suddenly limber up their pieces and disappear into the woods beyond. . . . The loss in killed and wounded on the Union side was less than one hundred. During the engagement [General Abner] Doubleday's division of infantry arrived. It was nearly dark when the Confederates abandoned their position."

Heros von Borcke describes the withdrawal: "We marched back along the road to Middleburg, near which place General Stuart intended to camp, having ordered me to gallop ahead of the column into the village to make the necessary arrangements for food and forage with the cavalry quartermaster stationed there. Middleburg is a pleasant little place of some fifteen hundred inhabitants. . . .

"Riding up the main street of the village, I was brought to a halt by a group of very pretty young girls who were carrying refreshments to the soldiers and invited me to partake of them, an offer which I was not strong enough to decline. In the conversation which followed, my fair entertainers expressed the greatest desire to see General Stuart, and were delighted beyond measure to hear that the bold cavalry leader was my personal friend, and that I should probably have little difficulty in persuading him to devote a quarter of an hour to their charming company. This spread like wildfire through the village, so that half an hour later, when Stuart galloped up to me, I was attended by a staff of fifty or sixty ladies of various ages from blooming girlhood to matronly maturity.

"The general very willingly consented to remain for a while that everyone might have an opportunity of seeing him, and was immediately surrounded by the ladies, all eager to catch the words that fell from his lips, and many, with tears in their eyes, kissing the skirt of his uniform coat or the glove upon his hand. This was too much for the gallantry of our leader, who smilingly said to his gentle admirers, 'Ladies, your kisses would be more acceptable to me if given upon the cheek.'

"Thereupon the attacking force wavered and hesitated for a moment. But an elderly lady, breaking through the ranks, advanced boldly and, throwing her arms around Stuart's neck, gave him a hearty smack, which served as the signal for a general charge. The kisses now popped in rapid succession like musketry, and at last became volleys, until our general was placed under as hot a fire as I had ever seen him sustain on the field of battle."

The fighting continued on succeeding days. On November 3, Stuart and his outmatched troopers had a bad time of it in a clash that occurred near Upperville, just east of Ashby's Gap in the Blue Ridge. The Confederates were assailed both by cavalry and infantry. Again in Von Borcke's words: "The tremendous hosts of the Yankees advancing upon us across the fields, which I could compare only to a mighty avalanche, seemed likely to crush everything before them; but the gallant fellows of Fitz Lee's brigade stood the shock of their attack nobly, and succeeded for a time in checking the onward movement of their columns. Stuart perceiving, however, that he could not long maintain his ground, sent me off in the direction of Paris to select a new position, where the nature of the country would facilitate further resistance. This I soon found near Ashby's Gap, a few miles from Upperville, where a range of mountains, spurs of the Blue Ridge, accessible for a long distance only by a single road, made successful opposition to a far superior force possible.

"On my return to the general, the conflict had reached its height, and, in my opinion, the urgent necessity of immediate retreat was patent to all. Nevertheless, Stuart was for continuing the struggle. Again and again animating his men by his presence and the exposure of his own person, he led our admirable soldiers to the conflict. Not until one of our caissons had been exploded by a well-aimed shot; not until Colonel [Williams C.] Wickham, temporarily commanding Fitz Lee's brigade, had been wounded at my side, a fragment of shell striking him in the neck; not until the hostile infantry was outflanking us on either side—was the order given for the withdrawal, which, in consequence of the long delay of our commander in issuing the order, was managed, I am sorry to say, with a great deal of haste and confusion, and came very near being a rout.

"The dismounted sharpshooters, running back hurriedly to their horses, upon gaining them, rode off, without forming, in every direction. The regiments themselves, exposed to a concentrated withering fire of the enemy, galloped confusedly, and in precipitation, through the narrow streets of Upperville, followed by the hostile cavalry in eager pursuit.

"General Stuart and myself were the last of our column to ride through the village, escaping almost miraculously the Yankee balls and bullets that whistled after us, and both receiving slight injury from a falling chimney, which, at the very moment of our passing by it, was struck by a shell and toppled over by the explosion, the shattered stones and bricks flying far and wide.

"We had not left the village when the enemy entered it on the opposite side; and yet many heroic young ladies, regardless of the great danger, ran out of the houses to wave a last farewell to us with their cambric handkerchiefs; and, what was better still, to seek out, amidst this fearful tempest of shells and bullets, our poor wounded, who, unable to follow their flying comrades, were lying about, in their agony, anywhere in the dusty streets.

"Too much credit cannot be given to Pelham for the great forethought and coolness with which he had taken his artillery along a little bypath around the village to a point about a mile distant, where, placing his guns in a favorable position, he skilfully covered our retreat, and, by the accuracy and rapidity of his firing, saved us from greater disaster. [Pelham] was himself hard at work in his shirtsleeves, taking a hand with the cannoneers in loading and aiming the pieces.

"Meanwhile the united efforts of General Stuart and the members of his staff had availed to put a stop to the stampede. Our regiments were re-formed, and our lines reestablished. But the scene was still frightful. Wounded men on foot were limping to the rear, or riding two on one horse; wounded animals were galloping wildly over the field; ambulances and army wagons were being hurried along the road, on which was concentrated a heavy fire of the hostile batteries, and over which canister and shell were howling in the air or ricocheting on the hard dry ground.

"Pelham's guns were now in a very dangerous situation, a squadron of Federal cavalry having advanced against them at a gallop, and having dismounted and placed a number of men behind a stone fence not more than two hundred yards distant, from which they poured a fatal carbine fire upon the gunners and artillery horses. I tried my best to lead two squadrons of one of our regiments forward to a charge, that I might drive the Yankees from this position; but, after following me at a gallop to within eighty yards of the wall, they broke into rapid flight at the murderous volley of the sharpshooters.

"Pelham was doing his best, in the meantime, to dislodge the bold riflemen, by firing canister at the wall, but this had not the desired effect in consequence of the thickness of the barrier, so I shouted to him, 'Try solid shot!' which he did at once, and with the best results. Every ball demolished large sections of the fence, scattering the fragments of the stones all around, killing and wounding many of the sharpshooters behind it, and driving off the rest, whom we pursued, cutting down and taking prisoners nearly all of them.

"About six o'clock in the evening we arrived at the heights near Ashby's Gap, from which we could overlook the whole lower country towards Upperville. In the waning light of day we could plainly discern that for a considerable distance it was covered with the dark masses of the enemy, with their long cavalry columns and artillery trains, so that we had no reason to indulge chagrin at having been put to flight by numbers more than ten times superior to our own. The exceeding narrowness of the approach, and the two mountain ridges stretching out on either side of it, made defense an easy affair. . . .

"Firing ceased entirely with the coming darkness; and, as we saw by the Yankees going into camp that the pursuit would not be continued by them until the following day, we determined to give rest to our weary men and horses, and the glow of our bivouac fires was soon reflected from the mountains around us."

15

Burnside Succeeds McClellan

Until this point in the campaign, Jeb Stuart had kept in contact with Stonewall Jackson's command through gaps in the Blue Ridge. Now, with McClellan continuing southward, the time had come when this contact would have to be discontinued, and Stuart decided to discuss the development with Jackson in person, by way of Ashby's Gap. According to Von Borcke, the episode of the visit to Jackson began about 10 P.M. on November 3, only a few hours after the Upperville fight:

"The deep sleep which succeeded the fatigues of the . . . day had hardly fallen upon me when I was aroused by the touch of Stuart's hand upon my shoulder. The general's wish was that I should bear him company, with several of our couriers and Dr. Eliason, who was well acquainted with all the roads. . . . General Jackson . . . had encamped about twelve miles off, on the opposite side of the Shenandoah [River], near the village of Millwood. The command of our cavalry had been temporarily transferred to Colonel [Thomas L.] Rosser. . . .

"A cold wind was blowing in our faces as we trotted through the village of Paris in the direction of the Shenandoah, and it was freezing hard when we reached the stream, about midnight, at a point where ordinarily it was easily fordable, but where we found it so much swollen by the recent rains in the mountains that we were compelled to cross it swimming [our horses]. We reached the opposite bank in safety, but chilled through and with soaking garments. Such was the intensity of the frost that in a very few minutes our cloaks and blankets were frozen quite stiff; and the water, as it dripped from the flanks of our horses, congealed into icicles, and the legs of the animals were rough with ice. But a sharp ride, as it promoted the circulation of the blood, kept us tolerably warm, and at two o'clock in the morning we arrived at Jackson's encampment.

"Stuart, being unwilling in his great tenderness for Old Stonewall to disturb his slumbers, proposed that we should seek rest for the remaining hours of the night; but in our frozen condition, it being first necessary that we should thaw out our garments before we could dry them, we preferred building a huge fire of logs, around whose cheerful blaze we sat and smoked our pipes—though, with teeth chattering like castanets, this was smoking under difficulties.

"Jackson, who, in accordance with his usual habit, awoke with the earliest glimmer of day, no sooner discovered us than he expressed his regret at our evident discomfort, but gave us the readiest consolation by ordering breakfast to be immediately prepared. Nothing was better calculated to restore our good spirits than the summons to the general's large breakfast table, where the aroma rose in clouds of vapor from an immense coffee pot, and where stood a magnificent haunch of venison, cold, a present from a neighboring planter.

"The good cheer had the happiest effect on Stuart, who enlivened our repast with abundant anecdote and the recital of many a joke at [my] expense. . . . It was his special delight to tease me on account of the little mistakes I still frequently committed in speaking the English language, which he always cleverly turned so as to excite the merriment of his auditors. During one of our many [previous] conversations concerning Old Stonewall . . . while intending to say 'It warms my heart when he talks to me,' I had employed the expression, 'It makes my heart burn,' etc.

"Stuart now took occasion to repeat my remark, and represented me most absurdly as having declared that 'it gave me the heartburn to hear Jackson talk,' which of course provoked the roaring laughter of our little company. Jackson himself alone did not participate in the boisterous mirth. Looking me straight in the face with his large expressive eyes, and pressing my hand warmly across the table as just the faintest smile broke over his features, he said, 'Never care, Major, for Stuart's jokes. We understand each other, and I am proud of the friendship of so good a soldier and so daring a cavalier as you are.'

"I was conscious of a blush reddening my cheeks under my beard at this, but I felt also a glow of pride, and I would not at that moment have exchanged the simple, earnest tribute of the great warrior for all the orders and crosses of honor of Europe.

" 'Hurrah for Old Von! And now let us be off,' said Stuart; and, slapping me on the back to conceal his own slight embarrassment, he rose from the table, followed by his companions. In a few minutes we rode off at a gallop to fresh scenes of excitement and activity."

On the Union side, the main columns of the infantry had been moving slowly southward past Leesburg. McClellan's Second Corps, now commanded by Darius Couch, had approached Upperville during the final moments of the November 3 cavalry fight and had heard its concluding sounds.

The narrative is taken up by the Second Corps staff officer, Francis Walker: "The night of reaching Upperville was cold and gloomy. General Couch had an inveterate repugnance to making his headquarters in a house, greatly preferring the benignant shelter of a Virginia rail fence. But on this occasion, there being great probability of frequent despatches to be received and sent, he gave Captain [Charles H.] Morgan, his chief of artillery, permission to select a house for headquarters.

"Delighted at this concession to the bodily infirmities of the staff, Morgan galloped gayly into the yard of a spacious mansion on the outskirts of the town. Here was an old man, evidently the propri-

Darius N. Couch

etor, somewhat shaken by the recent artillery fire and the galloping and pistol shots of the cavalry. 'Good evening,' said Morgan. 'Good evening,' responded the native. 'General Couch proposes to make his headquarters at your house tonight—that is, if you have no objection.'

"Now the old gentleman had a great many objections, but as he did not dare to express them, he straightway began with one accord to make excuse. Of course he would be delighted to have the general with him, but he was afraid he could not make him comfortable. Perhaps the general had better go where he could be better accommodated. 'But,' quoth Morgan argumentatively, 'you have a large house.' This could not be denied, as anyone could see it at a glance, so the luckless proprietor had to admit that the house was large. 'But,' he added eagerly, 'I have a large family.' 'Well now,' asked Morgan, 'what family have you got?' 'In the first place,' said the old gentleman, 'I have three nieces.' 'Say not another word! We'll take the house!' And we did take the house; and three saucier vixens could hardly be found in all rebeldom.

"During the movement along the Blue Ridge . . . a curious psychological phenomenon appeared. Although this was one of the best-disciplined commands of the army, with a high repute for good order, a mania seized the troops for killing sheep. On the Peninsula there had been no sheep to kill; and, while on the march to Antietam our men had scrupulously respected the loyalty of western Maryland. But when the fat and fleecy flocks of the country through which we were now called to pass came in sight, discipline for the moment gave way, at least *quoad* mutton.

"At first the night was taken for forays, but soon the passion rose to absolute fury. In vain did officers storm and swear; in vain was the saber used freely over the heads of the offenders who were caught; in vain, even, did the provost guard of one division turn about and fire ball-cartridge, from the road, at fellows who deliberately left the ranks to go across the fields. General Couch was outraged. He instructed each division commander to assemble a court-martial for the trial of these offenders. And soon, every evening after coming into camp, three courts were in session in the Second Corps, with sheep-stealers before them; and sharp and summary were the punishments inflicted. But all to no purpose—the killing went on as bad as ever.

"Of the three division commanders, General [Winfield S.] Hancock was peculiarly sensitive to the slightest imputation of indiscipline. Accordingly, of all three it was he who issued the sternest orders and swore the loudest oaths. One day Hancock, having observed some soldiers of the Irish Brigade, after falling out of ranks upon some pretense, steal around a bit of woods manifestly bound on plunder, determined to make an example. Accordingly he left the column with his staff, and, galloping rapidly around the woods from the opposite side, he came upon the group gathered around an unfortunate victim [stretched on the ground], upon which one of the number was just proceeding to make anatomical observations.

"The less guilty members of the party, being less closely engaged, caught a glimpse of the coming doom in time to climb over a high stone fence and escape; but upon the principal offender, taken *in flagrante delictu*, Hancock pounced with drawn sword and eyes flashing fire. Down on his knees went the wretch, scared by the general's aspect. 'Arrah, dear general, don't be the death of me. I didn't do it; indade I didn't.'

" 'You infernal liar,' shouted the general, 'what do you mean by telling me that? I saw you, you scoundrel! I'll teach you to disobey orders! I'll teach you to kill sheep!' And, with this, crushing out the last hope of poor Paddy, he flourished his sword as if about to begin execution—when, in the most opportune moment, up jumped the innocent subject of the controversy, and, giving vent to its feelings in a quavering 'Ba-a!' ran off; while, amid the shouts of the staff, the general put up his saber and rode away."

By November 4, McClellan's leading units were about forty miles south of the Antietam battlefield. A captain from Massachusetts, William F. Draper, gives an anecdote of the moment: "On the march between Rectortown and Salem we passed a house, duly guarded by our soldiers [against the army's thievery], where an irate woman stood at the door and addressed us. 'Where are you-uns all going?' said she. 'To Richmond,' some of the boys replied. 'Well,' said she, 'You'll have a *Longstreet* to go through, and a big *Stonewall* to get over before you get there!' "

As it happened, Jackson was still in the northerly regions of the Shenandoah Valley, but Longstreet, screened by Jeb Stuart's activities, had speeded his march, drawing well ahead of McClellan and issuing from the Valley to settle in at Culpeper, about twenty-five miles south of the Union van.

A Confederate staff officer, Major Jedediah Hotchkiss, makes this comment about the situation: "With his usual boldness, Lee did not hesitate to post the two wings of his army sixty miles apart . . . well satisfied that with Longstreet's ability as a stubborn fighter when once in position, he could resist a front attack from McClellan and trust to Jackson to descend the mountains in ample time to fall on the enemy's flank and join in the fray, knowing also that the Federal authorities would hesitate to push forward the Army of the Potomac and leave Jackson so near the gateway to the Federal Capital.

"Could Lee have followed his own desires, he would have ordered Jackson to descend upon McClellan's flank while he moved to attack his front with Longstreet; but reasons of state required him to guard the approaches to the Confederate capital, and compelled him to stand upon the defensive."

Jeb Stuart was now south of Waterloo Bridge on the Rappahannock River, in a position to cover Longstreet's bivouac at Culpeper. Stuart and his staff, according to Von Borcke, "established their headquarters at the house of a Mr. M. . . . During the night [of November 5–6] there came a telegram for General Stuart, which, in accordance with his instructions, habitually observed by me, I opened with his other despatches, and found to contain the most painful intelligence. It announced the death of little Flora, our chief's lovely and dearly-loved daughter, five years of age, the favorite of her father and of his military family. This sweet child had been dangerously ill for some time, and more than once had Mrs. Stuart [tried to summon] her husband to Flora's bedside; but she received only the response of the true soldier, 'My duty to the country must be performed before I can give way to the feelings of the father.'

"I went at once to acquaint my general with the terrible tidings; and, when I had awakened him, perceiving from the grave expression of my features that something had gone wrong, he said, 'What is it, Major? Are the Yankees advancing?' I handed him the telegram without a word. He read it, and, the tenderness of the father's heart overcoming the firmness of the warrior, he threw his arms around my neck and wept bitter tears upon my breast."

Stuart wasn't granted much time to nurse his grief, for Pleasonton's troopers had reached the Rappahannock and were intent upon keeping him busy. The Union foot soldiers, however, became less of a problem. On November 6 their van units began drawing up in the Warrenton area and establishing camps.

Among the Federals who completed the march on the sixth were those of George Stoneman's division, one of the brigades of which was that of the French-born New Yorker, Regis de Trobriand. It was late in the day when the unit settled in. "The night was really glacial. Happily, fuel was plentiful. The great fires lighted on all sides continued to blaze until morning. Then the snow began to fall, at first in light flakes and soon in a thick whirlwind, whipped by continual squalls. The trees groaned, the ground trembled, and the men shivered.

"In the midst of the storm, General Stoneman sent for me, and, looking like a snowman, I entered the country church where he was quite comfortably installed with his staff. When I had warmed myself a little, he told me that the first two brigades of the division were camped in a forest of tall pines which the road passed through a short distance away. 'You can also go there and choose a place for your regiments,' he added. 'They will be better protected than in this position where you are now.'

"I mounted my horse, accompanied by an officer of my staff, and we found, without much trouble, a place with the desired conditions. But the snowstorm did not abate, and, the day being nearly spent, I concluded to see the general again on my return, to ask him to let me put off the changing of camp for my brigade until morning.

"He consented immediately, with an air that made me think that our advance movement was suspended. Why? I could not imagine. But there was something new in the air, and something indefinable in the manner of the general and his staff which struck me."

Events leading to this moment had begun in Washington during the days just previous. Lincoln had decided to replace McClellan without further delay.

To a group of White House visitors the President said: "General McClellan thinks he is going to whip the rebels by strategy, and the army has got the same notion. . . . Don't you see that the country and the army fail to realize that we are engaged in one of the greatest wars the world has ever seen, and which can only be ended by hard fighting? General McClellan is responsible for the delusion that is untoning the whole army—that the South is to be conquered by strategy."

Selected for a major role in McClellan's replacement was General C. P. Buckingham, of the Capitol staff. "I was at the time on special duty at the War Department. . . . On the evening of the 6th of November, about ten o'clock, the Secretary [Edwin Stanton] sent for me to come to his office, where I found him with General Halleck.

He told me that he wanted me to go and find the Army of the Potomac, and spent some time in giving me minute directions as to the route I should take [by special train]. Just before I left he handed me two envelopes, unsealed, telling me to take them to my room, and, having read them, seal them up.

"I was thunderstruck to find that one of the envelopes contained two orders for McClellan—one from the President, relieving him from the command of the army, and the other from General Halleck, ordering him to report to [his home] in New Jersey. . . . The other envelope contained two orders to Burnside—one from the President, assigning him to the command of the army . . . and the other from General Halleck, directing him to report what his plans were.

"Before leaving next morning, I saw the Secretary at his home, and he explained to me his reasons for sending an officer of my rank on an errand like that. The first was that he feared Burnside would not accept the command, and my instructions were to use, if necessary, the strongest arguments to induce him not to refuse. The second reason, though a characteristic one [on the part of Secretary Stanton, who was inclined to make impetuous judgments], had very little foundation.

"The Secretary not only had no confidence in McClellan's military skill, but he very much doubted his patriotism, and even loyalty, and he expressed to me some fear that McClellan would not give up the command; and he wished, therefore, that the order should be presented by an officer of high rank, direct from the War Department, so as to carry the full weight of the President's authority. He directed me to see Burnside first and get his decision. If he consented to accept, I was to see McClellan; but if not, I was to return to Washington.

"I found Burnside about fifteen miles south of Salem, where his division [actually, a grand division composed of two corps] was halted, and he alone in a little chamber. Closing the door, I made known my errand. He at once declined the command. . . . Among other objections, he urged his want of confidence in himself, and his particularly friendly relations to McClellan, to whom he felt under the strongest obligations.

"I met these objections by stating that McClellan's removal was resolved upon at any rate, and that if he, Burnside, did not accept the command, it would be given to [Joseph] Hooker. . . . He at length consented to obey the order, and I requested him to go with

Ambrose E. Burnside

me to find McClellan. We returned to Salem, whence I had ridden on horseback through a snowstorm, and I had my locomotive fired up the same evening, and on it we proceeded about five miles up the railroad to McClellan's camp."

The news of Buckingham's trip from Washington had already reached McClellan, and he had a strong suspicion as to what was about to happen. He himself assumes the narrative: "Late at night I was sitting alone in my tent, writing to my wife. All the staff were asleep. Suddenly someone knocked upon the tent-pole, and, upon my invitation to enter, there appeared Burnside and Buckingham, both looking very solemn. I received them kindly and commenced conversation upon general subjects in the most unconcerned manner possible.

"After a few moments, Buckingham said to Burnside, 'Well, General, I think we had better tell General McClellan the object of our visit.' I very pleasantly said that I should be glad to learn it. Whereupon Buckingham handed me the two orders of which he was the bearer. . . . I saw that both—especially Buckingham—were watching me most intently while I opened and read the orders. I read the papers with a smile, immediately turned to Burnside and said, 'Well, Burnside, I turn the command over to you.' "

When the interview ended and the visitors left, McClellan sat down in the fitful candlelight and added the news to the letter he was writing to his wife. "They have made a great mistake. Alas for my poor country!" He insisted later that at the time he was relieved he had the army "perfectly in hand" and in "excellent condition to fight a great battle," with all of the signs pointing toward "a brilliant victory."

Be that as it may, McClellan's association with the army came to a permanent end that snowy November night. After finishing the letter to his wife, the general composed a brief farewell address to be read before the troops: "In parting from you I cannot express the love and gratitude I bear to you. As an army you have grown up in my care. In you I have never found doubt or coldness. The battles you have fought under my command will probably live in our Nation's history. The glory you have achieved over mutual perils and fatigues; the graves of our comrades fallen in battle and by disease; the broken forms of those whom wounds and sickness have disabled—the strongest associations which can exist among men unite us by an indissoluble tie. We shall ever be comrades in supporting the Constitution of our country and the Nationality of its people."

As explained by George Stevens, the army surgeon from New York: "No sooner had the farewell order of General McClellan been read to the troops than the whole army was ordered into line for review by corps. The retiring and the incoming generals, each with his long train of followers, galloped along the whole line of the army, while batteries fired salutes and bands played 'The Star Spangled Banner' and 'Hail to the Chief.' Many of the regiments cheered the departing general with great enthusiasm, while others observed a studied silence."

Among the cheerers was staff officer Francis Walker, who later used these words to sum up the feelings of the many thousands who shared his viewpoint: "When the chief had passed out of sight, the romance of war was over for the Army of the Potomac. No other commander ever aroused the same enthusiasm in the troops, whether in degree or in kind. The soldiers fairly loved to look upon him; the sight of him brought cheers spontaneously from every lip; his voice was music to every ear. Let military critics or political enemies say what they will, he who could so move upon the hearts of a great army as the wind sways long rows of standing corn was no ordinary man; nor was he who took such heavy toll of Joseph E. Johnston [on the Peninsula] and Robert E. Lee [on the Peninsula and at Antietam] an ordinary soldier." The Federals who viewed

McClellan's departure with "a studied silence" included the letter-writing chaplain from Pennsylvania, A. M. Stewart, who, earlier in the war, had been one of the general's partisans. "We then fully believed in Little Mac; we trusted in Little Mac; we gloried in Little Mac; yea, we almost worshipped Little Mac. It is true, we knew nothing about Little Mac. Not what he had done, but what he was *about to do*, made Little Mac great.

"The truth is, our magnificent army much needed a transcendent leader, and the crisis prompted us both to crave and expect one fit for the occasion—one whom we could afford to idolize. At the seeming opportune moment, Little Mac was ushered upon the military stage. We all accepted Little Mac as one chosen of the Lord and sent in the nick of time by a kind Providence to save the nation.

"A long, a varied, a painful trial and experience of Little Mac has forced the humbling impression that Little Mac was sent by the *President*, in his haste, in his earnestness, eagerness, and *ignorance*. . . .

"The writer can truly say it cost him many a struggle, long reluctance, commingling with sadness, to have his high conceptions of Little Mac so gradually, yet effectually, ooze out, as to make him appear, in very deed, Little Mac."

During the week in November that saw McClellan replaced, there was another occurrence—a political development—that caused a stir among the troops. Regis de Trobriand explains (with his viewpoint, like that of many others, being emphatically pro-Republican):

"We were still [in the Warrenton area] when the papers brought the news more discouraging to the army than all the privations it had been compelled to undergo. The pseudo-democratic party had prevailed in the elections in several states. By force of agitating, of intriguing, and inveighing against all the measures taken by [the] government . . . the *Copperheads* [i.e., the Peace Democrats] had succeeded in deceiving the people and getting hold of the power in New York and several other states. . . . Many loyal men said . . . that the Republic was lost, and that the war would end only in a shameful compromise, or even in a peace which would be that of dismemberment."

The Peace Democrats, it must be noted, saw the deposed McClellan as Presidential timber, and he would be their choice to run against Lincoln in 1864.

16

November Interlude

As explained by Northerner William Swinton, the newsman-historian: "To the general on whose shoulders was placed at this crisis the weighty burden of the conduct of the Army of the Potomac, the great responsibility came unsought and undesired. Cherishing a high respect for McClellan's military talent, and bound to him by the ties of an intimate affection, General Burnside naturally shrank from superseding a commander whom he unfeignedly regarded as his superior in ability. The manly frankness with which Burnside laid bare at once his feelings towards his late chief and his own sense of inadequacy for so great a trust was creditable to him. . . .

"To the public his modest shrinking and solicitude appeared the sign of a noble nature, wronging itself in its proper estimate, and it was judged that he was a man of such temper that the exercise of great trusts would presently bring him a sense of confidence and power. And indeed, severely just though Burnside's judgment of his own capacity afterwards proved, there was at the moment no man who seemed so well-fitted to succeed McClellan. Of the other corps commanders in the Army of the Potomac, no one had yet proved his capacity in the exercise of independent command. But Burnside, as chief of the North Carolina expedition, brought the prestige of a successful campaign; and it was known that he had energy, perseverance, and, above all, a high degree of patriotic zeal.

"Frank, manly, and generous in character, he was beloved by his own corps, and respected by the army generally. To the troops he was recommended as the friend and admirer of McClellan; and in this regard, as representing a legitimate succession rather than the usurpation of a successful rival, he seemed the man of all others best fitted to smooth over the perilous hiatus supervening on the lapse from power of a commander who was the idol of [a great part of] the army."

Adds Colonel Theodore Gates, the New Yorker who led the Ulster Guard: "When General Burnside was placed in command of the Army of the Potomac, the Administration and the loyal people of the country were impatient of the long delay that had followed the Battle of Antietam. They were likewise dissatisfied with the results of that battle and the escape of the Confederate army. . . . Burnside knew he was expected to do what McClellan had failed to do. . . .

"In view of the relative positions and conditions of the two armies, and of the public expectations . . . Burnside should have made it his instant business to find the rebel army and fight it. He knew where to look for it, and two days' march would have brought Lee to battle or compelled him to flee. . . . Instead of this, Burnside spent ten days at Warrenton, deliberating and reorganizing the army."

"The following," says the Second Corps staff officer, Francis Walker, "was the organization effected: Right Grand Division, Major-General E. V. Sumner, commanding. . . . Center Grand Division, Major-General Joseph Hooker, commanding. . . . Left Grand Division, Major-General William B. Franklin, commanding. . . . The artillery was, in the main, distributed among the divisions of the several corps, though with a strong reserve. The cavalry remained under the command of General Pleasonton."

Even as the adjustments progressed, Pleasonton was out in front of the army contending with Jeb Stuart. On the evening of November 9, General Lee (with Longstreet at Culpeper) ordered Stuart to conduct a reconnaissance in force toward Warrenton. According to Heros von Borcke's lively chronicle, Stuart "was to take with him Fitz Lee's brigade, one battery, and two regiments of infantry, the latter having been detached to him for this special purpose.

"We were roused at daybreak next morning by the roll of the drums of our reinforcements, and at eight o'clock we crossed Hazel River [a tributary of the Rappahannock], sending one regiment of cavalry to the right towards Jefferson[ton], and proceeding with the main column to the left towards the village of [Amissville]. About ten o'clock our advanced-guard came up with the enemy, with whom we were soon hotly engaged, the Yankees falling back slowly before us.

"I could not help admiring on this occasion the excellent behavior of a squadron of the 5th New York Cavalry, who received with the greatest coolness the heavy fire of our battery, maintaining perfect order . . . and finally only giving way when we charged them with several squadrons.

"During the early part of the fight the Federals had been wholly without artillery, but several batteries now came to their assistance, opening a vigorous and well-directed fire upon our guns. . . . I had halted near two of our pieces, and was talking with . . . the officer in command of them, when a shell, bursting within thirty feet of us, sent its deadly missiles in every direction, several fragments of the iron passing directly between us, and one of them shattering the leg of the brave young fellow so that it dangled loosely. . . . He insisted, however, on remaining with his guns, and it required the joint persuasions of General Stuart and myself to induce him to withdraw from the field and place himself in the hands of the surgeon.

"Our infantry now joining in the fight, we drove the Yankees back to the neighborhood of [Amissville], when I was ordered by my chief to reconnoiter the position there before he could attempt pushing his success further. Climbing a high hill about a mile on our right, I soon obtained a magnificent view of the surrounding country, extending for many miles towards the town of Warrenton, where numerous encampments indicated the presence of the entire Federal army.

"In the immediate front, towards [Amissville], I could see the force opposing us about being reinforced by . . . infantry and . . . artillery, which were advancing at a double-quick along the turnpike road. In full haste I galloped back to inform General Stuart of the danger of his position, but before reaching him I saw our troops falling back, my chief having himself quickly perceived the additional strength of his opponents.

"The enemy's [horsemen] were now moving rapidly forward in admirable order, and by their spirited and accurate fire greatly harrassed the retreat of our troops, which was covered by two pieces of our artillery and our cavalry sharpshooters. Stuart, seeing his cavalrymen rapidly driven back, and greatly provoked at the successful advance of the foe, called to him twenty-five or thirty of our infantry riflemen and posted them at the corner of a wood, with orders not to fire until the enemy had arrived within two hundred yards of them, that they might punish effectively the impudence of the Yankees, as he called it.

"Stuart here, as usual, greatly exposed his own person on horse-back, by riding out of the wood into the open field, and I felt it my duty to say to him that in my opinion he was not in his proper place, as in a few minutes the whole fire of the enemy would be concentrated upon him. But, as J. E. B. was in a very bad humor, he answered me curtly that if this place seemed likely to become too hot for myself I was at liberty to leave it; whereupon I made response that, my duty attaching me to his side, no place could be too hot for me where he chose to go.

"Nevertheless I changed my position, cautiously bringing a large tree, in front of which I had been standing, between myself and the enemy. In an instant the firing commenced, and three bullets struck the tree at just the height to show that, had I remained where I was, they would certainly have gone through my body.

"Looking at Stuart, I saw him pass his hand quickly across his face, and even at this serious moment I could not help laughing heartily when I discovered that one of the numberless bullets that had been whistling round him had cut off half of his beloved mustache as neatly as it could have been done by the hand of an experienced barber.

"The Yankees having kept up the pursuit for only a short distance, we continued our retreat quietly towards Hazel River. Altogether our reconnaissance had been highly successful. We had found out all we desired to know without much loss. . . . Being ordered by General Stuart to report immediately to General Lee what had been done, I galloped rapidly ahead, about dusk, passing en route our [cavalry] headquarters . . . and hurried onward without stopping. With some trouble I found General Lee's encampment. . . . His modest tents had been pitched in a dense pine thicket.

"Supper was announced just as I arrived, and, having accepted the general's kindly invitation to join him at the table, I there recited to an eager audience our recent adventures. The Commander-in-Chief and the members of his staff were all greatly amused at the loss of half of Stuart's mustache, a personal ornament upon which they knew our cavalry leader much prided himself.

"It was late at night when I got back again to our headquarters, where Stuart and my comrades of his staff had arrived long before me.

"All was quiet next day at headquarters, and we had the pleasure of seeing there Mrs. Stuart, who had arrived at Culpeper Court

House the previous evening. She had come to spend some days with her husband, to share with him her sacred grief in the calamity that had befallen them both. It was a melancholy pleasure to see how well that admirable lady bore up under the weight of her affliction. . . . Her manner was composed, but her eyes betrayed [by redness] their frequent overflow of tears. . . .

"Mrs. Stuart had brought with her to camp her son, Jemmy, a stout little three-year-old, who, in his vivacity, in his passion for horses, and in his whole appearance, strongly resembled his father. Whenever his mother or his Negro 'mammy' left him unguarded for a moment, Jemmy was immediately among the horses; and the greatest gratification I could give him was to take him for a rapid gallop before me in the saddle.

"During the morning General Lee came over to our camp on a short visit, and I was touched by the gentle, sympathizing way in which he talked with Mrs. Stuart."

Lee's own great loss had occurred only three weeks earlier.

Right now the general was experiencing a recess, granted him by Burnside, from the pressures of his job. The men in the ranks, too, found the Culpeper camps relaxing. Of course, the air was growing colder. General James Longstreet issued the following order: "The inclement season having set in, commanders will take every method of protecting and guarding their men from the weather in their present exposed situation. To this end, company and regimental commanders will take care that fires are kept burning during the entire day, and will at night see that they are moved a short distance, so that the men can make their bivouacs on the earth thus warmed during the day."

The rigors of the season did not prevent the troops from enjoying their off-duty hours. In the words of Adjutant William Miller Owen, of the Washington Artillery of New Orleans: "Our newly organized 'Literary and Dramatic Association' gave their first entertainment in this camp. An immense fire was built, around which logs were placed, in horseshoe form, for the audience. Upon a platform, seated in an armchair improvised from a flour-barrel, sat the president, Corp. R. McK. Spearing.

"The president opened the meeting by stating the objects of the society, which were—by the contribution of whatever varied talents the boys possessed—to assist, upon stated occasions when we were at leisure, in the amusement and instruction of the command.

"A certain number were booked for the opening night, and, in all

sincerity, it can be recorded the entertainment was highly creditable. George Meek was especially praised for his recital of Poe's
'Raven.'"

Social entertainments were also a part of the Culpeper scene, for
many of the town's civilians invited the troops into their homes. A
visitor to Culpeper at the time was the wife of one of Lee's generals,
Mrs. Roger A. Pryor, a native of Petersburg. Mrs. Pryor relates: "I
had not imagined there were so many soldiers in the world as I saw
then. 'You cannot take a step anywhere,' said a lady, 'without treading on a soldier!' They were in the finest spirits, notwithstanding
their long marches and short rations.

"Thousands on thousands of Federal troops were in Virginia.
The highways of our chief rivers were closed, our railroads menaced. Everything we needed was already scarce and held at high
prices. Nobody had comforts or luxuries. Nobody murmured because of such privations.

"We made our host's drawing-room a camping-ground, his fire
our campfire. Around it gathered a nightly crowd of gay young
soldiers. They wished no serious talk, these young warriors! They
had a brief respite from fatigue and sorrow, and they intended to
enjoy it.

"They sentimentalized, however, over the tender and mournful
song, 'Lorena,' which . . . touched a chord in every heart. . . .

> " 'It matters little now, Lorena;
>   The past is the eternal past.
> Our heads will soon lie low, Lorena;
>   Life's tide is ebbing out so fast.
> But there's a future—oh, thank God!
>   Of life this is so small a part.
> 'Tis dust to dust beneath the sod,
>   But *there*, up *there*, 'tis *heart* to *heart!*'

"With pretty Nelly at the piano, her blue eyes raised to heaven,
and Jack Fleming accompanying her on the guitar, his dark eyes
raised to Nelly, the effect was overwhelming; and lest somebody
should quite finish us by singing [an even sadder song], we would
hasten to demand the 'Bonnie Blue Flag,' or 'Dixie,' or . . . better
still, a good story.

"The latter call would bring many we had heard before—there

are so few good stories in the world—but we would welcome each one with applause. . . .

"The soldier from rural districts was a trial to his officers in the early days of the war. . . . He never could be made to understand that freedom of speech with an officer, who had been perhaps a

A Confederate hero

neighbor, was denied him—nor yet that he could not indulge in good-natured chaff or criticism.

" 'Are you a sentinel here?' asked an officer, who found a sentry sitting down and cleaning his gun, having taken it entirely to pieces.

" 'Well, I am a sort of sentinel, I reckon.'

" 'Well, *I* am a sort of officer-of-the-day.'

" 'Is that so? Just hold on till I get my gun together, and I will give you a sort of a salute.'

". . . In the hardest times of starvation and weariness, according to our soldier boys, the situation would be relieved by . . . drollery. . . . Officers who had an easy place, and musicians, for a similar reason, were . . . special targets. . . . These fellows who didn't fight were all classed under the general term of 'bomb-proofs.'

". . . If a bomb-proof officer—a fellow who had a position in the rear—should happen to be smartly dressed when cantering along near a regiment, he would be apt to change his canter to a gallop as the men would shout and whoop: 'Oh, *my!* Ain't he pooty? Say, mister, whar'd ye git that biled shut? . . . Sich a nice-lookin' rooster oughter git down an' scratch for a wurrum!'

". . . They made great fun, too, of their own fears. . . . A number of militia having given way under fire, their commanding officer called out to one of the fugitives, 'What are you running away for, you ——— coward? You ought to be ashamed of yourself.'

" '. . . Them fellers over thar are shootin' bullets as big as water-millions. One of 'em went right peerst my head—right peerst. . . .'

" 'Well, why don't you shoot back, sir? You are crying like a baby.'

" 'I knows it, Gin'ral—I knows it! I wish I *was* a baby, and a gal-baby, too, and then I wouldn't hev been cornscripted.'

". . . A good story had found its way into our lines from a Federal officer. He was commenting upon the fact that all Southern women were intense rebels—with one exception. He had been with others marching down a wooded lane which ended in a sharp curve. As they rounded it, they suddenly came upon a house, before which was a woman picking up chips. As she had evidently not seen them, the officer tiptoed up to her, put his arm around her waist, and kissed her—and stepped back to avoid the box on the ear he knew he deserved. The woman, however, straightened herself, looked at him seriously for a moment, and said slowly, 'You'll find me right here every mornin' a-pickin' up chips.'

"It would seem that the telling of stories of a mildly humorous nature, with the characteristic of dialect, was a feature of the wartime. . . . The poor little stories that went the rounds among the rank-and-file at the campfires in Virginia had their uses. Whatever the weariness, the discouragement, the failure of the wagons to come up with provisions, by such simple means did the brave boys lighten their own and each others' hearts. . . .

"Many of these soldier boys—'boys' now no longer, but 'veterans'— were from Petersburg, and had stood in line on the day when Alice and Tabb and Marian and Molly and all the other girls had waited with me to see them off. It was delightful to meet them [now] and to hear news of the others. Where was Will Johnson? Where was Berry Stainback? Will had been captured 'for no other reason whatever except that he and Berry had but one blanket between them, and Will had to get himself captured when he found Berry had been, in order to continue to share the blanket, which was in Berry's possession,' a story which Will's friends could safely invent for their amusement, as his known courage was beyond all doubt.

"General Jeb Stuart was a great hero with these soldier boys, dashing as he did all over the country with his eight thousand mounted men. He was our plumed knight, with his gold star and long feather. They never wearied of stories of his promptness, his celerity, his meteorlike dashes.

" 'They'll never catch him!' said one proudly. 'They'll always reach the place where he recently was.'

" 'He reminds me of the knights of the olden time,' said a young lady.

" 'The mediaeval knight, my dear young lady,' said [a general officer], 'would be of little use in this war. He would have stood no chance with one of Stuart's men.'

" 'Fancy him,' said another, 'with his two hundred weight of iron on him, and as much on his big cart-horse. Imagine him, armed with a maul or a lance, a battle-axe, and six-foot pole, going into a fight at Manassas or Antietam.'

" 'He would never get there,' said the General. 'A light cavalryman of the 1st Virginia would have ridden around King Arthur or Sir Launcelot half a dozen times while the knight was bracing himself up for action; and the Chicopee saber would have searched out the joints under his chin, or his arm, or his sword-belt, and would have shucked him like an oyster. . . .'

"And Jackson was another of their idols. Stories of his strategy, his courage, his faith in God, his successes, filled many an hour around the campfire in the hospitable Culpeper mansion.

"But the chief idol of their hearts—of all our hearts—was our beloved commander, our Bayard *sans peur et sans reproche*, General Lee. The hand instinctively sought the cap at the mention of his name. . . . Happy was the private soldier who had seen General Lee, thrice happy the one who had spoken to him."

17

Toward a Meeting at Fredericksburg

Union General Burnside began to move from Warrenton on November 15. "At that time," says newsman-historian William Swinton, "the Confederate right, under Longstreet, was near Culpeper, and the left, under Jackson, in the Shenandoah Valley— the two wings being separated by two marches. And it had been General McClellan's intent, by a rapid advance on Gordonsville [south of Culpeper], to interpose between Lee's divided forces. But this was not a matter that touched Burnside's plan; for he had already resolved to abandon offensive action on that line, and was determined to make a change of base [southeastward] to Fredericksburg on the Rappahannock. . . .

"The project of changing the line of operations to Fredericksburg was not approved at Washington, but it was assented to. . . . In the march towards Fredericksburg, it was determined that the army should move by the north bank of the Rappahannock to Falmouth [opposite Fredericksburg], where by a pontoon-bridge, the boats for which were to be forwarded from Washington, it would cross to Fredericksburg and seize the bluffs on the south bank [before Lee fathomed the move and launched a reaction from Culpeper]. . . . Sumner's Grand Division led the van."

Riding with the foremost troops (the Second Corps, under Couch) was staff officer Francis Walker. "Marching steadily, but with all-night rests [we] reached Falmouth . . . in the early afternoon of the 17th. The few pickets of the enemy who were on this bank retired as the head of the corps came up. Fredericksburg was at this moment occupied by a regiment of cavalry, four companies of infantry, and a light battery. The guns of the latter were to be seen in

position on the northern outskirts of the city, the drivers and cannoneers lying idly about in groups. . . .

"It pleased General Couch . . . to order Captain [Rufus D.] Pettit
to take his guns by a roundabout way through some deep ravines
well to the rear of Falmouth, and to climb, from behind, a steep hill
of considerable height exactly [across the river from] the Confederate battery; the result of which was that Pettit's six Parrotts began
slinging solid shot and shell in among the enemy's guns and gun-

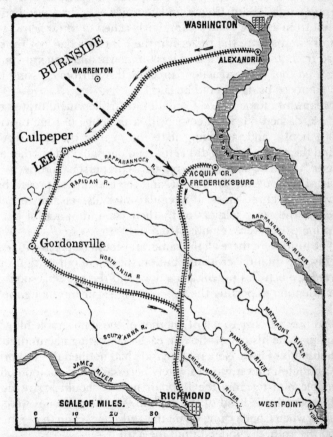

Burnside, at Warrenton, might have attacked through Culpeper toward
Gordonsville, with a view to approaching Richmond from the west, his supplies
coming by way of Alexandria. This was the maneuver favored by Washington.
Instead, Burnside tried to steal a march on Lee, heading for Richmond by way of
Fredericksburg, his supplies coming from a base established at the mouth of
Acquia Creek, on the Potomac about thirty miles below Alexandria.

ners before they had the faintest notion that the ball was about to open.

"Gallantly they sprang to their pieces, but it was of no use. Pettit had the advantage in elevation; his guns were six to their four; and, besides, he had cannoneers who could hardly be matched in any battery of the regular army. Within five minutes every man had been driven from the pieces and had taken refuge behind the adjacent houses and walls.

"There stood the four guns abandoned in plain view. It was a tempting sight. Both Couch and Sumner, who had watched the contest from among Pettit's guns, fairly ached to throw across some infantry and secure the prize. But the pontoons had not yet been heard from; the Falmouth ford was unknown; and General Sumner conceived that his instructions precluded him from crossing until [the pontoon] bridges could be laid.

"Meanwhile some of the Confederate artillerymen, braver than the rest, dashed out from cover with a prolonge [a rope provided with a hook], and, attaching it to the nearest piece, dragged it behind the house. In vain did Pettit send one shot and another after the gun, which he had come to regard as his personal property. The whole affair took but an instant, and the marauders proved but a flying mark. Three times, at irregular intervals, was this repeated, either by the same soldiers or by their comrades; and at last the tempting prizes were removed from sight.

"The guns were there all the same, and could be taken with equal ease by any infantry crossing; but, as they were out of sight, they exerted a much less potent attraction, and the generals soon gave their attention to posting the fast-arriving regiments along the left bank.

"And now we have to tell of another of those miserable blunders which mar the history of the war, each one costing its hundreds or its thousands of lives. General Burnside had notified the authorities at Washington that it was absolutely necessary that pontoon boats, to enable him to cross the Rappahannock, should arrive simultaneously with the head of the column. Yet the pontoons were not on hand when Couch came up on the 17th, nor yet on the 18th, nor yet on the 19th, nor indeed until the 25th.

"In consequence General Sumner was obliged by his instructions to concentrate the Second and Ninth Corps, subject to the mortification of every day seeing fresh Confederate brigades occupying and fortifying the strong positions behind Fredericksburg."

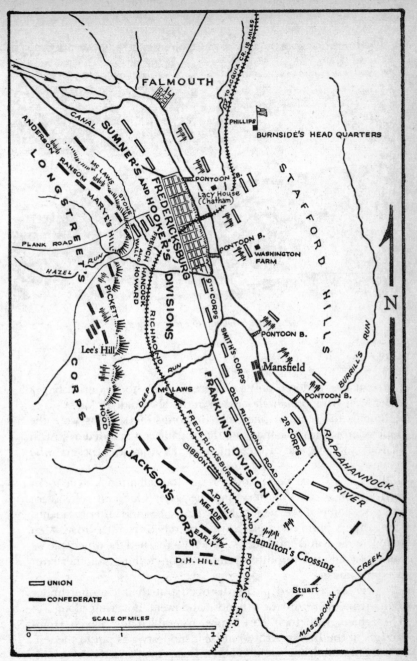

The Battle of Fredericksburg

Looking from Falmouth to Fredericksburg

Lee at first ordered only Longstreet's corps to Fredericksburg's defense, leaving Stonewall Jackson in the Shenandoah Valley.

Among the leading marchers in Longstreet's corps were the South Carolinians who made up the brigade commanded by Joseph B. Kershaw, and one of these men was D. Augustus Dickert, who relates:

"We crossed the north fork of the Rappahannock at a rocky ford ... on a cold, blustery day, the water blue and cold as ice itself. ... Some of the men took off their shoes and outer garments, while others plunged in just as they marched from the road. Men yelled, cursed, and laughed. ... When we reached the other side we were told, 'No use to put on your shoes or clothing; another river one mile ahead.'

"... Those who had partly disrobed put their clothing under their arms, shoes in their hands, and went hurrying along. ... These men, with their bare limbs, resembled the Scotch Highlanders in the British Army, but their modesty was put to the test. When about halfway to the other stream, they passed a large old-fashioned Virginia residence with balconies above and below—and these filled with ladies of the surrounding country, visitors to see the soldiers pass. It was an amusing sight . . . to witness this long line of soldiers rushing by with their coattails beating a tatoo on their naked nether limbs.

"The other stream was not so wide, but equally as cold and deep. General Kershaw, sitting on his horse at this point amusing himself at the soldiers' plight, undertook to encourage and soothe their ruffled feelings by giving words of cheer. 'Go ahead, boys . . . and don't mind this. When I was in Mexico—'

" 'But, General, it wasn't so cold in Mexico, nor did they fight war in winter, and a horse's legs are not so tender as a man's bare shins' were some of the answers given, and all took a merry laugh and went scudding away.

"Passing over, we entered the famous Wilderness. . . . We found, too, the 'Chancellor House,' this lone, large dismal-looking building standing alone in this Wilderness and surrounded on all sides by an almost impenetrable forest of scrubby oaks and tangled vines. The house was . . . situated on a cleared plateau, a piazza above and below, reaching around on three sides. It was called 'Chancellorsville,' but where the 'ville' came in . . . I am unable to tell. . . .

A Federal pontoon train

"We took up camp in rear of Fredericksburg, about two miles south of the city."

General Longstreet himself made for Fredericksburg's overlooking heights, and he was headquartered there when, on November 21, Union General Sumner sent the following communication to the mayor and his council:

"Under cover of the houses of your city, shots have been fired upon the troops of my command. Your mills and manufactories are furnishing provisions and the material for clothing for armed bodies in rebellion against the government of the United States. Your railroads and other means of transportation are removing supplies to the depots of such troops. This condition of things must terminate, and, by direction of General Burnside, I accordingly demand the surrender of the city into my hands . . . at or before five o'clock this afternoon.

"Failing an affirmative reply to this demand by the hour indicated, sixteen hours will be permitted to elapse for the removal from the city of women and children, the sick and wounded and aged, etc., which period having expired I shall proceed to shell the town."

The Chancellor House

The paper was referred to Longstreet's headquarters. "I asked the civil authorities to reply that the city would not be used for the purposes complained of, but that neither the town nor the south side of the river could be occupied by the Union army except by force of arms."

Longstreet's proposal was adopted, with the civil authorities adding to their communication that the town's limited transportation facilities precluded a rapid evacuation of the specified people. To this General Sumner responded:

". . . In consideration of your pledges that the acts complained of shall cease, and that your town shall not be occupied by any of the enemy's forces, and your assertion that a lack of transportation renders it impossible to remove the women, children, sick, wounded, and aged, I am authorized to say to you that our batteries will not open upon your town at the hour designated."

Again in Longstreet's words: "As the inference from the correspondence was that the shelling was only postponed, the people were advised to move with their valuables to some place of safety as soon as possible."

Stonewall Jackson's corps was now leaving the Winchester area and starting southward through the Shenandoah Valley. An unidentified staff officer relates an incident of the earliest part of the march:

"While passing through Middletown . . . General Jackson, with his staff, riding some two or three miles in front of his army . . . met a very old woman looking for her grandson, who was somewhere in the army. As we passed, she hailed the General, saying, 'Are you Mr. Jackson?'

"He told her he was, and asked what she wanted.

" 'I want to see my grandson, George Martin. He belongs to your company. I've brought him these clothes and victuals.'

"The General asked her what regiment her grandson was in, but she could not tell. She did not know what company he was in, the name of his captain—even whether he was a private or an officer. All she could tell was that 'he was in Mr. Jackson's company.'

"In her disappointment, she cried, 'Why, Mr. Jackson, don't you know little George Martin—George Augustus Martin? He's been with you in all your battles. And they say,' she added, with tears streaming down her furrowed cheeks, 'that he fit as hard as the best of them.'

"At this point some of the younger members of the staff laughed.

The General turned around quickly with his brow contracted, his lips compressed, and his eyes flashing with anger. He looked as if he was trying to find the guilty ones. Dismounting from his horse and approaching the old woman, he, in the kindest manner and simplest words, explained why he did not know her grandson, but gave her such simple and repeated directions as would enable her to find him."

It was while Stonewall was making his march that, down in Charlotte, North Carolina, Mary Anna Jackson gave birth to a baby girl. This event, according to Mary Anna, gladdened her husband's heart "more than all his victories." It will be recalled that Jackson's first wife died in childbirth, the baby stillborn, and that Mary Anna's first baby lived for only a few weeks.

On the Union side, the migration from Warrenton to the Fredericksburg area had continued. "The region," wrote Pennsylvania's Chaplain Stewart in one of his letters, "is less hilly than was supposed, being no more than what is usually termed undulating. . . . The farming interests . . . appear wretched in the extreme . . . and wherever the contending armies have gone the desolation has become almost complete. Fences burned and fields thrown into commons. Very few horses, cattle, sheep, hogs, or fowls are to be found; and wherever discovered they are at once appropriated by our straggling soldiers.

"Once or twice I saw our soldiers catch some turkeys and chickens, and then offer the wretched-looking owners a fair price in good Federal money, greenbacks or postage currency. In every instance they were utterly refused with the assertion such money was worth nothing whatever. So ignorant and infatuated are those poor rebels. . . .

"Many of the old farmhouses are tenantless. What has become of the miserable owners seems an utter puzzle to understand. The families which have remained, and by whose sorry-looking tenements our columns passed, peered out at us with timid and sinister looks.

"With some of them I conversed . . . ask[ing] the question, 'How do you expect to get through the coming winter?' The men were sullen as baited bulls. The women, gazing at me with looks in which were commingled fear, rage, and sadness, would generally answer, 'The Lord only knows!' The Lord certainly does know, and unless He interposes, many of them will surely perish. . . .

"The towering pride of old Virginia is being fearfully humbled.

Some slave women and children were seen gazing curiously upon our grand cavalcade. But two or three able-bodied colored men did I see in two days' march. One of these was accosted by a soldier from our regiment, 'Wouldn't you like to go along, and have a gun?' His voice seemed to tremble as he answered, 'O, I couldn't leave de pore children!'

"Poor fellow. The ties which bound him to his children were stronger than his evident desire for freedom. His redemption, however, draweth nigh."

For Union Private Theodore Gerrish of the 20th Maine, the trip between Warrenton and Fredericksburg became a terrible trial, for his health broke down. His story begins as his regiment ended its first day's march:

"We halted in a large field on a hillside, just as the sun was sinking from view. . . . The little shelter tent was soon spread over its framework of small poles, and the work for the night was quickly divided among our tent's company of three. William was to get the water, Charley was to act as cook, and I was to secure rails for firewood. . . .

"The supper [of coffee, hardtack, and salt pork] was eaten with a keen relish. I arose to my feet, but to my surprise everything around me seemed to be changing its position. My head whirled, and I fell to the ground. . . . The surgeons were summoned, and decided that it was an attack of typhoid fever.

"In the evening it began to rain in torrents. . . . The rain poured upon the thin cotton above my face, and . . . tiny streams of water were running upon the ground on which I was lying. William and Charley exposed themselves to that fearful storm to protect me. With their bayonets they digged trenches around the tent to prevent the water from pouring in. They piled their blankets and overcoats upon me to keep me warm and dry. They carried wood from a great distance through the darkness and kept a great fire burning at the tent door. . . .

"It was at an early hour in the morning I was awakened from a troubled sleep. The rain had ceased to fall, but the air was chilly and damp. . . . Charley was speaking to me, 'Come, my boy, we are to march in a few moments. The surgeon says there is no room for you in the ambulance, but if William and I can get you down there I will find you a place or I will know the reason why.'

"Sick, weak, and half delirious, they bore me to where the ambulances were standing, near the regimental headquarters. They were all loaded, with one exception, and in this they quickly placed me with my blankets and baggage. Just at this moment a surgeon emerged from one of the tents and approached the ambulances. . . .

"Charley, with a military salute and much politeness, remarked, 'Surgeon, that sick man in Company H is unable to march. If we leave him on the ground he will die, and I have put him in that ambulance.'

"With a fearful oath the surgeon answered, 'Sergeant, that ambulance is reserved for the use of the officers if they should need it. So pull your man out, and if he is too cowardly to march to the front, let him die like a damned dog on the ground.'

"With a voice perfectly cool, and yet as keen as a scimitar, Charley replied, 'You are mistaken in the man, sir. He has always done his duty. He is now very sick. If he is taken from the ambulance, you will do it; and, if it is done, I will report it to every officer in the regiment, and will publish the facts in every newspaper in the state of Maine.'

"I trembled as I thought what the results of the controversy might be to Charley. I knew him well. He had seen much of the world. As a sailor, he had frequently weathered Cape Horn, and four years of his life had been passed in a whaling voyage amid the icebergs of the northern seas. He was a kindhearted Christian gentleman, yet as immovable as the hills of his native Vermont.

"The surgeon evidently saw that he had caught a Tartar, and with a volley of oaths turned on his heel and walked away. Another sick man was placed in the other compartment of the ambulance, and we moved forward. . . .

"The day was cold and raw. The rain came pouring down at intervals. The roads were rough and muddy. Our ambulance formed a part of the long line of ambulances, baggage wagons, and artillery filling the road for many miles. At times we moved very slowly. Perhaps for an hour we would not move at all. Then the train in front would close up rapidly, and for a mile or more our horses would gallop over the rough road.

"The space that I occupied in the carriage was about two feet in width by six in length. Lying upon my back with my head toward the horses, a thin, low partition separated me from my sick companion, whose groans of pain sounded hoarse and hollow. I was burning up with a fearful heat, and I was so *tired*. At times I would distinctly understand my situation, and could hear my driver as he talked to his horses or sang songs. . . . Then all would become blank. Dark, weird forms would flit around me. I would see green hills, great forests, crystal streams of water, and familiar faces. Then there would be rushing columns of soldiers and scenes of carnage and death. . . .

"The train had been slowly toiling along . . . through a dense forest. It finally came to a dead halt. My driver, whom I had learned by his language to be a coarse, rough fellow, was growling because the train did not move on. An officer who had charge of the train came riding back and accosted the driver with, 'Well, Sam, unhook your horses. We are to stop here for the night.'

" 'Stop here?' answered the astonished Sam. 'What shall we do with the sick fellers? I reckon they're pretty well gone for it, by the way they have groaned and raved all day.'

" 'That is none of my business,' gruffly replied the officer. 'All I have to do is to haul them as long as they are alive. The more that die, the fewer we shall have to haul.' And with a coarse laugh he rode on.

" 'Perhaps it don't matter,' I heard Sam mutter as he hitched his horses close by the side of the carriage, 'but I swear I do like to see men [treated] a little human like. I pity these poor cusses groaning and talking about home. . . . The Lord only knows what is to become of us all before we get out of this infernal scrape. A fellow can't look a foot ahead and see how soon his own time will come.'

"I heard this much, and then his voice grew indistinct. I experienced dizzy sensations, and soon all was dark.

"It must have been midnight. I thought I heard familiar voices. I could not be mistaken. The curtain at the rear of the ambulance was raised, and William's voice was heard saying, 'Yes, here he is.' And Charley broke in with, 'Say, old fellow, how are you? We have come back to find you, and for three blessed miles we have looked in every ambulance to see if you were there.'

"Three miles they tramped, after a hard day's march, in search of me! But he continued, 'We have brought your supper. . . . I found a piece of soft bread at a sutler's today, and I have toasted that and sprinkled sugar upon it. . . .' The food was held to my lips. It was sour, dry, tough, and smoky—but had it been ever so tempting I could not have eaten it. . . .

"With kind words of encouragement, and promising to visit me again as soon as possible, they bade me good-bye and were gone.

"It was about the hour of noon on the second day of my ambulance ride when Sam thrust his head inside the carriage with, 'Here is a biling spring. Guess I will fill your canteen with water.'

"A few moments after, the canteen was placed at my side, and the ambulance rolled swiftly on. My lips and throat were parched with a burning heat. With weak and eager hands I seized the canteen and pressed it to my lips. The water was so cool and delicious. Suddenly the carriage came in contact with some obstacle. There was a fearful jolt, and the canteen slipped from my nerveless grasp. The water went pouring down my neck. I had not the strength to take the canteen up again. . . .

"The second night came, and we halted again on the muddy road in the great dark forest. The regiment was now so far away that my comrades could not return. I knew that I was better; the fever had partially subsided. But I was so weak and faint!

"Slowly the hours passed away. My companion had ceased to groan, and I supposed he was sleeping. I knew that Sam was busily at work over a fire that he had built by the roadside. I could hear him mutter and talk as he stirred the fire or piled more fuel upon it. A savory odor seemed to fill the air. He is preparing his supper, I thought; and then I fell asleep.

"I was awakened. Someone was speaking to me. . . . It was Sam's voice. 'Say there, old feller, don't you want some supper?' And before I could reply he rattled on, 'I drew a Secesh chicken back along the road today, and have made some broth for you fellers. But I find that your companion has become uncommon quiet, so I will give it to you.'

"He rolled up the side curtains of the carriage. A great fire was burning close at its side, sending its light far out in the darkness among the great pine trees, until each one looked wild and weird, like grim giants standing as sentinels in the gloom.

"My head was bolstered up, and the change of position afforded so much relief! The fire was warm and nice, and flooded the interior of the carriage with its cheerful light. And, as tenderly as a woman the rough fellow, with a spoon, fed me the delicious broth. It was to me the elixer of life. . . . The tears ran thick and fast from my eyes and fell upon the great hard hand that was so kindly ministering to my wants. Sam pretended not to notice them, but in his comical way continued to talk.

". . . Chickens are mighty hard to find. I hardly know when I can draw another. The old woman where I got this one flourished her broomstick over my head and threatened my life if I did not drop her chicken. . . .'

"I tried to thank him, but gratitude choked my utterance. My head was laid back upon its hard pillow. The fire continued to make the inside of the carriage comfortable and warm. . . .

" 'Cheer up!' shouted Sam on the afternoon of the third day. 'You are almost home.' He gave his whip a sharp crack, the weary horses went on at a sharp gallop, and the ambulance stopped at the street of Company H. I was indeed at home.

"Kind comrades were there to welcome me: William, Charley, and a dozen others to assist them. I was quickly taken from the ambulance and led to a tent. I glanced over my shoulder and saw some men as they removed my companion from the carriage. His form seemed cold and rigid. He was dead. . . .

"My tent-mates went to thank Sam for his kindness to me. The noble fellow brushed his rough hand across his eyes and drove rapidly away.

"Our camping ground was a small pine knoll at Stoneman's Switch, near Falmouth."

At Fredericksburg, many of the civilians had begun moving out. Some went directly southward by rail, destined for towns along the route to Richmond, or for Richmond itself. One of the intermediate towns was Ashland, and one of the people living there at the time was Judith McGuire, the talented diarist. She wrote on November 23:

"Poor Fredericksburg! The enemy on the Stafford side of the river in force, their cannon planted on the hills. . . . Women and children are being hurried off, leaving everything behind except what they can get off in bundles, boxes, etc. There is no transportation for heavy articles.

"The Vandals threw a shell at a train of cars filled with women and children. It burst very near them, but they were providentially protected. A battle is daily expected. In the meantime the sufferings of wandering women and children are very great.

"*November 25.* Just from the [Ashland] depot. The cars have gone to Richmond, filled with noncombatants from Fredericksburg— ladies with their children, many of whom know not where to go. They will get to Richmond after dark, and many propose staying in the cars this cold night, and seeking a resting place tomorrow. The feeling of desolation among them is dreadful. Oh, how I wish that I had even one room to offer!

"The bombardment has not commenced, but General Lee requested last night that the women and children who had not gone should go without delay. This seems to portend hot work."

But the hot work was not yet at hand. Something quite different is described by the Union's Surgeon George Stevens: "The 27th of November was Thanksgiving Day in nearly all the loyal states; and doubtless our friends at home, as they gathered in many a family circle that day to partake of bounteous Thanksgiving dinners, spoke of those who were away at the war, and thought that with them Thanksgiving could only be a hard day's march in the rain or mud, with rations of hard bread and pork; and so, many kind hearts pitied the soldiers as they thought that we were deprived of the luxuries which they were enjoying.

"But we, too, enjoyed a pleasant Thanksgiving. In the morning, throughout the corps there was a brigade inspection. We put on our good clothes and presented ourselves to our generals looking our best. Then, as we marched back into the various camps we found dinner smoking in many a cook-tent, and the odor of roast meats rising throughout the whole corps like an odor of sweet incense. Fresh sheep pelts hanging here and there in considerable profusion told of good cheer among all men.

"As evening approached, the voice of singing was heard from all the camps, and groups were gathered under the shadow of the chestnut trees, where many pairs of government shoes were shuffling to the music of violins. Throughout the limits of the corps, good humor and mirth prevailed. The sick forgot their pains; and the homesick ones, for the time, looked bright as they yielded to the general feeling of happiness."

Returning to the Confederate side and to Mrs. McGuire at Ashland:

"*29th*. Nothing of importance from the army. The people of Fredericksburg suffering greatly from the sudden move. I know a family, accustomed to every luxury at home, now in a damp basement-room in Richmond. The mother and three young daughters cooking, washing, etc. The father, a merchant, is sick and cut off from business, friends, and everything else. Another family, consisting of mother and four daughters in one room, supported by the work of one of the daughters, who has an office in the Note-Signing Department. . . . Their supplies in Fredericksburg can't be brought to them—no transportation.

"I cannot mention the numbers who are similarly situated. The country is filled with them. . . . Every cottage in this village is full. And now families are looking with wistful eyes at the ballroom belonging to the hotel, which, it seems to me, might be partitioned off to accommodate several families. The billiard rooms are taken, it is said, though not yet occupied. But how everybody is to be supported is a difficult question to decide.

"Luxuries have been given up long ago by many persons. Coffee is $4 per pound, and good tea from $18 to $20; butter ranges from $1.50 to $2 per pound; lard 50 cents; corn $15 per barrel; and wheat $4.50 per bushel. We can't get a muslin dress for less than $6 or $8 per yard; calico $1.75, etc. This last is no great hardship, for we will all resort to homespun. We are knitting our own stockings, and regret that we did not learn to spin and weave. . . .

"*30th*. The Yankee army ravaging Stafford County dreadfully, but they do not cross the river. Burnside . . . is quietly waiting and watching our little band on the opposite side. Is he afraid to venture over? His 'On to Richmond' seems slow."

18

The Fateful Plans Completed

T HE FACT that Stonewall Jackson's corps was now arriving from the Valley to reinforce Longstreet did nothing to fan Burnside's ardor for speed. The Union commander, in fact, had become literally sick with worry about his position. He might have considered going into winter quarters at Falmouth and delaying matters till spring, but he knew that Washington wanted action.

Surprisingly, Burnside still felt that his best bet was to push for Richmond through Fredericksburg. Lincoln had been down the Potomac for a parley at Acquia Creek, about ten miles northeast of Falmouth, the army's new base of supplies; and Burnside, in turn, had attended a meeting in Washington. Alternative plans were discussed, but the general was allowed to shape the effort as he desired.

The decision to attack Lee at Fredericksburg was an incredibly bad one, for the heights behind the town, which formed a rough parallel with the river, were supremely defensible.

The arrival of December 1 found Burnside making his final preparations. The base at Acquia Creek, of course, figured largely in these, and he had a special force stationed there. One of the regiments was that to which Chaplain Stewart belonged. The good reverend, however, was not privy to the general's plans. He thought it probable that the fighting was over for the winter, and his chief concern was the state of the army's morality. He could not see how a righteous God could grant victory to men of such dissolute ways.

"Clever, well-meaning Uncle Abe," the letter-writer stated, "has issued a proclamation for the better observance of the Sabbath and a restraint of wickedness in the army. Intentions good, no doubt. Yet is the language of the President's manifesto so entirely indefinite that scarcely the least attention is likely to be given thereto. Common law will not answer in the army. Its officers and privates as a whole are entirely too wicked to be much influenced by well-meant generalities in Presidential proclamations or vague and powerless Congressional enactments as to morality. In order to meet the case, all want positive enactments, as God gave to ancient Israel, with specific penalties surely to be executed for each violation.

"Acquia Creek . . . is a small stream emptying itself into the Potomac on the Virginia side. . . . It became somewhat famous during last winter as the place where the rebels erected a number of batteries, and, for a series of months, kept the Potomac pretty effectually blockaded, thus cutting off nearly all water communication with the Capital. A railroad fifteen miles in length connects this point with Fredericksburg. . . . This route has of late years become quite a favorite one for travelers from North to South, going down in steamboats from Washington to Acquia Creek.

"This railroad was in the possession of our troops when General Burnside came up from North Carolina last summer . . . and landed his troops at this point. Afterwards, when directed to abandon this region and join General Pope . . . Burnside ordered everything to be destroyed which might in any way aid the military operations of the rebels. The railroad pier extending far out into the river, the temporary buildings on the wharf, together with the cars, the engines, and the bridges along the road, were all burnt, and the track itself torn up.

"Two weeks since, when Burnside . . . marched from Warrenton to the neighborhood of Fredericksburg . . . the ruined railroad presented the only feasible route along which to convey provisions in quantities sufficient for such a host. Modern skill, energy, and speed in construction are truly marvellous. Fifteen days ago this railroad was . . . an utter desolation. Yet for seven days past have trains of cars been carrying along it, and distributing to the various camps . . . enormous quantities of beef, pork, crackers, oats, corn, and hay, together with every [other] variety of army supplies.

"The engineer corps of the army had materials brought from a distance, and reconstructed the long dock, erected temporary depots, rebuilt the bridges, relaid the track, brought four large engines from the North, with a sufficient number of cars, got them on the track and in running order—all within a week. . . .

"Our regiment . . . [had] instructions to take a general military supervision of the place and its connections; to brush away any marauding secesh who might chance to interfere, to guard the railroad, and protect public property. . . .

"As the service upon which we were sent must, from present appearance, be required all winter, our boys took it into their heads—and quite naturally, too—that this was to be their location, and these their duties, for months to come. Our campground was on an open space fronting the river. Plans were speedily set on foot for building winter quarters. The rebel regiments which spent last winter here had . . . built themselves very comfortable and convenient habitations—log houses, shingled roofs, floors, windows, and brick chimneys. These, however, were not in a location to suit our present purpose. In order to avoid the range of the [Union] gunboats from the river, their quarters had been built nearly a mile back behind the hills. . . .

"Away went our boys in long files, like ants to a sugar drawer, and . . . long rows of secesh cabins were torn down and carried, piecemeal, that long distance upon their shoulders. While some carried, others builded. Busy as beavers did they thus labor for a whole week, working often far into the night. . . . By Saturday last the new city was well-nigh completed. . . .

"On Sabbath afternoon, two dilapidated regiments from New York were sent down to take our place, and we ordered back to our brigade. . . . Our boys, in consequence, felt a little disappointment in not being allowed to inhabit, even for a few days, the city they had with so much labor built. This feeling was also aggravated by various squads of the newcomers passing along the streets and boasting, so as to be heard, what fine winter quarters our regiment had built for them.

"When the city was about being abandoned early on Monday morning, by some untoward accident, in the haste of preparations for starting, flames were seen to burst out from a number of the newly built houses. Nearly all the material being seasoned [and] the weather for some days dry . . . the entire city was in a few minutes in flames. Grand was the conflagration, and worthy of an artist's pencil."

The situation on the Confederate side at this time is given by William Miller Owen, of the Washington Artillery, in the form of a journal entry:

"Lee's army now confronts the Federal commander, who can see

View from Marye's Heights showing stone wall and open ground extending toward Fredericksburg.

the bristling bayonets of the Army of Northern Virginia, 78,000 strong, surmounting the range of hills that overlook the plain and city of Fredericksburg. [Jackson's units, who held the right, were not concentrated. With Burnside's intentions unfathomed, they extended far down the river.] The enemy shows a large force on Stafford Heights ... but Lee, Longstreet, and Jackson, and their men stand before them and again bar their way to Richmond.

"The line of heights on our side is being strengthened with earthworks, rifle pits, and redoubts for artillery. The Washington Artillery has been assigned to Marye's Hill, which juts out towards the town, forming a sort of salient, and nearer to it than any of the other fortifications.... On the right ... is Lee's Hill [so named because the general chose the eminence as a combination headquarters site and observation post].

"In front of Marye's Hill ... is a sunken road, and on the side towards the town is a stone wall about breast high. The field beyond is [nearly] flush with the top of the wall. Before Marye's Hill is an open plain, with a few cottages and market gardens, and divided up into lots by board fences until the outskirts [of the town] are reached.

"In front of the town flows the Rappahannock, and opposite are the Stafford Heights, upon which the enemy has posted more than a hundred pieces of artillery, commanding the town. Thus, between our position on Marye's Hill and the enemy on Stafford lies the old-fashioned Revolutionary [War] town of Fredericksburg.

"For the first time our army will fight behind dirt. On Marye's the engineers have laid out works for three of our batteries, *en barbette*—that is, with the work only as high as a man's breast or as the muzzle of a cannon; but we improve upon their work by raising the earth higher and arranging embrasures to fire through. The engineers say we spoil their work, but as *we*, not they, have to stand here in case Burnside comes across, they will remain as we have altered them. Longstreet says, 'If we only save the finger of [one] man, that's good enough.' As the position is enfiladed by the enemy's batteries at Falmouth, strong traverses are built to protect us from a flank fire.

"Officers of other batteries have already dubbed our [exposed] position a 'slaughter pen.' It may turn out so; but the Old War Horse, Longstreet, says he hardly thinks Burnside will cross here and make a direct attack, but go around our left flank."

Stationed in the same zone of Longstreet's lines as William Miller Owen and his comrades was another artillery battalion, that of Colonel E. Porter Alexander. This unit had just received a replacement—a private soldier, and a stranger to all—who aroused a lot of speculation. As explained by W. C. Elam, one of the battalion's members:

"He had fitted himself out with a fine new uniform, from head to foot, with a great deal of gilt lace and red about it. His cap was particularly flashy, and he wore it with a jaunty and devil-may-care air. In a belt around his waist he habitually carried a five-shooter and a large bowie-knife—weapons with which he had already done good service for the Confederacy, as he boasted.

"According to his story, he had been amongst the earliest volunteers for six months, and had captured a Federal battery at [First] Manassas—if he had not really won that battle. [General Pierre] Beauregard had complimented him on the field, and would have promoted him at the same time, but . . . he had declined the office—preferring the careless and irresponsible life of the private soldier.

"He was enrolled as Augustus Forbes, and . . . he showed us some

THE MARYE MANSION

of his wounds. They looked like briar-scratches, but he said his flesh healed with remarkable rapidity and smoothness. . . . He was soon pretty well known as 'The Hero of Manassas.'

" 'I tell you, fellows' said he to us, who had seen no greater battles then than skirmishes and affairs of outposts, 'it's a little ticklish making your first charge on a battery in full play; but you get your blood up, you know, and then you feel like you are waltzing to the band with your best girl. It's so with me anyhow. Most fellows always feel somewhat scared; but after my first fight I've been cool as ice, but eager to be in the thickest of it.'

"Our junior lieutenant, Mitchell, was standing nearby, and he heard Forbes. 'You are the man for me, Forbes,' he said, 'and I'm glad you are on my gun. You'll set myself and my other men a good example, and keep us to our duty if we flinch.'

" 'All right, lieutenant,' responded Augustus assuringly. 'You may rely on me. I trust it won't be too long before we have a battle, as camp life is mighty dull without plenty o' fighting.'

"On the strength of his alleged record, Private Forbes assumed all the privileges of the veteran, and largely shirked his duties, even including his share of the mess-work. But he was tolerated by the boys in this shirking, not only on account of his accredited prowess in battle . . . but because he was the most skilful and successful forager in our part of the army.

"Some carpers declared that he must be a trained sneak-thief. Yet we all regarded him very highly as we partook of the dainties he had purveyed from smoke-house, sty, hen-roost, dairy, field, orchard, and garden."

There is more to the story of Augustus Forbes, but the telling must wait till later.

At this point we'll turn again to the journal of the Washington Artillery's William Miller Owen:

"We ride into Fredericksburg almost daily and visit a few of the citizens who are still at home, among the rest Temple Doswell and T. S. Barton, a venerable citizen who says he will stay in his old house and die there, if need be. He keeps open house for all who choose to call, and his dining table is always set with cold saddles of mutton, bread and butter, flanked by bottles of old wines from his ancient stock in the garret. He says he would rather we would consume every bottle of it than let the Yankees get it. We will try and carry out the patriotic idea.

"[William] Barksdale's Mississippi brigade is in the town on picket, and the enemy's pickets across the river only a biscuit's toss. There is no firing [allowed], so they chaff each other fearfully."

Some of the Union pickets were stationed on the old "Ferry Farm," boyhood home of George Washington. This was the place, according to Captain William Draper, whose company did numerous stints there, "where he cut the cherry tree with his little hatchet but could not tell a lie. The old homestead served as my headquarters several times, but it finally was entirely torn down for fuel and to assist in making comfortable the headquarters of the nearest regiments."

Returning to the Confederate side and to William Miller Owen:

"Our camp is about a mile back from the line. The redoubts are all ready on Marye's for our occupation, and we are to get into position at once should the enemy attempt to cross the river. Each officer knows the position to be occupied by his guns. The signal is to be two guns fired in quick succession, and the army will go into the works without further orders."

Writing a few days later, Owen added: "Our 'Literary and Dramatic Association' has erected a stage and side-scenes for a theatrical performance in the open air. The side-scenes are blankets, and the drop-curtain an old tent-fly, with crossed cannons and 'W. A.' [Washington Artillery] in charcoal letters. The circular enclosure is protected from the cold winds by pine brush; the seats are of logs, and huge fires light the 'house' and warm it at the same time. The play is the 'Lady of Lyons,' with Lieutenant Stocker as *Claude Melnotte* in braided artillery jacket and red kepi, and Sergeant John Wood as *Pauline*.

"The play went off admirably well, both parts being well-performed; but where the sergeant got his petticoats from he won't tell!

"The after-piece was a roaring farce. Our guests were much

pleased; and the boys say they are well organized now, and will soon give a series of entertainments.

"We have at last persuaded old Mr. Barton to pack up what he can and retreat to Richmond. Lieutenant Norcom, Captain Barton, and myself devoted a day and night to packing up his library, some of his old wines, and clothing, etc., and saw him aboard the cars and out of harm's way.

"The citizens are still leaving the town to avoid the coming clash of arms, and very rightly, too."

The plight of the evacuees was complicated by a heavy snowfall. In the words of Robert Stiles, a young Virginian serving as adjutant of the Richmond Howitzers: "I never saw a more pitiful procession than they made trudging through the deep snow. . . . I saw little children tugging along with their doll-babies, some bigger than they were, but holding their feet up carefully above the snow; and women so old and feeble that they could carry nothing and could barely hobble themselves. There were women carrying a baby in one arm, and its bottle, its clothes, and its covering in the other. Some had a Bible and a toothbrush in one hand, a picked chicken and a bag of flour in the other.

"Most of them had to cross a creek swollen with winter rains and deadly cold with winter ice and snow. We took the battery horses down and ferried them over, taking one child in front and two behind, and sometimes a woman or a girl on either side with her feet in the stirrups, holding on by our shoulders. Where they were going we could not tell, and I doubt if they could."

During this period the opposing cavalry forces were spread up and down the banks of the Rappahannock for fifty miles, watching each other across the various fords. Little action developed. Confederate horse artilleryman John Pelham, however, performed a special mission at Port Royal, about twenty miles downriver from Fredericksburg, turning back some Yankee gunboats that were ascending from the Chesapeake. Jeb Stuart took a personal part in the episode, afterward returning to his Fredericksburg camp, on the right of the line with Jackson's corps. It was now December 3.

"The following morning," says Heros von Borcke, "we were enlivened by snowball fights which commenced as skirmishes near our headquarters but extended over the neighboring camps and assumed the aspect of general engagements. In front of our headquarters, beyond an open field of about half a mile square, Hood's division lay encamped in a piece of wood. In our immediate rear stretched the tents and huts of a part of [Lafayette] McLaws's division.

"Between these two bodies of troops animated little skirmishes had frequently occurred whenever there was snow enough on the ground to furnish the ammunition; but on the morning of the 4th, an extensive expedition having been undertaken by several hundred of McLaws's men against Hood's encampments, and the occupants of these finding themselves considerably disturbed thereby, suddenly the whole of the division advanced in line of battle, with flying colors, the officers leading the men as if in real action, to avenge the insult.

"The assailants fell back rapidly before this overwhelming host, but only to secure a strong position from which, with reinforcements, they might resume the offensive. The alarm of their first repulse having been borne with the swiftness of the wind to their comrades, sharpshooters in large numbers were posted behind the cedar bushes that skirt the Telegraph Road, and hundreds of hands were actively employed in erecting a long and high snow wall in front of their extended lines.

"The struggle had now the appearance of a regular battle, with its charges and countercharges—the wild enthusiasm of the men and the noble emulation of the officers finding expression in loud commands and yet louder cheering, while the air was darkened with the snowballs as the current of the fight moved to and fro over the well-contested field.

"Nearer and nearer it came towards our headquarters, and it was soon evident to us that the hottest part of the engagement would take place in our neutral territory. Fruitless were the efforts of Stuart and myself to assert and maintain the neutrality of our camp, utterly idle the hoisting of a white flag. The advancing columns pressed forward in complete disregard of our signs and our outspoken remonstrances; clouds of snowballs passed across the face of the sun; and ere long the overwhelming wave of the conflict rolled pitilessly over us.

"Yielding to the unavoidable necessity which forbade our keeping aloof from the contest, Stuart and I had taken position, in order to obtain a view over the field of battle, on a big box containing ordnance stores in front of the General's tent, where we soon became so much interested in the result, and so carried away by the excitement of the moment, that we found ourselves calling out to the men to hold their ground, and urging them again and again to

Union cavalry reconnaissance along the Rappahannock.
Alfred Pleasonton on left.

the attack, while many a stray snowball, and many a well-directed one, took effect upon our exposed persons.

"But all the gallant resistance of McLaws's men was unavailing. Hood's lines pressed resistlessly forward, carrying everything before them, taking the formidable fortifications and driving McLaws's division out of their encampments. Suddenly, at this juncture, we heard loud shouting on the right, where two of [Richard H.] Anderson's brigades had come up as reinforcements. The men of McLaws's division, acquiring new confidence from this support, rallied, and in turn drove, by a united charge, the victorious foe in headlong flight back to their own camps and woods.

"Thus ended the battle for the day, unhappily with serious results to some of the combatants, for one of Hood's men had his leg broken, one of McLaws's men lost an eye, and there were other chance wounds on both sides.

"This sham-fight gave ample proof of the excellent spirits of our troops, who, in the wet, wintry weather, many of them without blankets, some without shoes, regardless of their exposure and of the scarcity of provisions, still maintained their good humor, and were ever ready for any sort of sport or fun that offered itself to them.

"On the morning of the 5th, General Stuart and myself, with several other members of the staff, again set out for Port Royal, where some of the Federal gunboats were renewing their demonstrations. The day was bitterly cold, and the road exceedingly slippery from the frost, so that the ride was anything but pleasant.

"All along our route we found our troops, chiefly those of Jackson's corps—Old Stonewall having established his headquarters midway between Fredericksburg and Port Royal at the plantation of James Parke Corbin, Esq., known as 'Moss Neck'—busily employed in throwing up fortifications. . . . They had greatly improved the highway also, erected lines of telegraphic communication to the headquarters of the different corps of the army, and cut military roads through the woods to various points along our lines.

"It was late in the evening, and darkness had overtaken us, when

Drivers of Pleasonton's baggage wagons watering their mules in the Rappahannock's shallows.

we reached the charming country seat of 'Gaymont,' within a short distance of our place of destination, where a most cordial hospitality was extended to us, and where, in the snug library before a glorious wood fire, we warmed our half-frozen limbs and remained in delightful conversation with the ladies till a late hour of the night.

"The following day it was reported by our scouts and patrols that the gunboats had disappeared. It was Sunday, and we spent it as a day of rest in the most blissful quietude.

"On Monday morning we reluctantly took leave of our kind hosts and started on a reconnaissance . . . with General D. H. Hill, who with his division formed the extreme right of our infantry lines. . . . The Yankees were in plain view on the other side of the river, and were evidently very active in erecting fortifications, marching and countermarching small bodies of troops, and in communicating with other parts of their lines by signal-flags.

"Night was far-advanced when we returned to our headquarters."

19

Burnside Crosses the Rappahannock

U P IN Fredericksburg, the Confederate troops that were spread along the riverfront—Barksdale's Mississippians—had been perfecting their defenses, working during the hours of darkness. A series of rifle pits, some with connecting trenches, lined the edge of the bank. Men were also stationed at cellar windows in the houses just to the rear.

In the words of Barksdale's superior, Lafayette McLaws: "Two or three evenings previous to the Federal attempt to cross, I was with General Barksdale, and we were attracted by one or more of the enemy's bands playing at their end of the railroad bridge [a ruined structure located where the tracks entered the town]. A number of their officers and a crowd of their men were about the band cheering their national airs, the 'Star Spangled Banner,' 'Hail Columbia,' and others, once so dear to us all.

"It seemed as if they expected some response from us, but none was given until, finally, they struck up 'Dixie,' and then both sides cheered, with much laughter. Surmising that this serenade meant mischief, I closely inspected our bank of the river, and at night caused additional rifle pits to be constructed."

Switching to the Union side and to Edwin Sumner's top subordinate, Darius Couch: "On the night of the 9th, two nights before the crossing, Sumner called a council to discuss what we were to do, the corps, division, and brigade commanders being present. The result was plain, free talk all around, in which words were not minced, for the conversation soon drifted into a marked disapprobation of the manner in which Burnside contemplated meeting the enemy. Sumner seemed to feel badly that the officers did not agree to Burnside's mode of advance. That noble old hero was so faithful and loyal that he wanted, even against impossibilities, to carry out everything Burnside suggested. . . .

"Somebody told Burnside of our views, and he was irritated. He asked us to meet him the next night. . . . He said he understood, in a general way, that we were opposed to his plans. He seemed to be rather severe on Hancock—to my surprise, for I did not think that officer had said as much as myself in opposition to the plan of attack. Burnside stated that he had formed his plans, and all he wanted was the devotion of his men.

"Hancock made a reply in which he disclaimed any personal discourtesy, and said he knew there was a line of fortified heights on the opposite side, and that it would be pretty difficult for us to go over there and take them. I rose after him, knowing that I was the more guilty, and expressed a desire to serve Burnside. . . . French came in while I was talking. He was rather late, and in his bluff way exclaimed, 'Is this a Methodist camp-meeting?'"

According to Union narrator Regis de Trobriand: "On the evening of the 10th the order arrived to hold ourselves ready to march the next morning. 'This time,' it was said, 'the ball is going to begin.'

The ruined railroad bridge

The night was full of suppressed agitation. . . . The fires remained burning longer than usual. In different directions was heard the rolling of wagons . . . and cannon. . . . Confused noises indicated the march of regiments changing position. Their bayonets flashed through the obscurity, lighted up by the bivouac fires."

On the Confederate side, according to Lafayette McLaws, suspicions were aroused while the night was still young. "General Barksdale reported that his pickets had heard noises, as if the enemy were hauling pontoon-boats to the brink of the river. A dense fog had prevented a clear view. About 2 A.M. of the 11th, General Barksdale notified me that the movements on the other side indicated that the enemy were preparing to lay down the pontoon-bridges. I told him to let the bridge-building go on until the enemy were committed to it and the construction parties were within easy range."

An observer on the Union side was William Swinton, who recorded these details for the *New York Times*: "Five pontoon-bridges were to be thrown across the river—the first at the Lacy House [known also as Chatham], which lies directly opposite the end of the main street of Fredericksburg, half a mile below Falmouth; the second and third within a few hundred yards from the first. The remaining two were to be thrown over a mile and a half or two miles further down the stream, and on these the grand division of General Franklin—the left—would cross, while Sumner's and Hooker's grand divisions—right and center—would use the three upper ones.

"It was about three o'clock this morning [he was writing on December 11] when the boats were unshipped from the teams at

The Lacy House, or Chatham

the river's brink. Swiftly and silently the Engineer Corps proceeded to their work. A dense fog filled the valleys and water margin, through which the bridge-builders appeared as spectral forms. . . . The construction of the two lower—Franklin's—bridges . . . was performed with perfect success—the engineers being allowed to complete the first without any interruption whatever, while the construction of the other was but slightly interrupted by the fire of the rebel sharpshooters.

"We were not so fortunate with the upper bridges. The artificers had but got fairly to work when at five o'clock the firing of two guns from one of the enemy's batteries announced that we were discovered. They were signal guns. Rapid volleys of musketry, discharged at our bridge-builders, immediately followed. This was promptly responded to on our side by the opening of several batteries.

"The fog, however, still hung densely over the river. It was still quite dark, and the practice of the artillerists was necessarily very much at random. The Engineer Corps suffered severely from the fire of the sharpshooters concealed in the town. The little band was being murderously thinned, and presently the work on the bridges slackened, and then ceased.

"Meanwhile, the firing from our batteries, posted about a mile from the river, was kept up vigorously. The effect was singular enough, and it was difficult to believe that the whole affair was not a phantasmagoria. It was still quite dark, the horizon around being lit up only by the flash of projectiles which reappeared in explosive flame on the other side of the river.

"Daylight came, but with it came not clearness of vision for onlookers. The mist and smoke not only did not lighten, but grew more opaque and heavy, hugging the ground closely. Our gunners, however, still continued to launch their missiles. . . . The rebel batteries hardly returned our fire. . . .

"Toward eight o'clock a large party of general officers, among them General Burnside, the corps commanders, and many others of high rank had congregated in front of, and on the balcony of, General [Burnside's] headquarters, Phillip's House, situated about a mile directly back of the Lacy House. The performance could be heard but not seen. The stage was obstinately hidden from view, and all were impatient that the curtain should rise. Aides and couriers came and went with messages to and from the batteries and bridges.

"At half-past nine o'clock official notification was received that the two bridges on the extreme left were completed, and General Franklin sent to General Burnside to know if he should cross his force at once. The reply was that he should wait until the upper bridges were also completed.

"Meantime, with the latter but little progress was made. During the next couple of hours, half a dozen attempts were made to complete the bridges, but each time the [parties were] repulsed with severe loss. . . . It was a hopeless task. . . . The rebel sharpshooters, posted in the cellars of the houses of the front street, not fifty yards from the river, behind stone walls, and in rifle pits, were able to pick off with damnable accuracy any party of engineers venturing on the half-completed bridges.

"The case was perfectly clear. Nothing can be done till they are dislodged from their lurking-places. There is but one way of doing this effectually—shell the town. . . . General Burnside gives the order: 'Concentrate the fire of all your guns on the city, and batter it down!' You may believe they were not loth to obey. . . . In a few moments . . . a total of one hundred and seventy-nine guns [actually, a number nearer one hundred], ranging from ten-pounder Parrotts to four-and-a-half-inch siege guns . . . opened on the doomed city."

Barksdale's sharpshooters

Switching to the Confederate side and to General Longstreet: "From our position on the heights we saw the batteries hurling an avalanche upon the town whose only offense was that near its edge in a snug retreat nestled three thousand Confederate hornets that were stinging the Army of the Potomac into a frenzy."

As added by Confederate General McLaws: "It is impossible fitly to describe the effects of this iron hail hurled against the small band of defenders and into the devoted city. The roar of the cannon, the bursting shells, the falling of walls and chimneys, and the flying bricks and other material dislodged from the houses by the iron balls and shells, added to the fire of the infantry from both sides and the smoke from the guns and from the burning houses, made a scene of indescribable confusion—enough to appall the stoutest hearts!"

General Lee's reaction to the bombardment is given by the lettered staff officer, John Esten Cooke. "The destruction . . . and the suffering of the inhabitants [still in the town] aroused in him a deep melancholy, mingled with exasperation, and his comment . . . was probably as bitter as any speech which he uttered during the whole war. Standing wrapped in his cape, with only a few officers near, he looked fixedly at the flames rising from the city, and, after remaining for a long time silent, said in [a] grave, deep voice, 'These people delight to destroy the weak, and those who can make no defense. It just suits them.' "

The citizens, many of whom were huddling in their cellars, were not being destroyed. Few, indeed, were being hurt. And there was at least one who even refused to cower in hiding. As told by Robert Stiles of the Richmond howitzers:

"During the bombardment I was sent into Fredericksburg with a message for General Barksdale. As I was riding down the street that led to his headquarters, it appeared to be so fearfully swept by artillery fire that I started to ride across it, with a view of finding some safer way of getting to my destination, when, happening to glance beyond that point, I saw walking quietly and unconcernedly along the same street I was on, and approaching General Barksdale's headquarters from the opposite direction, a lone woman. She apparently found the projectiles which were screaming and exploding in the air, and striking and crashing through the houses, and tearing up the streets, very interesting—stepping a little aside to inspect a great, gaping hole one had just gouged in the sidewalk, then turning her head to note a fearful explosion in the air.

The bombardment of Fredericksburg

"I felt as if it really would not do to avoid a fire which was merely interesting, and not at all appalling, to a woman; so I stiffened my spinal column as well as I could and rode straight down the street toward headquarters and the self-possessed lady; and, having reached the house, I rode around back of it to put my horse where he would at least be safer than in front.

"As I returned on foot to the front, the lady had gone up on the porch and was knocking at the door. One of the staff came to hearken, and, on seeing a lady, held up his hands, exclaiming in amazement, 'What on earth, madam, are you doing here? Do go to some safe place, if you can find one.'

"She smiled and said, with some little tartness, 'Young gentleman, you seem to be a little excited. Won't you please say to General Barksdale that a lady at the door wishes to see him?'

"The young man assured her General Barksdale could not possibly see her just now; but she persisted. 'General Barksdale is a Southern gentleman, sir, and will not refuse to see a lady who has called upon him.'

"Seeing that he could not otherwise get rid of her, the General did come to the door, but actually wringing his hands in excitement and annoyance. 'For God's sake, madam, go and seek some place of safety. I'll send a member of my staff to help you find one.'

"She again smiled gently—while old Barksdale fumed and almost swore—and then she said quietly, 'General Barksdale, my cow has just been killed in my stable by a shell. She is very fat, and I don't want the Yankees to get her. If you will send someone down to butcher her, you are welcome to the meat.' "

The bombardment was maintained for about two hours. Again in the words of Northern newsman William Swinton: "Fifty rounds being fired from each gun . . . I know not how many hundred tons of iron were thrown into the town. The congregated generals were transfixed. Mingled satisfaction and awe was upon every face. But what was tantalizing was, that though a great deal could be heard, nothing could be seen, the city being still enveloped in fog and mist. Only a dense pillar of smoke, defining itself on the background of the fog, indicated where the town had been fired by our shells. Another and another column showed itself, and we presently saw that at least a dozen houses must be on fire.

"Toward noon the curtain rolled up, and we saw that it was indeed so. Fredericksburg was in conflagration.

"Tremendous though this firing had been, and terrific though its effect obviously was on the town, it had not accomplished the object intended. It was found by our gunners almost impossible to maintain a sufficient depression of their pieces to shell the front part of the city, and the rebel sharpshooters were still comparatively safe behind the thick stone walls of the houses.

"During the thick of the bombardment a fresh attempt had been made to complete the bridges. It failed, and evidently nothing could be done till a party could be thrown over to clean out the rebels and cover the bridge-head. For this mission, General Burnside [in mid-afternoon] called for volunteers, and Colonel [Norman J.] Hall . . . immediately responded that he had a brigade that would do the business. Accordingly, the 7th Michigan and 19th Massachusetts . . . were selected for the purpose.

"The plan was that they should take the pontoon-boats of the first bridge, of which there were ten lying on the bank of the river, waiting to be added to the half-finished bridge, cross over in them, and, landing, drive out the rebels.

"Nothing could be more admirable or more gallant than the execution of this daring feat. Rushing down the steep banks of the river, the party found temporary shelter behind the pontoon-boats lying scattered on the bank, and behind the piles of planking destined for the covering of the bridge, behind rocks, etc. In this situation they acted some fifteen or twenty minutes as sharpshooters. . . . In the meantime, new and vigorous artillery firing was commenced on our part; and just as soon as this was fairly developed, the 7th Michigan rose from their crouching places, rushed for the pontoon boats, and, pushing them into the water, rapidly filled them with twenty-five or thirty each.

"The first boat pushes off. Now, if ever, is the rebels' opportunity.

The assault on Barksdale's position

Crack! Crack! Crack! From fifty lurking-places go rebel rifles at the gallant fellows who, stooping low in the boat, seek to avoid the fire. The murderous work was well done. Lustily, however, pull the oarsmen, and presently, having passed the middle of the stream, the boat and its gallant freight come under cover of the opposite bluffs.

"Another and another boat follows. Now is their opportunity. . . . Instantly they see a new turn of affairs. The rebels pop up by the hundred, like so many rats, from every cellar, rifle pit, and stone wall, and scamper off up the streets [toward secondary defensive positions in the town]. . . . With all their fleetness, however, many of them were much too slow. With incredible rapidity, the Michigan and Massachusetts boys sweep up the hill . . . capturing . . . prisoners. The pontoon-boats, on their return trip, took [the prisoners] over."

According to another newsman who was present, the *Boston Journal*'s Charles Carleton Coffin, there was a special story behind one of the captures, a story that began while the assailants were still on the Union side of the river.

"When the soldiers of the 7th Michigan leaped into the boats, a drummer-boy joined them—Robert Henry Hendershot. He was only twelve years old, but his dark eyes flashed brightly under the excitement of the moment. His drum was upon his neck.

" 'Get out; you can't go,' said an officer.

" 'I want to go,' said Robert.

" 'No, you will get shot. Out with you.'

"Robert jumped into the water, but instead of going ashore, remained to push off the boat; and then, instead of letting go his hold, clung to the gunwhale, and was taken across.

"As the boat grounded upon the other shore, a piece of shell tore through his drum. He threw it away, seized the gun of a fallen soldier, rushed up the hill, and came upon a Rebel soldier, slightly wounded.

" 'Surrender!' said Robert, pointing his gun at him.

"The Rebel gave up his gun, and Robert marched him to the rear."

Another early incident is given by W. A. Hill, a captain in the 19th Massachusetts: "We came upon a rebel lying . . . with his eyes closed, and just breathing. He had been disemboweled, apparently by a shell. And there was a hog, one of the wild kind common in the South, who had been sniffing round, and had begun to eat him. . . . One of our boys shot the hog."

A third regiment, the 20th Massachusetts, joined the first two, and some sharp street fighting ensued. Meanwhile, as explained by William Swinton (who had crossed the river in one of the assault boats), "it took the engineers but a brief period to complete the bridge. They laid hold with a will, plunging waist-deep into the water and working as men work who are under inspiration. In less than half an hour the bridge was completed, and the head of the column of the right grand division, consisting of General Howard's command, was moving upon it over the Rappahannock. A feeble attempt from the rebel batteries was made to shell the troops in crossing, but it failed completely."

Work on the other bridges was now pressed. At the same time, with twilight at hand, the street fighting continued. Newsman Coffin was watching. "The Rebels were falling back from street to street, and the men from Michigan and Massachusetts were pressing on. . . . Far up the streets there were bright flashes from the muskets of the Rebels, who fired from cellars, chamber windows, and from sheltered places. Nearer were dark masses of men in blue, who gave quick volleys as they moved steadily on, demolishing doors, crushing in windows, and searching every hiding place.

"Cannon were flaming on all the hills, and the whole country was aglow with the campfires of the two great armies. The Stafford Hills were alive with men—regiments, brigades, and divisions moving in column from their encampments to cross the river. The sky was

Street fighting in Fredericksburg

without a cloud. The town was lighted by lurid flames. The air was full of hissings—the sharp cutting sounds of the leaden rain. . . . There were shouts, hurrahs, yells, and groans from the streets."

The fighting wound down with the Confederates making their final withdrawal by plan. Southerner Robert Stiles relates:

"The 21st Mississippi was the last regiment to leave the city. The last detachment was under the command of Lane Brandon. . . . In skirmishing with the head of the Federal column—led, I think, by the 20th Massachusetts—Brandon captured a few prisoners and learned that the advance company was commanded by [Henry L.] Abbott, who had been his chum at Harvard Law School when the war began.

"He lost his head completely. He refused to retire before Abbott. He fought him fiercely and was actually driving him back. In this he was violating orders and breaking our plan of battle. He was put under arrest, and his subaltern brought the command out of town.

"Buck Denman . . . a Mississippi bear hunter and a superb specimen of manhood, was color-sergeant of the 21st and a member of Brandon's company. He was tall and straight, broad shouldered and deep-chested, had an eye like an eagle and a voice like a bull of Bashan, and was full of pluck and power as a panther. He was rough as a bear in manner, but withal a noble, tenderhearted fellow, and a splendid soldier.

"The enemy, finding the way now clear, were coming up the street, full company front, with flags flying and bands playing, while the great shells from the siege guns were bursting over their heads and dashing their hurtling fragments after our retreating skirmishers.

"Buck was behind the corner of a house taking sight for a last shot. Just as his fingers trembled on the trigger, a little three-year-old, fair-haired baby girl toddled out of an alley, accompanied by a Newfoundland dog, and gave chase to a big shell that was rolling lazily along the pavement, she clapping her little hands, and the dog snapping and barking furiously at the shell.

"Buck's hand dropped from the trigger. He dashed it across his eyes to dispel the mist and make sure he hadn't passed over the river and wasn't seeing his own baby girl in a vision. No, there is the baby, amid the hell of shot and shell; and here come the enemy. A moment and he has grounded his gun, dashed out into the storm, swept his great right arm around the baby, gained cover again; and, baby clasped to his breast and musket trailed in his left hand, is trotting after the boys up to Marye's Heights."

Night was falling when Union newsman Swinton turned his attention from affairs at the bridges and began to inspect Fredericksburg.

"As the rebels were in very considerable force on the heights back of the city, one could not extend his perambulations beyond the street fronting on the river. Every one of the houses which I here entered—a dozen or more—[was] torn to pieces by shot and shell, and the fire still hotly [raged] in a dozen parts of the city.

"A few citizens—a score or two, perhaps—male and female, presently made their appearance, emerging out of the cellars. . . . Three women . . . whom we found in a cellar, told us that they, with a majority of the inhabitants, had moved out of Fredericksburg a fortnight or so previously, but that, growing reassured by our long delay, they, with a good many others, had come back the evening before. The [absent] inhabitants they report as now living in various parts of the environs, some in Negro huts and others in tents made with bed-clothes, etc. . . .

"During the . . . bombardment we [had] observed a couple of white handkerchiefs waved out of the windows in a house in the city. This was taken by some for a flag of truce, and the Chief of Artillery was on the point of causing the shelling to cease. General Burnside, however, decided that it was probably merely . . . [a] rebel ruse, and ordered operations to be continued. We found out that the demonstrations were made by two of the women referred to, with the desire that we should send over a boat and convey them away from Fredericksburg. . . .

"A number of rebel dead were found in various parts of the city, some exhibiting frightful mutilations from shells, and I took as a trophy a rifle, still loaded, out of the grasp of a hand belonging to a headless trunk.

"Those . . . that we took prisoners were wretchedly clad, and mostly without blankets or overcoats, but they generally looked stout and healthy, and certainly in far better condition than they could have been were there any truth in the report of some deserters the other day, to the effect that for three weeks they had nothing to eat but the persimmons they were able to pick up."

During the hours that saw the conquest of Fredericksburg by Sumner (with Hooker standing by on the Stafford shore), Franklin had begun his downstream crossing, the sector largely one of open expanses. Only light resistance was met, since the terrain favored the movement's artillery cover. One of the bluecoats present here, surgeon George Stevens, explains that "Franklin [posted] but a small force across the river—a strong picket-line, well-supported, holding a semicircular tract of the plain." Stevens himself remained on the Stafford shore with the bulk of Franklin's troops. "Night came on, and the spectacle was unutterably grand as the sheets of fire burst from the mouths of the opposing batteries. But at length the roar of battle subsided, and, except [for] the firing of pickets, all was quiet."

In Fredericksburg, the battle sounds were replaced by sounds of another kind—those of rampaging Yankees. Since the Confederates had violated their agreement to keep the town a neutral zone, the bluecoats felt that it was now fair game.

Looting the captured town

Union newsman Coffin says that "the soldiers . . . made themselves at home in the deserted houses. They tumbled the furniture into the streets, brought out featherbeds and mattresses—which the surgeons soon appropriated for the use of the wounded.

"Some were boiling their coffee in the kitchens; others were cooking eggs or frying flapjacks from flour found in the pantries. They were rummaging closets and taking whatever pleased their fancy. . . .

"One soldier was strolling the streets wearing an old-fashioned scoop bonnet; another had on a chemise [a female undergarment] over his uniform; a third was wearing a gown; a fourth had a mantle thrown over his shoulders; another appeared with a string of custard cups which he was wearing as a necklace; another had found an old-fashioned bell-crowned hat, in fashion thirty years before the war."

No street scene was more novel than that of the groups of men who sang and danced to the music of fine old pianos that were speedily banged into discord.

The pilfered goods included large quantities of tobacco, and this item was treasured, in particular, by the outpost men, who, Coffin explains, "through the long night, while keeping watch, enjoyed their pipes at the expense of the enemy."

20

Establishing the Front

I T WAS supposed by many soldiers on both sides that December 12 would see major fighting, but the day became yet another one of preparation. Burnside had more than 100,000 men to deploy. The Confederates, as they continued fortifying, had a fine view of the show taking place a mile or two from their elevated position. Although Union General Sumner's troops vanished as they descended the Stafford slopes and crossed their bridges into Fredericksburg, Franklin's wing, down the river, remained clearly visible while crossing to the plain.

"As the fog lifted," says Confederate observer D. Augustus Dickert, "Stafford Heights and the inclines above the river were one field of blue. Great lines of infantry, with waving banners, their bright guns and bayonets glittering in the sunlight, all slowly marching down the steep inclines between the heights and the river, on over the bridges, then down the riverside at a double-quick to join their comrades of the night before.

"These long, swaying lines ... resembled some monster serpent.... Light batteries of artillery came dashing at breakneck speed down the hillsides, their horses rearing and plunging, as if wishing to take the river at a leap. Cavalry, too, with their heavy-bodied Norman horses, their spurs digging the flanks, sabers bright and glistening and dangling at their sides, came at a canter, all seeming anxious to get over.... Long trains of ordnance wagons, with their black oil-cloth covering, [and] the supply trains and quartermaster departments, all [followed] in the wake of their division or corps headquarters, escorts, and trains.

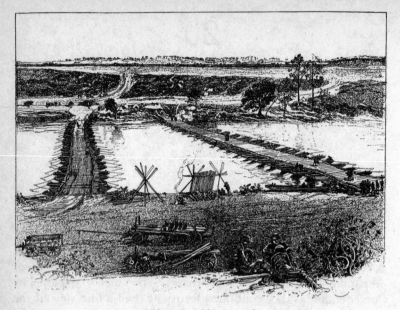

Where Franklin crossed

"All spread out over the hills and in the gorges lay men by the thousands, awaiting their turn to move. . . . Bands of music enlivened the scene by their inspiring strains, and when some national air, or especially martial piece, would be struck up, shouts and yells rended the air for miles, to be answered by counter yells from the throats of fifty thousand Johnny Rebs. . . . The Confederate bands were not idle, for as soon as a Federal band would cease playing, some of the Southern bands would take up the refrain, and as the notes, especially 'Dixie,' would be wafted over the water and hills, the bluecoats would shout, sing, and dance. Hats and caps went up, flags waved in the breeze—so delighted were they at the sight and sound of Dixie."

Adds the South's Prussian ally, Heros von Borcke: "From the many heavy batteries over the river rose, from time to time, little white puffs of smoke; and the deep, dull boom of the big guns was almost immediately followed by the angry whirr of a 50- or 100-pound shell, which, falling, in the majority of instances, too short, did little or no damage. Our artillery, from different points along our line, occasionally answered the enemy's guns with just as little effect."

A Union participant, Private George E. Jepson of the 13th Massachusetts, Franklin's wing, assumes the narrative: "On reaching the southern bank of the river, we were deployed as skirmishers. Not an enemy was at first in sight. . . . As the bugles sounded to advance, the long line of skirmishers stepped briskly forward, until, passing over a rising ground, the broad plain . . . burst upon the view. Bisecting this plain could be seen a long row of evergreen trees . . . indicating one of those beautiful roadways for which this section of the Old Dominion is justly celebrated. . . .

"And now, midway of the plain, and against this dark background, suddenly emerged into view an opposing line of gray-clad riflemen. The enemy was before us, prepared, apparently, to dispute the right of way. In appearance only, however, for as we advanced the Johnnies slowly retreated, and we wonderingly saw them clamber over the roadbank and disappear.

"Thus far not a shot had been fired, which told to each side that the opposing force was composed of veteran troops with nerves too well schooled to lose self-control, forget discipline, and become rattled at the first sight of an enemy.

"Undoubtedly each man's pulse was a little quickened as we drew nearer and nearer, at the seeming certainty that behind the frowning embankment hundreds of death-dealing tubes were leveled at us. But—sounded the bugles, and on we went, mounted the bank, and, through the gaps in the cedars, beheld our foe slowly retiring behind a ridge of land on the other side of the road, and which ran for a long distance parallel with it.

"Once in the roadway, the bugles signaled to halt; and the strain upon both moral and physical powers was relaxed, for the present at least. . . .

"It was apparent that the Confederates had established their outposts along the parallel ridge in front of us; and it soon became equally evident that the battle was not to be joined that day, and that our skirmish line was as far advanced as was practicable without precipitating an engagement.

"All remained quiet in our front. Not a shot had been fired, and a mutual understanding not to begin hostilities appeared to have been established in some indefinable way between the two picket lines. Moreover, from time to time a Confederate would come out a few paces from the ridge and shout some good-natured badinage at us, to which we responded in a strain pitched to the same tune.

"At length a 'grayback' was seen to advance, waving a handkerchief and offering to meet one of 'you-uns' halfway for a friendly confab. A ready response greeted the proposal, and one of the 13th was soon sent forth with a well-filled haversack containing sugar, coffee, salt, and hardtack, the joint contribution of his messmates.

"The advance of the friendly foes, deliberately timed so that they would meet at a point equidistant from either line, was eagerly and excitedly watched by both sides. As the men neared each other they were seen to extend a welcoming hand; and then, as the palms of the Johnnie and Yank met in a fraternal grasp, an electric thrill went straight to the heart of every beholder.

"Such a wild, prolonged, and hearty cheer—such a blending of Yankee shout and Rebel yell as swelled up from the opposing lines— was never before heard, even in battle!

"The contents of the haversack were soon transferred to the adventurous Reb, who, in turn, loaded our man down with native tobacco and bacon. . . .

"Numerous similar affairs occurred, the utmost good fellowship being manifested. It was learned that our immediate opponents were the 19th Georgia Regiment. They told us that they had tasted neither coffee, sugar, nor salt for months."

Back at the river, where Franklin's troops had continued crossing, something of a soberer nature was afoot. As explained by Surgeon George Stevens: "A fine stone mansion of large dimensions ["Mans-

A handshake between the lines.

field" or "Bernard's"], situated on the south bank ... a little below the bridge, was taken by the surgeons of our Second division for a hospital. The position was exposed to the rebel fire, but it was the best that could be found. ... The owner of this magnificent mansion still remained in it. He was an old secesh bachelor, very aristocratic in his notions, and highly incensed at the use his house was put to by the 'hireling Yankees.' But he was taken care of by a guard. ... His fine larder furnished us delicacies, and his cellar rich old wines."

At the front, peaceful relations were not everywhere the rule. Returning to Confederate narrator Heros von Borcke:

"About eleven o'clock I was asked by General Stuart to accompany him on a ride along our line of battle to the extreme right, that we might look after our horsemen, reconnoiter the position and movements of the enemy in that direction, and ascertain whether the nature of the ground was such that a charge of our whole cavalry division during the impending fight might be profitably attempted.

"It was a pleasure and an encouragement to pass the extended lines of our soldiers, who were lying carelessly behind their earthworks, or actively engaged in throwing up new ones—some cooking, others gaily discussing the designs of the enemy and greeting with loud cheers of derision the enormous shells, which they called 'Yankee flour barrels,' as these came tumbling into the woods around them, and to read in every bronzed face of them all eagerness for the conflict, and confidence as to the result.

"The atmosphere had now again become obscure, and the fog was rolling up from the low swampy grounds along the margin of Deep Run Creek. ... Here we turned off into a narrow bridle path which bore away some distance from our lines but would shorten our ride by nearly a mile. We had proceeded but a few steps at a careless trot when suddenly a long line of horsemen in skirmishing order appeared directly before us in the mist.

"I felt very certain they were Federal horsemen, but Stuart was unwilling to believe that the Yankees would have the audacity to approach our position so closely; and, as the greater part of them wore a brownish dust-colored jacket over their uniforms, he set them down as a small command of our own cavalry returning from a reconnaissance.

"So we continued upon our route yet a little farther, until, at a distance of about forty yards, several carbine shots, whose bullets

A Rappahannock mansion, "Mansfield" or "Bernard's," used as a Union hospital and as Franklin's headquarters.

whistled around our heads, taught us very plainly with whom we had to deal. At the same moment, ten or fifteen of the dragoons spurred furiously towards us, demanding, with loud outcries, our surrender—hearing which, we galloped in some haste back to our lines, where our bold pursuers were received and put to flight by Early's sharpshooters.

"A considerable number of our infantry skirmishers now moved forward to drive the dashing cavalrymen off. But the latter held their ground gallantly, and kept up so annoying a fire with their long-range carbines, that our men did not obtain any advantage over them, while Stuart and myself could not look without admiration upon the address and intrepidity our enemies displayed.

"General Hood, who had been attracted by the noise of the brisk fusillade, soon came riding up to us, and seeing at a moment what was going on, said, 'This will never do. I must send up some of my Texans, who will make short work of these impudent Yankees.'

"One of Hood's adjutants galloped off at once with an order from his general, and soon a select number of these dreaded marksmen, crawling along the ground, after their wild Indian fashion, advanced upon the Federal dragoons, who had no idea of their approach until they opened fire at a distance of about eighty yards. In a few seconds several men and horses had been killed; and the whole Federal line—stampeded by a galling fire from an unseen foe in a quarter wholly unexpected—broke into confused and rapid flight.

"This opened the way for us, and we continued our ride without further interruption. . . . We found our horsemen in good spirits, and occupying their position on the Port Royal road, where the right wing was engaged in a lively skirmish with a body of Federal cavalry, which ended in the withdrawal of the latter.

"Our comrades of the other arms of the service had [from time to time] indulged in . . . captious criticism of the cavalry for not having given the decisive finishing stroke to great battles by grand and overwhelming charges, as had been done in the times of Frederick the Great and Napoleon—criticism that was unwarranted and unjust, since the nature of the ground in Virginia did not favor the operations of cavalry, and since the great improvement in firearms in our day had necessitated a very material change in cavalry tactics. . . .

"Nevertheless, General Stuart was anxious, with every officer and private under his command, to show that we were able to do what other cavalry had accomplished before us; and all burned with the noble ambition of winning an enduring fame [in the coming battle] . . . with the eyes of the whole army resting upon us. . . .

"The open plain [stretching toward the enemy] . . . cut by only a few ditches, and with only here and there a fence running across it, seemed to offer us the arena for the realization of our dreams of glory. But, upon a closer survey of the ground, we found it much too soft for a charge with any chance of success, as the horses, moving even at a moderate speed, would sink several feet into the mire. . . .

"On the road between Hamilton's crossing and Fredericksburg, thousands of Yankees were working like beavers in digging rifle pits and erecting works for their artillery. Stuart being anxious to discover exactly what they were about, I rode with him in that direction to a small barn, where we dismounted and tied our horses, and thence carefully approached the hostile lines by creeping along a ditch . . . constituting the boundary of an inconsiderable plantation. Thus we proceeded until we reached a slight eminence only a few hundred yards from the Yankees, where two big posts, the remains of a dismantled gate, concealed us from their observation.

"Our own view was so satisfactory that, with our field-glasses we could distinctly mark the features of the men. It was evident enough to us that they were engaged in converting the simple road into a most formidable work of defense, and that in Jackson's front they were massing large forces of infantry and artillery."

This was important intelligence. Until this moment the Confederates had not been sure of Union General Franklin's intent. He might have been planning to move down along the bank of the river with a view to turning Jackson's flank. Now it was clear that Franklin's attack would come from the front. Jackson's units, some of which had continued in positions farther down the river, could be concentrated.

Von Borcke continues: "Quite content with what we had seen, we returned to our horses, and I received orders to ride at once to General Lee to make report of our reconnaissance, General Stuart himself galloping over to A. P. Hill. After a ride of a few minutes I met Generals Lee and Jackson, who were taking a turn to inspect our own lines and to reconnoiter those of the enemy. Upon hearing what I had to tell them, both generals determined at once to repair themselves to the point of lookout from which we had just withdrawn; and, leaving their numerous escort behind, accompanied only by an orderly, they rode forward under my guidance to the barn already mentioned. Here the horses were placed in charge of the orderly, and we made our way on foot to the gateposts.

"Fearing to augment the danger of their situation by my presence, I retired to the roadside some twenty yards distant and left the two great leaders to their conference and survey. I must confess I felt extremely nervous as regards their safety, so close to the enemy, who surely little expected that the two greatest heroes of the war were so nearly in their clutches. One well-directed shot, or a rapid dash of resolute horsemen, might have destroyed the hopes and confidence of our whole army. The sensation of relief on my part was therefore great when, after many minutes of painful anxiety and impatience, the generals slowly returned, and we reached our horses without accident.

"We were soon joined by Stuart, and all—except Jackson, who parted from us to regain the troops under his command—rode . . . to Lee's Hill."

The crowd of observers on the hill included an unidentified correspondent of the *London Times*, who noted: "It became more and more obvious, even to the least experienced eye, what a magnificent position was occupied by the Confederate army, and how wisely and sagaciously the ground had been chosen by General Lee. It must have been a moment of proud gratification to General Lee and those captains who, under him, have gained ever-increasing distinction, when they realized beyond all question that the enemy was about to force an attack under circumstances which would have insured defeat had the onslaught been made by the bravest disciplined troops of Europe. . . .

"Even in its weakest points the Confederate line possessed great advantages of position; and it is no wonder that every Southerner, from the commander-in-chief down to the youngest drummer boy, understood and appreciated the strength of the ground, and contemplated the coming shock of battle with serene confidence and composure."

It was the ground behind Fredericksburg that was the strongest. This was the zone facing Union General Sumner's command, which was still in the process of settling into the town, with each newcomer finding its scenes a fascination. In the words of Private W. H. Spiller, who belonged to the newly formed 13th New Hampshire Volunteers:

"I took a little stroll around through some of the streets looking for trophies and observing the results of our bombardment of the day before. Our shells had raised sad havoc with most of the buildings. The brick ones—many of them—were in ruins, and the wooden ones were shattered and honeycombed with holes from an inch in diameter to those as large as a hogshead.

"I came to quite a nice-looking dwelling-house surrounded by a lawn filled with shrubbery and trees. Thinking I would like to look the place over, I opened the gate and walked in. As I approached the back of the house, a sight met my eyes that brought me to a standstill. There upon the lawn on its back, stretched stiff and stark, was the body of as handsome a man as I ever saw, dressed in a new Confederate uniform.

"He was an officer. His rank, in my horror at the sight—for this is the first body whose death resulted from violence I had ever seen—I forgot to notice. In life he must have been a noble-looking man. His features were as fine and clean-cut as though chiseled from marble, and as white. He had a long black mustache and goatee, and black curly hair.

"As he lay there, cold and stark in death . . . I could not help wishing that he were alive and well and up on the heights with the rest of the Johnnies. He had been killed the day before by one of our shells, which had taken off the top of the back of his head. I had seen enough, and went back and told the rest of the boys, many of whom wished to see a rebel at short range, either dead or alive.

"During the day quite a number of dead rebels were found in the yards and houses, where they had been killed by our shells or the bullets of our sharpshooters. We spent this day . . . in the streets, doing nothing in particular, but ready to fall in at a moment's warning. . . .

"We ran across an old darky who told us where the rebs had sunk several tons of tobacco close by the river bank to keep it from falling into our hands. We procured poles and drove spikes into the ends of them, then began hunting for the weed. We found it readily. As fast as a box was brought to the surface, plenty of hands were ready to pull it on shore. In less than an hour we had captured enough tobacco for our whole brigade. We all filled our knapsacks and pockets with it, and left lots of it to be kicked about the streets."

Adds a Northern newsman, a representative of the *Cincinnati Commercial*: "The town in the afternoon literally swarmed with troops. The enemy's batteries were ominously silent. If the rebel general had any particular objections to the presence of our troops in the town, why did he not open upon them from his batteries? What was to prevent the enemy from shelling the town, as we had done? I asked several military gentlemen the question, for the situation appeared to me to be one of the deepest peril.

"One said, 'The enemy have not ammunition to spare.' Another: 'Oh, a bombardment don't amount to anything anyhow.' Another: 'They don't care about bombing us. It is an inconsequential sort of business. We threw four thousand shells yesterday, and it amounted to nothing.' Another: 'They're afraid of our siege guns. . . .' Another: 'General Lee thinks he will have a big thing on us about the bombardment of this town. He proposes to rouse the indignation of the civilized world, as they call it. You'll see, he won't throw a shell into it. He is playing for the sympathies of Europe.'

"Another thought the enemy were skedaddling. . . . But I think a private soldier came nearer the mark than anyone else. He said, with the usual expletives, 'They *want* us to get in. Getting out won't be quite so smart and easy. You'll see if it will.'"

The looting of the town had continued. Says General Darius Couch: "I placed a provost guard at the bridges, with orders that nobody should go back with plunder. An enormous pile of booty was collected there by evening. But there came a time when we were too busy to guard it, and I suppose it was finally carried off by another set of plunderers. . . .

"Late on that day we had orders to be ready [to move down the river] . . . which meant that we were to join Franklin. That was the only proper move to make, since we had done just what the enemy wanted us to do—had divided our army. The conditions were favorable for a change of position unknown to the enemy, since the night was dark. . . . But the order to march never came. The orders that were given by Burnside showed that he had no fixed plan of battle. After getting in the face of the enemy, his intentions seemed to be continually changing."

Union staff officer Francis Palfrey adds that "it is a pitiful picture, but is probably a true one, that Burnside passed the evening of the 12th riding about, not quite at his wits' end, but very near it. As far as can be made out, he finally came to the conclusion that he would attempt to do something—he did not quite know what—with his left [under Franklin]; and if he succeeded, to do something with his right [under Sumner]."

On the Confederate side, according to the *London Times* correspondent, the latter part of the day found the troops in an altered mood. "The solemnity of the immediately approaching battle cast its shadows over the scene, and that earnestness . . . of demeanor which, on the eve of momentous events, overtake even the most garrulous and thoughtless, reigned unmistakably upon every countenance.

"At night, as the pickets of the two armies were stationed within a hundred yards of each other, the Confederates could hear the earnest and impassioned speeches of Federal orators rousing the spirit of their troops and making vehement appeals to the sanctity of the 'old flag.'

" 'The old flag is played out!' shouted the Confederates in reply. 'Somehow,' remarked one of the Confederates to me, 'there must be a want of grit among the Yankees, otherwise they wouldn't want all this talking to.' "

In Fredericksburg, the *Cincinnati Commercial* correspondent, seeking impressions with which to round out his story of the day, paid a visit to one of Sumner's division commanders, General William W. Burns. "He occupied the large and recently showy residence of the Mayor. . . . It had been riddled during our bombardment of the place. . . . Every room was perforated by shot and had been shattered by shells. The plastering, pulverized by the shock of the explosions, was thick upon the floors, which, in turn, were ripped as if ploughshares had been driven through them. The mantelpieces were knocked from the walls, the partitions mere rags of lath.

"In the midst of the ruins, the General and his aides enjoyed their coffee, mutton-chops, hard-bread, and their pipes; and wrote letters to their wives, giving them the pleasing intelligence that they were to march upon the enemy in the morning. . . .

"The streets were full of soldiers, lounging and smoking about their fires, or wrapped in their blankets and sleeping, their muskets stacked. . . . The sky was clear, and thickly as the stars sparkled overhead the [Union] campfires blazed along the Rappahannock [on both sides, for many troops, including the army's reserve, under Hooker, remained on the Stafford slopes]. . . . Behind the dark and gloomy hills compassing the town on the enemy's side, there was a wide glare . . . marking the presence of the rebel army of Virginia."

21

The Battle Is Joined

CONFEDERATE GENERAL James Longstreet takes up: "Before daylight on the morning of the eventful 13th I rode to the right of my line, held by Hood's division. [See battle map, page 219.] General Hood was at his post in plain hearing of [Franklin's] Federals south of Deep Run, who were marching their troops into position for the attack. The morning was cold and misty, and everything was obscured from view, but so distinctly did the mist bear to us the sounds of the moving Federals that Hood thought the advance was against him. . . .

"The position of Franklin's men on the 12th, with the configuration of the ground, had left no doubt in my mind as to Franklin's intentions. I explained all this to Hood, assuring him that the attack would be on Jackson. . . . I then returned to Lee's Hill, reaching there soon after sunrise. . . .

"Along the Stafford Heights 147 guns were turned upon us, and on the level plain below, in the town, and hidden on the opposite bank, ready to cross, were assembled nearly 100,000 men [the number was actually about 115,000]. . . . The valley, the mountaintops, everything was enveloped in the thickest fog, and the preparations for the fight were made as if under cover of night. The mist brought to us the sounds of the preparation for battle, but we were blind to the movements of the Federals."

Longstreet was in the company of General Lee at this time, and the two were about to be joined by another high commander. In the words of James Power Smith, of Stonewall Jackson's staff:

"I rode with Jackson to Lee's position on top of the hill . . . and

Union gun used at Fredericksburg.

well remember the grand old chief, his serious, dignified demeanor, his cheerful greeting of Jackson; then of their studying together what little they could see through the fog lying over the town, and Lee's confident words at parting. General Lee [afterward] . . . told . . . how from that hill he looked anxiously to see whether there was yet standing back of the Chatham House [Lacy's] the chestnut tree, under which long years before he had addressed the young woman who became his wife.

"As Jackson rode back along the lines, the enthusiasm of the troops was simply boundless. It was impossible to restrain the cheers, which rolled like waves up and down the ranks and broke out again and again, revealing to the enemy the exact positions of our lines. . . .

"He wore the new and handsome coat, the present of General J. E. B. Stuart, and a new cap . . . with a wide braid of gilt about it. . . . He had a new officer's saber and spurs, sent him by Colonel [E. V.] White of the cavalry.

"Altogether he looked so very spick-and-span that the boys could scarcely believe their eyes, so unlike was he to the battered, sun-burnt 'Old Jack' of the Valley. But the sorrel horse he rode, and the same following of staff and couriers reassured the troops, and they were more than ever delighted with him. The unwonted splendor of their great general was greeted as a good omen on the morn of battle."

This feeling was not universal. Here and there a grumble was heard, with one man saying, "Old Jack will be afraid of spoiling his clothes and will not get down to work."

Returning to James Longstreet:

"Suddenly, at 10 o'clock, as if the elements were taking a hand in the drama about to be enacted, the warmth of the sun brushed the mist away and revealed the mighty panorama in the valley below.

"Franklin's forty thousand men, reinforced by two divisions of Hooker's grand division [detached from that body, which remained in reserve on the Stafford bank], were in front of Jackson's thirty thousand. The flags of the Federals fluttered gayly, the polished arms shone brightly in the sunlight, and the beautiful uniforms of the buoyant troops gave to the scene the air of a holiday occasion rather than the spectacle of a great army about to be thrown into the tumult of battle.

"From my place on Lee's Hill I could see almost every soldier Franklin had, and a splendid array it was. But off in the distance was Jackson's ragged infantry, and beyond was Stuart's battered cavalry, with their soiled hats and yellow butternut suits, a striking contrast to the handsomely equipped troops of the Federals.

"About the city, here and there, a few soldiers could be seen, but there was no indication of the heavy masses that were concealed by the houses. Those of Franklin's men who were in front of Jackson stretched well up toward [the open land in front of] Lee's Hill and were almost within reach of our best guns; and at the other end they stretched out to the east until they came well [within range] of Stuart's horse artillery under Major John Pelham."

As explained by Northerner William Swinton: "The nature of the ground manifestly indicated that the main attack should be made by Franklin on the [Union] left; for the field there affords ample space for deployment out of hostile range, whereas the plain in the rear of Fredericksburg, restricted in extent and cut up by ditches, fences, and a canal, caused every movement to be made under fire, presented no opportunity for maneuver, and compelled a direct attack on the terraced heights, whose frowning works looked down in grim irony on all attempt at assault.

"In the framing of his plan of battle, General Burnside conformed to the obvious conditions of the problem before him, and caused it to be understood that Franklin . . . should make the main

Federal skirmishers out in front.

attack from the left, and that upon his success should be conditioned the assault of the heights in rear of the town by Sumner. Such, at least, was the plan of action as understood by his lieutenants who were to carry it into execution.

"When, however, on the morning of the 13th, the commanders of the two bodies on the left and right, Generals Franklin and Sumner, received their instructions, it was found that, having framed one plan of battle General Burnside had determined to fight on another. I must add that the dispositions were such that it would be difficult to imagine any worse suited to the circumstances.

"Franklin, in place of an effective attack, was directed to make a partial operation of the nature of a reconnoissance in force, sending 'one division, at least, to seize, if possible, the heights near Hamilton's Crossing, and taking care to keep it well supported and its line of retreat open,' while he was to hold the rest of his command 'in position for a rapid movement down the old Richmond road [in order to swing around Jackson's right flank, if the opportunity developed].'

"General Sumner's instructions were of a like tenor: he was to 'form a column of a division ... for the purpose of seizing the heights in rear of the town,' and 'hold another division in readiness to support ... this movement.'

"General Burnside's plan thus contemplated two isolated attacks by fractional forces, each of one, or at the most two divisions, one on the right and the other on the left. Such partial attacks seldom succeed, and, directed against such a citadel of strength as the Confederate position at Fredericksburg, such feeble sallies were simply ludicrous. Not a man in the ranks but felt the hopelessness of the undertaking."

Says Regis de Trobriand, the brigade commander from New York: "I thought involuntarily of the gladiators of old, entering into the amphitheatre. *Ave, Caesar! Morituri te salutant!* If we had had there our Caesar, we also would have been able to exclaim, 'Those about to die salute thee!'"

To make the attack on the left, Franklin had chosen George Meade's division, with the divisions of John Gibbon and Abner Doubleday in support. The attack was opened with an artillery barrage.

How it felt to be on the receiving end of this fire is told by Heros von Borcke. The major had just seated himself on a box amid a deposit of Confederate supplies in a woods near Hamilton's Crossing.

"Suddenly it seemed as though a tremendous hurricane had burst upon us, and we became sensible upon the instant of a howling tempest of shot and shell hurled against our position . . . with a roar more deafening than the loudest thunder. Hundreds of missiles of every size and description crashed through the woods, breaking down trees and scattering branches and splinters in all directions.

"I was just calling out to the orderly who held my horse and had been walking the animal up and down at the distance of a hundred yards, to return to me at once, when, about thirty paces from me, a young officer of artillery, struck by the fragment of a shell, fell with a groan to the earth. I immediately rushed to his assistance, but reached him only to receive his parting breath as I lifted him from the spot. The incident, sad as it was, saved my own life, for, a few

A Union battery in action.

seconds after I had left my seat, a huge shell, falling into [the] pile of boxes and bursting there, shattered them to atoms, filling the air with the debris of wood, leather, and clothing. . . .

"We galloped to our post with the cavalry, which as yet had suffered not at all from the heavy fire of the enemy, this being concentrated chiefly upon our main line. [The cavalry, as shown on battle map on page 219, occupied its own spot adjacent to the main line's right flank.]

". . . I was [shortly] sent by Stuart to General Jackson with the message that the Yankees were about commencing their advance. I found Old Stonewall standing at ease upon his hill, unmoved in the midst of the terrible fire, narrowly observing the movements of the enemy through his field-glass. The atmosphere was now perfectly clear, and from this eminence was afforded a distinct view of more than two-thirds of the battlefield and the larger part of the whole number of the advancing foe, extending as far as the eye could reach—a military panorama the grandeur of which I had never seen equalled. . . .

"I could not rid myself of a feeling of depression and anxiety as I saw this innumerable host steadily moving upon our lines, which were hidden by the woods, where our artillery maintained as yet a perfect silence. . . .

"Upon my mentioning this feeling to Jackson, the old chief assured me in his characteristic way: 'Major, my men have sometimes failed *to take* a position, but *to defend* one, never! [Not quite true; they had been driven from the field at Kernstown during his famous Valley Campaign the previous spring.] I am glad the Yankees are coming!'

"He then gave me orders for Stuart to employ his horse artillery, and open fire at once on the enemy's flank.

"Pelham was accordingly directed to prepare for action, but, being exceedingly anxious to go to work without a moment's delay, he begged Stuart to allow him to advance two of his light pieces to the fork of the road where the Turnpike branches off to Fredericksburg, as from this point the masses of the enemy offered him an easy target. The permission being given, Pelham went off with his two guns at a gallop, amidst the loud cheering of the cannoneers; and in a few minutes his solid shot were ploughing at short range with fearful effect through the dense columns of the Federals.

"The boldness of the enterprise and the fatal accuracy of the firing seemed to paralyze for a time and then to stampede the whole of the extreme left of the Yankee army, and terror and confusion reigned there during some minutes. Soon, however, several batteries moved into position, and, uniting with several of those on the Stafford Heights, concentrated a tremendous fire upon our guns, one of which, a Blakely gun, was quickly disabled and compelled to withdraw.

"I was now sent by General Stuart to tell Pelham to retire if he thought the proper moment had arrived, but the young hero could not be moved. 'Tell the General I can hold my ground,' he said; and again and again pealed out the ringing report of his single gun, upon which at one time 32 pieces [officially recorded as "four batteries"] of the enemy's artillery were brought to bear in a sweeping crossfire, which killed and wounded many of his men, so that at last Pelham had to assist himself in loading and aiming it.

"Three times the summons to retire was renewed; but not until [nearly] the last round of ammunition had been discharged . . . did the gallant officer succumb to necessity in abandoning his position.

"The rest of our horse artillery had in the meantime joined in the cannonade, and the thunder soon rolled all along our lines, while from the continuous roar the ear caught distinctly the sharp, rapid, rattling volleys of the musketry, especially in the immediate front of General A. P. Hill, where the infantry were very hotly engaged. The battle was now fully developed, and the mists of the morning were presently succeeded by a dense cloud of powder smoke. . . . At intervals, above the tumult of the conflict, we could hear the wild hurrah of the attacking hosts of the Federals and the defiant yell of the Confederates. . . .

"Directly in our own front the cavalry sharpshooters had become occupied with long lines of hostile tirailleurs, and a vivid fusillade raged all along the Port Royal road. . . . The firing grew most animated near a number of stacks of straw, which a body of Federal infantry had taken possession of, and which offered them so efficient a shelter that all attempts to dislodge them had proved in vain.

"I had just been ordering our men not to waste their ammunition, and to fire only when they saw the person of a Yankee completely exposed, when close at hand I heard the dull thud of a bullet striking home, and turning round saw one of our soldiers . . . throw up his arms and fall heavily to the ground. Dismounting at once, I hastened to his side, but, finding that the ball had struck him right in the middle of the forehead, I regarded him as a corpse, and deemed all further assistance wholly unnecessary.

"Not many minutes had elapsed, however, before the apparently dead man began to move; and when the surgeon, who had already arrived, poured some brandy down his throat, to our infinite amazement he opened his eyes. . . . According to the surgeon's statement, the ball [had done little real harm], striking obliquely . . . [and] passing between the cuticle and skull all around the head, emerging at last from the very place it had first entered!"

The Federals that Von Borcke and his comrades were fighting were those of Abner Doubleday's division, which had advanced on Meade's left flank. Meade, supported by Gibbon, had engaged A. P. Hill.

In Meade's words: "The attack was for a time perfectly successful. The enemy was driven from the railroad, his rifle-pits, and breastworks, for over half a mile. Over three hundred prisoners were taken, and several standards."

The advance, however, had left many dead and wounded Federals in its wake. Streams of walking wounded extended to the rear, the men making their way either to the bridges across the river or to the hospital established at Mansfield, the Bernard estate.

An observer at Mansfield at this time was newsman Coffin, who relates:

"The cavalry under General [George D.] Bayard was drawn up in rear of the grove surrounding the fine old Bernard mansion. General Bayard was sitting at the foot of a tree, waiting for orders and watching the advancing columns of Meade and Gibbon. There was a group of officers around General Franklin [who was using the mansion-hospital as his headquarters]. . . . All of Franklin's guns were in play. The earth shook with the deep concussion.

"Suddenly the rebel batteries opened with redoubled fury. A shot went over my head, a second fell in front of my horse and ploughed a furrow in the ground; a third exploded at my right, a fourth went singing along the line of a regiment lying prostrate on the earth. . . .

"Meade was driving up the hill. Wounded men were creeping, crawling, and hobbling towards the hospital. Some, slightly wounded, were uttering fearful groans, while others, made of sterner stuff, though torn and mangled bore their pains without a murmur.

"A soldier, with his arms around the necks of two of his comrades, was being brought in. 'O, dear! O, Lord! My foot is torn all to pieces!' he cried.

"There was a hole in the toe of his boot where the ball had entered.

" 'It has gone clear through to the heel and smashed all the bones. O, dear! O, dear! I shall have to have it cut off!' he cried, moaning piteously as his comrades laid him upon the ground to rest.

"[I said,] 'Better cut off your boot before your foot swells.'

" 'Yes, do so.'

"I slipped my knife through the leather and took the boot from his foot. The ball had passed through his stocking. There was but a drop or two of blood visible. I cut off the stocking, and the bullet was lying between his toes, having barely broken the skin.

" 'I reckon I shan't help lug you any farther,' said one of the men who had borne him.

" 'Wal, if I had known that it wasn't any worse than that, I wouldn't have had my boot cut off,' said the soldier.

"Returning to the Bernard mansion, I saw a commotion among the cavalry, and learned that their commander was mortally wounded."

According to another witness, General William F. Smith: "Bayard, much endeared to us by his social qualities and his rare merits as a cavalry leader . . . [took] a round shot through the thigh. Bayard and his friend, Captain H. G. Gibson . . . were within ten feet of Franklin, and were just rising from the ground to go to luncheon when the shot came. It severed Gibson's sword belt without injury to him, and struck Bayard. Many generals could have better been spared from the service."

The mansion area continued to be a dangerous spot. As recounted by Chaplain Lung:

"Fragments flew into the door. A poor soldier had just reached the steps from the field with a wound in his arm, when a shell, dashing at his feet, most shockingly mangled his right leg. This lad, twenty minutes before, stood in the ranks full of bravery and life. Now, with broken arm and gory leg, he sits sighing and weeping with pain. A little while afterward, and we find this young warrior lying in the chamber upon a bunch of straw with only one leg and one arm. . . .

"The wounded came rapidly in from the field. . . . We stored these unfortunate creatures away as best we could. They lay scattered here and there all over the yard, in the corn-house, smoke-house, and slave shanties. In the hospital, we filled the rooms below and above, and many were carried into the cellar. . . .

"In every possible conceivable way men were wounded. I saw one man with gun in hand, walking with a firm step and a cheerful countenance, having been struck by a piece of shell in the forehead, laying bare the brain so I could see every pulsation.

"It is really surprising how soon one becomes accustomed to these scenes of suffering, so that broken bones and mangled limbs can be attended to with untrembling nerve."

Among the observers of the wounded who were crossing to Stafford Heights by way of the bridge above Mansfield was Captain Henry Blake of the 11th Massachusetts, who relates:

"Great vigilance was necessary to detect those that feigned sickness or wounds by tying a bandage stained with blood around their arms or heads, and prevent them from escaping across the river.

"An officer, assisted by two able-bodied men, slowly moved towards the bridge, until the colonel [on guard] halted them and directed the soldiers, in terms of the deepest kindness, to rejoin their company, and assured them that their commander should receive the best treatment.

" 'My good man, what is the matter with you?' he blandly asked the lieutenant, who had requested that those who bore him from the field might be allowed to remain and assist him.

" 'I am wounded,' he replied in a weak voice; and an expression of the most acute pain was visible in his face.

" 'Doctor, will you dress his wound? He is just in from the front.'

" 'I didn't say I was wounded. I am sick, and want to go over the river to be treated by my own doctor,' he said when he saw the surgeon approach.

" 'You can go as soon as you have been examined and reported unwell.'

" 'I will go anyway!' the officer exclaimed, and tried to rush by the guards, who arrested him.

"The colonel changed his soft words into hard oaths, struck him, and ordered the men to use the bayonet if he resisted them. And the skulker ran towards the front without showing any loss of physical strength.

"Many scenes like this occurred."

As for General Meade's work against Jackson's position, the outcome is succinctly told by Meade himself:

"The advancing line encountered the heavy reinforcements of the enemy, who, recovering from the effects of the assault and perceiving both our flanks unprotected, poured in such a destructive fire from all three directions as to compel the line to fall back. . . .

"With one brigade commander killed, another wounded, nearly

half their number *hors de combat*, with regiments separated from brigades, and companies from regiments, and all the confusion and disorder incidental to the advance of an extended line through wood and other obstructions, assailed by a heavy fire, not only of infantry but of artillery—not only in front but on both flanks—the best troops would be justified in withdrawing without loss of honor."

The *London Times* correspondent was watching from Lee's Hill. "The Confederates drove them . . . across the plain, and only desisted from their work when they came under the fire of [a fresh division and] the Federal batteries across the river."

With the Confederate group on the hill (the central figure of which was Lee himself) was the army's artillery chief, General William N. Pendleton, who discloses: "While the younger spectators near us gave expression to their feelings by shouts, clapping of hands, etc., the gratified yet considerate and amiable commander turned to myself, and with beaming countenance said, 'It is well war is so terrible, or we should get too fond of it.' "

Even as Lee spoke, something was happening that was illustrative of war at its worst. As explained by Union Colonel Regis de Trobriand, whose brigade helped to stop Jackson's pursuit:

"The cannonade had set the high grass on fire at several points, and the flame, quickened by light currents of air, extended rapidly

Lee at Fredericksburg

on all sides. Despairing cries were heard. They were the unfortunate wounded left lying on the ground and caught by the flames. Through the smoke they were seen exerting themselves in vain efforts to flee, half rising up, falling back overcome by pain, rolling on their broken limbs, grasping around them at the grass red with their blood, and at times perishing in the embrace of the flames. They were between the lines . . . and no one could help them."

Returning to Lee's Hill and the representative of the *London Times*:

"Meanwhile the battle which had dashed furiously against the lines of . . . A. P. Hill . . . was little more than child's play as compared with the onslaught directed by the Federals in the immediate neighborhood of Fredericksburg."

The newsman had begun to believe he was witnessing "a memorable day to the historian of the Decline and Fall of the American Republic."

22

Carnage at the Stone Wall

THE UNION divisions elected to make the assault on Lee's left, held by Longstreet, were two of those belonging to Darius Couch's corps of Sumner's wing. William French's division was to take the lead, with Winfield Hancock's division in support. Sumner himself remained on the Stafford shore, while Couch had established a command post in the town.

The series of heights—Marye's Hill and its adjuncts—that held the trenches and gun positions of Longstreet's main line were a formidable barrier; but it was the long stone wall at the foot of the heights that would be the Federal attack's undoing. "Behind this stone wall," says Longstreet, "I had placed about twenty-five hundred men, being all of General T. R. R. Cobb's brigade and a portion of the brigade of General Kershaw [actually, that of General Robert Ransom].... It must now be understood that the Federals, to reach what appeared to be my weakest point [on the heights], would have to pass directly over this wall held by Cobb's infantry...

"A little before noon I sent orders to all my batteries to open fire through the streets or at any points where the troops were seen about the city, as a diversion in favor of Jackson [who was at this time off balance in the face of Meade's attack]. This fire began at once to develop the work in hand for myself [or at least gave the appearance of precipitating a response]. The Federal troops swarmed out of the city like bees out of a hive."

Loud cries of "Hi! Hi!" carried to the heights as the attackers, after slowing to cross a bridged ditch, began deploying behind a ridge that gave them partial concealment.

"At last," relates Confederate artilleryman William Miller Owen, "the Federal line is formed, and appears above the ridge and advances. What a magnificent sight it is! We have never witnessed such a battle array before—long lines following one another, of brigade front. It seemed like some huge blue serpent about to encompass and crush us in its folds, their musket barrels gleaming brightly in the sunlight, their gay colors fluttering in the breeze. The lines advance at the double-quick, and the alignments are beautifully kept. The board fences enclosing the gardens [of the town's outlying cottages] fall like walls of mere paper.

"Then [on our side] the loud, full voice of Colonel [J. B.] Walton rings out, ' 'tention! Commence fi-ir-ng!' And instantly the edge of Marye's Hill is fringed with flame. The dreadful work of the Washington Artillery has begun. The boys soon warm up to their work, and aim and fire coolly and deliberately. Nearer and nearer the enemy's line advances, and now they are within range of canister, and we give it to them.

"Now they are near enough to the infantry in the sunken road [behind the stone wall], the Georgians and the North Carolinians . . . [who] are unseen by the enemy, for the smoke is beginning to cover the field.

"All at once the gray line below us rises. One moment to glance along the trusty rifle barrels, and volley after volley is poured into the enemy's ranks. Great gaps appear. We give them canister again and again. A few leave the ranks. More follow. The lines halt for an instant; and, turning, are seen running in great disorder towards the town. . . . The field before us is dotted with patches of blue . . . the dead and wounded of the Federal infantry.

"It was the division of French that had charged the hill and was shattered. . . . [Here the narrator begins to include information he learned through postwar studies.]

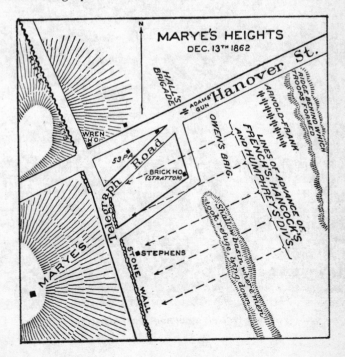

"Hancock's division now advances in splendid style, and, being joined by remnants of French's command, pushes on valiantly to and beyond the point French had reached; and then, in little more than fifteen minutes, like our first assailants, are forced back. Of the five thousand men Hancock led into action, two thousand fell in the charge.

"With Hancock came . . . the Irish brigade of [Thomas F.] Meagher, bearing aloft the green flag with the golden harp of Ireland. The brave fellows came within five-and-twenty paces of the stone wall and encountered such a fire of shot, shell, canister, and musketry as no command was ever known to live through. The result was that two-thirds [actually, about one-half] of this splendid and gallant brigade was . . . killed and wounded."

One of Hancock's wounded was Colonel Edward E. Cross, a regimental commander from New Hampshire, who describes his experience:

"As we were advancing to those fatal heights in line of battle, I was near my colors. A twelve-pounder shell from the Washington Artil-

Lines of Federals assaulting Marye's Heights.

lery burst right in front of me. One fragment struck me just below the heart, making a bad wound. Another blew off my hat. Another small bit entered my mouth and broke out three of my best jaw-teeth, while the gravel, bits of frozen earth, and minute fragments of shell covered my face with bruises.

"I fell insensible, and lay so for some time, when another fragment of shell, striking me on the left leg below the knee, brought me to my senses. My mouth was full of blood, fragments of teeth, and gravel; my breast-bone [was] almost broken in; and I lay in mud two inches deep. My brave boys had gone along. I always told them never to stop for me.

"Dead and wounded lay thick around. One captain of French's division was gasping in death within a foot of my head, his bowels all torn out. The air was full of hissing bullets and bursting shells. Getting on my knees, I looked for my flag. Thank God, there it fluttered right amid the smoke and fire of the front line. I could hear the cheers of my brave men. Twice the colors dropped, but were up in an instant. I tried to crawl along, but a shot came and struck the steel scabbard of my saber, splitting it open and knocking me down flat.

"Dizzy and faint, I had sense enough to lay myself out decently. . . . Two [advancing] lines passed over me, but soon they swayed back, trampling on the dead and dying. Halting about thirty yards in the rear, one line laid down and commenced firing. Imagine the situation; right between two fires of bullets and shell—for our own artillery fire from over the river was mostly too short, and did great damage to our own troops. . . .

"As the [rifle] balls from our line hissed over me within a foot of my head, I covered my face with both hands . . . expecting every moment my brains would spatter the ground. But they didn't. The guardian angels—if there be such personages—or my destiny saved me."

(The colonel's destiny saved him for death at Gettysburg the following year.)

Union commander Darius Couch, then in Fredericksburg, takes up the narrative: "Without a clear idea of the state of affairs at the front, since the smoke and light fog veiled everything . . . I climbed the steeple of the court house and, from above the haze and smoke, got a clear view of the field. Howard [the one-armed general], who was with me, says I exclaimed, 'Oh, Great God! See how our men, our poor fellows, are falling!'

". . . The whole plain was covered with men, prostrate and drop-ping, the live men running here and there, and in front closing upon each other, and the wounded coming back. The commands seemed to be mixed up. I had never before seen fighting like that, nothing approaching it in terrible uproar and destruction.

"There was . . . on the part of the men . . . a stubborn determina-tion to obey orders and do their duty. I don't think there was much feeling of success. As they charged, the artillery fire would break their formation and they would get mixed. Then they would close up, go forward, receive the withering infantry fire, and those who were able would run to the [few] houses and fight as best they could; and then the next brigade coming up in succession would do its duty and melt like snow coming down on warm ground.

"I was in the steeple hardly ten seconds . . . [before] I . . . was convinced that we could not be successful in front, and that our only chance lay by the right. I immediately ordered Howard to work in on the right . . . and attack the enemy behind the stone wall in flank."

Howard's attack developed with one of his brigades, that of Colo-nel Joshua T. Owen, going against the stone wall itself, while an-other brigade, that of Colonel Norman Hall, swung to the right and moved upon a series of rifle pits adjoining the wall.

Hall's effort, the northernmost part of the Union front, is thus described by Confederate observer D. Augustus Dickert:

"Howard attempted . . . to turn Cobb's left. . . . He was met by some of [General John R.] Cooke's North Carolinians, and there, around the sacred tomb of Mary Washington [this tomb of Washing-ton's mother lay a half-mile to the north] was . . . [an] encounter between some New York and Massachusetts troops and those from the Pine Tree State.

"Sons of the same ancestry, sons of sires who fought with the Father of His Country in the struggle for the nation's independence, now fighting above [or at least "near"] the grave of the mother for its dissolution!"

Howard, of course, failed with this attack, and with his leftward effort as well.

"At each attack," explains James Longstreet, "the slaughter was so great that by the time the third attack was repulsed the ground was so thickly strewn with dead that the bodies seriously impeded the approach of the Federals.

"General Lee, who was with me on Lee's Hill, became uneasy

Confederates at the stone wall

when he saw the attacks so promptly renewed and pushed forward with such persistence.... After the third charge, he said to me, 'General, they are massing very heavily and will break your line, I am afraid.'

" 'General,' I replied, 'if you put every man now on the other side of the Potomac on that field to approach me over the same line, and give me plenty of ammunition, I will kill them all before they reach my line. Look to your right; you are in some danger there, but not on my line.' "

(Lee's right might well have been in danger if Union General Franklin had persisted in his attack with all of the power at his disposal.)

James Longstreet continues:

"I think the fourth time the Federals charged, a gallant fellow came within one hundred feet of Cobb's position before he fell. Close behind him came some few scattering ones, but they were either killed or they fled from certain death. This charge was the only effort that looked like actual danger to Cobb, and after it was repulsed I felt no apprehension, assuring myself that there were enough of the dead Federals on the field to give me half the battle.

"The anxiety shown by General Lee, however, induced me to bring up two or three brigades, to be on hand; and General Kershaw, with . . . his brigade, was ordered down to the stone wall. . . . Kershaw dashed down the declivity and arrived just in time to succeed Cobb, who, at this juncture, fell from a wound in the thigh and died in a few minutes from loss of blood."

Adds Cobb's immediate superior, Lafayette McLaws: "He and I were on intimate terms, and I had learned to esteem him warmly, as I believe everyone did who came to know his great intellect and his good heart. Like Stonewall Jackson, he was a religious enthusiast, and, being firmly convinced that the South was right, believed that God would give us visible sign that Providence was with us, and daily prayed for His interposition in our behalf."

When Cobb received his wound, according to a Confederate officer named W. Roy Mason, he was "at the foot of the stone wall

House by the stone wall where General Cobb died.

just at the door of Mrs. Martha Stevens. This woman . . . attended the wounded and the dying fearless of consequences, and refused to leave her house, although, standing just between the advancing line of the enemy and the stone wall, the position was one of danger [something of an understatement!]. It is said that after using all the materials for bandages at her command, she tore from her person most of her garments, even on that . . . [winter] day, in her anxiety to administer to necessities greater than her own."

By the time of Cobb's fall, additional Federal brigades were entering the fight, while the regiments of other brigades waited in reserve spots about the town, ready to go when called. Commanding the 13th New Hampshire, in reserve near the river, was Colonel Aaron F. Stevens, who became restless with the waiting.

"I rode up Caroline Street to the center of the city toward the point where our brave legions were struggling against the terrible combination of the enemy's artillery and infantry, whose unremitting fire shook the earth and filled the plain in rear of the city with the deadly missiles of war. I saw the struggling hosts of freedom stretched along the plain, their ranks ploughed by the merciless fire of the foe. I saw the . . . wounded . . . borne back on the shoulders of their comrades in battle and laid tenderly down in the hospitals prepared for their reception, in the houses on either side of the street as far as human habitations extended. I listened to the roar of battle and the groans of the wounded and dying. I saw in the crowded hospitals the desolation of war."

The narrator was presently ordered to move his regiment up from the river, and the men settled down for their next wait near a row of the hospital-houses. This was the regiment to which Private W. H. Spiller belonged, and he explains:

"Arms, legs, feet, and hands were being amputated; and every little while an arm or leg would be dropped from a window to the ground. . . . And before we moved from there, there were three or four piles of different members of the human body as large as bushel baskets. And all of this within fifty feet of where we were sitting or lying around on the grass."

It was now about two o'clock in the afternoon, and Union General Ambrose Burnside, who had been following the progress of the battle by means of reports sent to his headquarters at the Phillips house on the Falmouth side of the Rappahannock, had grown acutely anxious. Calling for his horse, the general rode to the river bank, where he was seen by Union newsman William Swinton.

"He walked restlessly up and down, and, gazing over at the

heights across the river, exclaimed vehemently, 'That crest must be carried tonight!'

"Already, however, everything had been thrown in except Hooker, and he was now ordered over the river.... Hooker went forward, reconnoitered the ground, consulted with those who had preceded him in action, saw that the case was hopeless, and went [back over the river] to beg Burnside to cease the attack. But Burnside insisted."

Hooker was away from the front for over an hour, during which time the fighting continued. On the Confederate side, the Washington Artillery persisted in its vital role. Again in the words of William Miller Owen:

"We are fighting under the very eyes of Lee and Longstreet. 'Now, boys, do your level best!' A solid rifle cannonball tears its way through the redoubt, scattering dirt and dust in our faces. Kursheedt picks it up and says laughingly, 'Boys, let's send this back to them again.' An instant later it is in the gun and dispatched on its mission back to the enemy.

"Corporal Ruggles, who, with sleeves rolled up, has been ramming his gun, suddenly throws up his hands and falls backwards with a ball in his spine. Perry seizes the sponge-staff as it falls from

Washington Artillery on Marye's Hill

Ruggles's hands, and takes his place. The sharp ring of a bullet, striking the face of the piece, is heard, and Perry's arm, having been shot through, drops helpless at his side. He has been severely wounded. Rodd is 'holding vent.' His elbow-joint is shot away. Everett steps into his place. A bullet strikes him and he falls. . . . Falconer passes in rear of the guns, and is struck by a bullet behind the ear, and falls a corpse. These casualties occurred in rapid succession from the accurate fire of the enemy's sharpshooters.

"We are now so short of men necessary to work Squires's guns that infantry soldiers are called in to help. The ground, which had been frozen hard, is now converted into mud and slush; and all hands, officers and men, have to put their shoulders to the wheels to run the guns up to the embrasures.

"There is a little brick house alongside of Squires's guns, and in it our wounded have taken shelter. A cannon shot comes crashing through the work, and, striking the edge of the wall, knocks brick and mortar right and left. Old Mr. Florence [a civilian on a visit to the army from Richmond] had been looking around the corner where the shot struck only a moment before, to see how his son was getting on at the gun. We think the old gentleman has gotten his quietus, but out comes his gray head again, as lively as ever.

"Major [Osman] Latrobe rides up to us, sent by Longstreet, to see how we are doing. We tell him, 'All right, except we are running short of ammunition,' and that we have not been able yet to get any sent to us, and asked to be supplied; but how can it be done under such a fire and the ammunition train so far away? He promises to see about it, and . . . he gallops away. . . .

"At this time Captain Squires is struck full in the chest by a spent ball, and reels and falls into my arms. Thinking he is dreadfully hurt, he says, 'Send for Galbraith to take command; I'm wounded.' But he is soon reassured, and gazes complacently at the leaden bullet-mark upon his gray overcoat.

"Kursheedt and Rossiter are at this moment badly wounded. Eshleman now comes over from the right, and reports his battery almost out of ammunition, only a few solid shot left. The other batteries are in the same condition. Nothing to do but to send to Colonel Alexander [whose artillery battalion was a mile behind the lines in reserve] for his limbers containing the ammunition we need to be sent to us. I scribbled a note to him, and Frank, the bugler, is dispatched with it.

"The enemy keeps up a brisk fire from his advanced lines . . .

aiming at our embrasures. Gunner Payne dislodged some sharpshooters from a frame house, with solid shot. The enemy's batteries
have been firing at us from positions they have taken upon the
plain; but we pay no attention to them, as they do us no harm,
reserving our fire always for the masses of infantry."

By this time, on the Union side, General Hooker had returned
from his meeting with Burnside, and he sought out Darius Couch at
the edge of town facing the front. The action was lulling. Couch
ventured to advise Hooker, who was his superior in rank, to try a
wide move around Lee's left. What followed is told by Second Corps
staff officer Francis Walker, who was present:

"To this suggestion, Hooker, in terribly bad temper, as was not
unnatural, replied contemptuously and insolently. Stung by the
insult, broken-hearted at the defeat of his corps and the massacre of
his gallant soldiers, and perhaps shrinking from the spectacle of a
fresh slaughter, Couch turned abruptly away and dashed up the
road [toward the right flank of his front].

"Passing [Captain John G.] Hazard's battery . . . he rode slowly up
to . . . [a] gun which was still being served in the road, and exchanged a few words with [its] officer. Then, putting spurs to his
horse, he proceeded to the point where [Colonel John R.] Brooke,
with his companions [of the 53d Pennsylvania], partially sheltered
behind [a] group of buildings . . . held the extreme advance.

"Sitting here, on horseback, at easy pistol-range from the enemy's
lines, Couch surveyed the field from right to left, conversed a moment with Brooke, who begged and prayed him to retire; and then,
turning to the left, rode *down the line of his corps.* [He was accompanied by an orderly and two of his staff, including the narrator.]

"A strange review it is, surely! There, prone on the ground—the
living mingled with the dead—are three or four thousand men, the
remains of twenty regiments. The line zigzags as the fortunes of
the several charges have left it, at some points fifty, at others one
hundred or two hundred yards from the stone wall. Except for those
who cluster for shelter at the rear of the few huts or houses on the
line [at least one or two of which were still occupied by their civilian
owners], not a man is erect.

"With rifle or sword tightly clutched, the private and the colonel
alike lie hugging the ground, while now and then strange shelter is
found. Here is a horse of the staff which has fallen near the point of
the farthest advance; it lies with its back to the enemy, and between
its legs is a very nest of men who press their heads against its belly.

Here two or three stones have been dragged together to make a pile somewhat bigger than a hat. There a lifeless body serves as a partial cover for the living."

When he was a distance across his front, Couch came to a brick house. The general himself says that he found the place "packed with men; and behind it the dead and the living were as thick as they could be crowded together. . . . I tried to shelter myself behind the brick house, but found I could not, on account of the men already there."

Returning to Francis Walker:

"The firing has almost ceased. Enough of our [able] men are sheltered behind the brick house, the huts, and [a] blacksmith's shop to make it hot for anyone who raises his head above the wall. The Confederates have been gorged with slaughter, or are awaiting the appearance of fresh columns of assault. . . . The batteries still pound each other, and the shells fly thickly over the plain.

"It is down such a line that Couch, with his three companions, rides, that winter afternoon, in his strange review."

Hooker's attack, the chief component of which was Andrew Humphreys' division, was soon under way. Humphreys himself led his men toward the stone wall.

On the Confederate side, the key artillery position on Marye's Hill had been provided with fresh guns. When William Miller Owen's appeal for ammunition was received by E. Porter Alexander in the rear, the colonel decided to fulfill the request by sending up replacement guns instead.

It will be recalled that one of Alexander's men was Private Augustus Forbes, the "Hero of Manassas." While Alexander, at his headquarters, was making his decision to enter the fight, Forbes and his comrades happened to be sitting around amid their guns, eating a freshly cooked batch of dried beans.

"So far," says W. C. Elam (the same narrator who gave us the first part of the boastful private's story), "Forbes had shown us no feats of daring, and had kept carefully under shelter, as far as possible, as we all had done. While we were still absorbing the beans, Lieutenant Mitchell came up and informed us that our battery, with others, was ordered into the trenches on Marye's Hill to relieve the Washington Artillery . . . and that we must get ready immediately.

" 'Oh, these horrid beans!' suddenly exclaimed Forbes, 'They have given me a dreadful colic. . . . I fear I shall be obliged to look up a doctor. . . .'

" 'Pshaw!' said the officer. 'There is nothing like gunpowder for colic, and we can't risk losing the battle by leaving you behind. Mount the limber chest, sir. And, Sergeant Brown, see that he doesn't stay back.'

"Forbes had to mount the chest, with Sergeant Brown on one side of him and Corporal Faxter on the other. 'I'm in dreadful pain!' he moaned. But he couldn't get away. And there he had to sit until we had galloped a mile or more amidst shrieking shells and singing rifle balls, to a deep ravine behind Marye's Hill. Here we were under shelter for a while, waiting for the trenches at the front to be cleared for our reception. We had all dismounted, and many were lying down. Forbes was groveling, face downward, in feigned spasms of colic.

"We had to make the rest of the run on foot, beside our guns and horses, across the plateau that crowned the hill. And it was indeed a frightful scene to traverse—every inch of ground continually struck, apparently, by bullets or fragments of shells. The hurly-burly, too, was terrific. It looked like certain death, or ghastly wounds at least, to venture on that storm-swept plain.

"Nevertheless, at the order to move, the guns were carried at a gallop, and we did our level best to keep up—all except the hero, Forbes. 'I won't go!' he yelled. 'I can't! I know I will be killed!'

" 'Fetch the infernal coward along, Sergeant Brown!' shouted Lieutenant Mitchell.

"Brown and Faxter seized the demoralized wretch, and dragged him up from the ravine to the level.

" 'Now, go on, you dog!' cried Brown, giving him the kick of a battering ram. And go Forbes did, on all fours, howling every jump, the sergeant following him closely and giving him a swinging kick for every howl.

"Brown's well-directed kicks carried Forbes to the trench to which his gun was assigned, and he tumbled in, lying flat on the earth, and still bellowing. He could be heard even above the din of artillery.

"The rest of us unlimbered the guns and took off the chests. But before we could place them in position, two men at Forbes's gun were hit pretty severely, and word was dispatched at once for help from the ambulance corps.

"We who were able were speedily working our guns with all our souls and bodies. The wounded men sat still and quiet, patiently awaiting succor. Augustus Forbes writhed in the dirt, as if suffering excruciating agonies, and his shrieks and screams rose high and higher with the tide of battle.

"The first men who arrived with a stretcher, of course, saw Forbes—and Forbes saw them. Up went his hands and heels, as signals of distress, and a piercing wail came from his wide-open mouth. They took him up tenderly and placed him on the stretcher. The wounded men sought to prevent the blunder, but the noise, confusion, and excitement were too great. Then, in a moment, Augustus Forbes was borne off to the rear at a double-quick step. The really wounded had to wait until later.

"The ambulance corps had established a station behind the brick walls of the cemetery that stood on Marye's Hill overlooking the deep ravine already mentioned. The bearers of Forbes, at a trot, brought him safely to shelter. But no sooner was he behind the walls than he leaped from the stretcher into the ravine and dashed away like a wild deer, leaving the stretcher-men agape with unbounded amazement.

"He fled swiftly out of sight, and we never heard of Forbes again during the war."

Dusk was now at hand, and Union General Humphreys' attack had reached its climax. Humphreys had had two horses shot from under him, and was leading on foot.

The final moments of the effort are thus described by an unidentified member of the 129th Pennsylvania Volunteers:

"The batteries began to play upon us from every side, and there was a continuous line of fire from the top of the stone wall right into our ranks. How the bullets whistled and hissed about our heads, and the shell exploded right in our midst! Nothing could withstand that withering line of fire. Men fell around me on all sides, and it seemed almost a miracle that I was untouched.

"The line was kept in as good order as was possible under the circumstances. We advanced to within a short distance of the wall . . . and then flesh and blood could stand it no longer. The line began to waver and part. Our advance was checked. We could not keep the gaps in the ranks filled up. The officers did their best to urge the men forward, but it was worse than useless, as nothing but death stared them in the face.

"We began to retire, and the enemy, seeing this, poured in a more destructive fire than ever. Still there was no panic among the men, and, although some confusion occurred in the ranks, we retired slowly and deliberately to our first position. . . . By this time it had grown quite dark. Still the rattle of musketry and the thundering of the cannon continued."

"This charge," says Confederate staff officer John Esten Cooke, "was the real termination of the bloody Battle of Fredericksburg. But, on the Confederate right, Jackson had planned and begun to execute a decisive advance on the force in his front. . . . His intention was to depend on the bayonet, his military judgment or instinct having satisfied him that the morale of the Federal army was destroyed. The advance was discontinued, however, in consequence of the lateness of the hour and the sudden artillery fire which saluted him as he began to move. . . . As darkness settled down, the last guns of Stuart, who had defended the Confederate right flank . . . were heard far in advance, and apparently advancing still."

Stuart was indeed advancing, but he turned back upon notification from Jackson that the attack had been called off.

Except for sporadic musketry, hostilities soon ceased along the entire front.

23

Incidents of the Aftermath

I<small>T WAS</small> true that the battle was over, but no one knew it at nightfall on December 13. Burnside was planning to renew his attack in the morning, and Lee, surprised at how easily the Yankees had been repelled, believed he'd have to make another stand—which he was quite willing to do.

The evening hours found the terrain between Fredericksburg and Marye's Heights seething with Union activity. Some of the bloodied units were settling into restless bivouac on the battlefield spots they'd occupied when the fighting ended. They were "holding the ground" as a base for the next day's work. Other combatants were trudging back into the town. Reserve units were making their way from the town to positions up near the stone wall, their mission to shield the ambulance corps as it started its massive task of removing the helpless wounded.

As related by Colonel D. Watson Rowe, of Erastus B. Tyler's brigade of Humphreys' division:

"At nine o'clock at night, the command was withdrawn from the front, and rested on their arms in the streets of the town. Some sat on the curbstones, meditating, looking gloomily at the ground. Others lay on the pavement, trying to forget the events of the day in sleep. There was little said. Deep dejection burdened the spirits of all. . . . When anyone spoke, it was of a slain comrade—of his virtues, or of the manner of his death; or of one missing, with many conjectures respecting him. . . . The conversation was with bowed head and in a low murmur, ending in a sigh. . . .

"It was December. . . . There was no campfire, and there was neither blanket nor overcoat. They had been stored in a warehouse preparatory to moving out to the attack. But no one mentioned the cold; it was not noticed. [The temperature was moderate for the season.]

"Steadily the wounded were carried by to the hospitals. . . . Someone, now and then, brought word of the condition of a friend.

"The hospitals were a harrowing sight. . . . Downstairs, upstairs, every room full. Surgeons with their coats off and sleeves rolled up above the elbows, sawed off limbs, administered anesthetics. They took off a leg or an arm in a twinkling, after a brief consultation. It seemed to be, in case of doubt—off with his limb.

"A colonel lay in the middle of the main room on [a] first floor, white, unconscious. When the surgeon was asked what hope, he turned his hand down, then up, as much as to say it may chance to fall either way.

"But the sights in a field hospital, after a battle, are not to be minutely described. Nine thousand was the tally of the wounded—nine thousand, and not all told."

The narrative is taken up by John W. Ames, a captain in the 2nd brigade of George Sykes's division, also in Fredericksburg that evening:

"We finally slept, but we were roused before midnight, and formed into line with whispered commands, and then filed to the right; and, reaching the highway, marched away from the town [onto the battlefield]. There were many dead horses at exposed points . . . and many more dead men.

"Here stood a low brick house, with an open door in its gable end, from which shone a light, and into which we peered when passing. Inside sat a woman, gaunt and hard-featured, with crazy hair and a Meg Merrilies face [a face like that of a gypsy in Sir Walter Scott's *Guy Mannering*], still sitting by a smoking candle, though it was nearly two hours past midnight. But what woman could sleep, though ever so masculine and tough of fiber, alone in a house between two hostile armies—two corpses lying across her doorsteps, and within, almost at her feet, four more! So, with wild eyes, and face lighted by her smoky candle, she stared across the dead barrier into the darkness outside with the look of one who heard and saw not. . . .

"We formed in two lines—the right of each resting near and in front of this small brick house, and the left extending into the field at right angles with the highway. Here we again bivouacked, finding room for our beds with no little difficulty because of the shattered forms of those who were here taking their last long sleep."

Erastus Tyler's brigade, after spending several hours in the town, also ended up bivouacking on this section of the field. Again in the words of D. Watson Rowe:

"The subdued sound of wheels rolling slowly along . . . told of the ambulance on its mission. . . . Cries were borne through the haze. . . . Now a single lament, again voices intermingled, and as if in chorus; from every direction, in front, behind, to right, to left, some near, some distant and faint. . . . They expressed every degree and shade of suffering, of pain, of agony; a sigh, a groan, a piteous appeal, a shriek, a succession of shrieks, a call of despair, a prayer to God, a demand for water, for the ambulance, a death rattle."

Federals who cast an eye toward Marye's Heights saw dying bivouac fires that seemed to mingle with the stars along the horizon. The vast majority of the Confederates were sleeping, but there were those who crept over the stone wall to strip the clothing from dead Federals close in front. (Body stripping was not confined to the Confederates. Federals did it too—not to replace tatters but to secure woolens to help keep them warm.)

One of the Confederates on guard behind the stone wall was Private Charles T. Loehr, of the 1st Virginia Infantry Regiment, who was disturbed by the chorus of Federal lamentations coming to his ears. "The horrors of the night were still more vividly brought before us by the appearance of an *Aurora Borealis*, or northern light, which for a time illuminated the heavens and exposed to our view the suffering wounded lying in front of us."

The display in the sky was viewed in a more positive way by Robert Stiles of the Richmond Howitzers. "It . . . surpassed in splendor any like exhibition I ever saw. Of course we enthusiastic young fellows felt that the heavens were hanging out banners and streamers and setting off fireworks in honor of our victory."

Burnside's hopes of upsetting the victory faded as the night wore away, for he found no support among his generals for his plan to resume the attack. He decided to revert to the defensive while pondering ways of resolving his situation. There was no immediate decision to recross the river, and the entire field remained on combat alert.

With the approach of dawn, Union Captain John Ames and his comrades, bivouacked beside the brick house of "Meg Merrilies," began a day of extraordinary conditions. Because these men had marched out of Fredericksburg in the dark, they did not know they had settled down in a shallow depression (shown on map "Marye's Heights") less than a hundred yards from the stone wall. In fact, they were not even aware that such a wall existed, for they had taken no part in the assaults of the previous day.

"We rose early," Ames recounts. "The heavy fog was penetrating and chilly, and the damp turf was no warm mattress to tempt us to a morning nap. So we shook off sloth from our moistened bodies willingly, and . . . set about breakfast [even building the usual camp-fires!]. The bivouac breakfast is a nearer approach to its civilized congener than the bivouac *bed*. . . . And a pipe! Who can estimate what that little implement has done for mankind? Certainly none better than those who have sought its solace after the bivouac break-fast that succeeds a bivouac bed, in December.

"We now began to take note, through the misty veil, of the wreck of men and horses cumbering the ground about us, and a slight lifting of the gray fog showed us the story of yesterday's repeated assaults and repeated failures. When our pipes were exhausted, we got up to inspect and criticize the situation. . . . Almost an army lay about us and scattered back over the plain toward the town. Not only corpses, but many of the badly wounded, hardly distinguishable from the dead, were [still] here too. . . .

"About eighty yards in front, the plowed field was bounded by a stone wall, and behind the wall were men in gray uniforms moving carelessly about . . . talking, laughing, cooking, cleaning muskets, clicking locks. There they were—Lee's soldiers! The Army of Northern Virginia!

"We were so absurdly near this host of yesterday's victory that we seemed wholly in their hands and a part of their great mass, cut off and remote from the Federal army and almost within the lines of the enemy—prisoners. . . . That was the immediate impression as we stupidly gazed in the first moment of the awkward discovery.

"But the sharp whistle of a bullet sounded in our ears, and a rebel's face peered through the puff of smoke as he removed the rifle from his shoulder. Then, rapidly, half-a-dozen more bullets whistled by us, and the warning sent us all to earth. . . . This had the effect of hiding us from the enemy, or partially so, for the fusillade slackened.

"It was irksome to keep one position . . . but the watch over us was very vigilant. Hardly a movement was made at any part of our line that did not draw fire from the wall. Necessity compelled us, however, to keep up something of a lookout upon the enemy at any risk. A cautious inspection showed great carelessness in their lines, the men still strolling and lounging—a group at cards, even, evidently ignoring or careless of our proximity.

"What to do about it was to us a topic second only in interest to the probable action of the enemy. Could we long lie thus without waking up the big guns, whose black muzzles looked down on us from the hilltops on our right? And if not, what then? From these guns there would be no possible shelter. Retreat . . . was more dangerous than to remain as we were. . . . The field behind us stretched away toward the town, level and exposed—the focus of an arc of battery-crowned hills. . . .

"We drifted into a common understanding. . . . Shots might rouse the enemy from his carelessness or ignorance. Certainly a volley from our line would not go unanswered. . . . Let them stick to their cards and forget us if they would!

". . . The enemy riddled every moving thing in sight: horses tied to the wheels of a broken gun carriage behind us; pigs that incautiously came grunting from across the road; even chickens were brought down with an accuracy of aim that told of a fatally short range. . . . They applauded their own success with a hilarity we could hardly share in, as their chicken-shooting was across our backs, leaving us no extra room for turning.

"But this was mere wantonness of slaughter, not indulged in when the higher game in blue uniform was in sight. The men who had left our ranks for water, or from any cause, before we were pinned to the earth, came back at great peril. Indeed, I believe not one of them reached our line again unhurt. Some were killed outright. Others were mortally wounded, and died within a few steps of us. And several who tried to drag themselves away flat upon their faces were put out of their misery. . . .

"This . . . showed us plainly what we might expect, and fixed our bounds to such segments of the field as were hidden from the enemy. . . . At one point the exposure was absolute. . . . A slight barrier was . . . formed at this point by a disposal of the dead bodies in front, so that the dead actually sheltered the living.

"After two or three hours of this experience we became somewhat accustomed to the situation—for man becomes accustomed to almost anything that savors of routine—and learned with considerable exactness the limit inside which we might move with safety. . . .

"It was somewhat curious to see how strong the tobacco hunger was with many—perhaps with most. Men would jump to their feet and run the length of a regiment to borrow tobacco, and in so doing run [a] gauntlet of . . . shots. This was so rarely accomplished in entire safety that it won the applause of our line and hearty congratulations to anyone fortunate enough to save his life and sweeten it with the savory morsel.

"All this would have been ludicrous but for the actual suffering inflicted upon so many. Men were mortally hit, and there was no chance to bind up their wounds. . . . A little was accomplished for their relief by passing canteens from hand to hand. . . . It was sad to hear the cries fade away to low moans and then to silence, without a chance to help.

"The laugh over a successful chase for tobacco would die away only to change into a murmur of indignation at the next cruel slaughter. A young officer, boyish and ruddy, fresh from a visit home . . . raised his head to look at the enemy, and a bullet at once pierced his brain. . . . Next a leg or arm was shattered as it became exposed in shifting from the wearisomeness of our position. . . .

"I suppose *ennui* is hardly the word where nerves are on the rack . . . yet something like *ennui* came over us. By chance I found a fragment of newspaper which . . . for a time banished the irksome present. Through this ragged patch of advertisements I . . . forgot . . . the grim war, the rifle's crack, and the bullet's whistle— forgot even the dead hand that had stretched itself toward me all the morning. . . .

"I was called back to the dull wet earth and the crouching line at Fredericksburg by a request from Sergeant Read, who 'guessed he could hit that cuss with a spy-glass,' pointing as he spoke to the batteries that threatened our right flank. [These were considerably more distant than the sharpshooters at the wall.] Then I saw that there was a commotion at that part of the Confederate works. . . . An officer on the parapet, with a glass, was taking note of us. Had they discovered us at last, after letting us lie here till high noon, and were we now to receive the plunging fire we had looked for all the morning?

"Desirable in itself as it might be to have 'that cuss with a spy-glass' removed, it seemed wiser to repress Read's ambition. The shooting of an officer would dispel any doubts they might have of our presence, and we needed the benefit of all their doubts. Happily, they seemed to think us not worth their powder and iron.

"Were we really destined to see the friendly shades of night come on and bring us release from our imprisonment? For the first time we began to feel it probable when the groups left the guns without a shot.

"I grew easy enough in mind to find that sleep was possible, and I was glad to welcome it as a surer refuge from the surroundings than the scrap of newspaper. It was a little discouraging to see a sleeping officer near me wakened by a bullet; but as his only misfortune, besides a disturbed nap, seemed to be a torn cap and scratched face, he soon wooed back the startled goddess.

"I had [all my life] enjoyed sleep for its quiet and rest, but never before for mere oblivion."

While Captain Ames is sleeping, we'll leave him for a time to note that things were occurring on other parts of the six-mile front. Here and there, artillerists were dueling. At some points, skirmishers were exchanging musketry. At other points, pickets were fraterniz-ing and exchanging coffee and tobacco. Away down on the Confed-erate right, Heros von Borcke was wondering about the meaning of the day.

"Hour after hour passed away in anxious expectation of the combat; but though the skirmishing at times grew hotter, and the fire of the artillery more rapid, long intervals of silence again suc-ceeded.

"As usual, the [Union] batteries were not chary of their ammuni-tion; and whenever a group of officers showed itself plainly within range, it was at once greeted with a couple of shells or solid shot.

"Having to ride over to Fitz Lee, who, with the greatest part of his brigade was in reserve, I met Doctor J., [a civilian] whose acquain-tance I had made during one of our raids. He was just driving up to the general in his buggy, which, besides its hospitable inmate, con-tained an excellent cold dinner and a bottle of whisky for our solace.

"We had scarcely, however, begun to unpack the chickens and biscuits, and the cork was still on its way [up] through the neck of the whisky bottle, when, instead of the 'cluck' announcing its complete extraction, our ears were greeted with a sound never pleasing at any time, but at this particular moment more than ever awakening disgust—the whizzing of a shell which plunged into the soft ground not more than twenty feet off, covering us instantaneously with an abundant coating of mud.

"This was too much for the nerves of our peaceful host, who drove off carrying with him the much-coveted refreshments, which had delighted our eyes, only to delude our remaining senses. We followed him, however, in eager pursuit, and succeeded several times in overtaking and arresting the flight of the precious fugitive, but each time our happiness was cut short by the enemy's artillery, whose aim pursued the buggy as tenaciously as ourselves, till at last we took refuge in a deep ravine, completely screened from the keen eyes of the Yankees, who, as we completed our meal, came in for a fire of maledictions for their want of common courtesy and consideration."

Getting back to John Ames, the Union captain we left pinned down, and asleep, in front of the fatal stone wall:

"When I returned to consciousness I found the situation unchanged, except that the list of casualties had been swelled by the constant rifle practice, which was still as pitiless and as continuous as before.

"It was almost startling to see, on looking at the brick house, the Meg Merrilies of the night before standing at her threshold. With the same lost look of helpless horror that her face had worn by candlelight, she gazed up and down our prostrate lines. . . . The desolate part she had to play suited well her gaunt and witchlike features.

"Shading her eyes with her hand at last . . . she searched our lines once more; then, with a hopeless shake of her head, she moved slowly back into the dismal little tomb she was forced to occupy. . . .

"Slowly the sun declined. He had been our friend all day, shining through the December air with an autumn glow that almost warmed the chill earth. But at his last half-hour he seemed to hang motionless in the western sky. His going down would set us free; free from the fire that was galling and decimating us; free from the fear of guns on the right, and advance from the front; free from numbness and constraint and irksomeness, and free from the cold, wet earth. Also it would bring us messengers from the town to call us back from the exposed position and the field of dead bodies.

"But he lingered and stood upon the order of his going, until it seemed as if a Joshua of the Confederates had caused him to stand still.

"When at last the great disc stood, large and red, upon the horizon, every face was turned toward it, forgetting constraint, thirst, tobacco, and rebel fire, in the eagerness to see the end of a day that had brought us a new experience of a soldier's life . . . with many new horrors. . . .

"At last the lingering sun went down. December twilights are short. The Federal line sprang to its feet with almost a shout of relief. The rebel fire grew brisker as they saw such a swarm of bluecoats rising from the ground, but it was too late to see the foresights on the rifles, and shots unaimed were not so terrible as the hated ground. So we contemptuously emptied our rifles at them; and before the smoke rolled away, the coming darkness had blotted out the wall and the hostile line.

"With our line rose also a few men from the ghastly pile of yesterday's dead, who hobbled up on muskets used as crutches. These poor fellows had bound up their own wounds, and the coffee we had given them [at dawn] had cheered them into life and hope. Their cheerfulness grew into hilarity and merriment as they found themselves clear, at last, of the dead, and facing toward home. . . . Poor fellows! Their joy was more touching than their sufferings— which, indeed, they seemed to have forgotten.

"In our own brigade we found we had lost nearly 150 out of a present-for-duty strength of about one thousand men. This would have been a fair average loss in any ordinary battle, but we had suffered it as we lay on the ground inactive, without the excitement and dash of battle, and without the chance to reply—a strain upon nerves and physical endurance which we afterward remembered as severer than many more fatal fields.

"In the midst of our buzz of relief and mutual congratulations, the expected summons came for us to fall back to the town.

"We marched past the court house, past churches, schools, bank buildings, private houses—all lighted for hospital purposes, and all in use, though a part of the wounded had been transferred across the river. Even the door-yards had their litter-beds and were filled with wounded men, and the dead were laid in rows for burial.

"The hospital lights and campfires in the streets, and the smoldering ruins of burned buildings, with the mixture of the lawless rioting . . . and the suffering and death in the hospitals gave the sacked and gutted town the look of pandemonium.

"In our new freedom, we wandered about for the first half of the night, loath to lie on the earth again after our day's experience. At last we . . . slept in the lurid firelight."

At the front, the night was a quiet one.

The morning of December 15, according to Heros von Borcke, "passed slowly away, the anxious silence maintained being broken only by the firing, from time to time, of the heavy batteries; and many of our leaders, Stuart and Jackson foremost, began to give up any hope of a renewal of the attack."

In the afternoon Burnside asked for a truce for the purpose of removing his wounded and beginning the task of burying his dead. Again in Von Borcke's words:

"Being one of the officers appointed on our side to superintend the proceedings, I rode forthwith down to the plain. . . . The burial parties of the Federals were ready and in excellent order, and . . . columns from 200 to 300 strong moved forward in double-quick and went at once to work, taking up the wounded and burying the dead, assisted by a large number of our own men. . . . The poor wounded were in a miserable state after their long exposure to cold and hunger."

Says Union Colonel Regis de Trobriand: "I will never forget the joy of the wounded when they were brought into our lines. One of them cried out, trying to raise himself on his litter, 'All right now! I shall not die like a dog in the ditch.' Another said to the men carrying him, while two great tears ran down his hollow cheeks, 'Thanks, my friends. Thanks to you I shall see my mother again.'

"The dead were hideous: black, swollen, covered with clotted blood, riddled with balls, torn by shells. The rebels . . . had left them neither shoes, nor trousers, nor overcoats.

"Among them I had the opportunity to recognize the body of young Dekone, aide to General Meade. His remains, at least, could be sent to his sorrowing family."

There were few Confederate victims on the plain. Most of Lee's casualties had occurred inside his own lines. By this time many of his wounded were being transported south.

For diarist Judith McGuire, living below Fredericksburg at Ashland, this day was a busy one.

"Trains have been constantly passing with the wounded for the Richmond hospitals. Every lady, every child, every servant in the village has been engaged preparing and carrying food to the wounded as the cars stopped at the depot—coffee, tea, soup, milk, and everything we could obtain. With eager eyes and beating hearts we watched for those most dear to us. Sometimes they were so slightly injured as to sit at the windows and answer our questions, which they were eager to do. They exult in the victory.

"I saw several poor fellows shot through the mouth—they only wanted milk; it was soothing and cooling to their lacerated flesh. One, whom I did not see, had both eyes shot out. But I cannot write of the horrors of this day. Nothing but an undying effort to administer to their comfort could have kept us up. The Bishop was with us all day, and the few gentlemen who remained in the village.

"When our gentlemen came home [from work] at five o'clock they joined us, and were enabled to do what we could not—walk through each car, giving comfort as they went.

"The gratitude of those who were able to express it was so touching! They said that the ladies were at every depot with refreshments. As the cars would move off, those who were able would shout their blessings on the ladies of Virginia: 'We will fight, we will protect the ladies of Virginia!'

"Ah, poor fellows! What can the ladies of Virginia ever do to compensate them for all they have done and suffered for us?"

Returning to the battlefield and to Heros von Borcke: "The approaching night brought with it a heavy storm and rain, and we were wet to the skin and shivering with cold when at a late hour we returned to headquarters. Stuart was in a very bad humor, and entertained no hope of a renewal of the fight the following day. 'These Yankees,' he said, 'have always some underhand trick when they send a flag of truce, and I fear they will be off before daylight.'

"This suspicion proved to be only too true."

Under cover of the darkness and the bluster of the night, the retreat across the bridges was performed with skill and dispatch, its progress undetected by the Confederates. Even some of the Federals who were left at the front on picket duty until the last moment did not know what was happening behind them. One of these was Warren Goss, the private from Massachusetts.

"About two o'clock at night, in the sleet and rain—by whose orders I know not—we stealthily crept back towards the river, which our forces had mostly crossed, though up to this time we had had no information of the army's crossing. . . .

"When morning dawned, we were boiling our coffee on the other side of the river; and the driving rain, coming down steadily, added not a little to our gloomy feelings. . . . There was universal despondency."

The mood on the Confederate side that morning is revealed by Heros von Borcke:

"On . . . Lee's Hill . . . a great number of the generals assembled around our commander-in-chief, all extremely chagrined that the Federals should have succeeded in so cleverly making their escape. . . .

"The tranquillity in which the day passed off was interrupted only by the firing from the enemy's batteries. . . .

"During the afternoon General Burnside renewed his request for

Franklin's division in retreat

the burial of the dead, which was at once granted; and the Federal troops destined to this duty, having crossed the Rappahannock in pontoons [i.e., in pontoon boats, since the pontoon bridges had been taken up], went to work without delay.

"Having been again ordered to assist in the superintendence of the proceedings, I was painfully shocked at the inevitably rough manner in which the Yankee soldiers treated the dead bodies of their comrades. Not far from Marye's Heights existed a hole of considerable dimensions, which had once been an ice-house; and, in order to spare time and labor, this had been selected by the Federal officers to serve as a large common grave, not less than eight hundred of their men being buried in it.

"The bodies of these poor fellows, stripped nearly naked [largely the work of Confederate prowlers of the past two days], were gathered in huge mounds around the pit and tumbled neck and heels into it—the dull thud of corpse falling on corpse coming up from the depths of the hole until the solid mass of human flesh reached near the surface, when a covering of logs, chalk, and mud closed the mouth of this vast and awful tomb.

"On my return to Lee's Hill I saw President Davis and Governor [John] Letcher with our commander. They had come up from Richmond to congratulate him and the troops under him on their success."

As a fitting cap to the success, William Barksdale and his Mississippians were ordered to reoccupy Fredericksburg. This was the brigade, it will be recalled, that included the 21st Mississippi, the berth of Buck Denman, the stalwart bear hunter who rescued the little girl from a street in the town the evening of the Union occupation.

For the outcome of the story of Denman and his precious charge we'll turn again to Robert Stiles, who begins by going back to the time of the battle:

"Behind that historic stone wall, and in the lines hard by, all those hours and days of terror was that baby kept, her fierce nurses taking turns patting her while the storm of battle raged and shrieked, and at night wrestling with each other for the boon and benediction of her quiet breathing under their blankets. Never was a baby so cared for. They scoured the countryside for milk, and conjured up their best skill to prepare dainty viands for her little ladyship.

"When the struggle was over and the enemy had withdrawn to his strongholds across the river, and Barksdale was ordered to reoccupy the town, the 21st Mississippi, having held the post of danger in the rear [during the retreat], was given the place of honor in the van, and led the column.

"There was a long halt, the brigade and regimental staff hurrying to and fro. The regimental colors could not be found.

"Denman stood about the middle of the regiment, baby in arms. Suddenly he sprang to the front. Swinging her aloft above his head, her little garments fluttering like the folds of a banner, he shouted, 'Forward, Twenty-first; here are your colors!' And without further order, off started the brigade toward the town, yelling only as Barksdale's men could yell.

"They were passing through a street fearfully shattered by the enemy's fire, and were shouting their very souls out—but let Buck himself describe the last scene in the drama:

" 'I was holding the baby high . . . with both arms, when above all the racket I heard a woman's scream. The next thing I knew I was covered with calico, and she fainted on my breast. I caught her before she fell, and, laying her down gently, put her baby on her bosom. She was most the prettiest thing I ever looked at, and her eyes were shut. And—and—I hope God'll forgive me, but I kissed her just once.' "

24

In Camp as the Year Ends

CASUALTY TOTALS for the Battle of Fredericksburg came to about 12,500 for the Federals and 5,000 for the Confederates. The victory gave Lee little satisfaction. He had merely repelled the Army of the Potomac when he might have crushed it. He should have counterattacked while its back was to the river. He had refrained from this because he expected a second frontal assault, which would have enabled him to renew the advantage of his supreme defensive position. And if Burnside had had his way, the situation would have developed in just such a manner.

The Confederacy took a mixed view of the victory. Those inclined to impulsive optimism felt that it was a major step toward independence, while others recognized it for what it was, the temporary check of a mighty foe.

In the North, according to one of the era's historians, Robert Tomes, "the disaster to the Union army at Fredericksburg created a great commotion. . . . The people, so often disappointed in their expectations of a success commensurate with the means which had been so profusely placed at the disposal of the Government, now became impatient of its conduct of the war. A general cry of indignation arose, artfully stimulated by the opposition, against the party in power. The President, Cabinet, and General-in-Chief [Henry Halleck, operating from Washington], held by popular opinion responsible for the repeated failures of the Union arms, and especially for the disaster at Fredericksburg, were respectively charged with incapacity. . . .

"General Burnside, however, with a generous self-sacrifice, came

313

to the rescue of his indicted superiors by assuming, in a letter, the full responsibility of the plan and conduct of the attack upon Fredericksburg."

Burnside even accepted the blame for the late arrival of the pontoons from Washington, which delayed his crossing of the river. He said that he had expected Halleck to make sure that the pontoons were sent in time, but added that he could have dispatched some of his own officers to Washington to check on the matter. "Perhaps I made a mistake in not doing so."

Burnside's forthrightness made little impression on his grumbling army. Staff officer Francis Walker explains: "The privates in the ranks knew just as well as their officers that they had not had a fair chance at Fredericksburg; and in their minds they dismissed Burnside from the command long before the Administration was prepared to act.

"This was strikingly shown at a review of the corps [the Second] held shortly after the battle, at which both General Burnside and General Sumner were present. The commander of the army was received with such freezing silence by the troops that General Sumner directed General Couch to have the men called upon for cheers. But although the corps and division commanders and their staffs rode along the lines waving their caps or their swords, only a few derisive cries were heard. . . .

"Had they but seen 'Little Mac' riding over the field to take command of them once more, [they] would have broken into cheers that would have made the welkin ring, and have asked nothing better than to be led against the enemy."

The narrator was one of those whom McClellan had managed to keep deluded. But even many who had understood McClellan for what he was, and had been heartily glad to see him go, began to have second thoughts about the change. "Masterly Inactivity," it seemed, had been replaced by something even worse: "Gigantic Stupidity."

The opposing armies now occupied about the same positions they'd held before the Battle of Fredericksburg. And it looked as though they'd be there for some time. As explained by Lieutenant Jesse Bowman Young of the 84th Pennsylvania Volunteers:

"While it was not definitely announced that no further movement against the enemy was to take place until spring, yet a general impression to that effect soon pervaded the army of Burnside. . . . The weather had [often] been very cold, and the regiments that had simply camped down in their shelter tents had suffered severely. Here and there were shrewd, farseeing commanders who had taken the responsibility on themselves of preparing huts and other shelters for their troops, but many regiments had been living thus far in mere tents in shivering discomfort. Now everybody went to work to build winter habitations. . . .

"It was singular what comfortable places the boys built for themselves. Here in a side hill we find a dozen officers quartered in a cavern dug out of the earth. A chimney has been excavated and a big fireplace carved out of the earth. And here, warm, dry, cheerful, and jocose, the occupants bunk together on the ground, on which has been thickly spread a covering of rubber coats, blankets, overgarments, and other bed material.

"Or perhaps we find bins and bunks arranged about the interior, with a table, rude benches, a camp chair or two, and other odds and ends. Now and then a picture is hung up. Sometimes the walls are covered with cuts taken from *Harper's Weekly* or *Frank Leslie's Illustrated Newspaper*, both of which had a large circulation in the army, while in almost every tent or other habitation we find in use some knickknack or handy trifle of comfort sent from home.

"Dugouts, log houses, mud huts, structures made of bushes, earth, and canvas, all mingled together in a curious mongrel fashion—if one can fancy these . . . each . . . reflecting the personality of its occupants and inventors . . . covering a large stretch of

Union winter camp

At ease inside a winter hut

country, twenty odd miles in length along the Rappahannock, and nearly that distance in breadth, and embracing a population of over a hundred thousand men—with no women or children, except a few nurses and drummer boys to give variety to the picture—if one can fancy this agglomeration of . . . habitations, he may form a fair idea of the army in its comfortable winter quarters."

Switching to the Confederate side of the river and to Heros von Borcke:

"The stroke of many axes rang through the surrounding forests and oak copses; and pine thickets dissolved from view to give place to complete little towns of huts and log-houses provided with comfortable fireplaces, from whose gigantic chimneys curled upwards gracefully and cheerily into the crisp winter air many a column of pale blue smoke.

"Longstreet's corps remained opposite Fredericksburg and its immediate neighborhood; Jackson's was stationed halfway between that place and Port Royal; and Stonewall himself had fixed his headquarters about twelve miles from us, [on] the well-known plantation of the Corbyn family, called Moss Neck."

General Lee, according to John Esten Cooke, was headquartered in a tent "pitched in an opening in the wood near the narrow road leading to Hamilton's Crossing, with the tents of the officers of the staff grouped near; and, with the exception of an orderly, who always waited to summon couriers to carry dispatches, there was nothing in the shape of a bodyguard visible, or any indication that the unpretending group of tents was the army's headquarters.

"Within, no article of luxury was to be seen. A few plain and indispensable objects were all which the tent contained. The covering of the commander-in-chief was an ordinary army blanket, and his fare was plainer, perhaps, than that of the majority of his officers and men. . . . Citizens frequently sent him delicacies, boxes filled with turkeys, hams, wine, cordials, and other things . . . but these were almost uniformly sent to the sick in some neighboring hospital. [One thing he kept was a live hen who, given the freedom of his camp, came into his tent to lay her daily egg.]

"Lee's principle . . . seems to have been to set a good example to his officers of not faring better than their men; but he was undoubtedly indifferent naturally to luxury of all descriptions. . . . In his other habits he was equally abstinent. He cared nothing for wine, whiskey, or any stimulant, and never used tobacco in any form.

"He rarely relaxed his energies in anything calculated to amuse him; but, when not riding along his lines or among the camps to see in person that the troops were properly cared for, generally passed his time in close attention to official duties connected with the well-being of the army, or in correspondence with the authorities at Richmond.

"When he relaxed from this continuous toil, it was to indulge in some quiet and simple diversion—social converse with ladies in houses at which he chanced to stop, caresses bestowed upon children, with whom he was a great favorite, and frequently in informal conversation with his officers. . . .

"The bearing of General Lee in these hours of relaxation was quite charming, and made him warm friends. His own pleasure and gratification were plain [to see], and gratified others, who, in the simple and kindly gentleman in the plain gray uniform, found it difficult to recognize the commander-in-chief of the Southern army."

One December day Lee received a special visitor from Richmond: his son Custis, who was serving as an aide to President Davis. Custis extended his time in camp to visit also with Jeb Stuart. Von Borcke says that Custis "wished to inspect the battlefield and the town of Fredericksburg; and . . . General Stuart and I gladly accompanied him on the expedition. I had thus the first direct opportunity presented to me of leisurely inspecting the ruins of poor Fredericksburg, which, with its shattered houses, streets ripped open, and demolished churches, impressed me sadly enough.

"The inhabitants had nearly all deserted the place, the only visible exceptions being here and there a wretched pauper or aged Negro, to whom no refuge elsewhere was open, creeping noiselessly along the silent street. The brave soldiers of Barksdale's brigade, however, who had so nobly resisted the first attempt of the enemy to cross the river, were reestablished in the town, and comfortably installed in several of the large buildings now abandoned.

"The firing of the pickets having once more ceased, a network of friendly relations had begun again to connect them, and an interchange of communications . . . recommenced. To carry on these, the most ingenious devices were resorted to. . . . On reaching the river, we beheld quite a little fleet of small boats, from three to four feet in length, under full sail with flying pennants, crossing backwards and forwards between the shores of the river, conveying tobacco and Richmond newspapers over to the Stafford side, and returning loaded in exchange with sugar and coffee and Northern journals. The diminutive craft were handled with considerable nautical skill, and rudder and sails set so deftly to wind and stream, that they always unerringly landed at the exact point of destination.

"Some days afterwards, this free-trade movement having outpassed the limits which were judged safe or convenient, a sudden embargo, in the shape of a severe and stringent order, was put upon the friendly traffic of foe with foe, to the mutual and unmitigated disgust of both sides."

It must be noted here that, during this period immediately following the battle, a change came over a great many of Barksdale's fierce Mississippians. They became absorbed in Christianity. Robert Stiles calls the proceeding "probably the most marked religious movement in our war. . . .

"The Baptist Church had been so injured during the bombardment that it could not be used. The meetings were first held in the Presbyterian Church and then in the Methodist, and finally were transferred to the Episcopal Church, St. George's, which was the largest in the city, and accommodated, I should say, packed as it invariably was, from a thousand to twelve hundred men. I have never seen such eagerness to hear the word of God. . . .

"The preacher was sometimes a distinguished divine from Richmond, sometimes one of the army chaplains, sometimes a private soldier from the ranks. . . . There was a soldier in a red blanket overcoat who had a voice like the sound of many waters, and who almost invariably sat or stood on the pulpit steps and led the singing. . . . [There were] many marks of cannonballs upon and in and through the building, and . . . it added to the thrill of the services to realize that we were gathered under the frowning batteries upon Stafford Heights."

The batteries were not a threat. Few Federals, artillerists or otherwise, were thinking in warlike terms as they completed work on their winter quarters and performed the usual duties inherent to army life in the field. For the hospital corps, the wounded remained a major problem, with great numbers lying in drafty tents awaiting room on the trains making the run to Acquia Creek, where special transports were loading.

Among the civilian nurses who were tirelessly active at this time was a young woman named Nellie Chase. As effused by one of her devoted charges:

"May the choicest blessings of Heaven be hers in all time to come! . . . She does, indeed, seem gifted in a most wonderful degree for scenes like this. . . .

"To the wounded she is all sympathy and kindness, but let anyone not a patient attempt familiarity, even in jest, and her black eyes flash such an indignant rebuke as is hardly equalled by her cool cutting rejoinder. More than one shoulder-strapped puppy has had occasion to rue the time he intruded his remarks upon her. . . .

"She has been in the army ever since the war broke out, nursing the sick and wounded, and 'ever in front.' Hospitals in the rear are no place for her. . . . Many a poor wounded soldier would lack his timely stimulant, soup, or delicacies if she did not pass through the tents at all hours of the day and night. . . .

"For all the labors and privations and sufferings of her campaigning life she receives no pay. She draws her rations as a private soldier, and the private soldiers who know her almost worship her. I overheard one say . . . that he would kill, as he would kill a dog, the man who would dare insult her, even in thought; and I believe it.

"War produces great developments of character, and Miss Nellie M. Chase is a most notable instance of it. She is not yet twenty-four years old, but in experience as a nurse or hospital matron on the battlefield, I think she has no living equal."

There were continued deaths among the wounded, and funerals were frequent. In the words of Color Sergeant D. G. Crotty of the 3rd Michigan Volunteer Infantry:

"When one of our men die in the hospital, all who can, go to his funeral. . . . One might suppose that a soldier is so used to seeing death on the battlefield that he is hardened to everything, but it is a mistake, for when one dies in camp he is mourned over. . . . The poor soldier dies away from home. No relative is nearby to comfort or sympathize with him in his last hour. But his comrades gather around him and give him the burial of the warrior.

"He is laid out in his uniform of blue, in a plain, rough coffin, over which hang the stars and stripes. The mournful procession commences its slow march, headed by the band. Oh, how solemn are the strains as they are taken up by the chilling breeze! His comrades follow close behind, marching with reversed arms. The solemn procession halts at the lonely grave, when the coffin is lowered into the earth. 'Ashes to ashes' are the words said by the man of God. The volleys are fired over the departed hero, and he is left to rest in peace."

A Union burial at Falmouth

In the hospitals, amid the suffering and dying, there was some-times humor. A badly wounded soldier who appeared to be los-ing ground was advised by a comrade to start praying. Smiling wanly, the victim responded: "What good would it do? Don't you know that the Lord will not hear a soldier's prayer unless it is forwarded through the regular military channels and has the en-dorsement of the Secretary of War?"

On the Confederate side, the salient events of the Christmas season involved Stonewall Jackson's headquarters down the river at Moss Neck. In the words of Jackson's aide, James Power Smith:

"The house was a large mansion, built a few years before when James Park Corbin had been a man of wealth, on the hills a mile or more back from the river and commanding a fine view.... It was exceedingly commodious, having a large number of rooms beau-tifully fitted and well-furnished. Mrs. Richard Corbin was the lady of the house, and gave the general a most cordial invitation to occupy as many rooms as he wished. But he would not listen to such a proposition. We must share the camp with the troops.... Our tents were pitched in the grove beyond the stables....

"Christmas was coming. Two days before, General Jackson told us he wished to entertain Generals Lee, Stuart, and Pendleton at din-ner on Christmas Day. I was the caterer.... An attempt to buy a turkey from a lady resulted in a present of two fine turkeys. A bucket of oysters arrived from somewhere down the river; and a box came to the general from Staunton ladies, with another turkey, a splendid ham, a large cake, a bottle of wine, and the spaces filled with white biscuit and the best of pickles.

"Jim, the general's cook, was altogether successful; and John, our waiting boy, had on a spotless white apron. Lee, in good humor, declared that we were only 'playing soldiers' and invited us to dine with him and see how a soldier ought to live. Stuart was in great glee ... playfully chiding Jackson for his bottle of wine. In the center of the table was a print of butter ... on which was [stamped] a gallant rooster. Stuart pronounced it to be Jackson's coat-of-arms.... Old General Pendleton said the grace, and [we] ate the dinner; and [everyone] said it was all good....

"We younger men were glad when the generals were gone, for we had an evening of entertainment before us—an invitation to a veritable old-fashioned party in Mrs. Corbin's beautiful parlors. There was a deal of preparation [by us] in the tents, and then a rare sight of beauty and grace, of lights and greenery, holly and mistletoe in the castle halls! And one young man, at least, our Sandy Pendleton [son of the general], met his fate in a pair of black eyes that night."

As for Jackson, it wasn't long before his rigorous tent life gave him an earache, and Dr. Hunter McGuire, the corps medical director, suggested that he switch to a room in the mansion. As continued by James Power Smith:

"The general then consented to occupy an office-building in the grounds. It was a small frame house, a story and a half high, which stood to the left and front of the mansion, under the fine trees. There was a little lobby in the front; on the left a wood closet, and on the right a narrow stairway leading to an attic room. An open fireplace was at the opposite end from the door. On either side of the door were bookshelves. . . . On the walls hung framed pictures of famous horses and fine cattle, and over the mantel was a tinted picture of a rat-worry [a terrier]. The general's cot was placed on one side, and a small table on the other. Two or three stools completed the furniture. . . .

"Stuart's first visit to the office was memorable. With clanking saber and spurs and waving black plume he came, and was warmly greeted at the door. Papers and work were all hastily laid aside. No sooner had Stuart entered than his attention turned to the pictures on the walls. He read aloud what was said about each noted racehorse and each splendid bull. At the hearth he paused to scan with affected astonishment the horrid picture of a certain terrier that could kill so many rats a minute.

"He pretended to believe that they were General Jackson's selections. With great solemnity he looked at the pictures and then at the general. He paused and stepped back, and in solemn tones said he wished to express his astonishment and grief at the display of General Jackson's low tastes. It would be a sad disappointment to the old ladies of the country, who thought that Jackson was a good man.

"General Jackson was delighted above measure. He blushed like a girl . . . and said nothing but to turn aside and direct that a good dinner be prepared for General Stuart. All the genial humor and frolic of that splendid cavalier were enjoyed exceedingly, with utter incapacity for response."

Stuart had just returned from a late-December foray behind the enemy's lines. This became known as his "Dumfries Raid," its memorability centering upon the fact that, after seizing some Federal army mules he found to be of poor quality, Stuart telegraphed a complaint about the animals to the Quartermaster General in Washington.

Union General Ambrose Burnside, impatient to redeem himself, chose the last days of December to instigate a new plan. As explained by newsman-historian William Swinton:

"General Burnside had determined to cross the Rappahannock seven miles below Fredericksburg, with a view to turn the Confederate position; and in connection with this operation he resolved to send a cavalry expedition to the rear of Lee's army for the purpose of cutting the railroad communications of the Confederates.

"Now the raiding column had actually got under way, and the whole army was in readiness for an immediate move, when ... General Burnside received a dispatch from President Lincoln instructing him not to enter on active operations without letting the President know of it.

"Surprised at this message, General Burnside recalled the cavalry expedition, and proceeded personally to Washington to ascertain the cause of the presidential prohibition. On seeing Mr. Lincoln, he was informed by him that certain general officers of the Army of the Potomac had come up to see him, and had represented that the army was on the eve of another movement; that all the preliminary arrangements were made; and that they, and every prominent officer in the army, were satisfied, if the movement was entered upon, it would result in disaster.

"In consequence of this condition of facts, the President, without [actually] prohibiting a move, judged that any large enterprise, *at that time*, would be injudicious. And General Burnside returned to his headquarters amazed at the revelation of the state of feeling in the army that was notorious to everyone in it save the commander himself."

As the year drew to a close, Union military fortunes were at a low ebb not only at Fredericksburg but also in other theaters of the war.

"There has been no other night in the history of our country," says the *Boston Journal*'s Charles Carleton Coffin, "like that of December 31, 1862. On the banks of Stone River, in Tennessee, the soldiers of the Army of the Cumberland were lying where they had fought through the day, with the dead and dying around them. They had been driven from their chosen position of the morning, and the conflict was still undecided. . . . The soldiers of the Confederate army opposing them were hovering around their bivouac fires congratulating themselves over the success which had attended them through the day. . . .

"On the banks of the Mississippi, between Memphis and Vicksburg, were the soldiers of the Union . . . who had vainly tried to gain the bluffs of Chickasaw near Vicksburg. . . . From the bluffs of Vicksburg the Confederate soldiers . . . could look down upon the winding river and behold in the distance, upon the moonlit waters, the fleet of Union gunboats which had opened the river southward to that point, but which were powerless to drive them from their stronghold. . . .

"On that last night of the year the soldiers of the Army of the Potomac, around their campfires on the Stafford hills opposite Fredericksburg . . . were thinking of loved ones at home, of peaceful scenes far away, of those who never again would keep step to the drum-beat. . . . They could look across the Rappahannock to the field where twelve thousand of their comrades had fallen in battle."

"New Year's Day," explains Regis de Trobriand, "passed more gayly than could have been expected."

The colonel goes on to describe the day as it was spent by a part of Hooker's command that came under his observation. "General [J. H. Hobart] Ward, who was well-fitted for all such details, organized diversions . . . which met with great success: foot-races, mule-races, sack-races, greased pole; burlesque procession; comic interludes. Nothing was lacking to the fete, in which the division joyfully participated.

"The higher officers paid their visits to the tents of the generals, where the inevitable drink watered the day's greetings. General [Daniel E.] Sickles, who at that time commanded Hooker's old division, did things in grand style. During the whole day he kept open house at his headquarters. The collation—which he had ordered from Washington—was abundant and choice. The champagne and whiskey ran in streams.

"I wish I could add that they were used in moderation; but the truth is that the subaltern officers, attracted by the good cheer, partook of them so freely that it was not to the honor of the uniform, nor to the profit of discipline."

25

Emancipation Is Proclaimed

Back in September, when Abraham Lincoln had issued the preliminary draft of the Emancipation Proclamation, he had committed himself to finalizing the measure on January 1, 1863. His position had weakened since then. The military situation had worsened. Public support for the war had diminished. The Democrats had made strong gains in the November elections.

All of these things convinced Lincoln that the proclamation's importance had grown. His war effort was more than ever in need of a new impetus.

Upon signing the final draft, the President said, "The South had fair warning that if they did not return to their duty I should strike at this pillar of their strength. The promise must now be kept, and I shall never recall a word."

In another statement, however, Lincoln revealed that he had some deep misgivings that the measure would have the kind of effect he hoped for. "We are like whalers who have been long on a chase. We have at last got the harpoon into the monster, but we must now look how we steer, or with one flop of his tail he will send us all into eternity."

The proclamation, as explained earlier, was aimed not only at the South and her "pillar of strength," but also at European inclinations to enter the war on the South's behalf. In England, newspaper reactions had begun to appear as soon as word of the preliminary announcement crossed the sea in autumn.

"It is not easy to estimate," said the *London Morning Post*, "how utterly powerless and contemptible a government must have become which could sanction with its approval such insensate trash. A few weeks since, trembling for the safety of its capital—at the present moment unable to force a passage into its enemy's territory—it still takes upon itself to dispose of property it is powerless to seize. . . . The President of the United States has no more power to liberate a slave in Virginia than Queen Victoria. . . .

"But the President of the United States has long since discontinued the antiquated custom of acting according to law. There are few, however, even of those who have manifested the greatest disregard for the laws they have sworn to administer, who have not been more or less sensitive to ridicule. . . . Mr. Lincoln seemingly cares as little for the ridicule as he does for the anger of the American people."

The *London Times* declared: "There is something ludicrous in such a proclamation, solemnly made by the Federal Government when its own capital is almost beleaguered." And the *Manchester Guardian*: "The proclamation is evidently nothing more than a compound of *bunkum* on a grand scale."

These diatribes notwithstanding, the British government was obliged to begin viewing the American war in a somewhat altered manner. The empire had freed its slaves years earlier, and it would not do for the government to seem to be pro-slavery now. Also a consideration was that there was a good deal of public support for Lincoln's proclamation, even among people thrown out of work for lack of the South's cotton. Said a "letter to the editor" published in the *London Gazette*: "We English have to open our eyes to the fact that the war in America has resolved itself into a war between freedom and slavery. . . . There is now no 'medium' course. Slavery or freedom must prevail. . . . Providence declares, as plainly as the handwriting on the wall: 'Choose this day which you will serve.'"

There was also support for Lincoln in the pro-Union *London Morning News and Star*. "The fiat has gone forth, and the heart of humanity will hail its execution. . . . Slavery will cease to defile the American flag and begin to disappear from the American soil."

In America itself, the Union states manifested no sudden upsurge in war spirit as Lincoln's decree was finalized. Only the antislavery people were unreservedly pleased. The Peace Democrats were chagrined, and many other citizens viewed the development with deep unease or angry disapproval. This was not a cause they considered worthy of a protracted expenditure of Northern blood and treasure.

The South was naturally outraged at this "triumph of the Abolition party." Edward Pollard, of the *Richmond Examiner*, called the proclamation "administrative madness," and added that Lincoln had "confessed to the world his inability and failure to accomplish his purposes by regular and honorable hostilities."

The slave insurrections the Confederates feared were never to develop. But the proclamation cleared the way for the official acceptance of black men, "defectors" from the South, into the Union service—and the number would grow rapidly.

"The forefathers of these Negro soldiers," protested President Jefferson Davis, "were gathered from the torrid plains and malarial swamps of inhospitable Africa. Generally they were born the slaves of barbarian masters, untaught in all the useful arts and occupations, reared in heathen darkness; and, sold by heathen masters, they were transferred to shores enlightened by the rays of Christianity.

"There, put to servitude, they were trained in the gentle arts of peace and order and civilization. They increased from a few unprofitable savages to millions of efficient Christian laborers. Their servile instincts rendered them contented with their lot, and their patient toil blessed the land of their abode with unmeasured riches.

"Their strong local and personal attachment secured faithful service to those to whom their service or labor was due. A strong mutual affection was the natural result of this life-long relation, a feeling best, if not only, understood by those who have grown from childhood under its influence. Never was there happier dependence of labor and capital on each other.

"The tempter came, like the serpent in Eden, and decoyed them with the magic word of 'freedom.' . . . He put arms in their hands, and trained their humble but emotional natures to deeds of violence and bloodshed."

According to the President's wife, Varina Davis: "The effect of the Emancipation Proclamation on the people of the South was unmistakable. It roused them to a determination to resist to the uttermost a power that respected neither the rights of property nor constitutional guarantees. . . .

"Almost every family in the South had lost some dear defender of their honor, who had died for liberty's sake; and the bonds of the old loving Union had been wrenched asunder. Our people were unwilling to yield an inch to the aggressions of the North, for they no longer loved the Union as it had been distorted by our enemies. . . .

"The condition of our servants began to be unsettled, and it was said there were clubs of disaffected colored men in Richmond, generally presided over by a white man, who were furnished with two thousand dollars for each servant who ran off from our service. However . . . we lost but two in that way. . . .

"One young woman, who was an object of much affectionate solicitude to me, followed her husband off, but systematically arranged her flight, made a good fire in the nursery, and came to warn me that the baby would be alone, as she was going out for a while.

"We never saw her afterward, and the following article . . . in a Washington paper filled us with grave apprehensions for the poor creature's safety:

" 'There are thousands of contrabands [ex-slaves] in Alexandria, and such another set of miserable beings I have never seen in this country. Some entire houses are set apart for them, and into these the abandoned flock in droves. Others live in tents, and others in the open commons of the town.

" 'There is already growing mortality among them, and an Alexandria physician told me that the smallpox had already broken out and would undoubtedly make great ravages in their midst. . . . There is little or no occupation for these contrabands. . . . They . . . seem impressed with the idea that it is the duty of the Government to provide for them.

" 'It is certain that Cuffee [the black male] finds small favor in the eyes of the troops who are now there, particularly since the issue of the emancipation decree. Every day Negroes are unmercifully beaten by white soldiers, and consider themselves lucky to get off with whole bones. Well-dressed darkies are the special aversion of the volunteers, and woe be unto them if they show themselves in fine feathers on King Street.' "

This was the sort of thing that General McClellan had had in mind when he informed Lincoln of his conviction that the Northern soldier would be unwilling to fight in a war based on the abolition of slavery. But such conduct was not general. The army was not a hotbed of unreasoning antiblack sentiment. The ranks, in fact, were graced with a good number of idealists.

One of these was Colonel Regis de Trobriand. The naturalized American had become devoted to the nation and its concepts, and he now thrilled to a sense of mission.

"It was no longer a question of the Union *as it was* that was to be reestablished. It was the Union as *it should be*—that is to say, washed clean from its original sin, regenerated on the baptismal font of liberty for all.

"Unless with that object, why this war, these immense sacrifices of every kind, these enormous immolations of men? To build up the crumbling edifice with the same stones which could not sustain it before? To . . . suppress the effect while retaining the cause? But that was no solution: it was a putting off. . . .

"The strife would have been eternally renewed, as long as the two incompatible and antagonistic elements, free labor and slave labor, existed together in the Republic. And we would have dragged behind us the heavy ball of slavery, which made us limp on the way of progress, and made us resemble rather the condemned criminals of civilization than its pioneers. . . .

"The war at last assumed its true character: a war for liberty against slavery. The time for disguise had passed. Congress . . . and the President . . . had in vain and repeatedly declared that the only objects of the war were 'the restoration of the Union, the maintenance of the supremacy of the Federal Government, and the reestablishment of constitutional relations between the United States and the States in which these relations were suspended or disturbed.'

"Congress and the President could not at first comprehend in its full extent the civilizing work of which they were the instruments— or, which is more probable, for political reasons they preferred not to proclaim them in advance. But, in any case, they could not have things any different from what they were. . . .

"The question was decided. Between the Republic and the accursed institution there was henceforth war to the death. The triumphs of the one [would lead] necessarily to the destruction of the other. And it was not the Republic that was destined to perish.

"Now we could march with a prouder step and fight with more confidence. We were no longer merely the soldiers of a political controversy. . . . We were now the missionaries of a great work of redemption, the armed liberators of millions . . . bent beneath the brutalizing yoke of slavery.

"The war was ennobled. The object was higher."

26

Burnside's Mud March

I T WAS men of a mold like that of Regis de Trobriand who held the Army of the Potomac together at this time when desertions were rising. Another stalwart was "Dunn Browne," who sermonized in a letter to his Massachusetts newspaper: "Shall we lie down in despair and give up the cause for which we took up arms? Or shall our spirit rise with the danger and meet the discouragements, and conquer all the obstacles that we have met? How can there be but one answer to this question in the hearts of a nation that has called itself the foremost nation on the globe?

"How dare we think of but one answer, after all our boastings and proclamations at the beginning of the contest? We are discouraged, wearied, indignant, disgusted. We have found war no boys' play, no easy game of glory and rewards, but a serious, terrible, heart-breaking, soul-sickening reality. But we are not yet fallen so low as to prefer a dishonorable peace."

No one in the army had more patriotic zeal than Ambrose Burnside himself, but it seemed to be impossible for the general to turn the zeal to practical use. He was more than ready, however, to keep trying. Two weeks after President Lincoln vetoed his second plan for getting at Lee (but did not confine him to inactivity), Burnside went ahead with another plan. William Swinton explains:

"The point at which General Burnside resolved this time to essay the passage of the Rappahannock was Banks' Ford ... about six miles above Fredericksburg. As, however, the enemy had a force in observation at all the practicable crossings of the Rappahannock, and as there was no possibility of making preparations for the passage at any one point with such secrecy that he should not become aware of it, it was resolved to make feints of crossing at several distinct points, both above and below Fredericksburg, and thus mask the real intent.

"Accordingly, new roads were cut through the woods to afford readier access to the fords, batteries were planted, rifle trenches were formed, and cavalry demonstrations made along the line; and these manifestations were made impartially at a variety of points."

Regis de Trobriand takes up: "The first preparatory order had been issued on the 16th [of January]. We did not expect it. What likelihood, in fact, was there that one would think of commencing active operations in the middle of the winter? . . . Nothing . . . indicated any immediate or even probable movement. A few indications, significant in appearance, rather denoted the contrary.

"For instance, the ladies were allowed passes to visit the army, which was only permitted in winter quarters when active hostilities were suspended for some time. [Our division commander] General [David B.] Birney, had been allowed, without objection, to go to Washington to meet Mrs. Birney, who was accompanied by quite a party of Philadelphians—ladies, sisters, or relatives of officers of his staff.

"They arrived at his headquarters on the 13th, where everything was ready to receive them, and for three days there was nothing but gaiety, rides on horseback and drives in carriages, collations, reviews, music, and improvised dances by moonlight.

"But here comes a fatal order. Immediately our visitors fly to the Acquia Creek Railroad like a flock of frightened grasshoppers. . . .

"On the 17th the weather turned cold in spite of the bright sunshine. On the 18th it froze hard. We were to break camp [for the main march up the river] in the afternoon. The prospect was not encouraging. In spite of himself, one thought of the amount of suffering such weather would entail. . . . It was a relief to receive the news that the departure was delayed twenty-four hours. We concluded from that that the movement was given up until the weather moderated."

The movement was not given up. Nor did everyone wish it to be. Many, in fact, saw it as a splendid opportunity to set things aright. Captain William Thompson Lusk of the 79th New York said in a letter to his mother:

"We are once more to meet the enemy. All gloomy forebodings engendered by the idleness of camp life have vanished before the prospect of impending action. My heart is as light as a feather. Hope is dominant, and I can think only of the glorious result if we are victorious. The gloom that now rests on our country will be lifted, and I already hear citizens repeating with joyous lips: 'We are victorious. Not in vain have been our sacrifices. We are proud of the army we have created.' "

New England's "Dunn Browne" tells how the march up the river began:

"Camps were broken up, tents struck, knapsacks packed; and soon long lines of troops were in motion over hill and dale. . . . The roads for miles were choked with supply-wagons, ammunition-trains and rumbling batteries. All was noise, confusion, and utmost activity. Trumpets sounded, drums beat, whips cracked, mules squealed, and teamsters cursed.

"In short, all things showed that a vast army was on the move. Excitement took the place of the quiet that had reigned in our midst for a month. Hearts beat high with hope and patriotic ardor—and spirits sank in dismay at the thought of approaching danger, wounds, and death. Some left couches of sickness, roused to new strength at the call to arms. Some, who had been perfectly well, paled into sudden sickness at the same prospect, and came sneaking round the surgeons' tents and crawling into hospitals."

"On the march," says New Yorker George Stevens, "an order from the commanding general was read to the troops, announcing to them that the auspicious moment had at length arrived when we were to reap the glorious fruits of our long toils."

As continued by Regis de Trobriand: "Over the roads still hard, through the fields, and under the forests our long columns of infantry marched till night, mingled with batteries of artillery, ammunition trains, and wagons carrying the pontoons.

"In the evening we arrived in rear of Banks' Ford in some woods composed of young pines with bushy tops, where the regiments which were to force the passage at daylight in the morning were crowded together. The glorious task was assigned to Ward's division, and my regiment was awarded the place of honor, the advance.

"But at the very time when we stacked arms, the fog, becoming more and more dense, turned to rain, which continued to fall, cold, heavy, incessant. The dull daylight was soon gone in the darkness of night, darker still amongst the pines. We were forbidden to light any fires or make any noise that might put the enemy on the alert. One saw nothing except here and there the dim light of a lantern.

Nothing was heard but the monotonous dropping of the rain and the murmurs of conversations carried on in a low voice."

According to William Swinton, the storm soon intensified. "It was a wild Walpurgis night, such as Goethe paints in the *Faust*. Yet there was brave work done during its hours, for the guns were hauled painfully up the heights and placed in their positions, and the pontoons were drawn down nearer to the river. But it was already seen to be a hopeless task; for the clayey roads and fields, under the influence of the rain, had become bad beyond all former experience; and by daylight, when the boats should all have been on the banks, ready to slide down into the water, but fifteen had been gotten up—not enough for one bridge, and five were wanted. Moreover, the night operations had not escaped the notice of the wary enemy, and by morning Lee had massed his army to meet the menaced crossing."

The Union assault troops continued to wait in the woods. "The rain," says Regis de Trobriand, "had been falling for twelve hours, and there were no indications of any cessation. The wind . . . ran through the trees with a roaring sound. At each gust, the water came down in showers from the branches, on the soaked soil, where the men were trampling around in the mud. No orders reached us. A few fires were tolerated at first, then authorized."

Smoke filled the woods, close to the ground, and eyes began to smart. The men nearest the river's bank, however, had no trouble seeing the rebels across the water. "They throw all kinds of slang at us," says Michigan soldier D. G. Crotty, "and have lots of fun at our expense."

Again in Swinton's words: "In this state of facts, when all the conditions on which it was expected to make a successful passage had been balked, it would have been judicious in General Burnside to have promptly abandoned an operation that was now hopeless. But it was a characteristic of that general's mind—a characteristic that might be good or bad, according to the direction it took—never to turn back when he had once put his hand to the plough; and it had already more than once been seen that the more hopeless the enterprise the greater his pertinacity.

"The night's rain had made deplorable havoc with the roads; but herculean efforts were made to bring pontoons enough into position to build a bridge or two withal. Double and triple teams of horses and mules were harnessed to each boat; but it was in vain. Long stout ropes were then attached to the teams, and a hundred and fifty men put to the task on each. The effort was but little more successful. Floundering through the mire for a few feet, the gang of Liliputians, with their huge-ribbed Gulliver, were forced to give over, breathless."

It had become equally hard to move the artillery and nearly every other wheeled possession of the army. But the impossible work was continued throughout the day. The rain persisted until it seemed to Lieutenant Jesse Bowman Young that "the bottom had dropped out of the entire region. Mud is no name by which to describe the sticky, miry, pitchy, unfathomable, and unexplorable semifluid beds of stuff which filled and overflowed the roads, every one of which was transformed into an abysmal slough of despond. The army was literally stuck in the mud . . . [with] everybody calling for help and no one able to render any, and the whole force . . . as absolutely helpless as though the rebel army had come upon them when asleep and bound them hand and foot."

From the start, even during the night, Ambrose Burnside, on horseback, had been slogging to every critical spot he could reach in a desperate effort to make things work. George Stevens recounts:

"As he rode through the camp of our division in the afternoon, with only two staff officers, himself and his horse completely covered with mud, the rim of his hat turned down to shed the rain, his face careworn with this unexpected disarrangement of his plans, we could but think that the soldier on foot, one oppressed with the weight of knapsack, haversack, and gun, bore an easy load compared with that of the commander of the army, who now saw departing his hopes of redeeming the prestige he had lost at Fredericksburg."

Swinton says that "night arrived, but the pontoons could not be got up, and the enemy's pickets . . . shouted out their intention to 'come over tomorrow and help build the bridges.'

"Morning dawned upon another day of rain and storm. The ground . . . now showed such a spectacle as might be presented by the elemental wrecks of another deluge. An indescribable chaos of pontoons, vehicles, and artillery encumbered all the roads—supply wagons upset by the roadside, guns stalled in the mud, ammunition-trains mired by the way, and hundreds of horses and mules buried in the liquid muck [dead through overexertion]. . . .

"It was no longer a question of how to go forward—it was a question of how to get back. The three-days' rations brought on the persons of the men were exhausted, and the supply-trains could not

Burnside's Mud March

be moved up. To aid the return, all available force was put to work to corduroy the rotten roads."

As added by Massachusetts Private Warren Goss: "The next morning the army wretchedly began its return to camp. Some ironically offered to get into the boats and row them to camp through the mud as the most expeditious manner of arriving there."

By this time the frolicsome Confederates across the river had erected a large sign that proclaimed: BURNSIDE STUCK IN THE MUD.

The outcome of the sorry venture is given by Colonel Theodore Gates of New York's Ulster Guard:

"With the utmost difficulty and in a state of demoralization that has no parallel in the history of the Army of the Potomac, the old camps were finally reached, and the 'Mud Campaign' was at an end. So, also, was General Burnside's usefulness as commander of the army.

"Burnside could not but feel that he was the victim of 'the slings and arrows of outrageous fortune' and the jealousy of some of his subordinates. Against the former there was no redress, but as to the latter he resolved to retaliate, and prepared 'General Order No. 8,' whereby Major General Hooker, Brigadier Generals W. T. H. Brooks and John Newton were named for ignominious dismissal from the service; and Major Generals W. B. Franklin and W. F. Smith, and Brigadier Generals John Cochrane and Edward Ferrero and Lieutenant-Colonel J. H. Taylor were relieved from duty [but retained their commissions] . . . .

"Before promulgating this order, General Burnside was persuaded to submit it to the President, who, after consultation with his Cabinet, decided to relieve General Burnside instead of approving the order; and on the twenty-eighth of January an order was issued by the Secretary of War relieving Burnside from the command 'at his own request.' And Hooker, whom he had proposed to 'ignominiously dismiss,' became his successor."

27

Hooker Restores Morale

O N JANUARY 27, 1863, Captain William Thompson Lusk of the 79th New York wrote his mother: "Joe Hooker commands the Army of the Potomac. Everybody appears entirely indifferent to the matter. Heroes of many defeats, we are not inclined to give gratuitous confidence to anyone. Whoever finally succeeds any better than McClellan did has a fine chance for immortality. The Army of the Potomac is splendid material, and [if] taught that their best efforts are not to be wasted, they will tell for themselves a splendid story. . . . Possibly we are adopting the right course to find the right man, possibly the right course to insure our ruin."

If there was no sweep of enthusiasm at Hooker's rise, there was at least a general feeling that he was the best man available. As explained by Regis de Trobriand:

"His brilliant services as general of division, the part he had played at Antietam as corps commander, the wound he had received there; finally, the efforts he had made to prevent the useless butchery attending the attack on the Fredericksburg heights, were so many recommendations to the favor and the confidence of the soldier. He exercised a direct influence on the troops of his old commands by his open manners, his military bearing, and by his intrepidity under fire. . . .

"Towards the officers his manners were generally pleasant, familiar even to taking a glass of whiskey with those whom he liked. In the high position in which he was placed, a little more reserve would not have been out of place. He was . . . accustomed to criticize freely . . . even in the presence of his inferiors, the conduct and acts

Joseph Hooker

of his superiors. On the other hand, when it concerned himself, he indulged in boastings that one hearing could not accept as gospel truth, or reckon modesty in the number of his virtues. . . .

"He had not acquired the cordial feeling of the generals as much as that of the troops. He had wounded some by openly criticizing them; he had alienated others by putting himself forward at their expense."

Abraham Lincoln, in one of the most apt of his wartime letters, admonished Hooker:

"I think it best for you to know that there are some things in regard to which I am not quite satisfied with you. I believe you to be a brave and skilful soldier. . . . You have confidence in yourself, which is a valuable, if not an indispensable quality. You are ambitious, which, within reasonable bounds, does good rather than harm.

"But I think that during General Burnside's command of the army, you have taken counsel of your ambition and thwarted him as much as you could, in which you did a great wrong. . . .

"I have heard, in such a way as to believe it, of your recently saying that both the army and the government needed a dictator. Of course it was not *for* this, but in spite of it, that I have given you the command. Only those generals who gain success can set up dictators. What I now ask of you is military success, and I will risk the dictatorship. The government will support you to the utmost of its ability. . . .

"I much fear that the spirit which you have aided to infuse into the army, of criticizing their commander, and withholding confidence from him, will now turn upon you. I shall assist you as far as I can to put it down. . . .

"And now, beware of rashness . . . but with energy and sleepless vigilance go forward and give us victories."

Hooker, it appears, was not altogether blind to his faults. Although his immediate reaction to the letter is not known, a little later he referred to it as the kind of letter a father might write to his son. "Although I think he was harder on me than I deserved, I will say that I love the man who wrote it."

Hooker's first act was to change the army's organization. The grand divisions were broken up, and the old corps system reinstated. George Meade, a rising star, became one of the corps commanders.

Next, says Regis de Trobriand, Hooker "applied himself . . . to raise the morale of the army and to perfect its organization in the different branches of the service by a series of well-considered measures, the effect of which proved the excellence of his judgment in such matters. He therein gained the incontestable honor of being

Hooker's headquarters

the first who had raised the Army of the Potomac to the level of the regular armies of the Old World, and above the other armies of the American continent—in the first place by the perfection of its discipline and instruction, and in the second by the reform of abuses and the improvement of its regulations."

As explained by Hooker himself: "At the time when the command was given to me, the condition of the army was deplorable. The desertions had reached an average of two hundred a day. The express offices were full of packages containing citizen's clothing, intended for the deserters, so eager were the parents, wives, brothers, and sisters to assist the flight of their relatives. . . .

"I turned my attention to the means necessary to bring back the absent, and to make the men present as comfortable and contented as circumstances would permit. I made regulations as to furloughs and leaves of absence, so that everyone could be away a few days in the course of the winter. . . . Convinced that idleness was the great evil in all armies, I made every effort to keep the troops busy, particularly at drill and maneuvers, as often as the weather permitted.

"The cavalry was consolidated into a separate corps and put in the best condition ever known in our service. Whenever the state of the roads and of the river permitted, expeditions were started out to attack the pickets and advance posts of the enemy, and to forage in the country he occupied. My object was to encourage the men, to

Union cavalry foragers

incite in their hearts, by successes—however unimportant they might be—a sentiment of superiority over their adversaries. . . .

"During this period of preparation the army made rapid progress."

Hooker was not overstating. "The army," says General Darius Couch, "assumed wonderful vigor. I have never known men to change from a condition of the lowest depression to that of a healthy fighting state in so short a time."

"During the bright winter days," adds the *Boston Journal*'s Charles Carleton Coffin, "the soldiers went through their drills and maneuvers. The bands played stirring tunes. The inspector kept close watch of their arms and equipments and clothing. The surgeons were careful of the health of the army. The men on furlough returned with bright faces. Stragglers were brought back to their regiments. The army . . . became larger day by day. Homesickness disappeared. Wherever General Hooker rode he was welcomed with a cheer."

During their maneuvers in the field, the men sometimes sang a ditty that included these lines:

> *For God and our country*
> *We're marching along.*
> *Joe Hooker is our leader;*
> *He takes his whisky strong.*

Supplies in abundance—including first-rate rations—arrived in the camps by way of the railroad from Acquia Creek on the Potomac. There was, however, a serious shortage of firewood. Regis de Trobriand explains:

"One can hardly form an idea of the rapidity with which the forests disappear around an army in winter quarters. When we arrived before Fredericksburg at the end of November the country surrounding the city was covered with great woods of oaks and pines. At the end of February everything was cleared off, not only around our camps but even at a considerable distance. The country, so picturesque a few months before, now had the dull aspect of a vast and muddy desert."

"The men of our . . . division," says New Yorker George Stevens, "lugged wood on their backs a mile and a half, with which to do their cooking and warm their tents."

The struggles of "Dunn Browne" with the firewood problem led to another letter for the *Springfield Republican*:

"The other morning, as I was taking the air a little before breakfast—in other words, lugging a big log of firewood a couple of miles through the mud to camp, on my shoulder—stopping a few moments . . . to rest my back a bit, I noticed quite a commotion in the water of a little stream that flows through the valley below where I was standing.

"Three men were up to their middle in the brook, pulling and lifting at some large object, which I took to be a stump or log of wood which they were trying to rescue from the flood for the fire. But soon up drove another man with a span of mules and a long chain attached, which he quickly passed to his comrades and they dexterously fastened round a projecting part of the object in their hands.

"Crack goes the whip, and out comes, with a strong pull, not the log I had expected to see, but the dead body of a mule. 'Well,' thought I to myself, 'it is a little queer here in the army to see so much pains taken to keep the soldiers on the stream below us from having mule and water to drink; but let us be thankful for one instance of comparative civilization and decency.'

"But, lo! The fellows, having waited a moment for the water to

Shoeing a mule in Hooker's camps.

Hooker's butchers dressing cattle.

drip from their pantaloons, begin to belabor the carcass with clubs and whips and kicks. And after some minutes of this process, as if brought to life by the cruel abuse, up springs the deceased mule and trots off to his tying-post as lively as ever.

"Investigating the matter, I learned that that mule, becoming disgusted with life in Virginia, or else being at heart a secesh mule, and wishing to deprive Uncle Sam of his valuable services, had deliberately availed himself of the pretext of going to water to lie down and attempt suicide. . . . And if the teamsters hadn't plunged in and held up his head, and actually hauled the creature out of the water by the chain round his neck, the deed would have been accomplished."

Returning to narrator George Stevens: "Notwithstanding the hardships they endured, the inclemency of the weather, and their severe picket duty, the men were gay. In many of the regiments the sounds of the guitar and accordion could be heard every evening. And on pleasant afternoons and evenings, parties [of men] assembled in the company streets and danced cotillions and polkas and jigs, to the music of violins. When snow covered the ground, mimic battles with snowballs were a frequent amusement. . . .

"Another favorite amusement in the corps was the game of baseball. There were many excellent players in the different regiments, and it was common for the ball-players of one regiment or brigade to challenge another regiment or brigade. These matches were watched by great crowds of soldiers with intense interest."

According to the Pennsylvania chaplain, A. M. Stewart, Washington's Birthday, February 22, gave rise to a curious development.

"This year it happened upon the Sabbath. Had we been at home, Monday would most likely have been selected on which to ooze out this birthday patriotism. As no Sabbath is allowed us in camp [Sunday was just another day], the actual birthday was observed.

"During the entire day a pitiless and furious eastern snowstorm beat upon our exposed condition, piling ... heavy drifts in and around our fragile dwelling-places. The effort of each one in camp was, in appearance, to squeeze through the day with what grains of comfort could be gathered under the conditions, letting birthdays and death-days take care of themselves.

"My ... veneration for the great *Pater Patriae* must have been very sadly at fault; for, during the entire forenoon, not the slightest consciousness or memory existed that an annual return of the day had come. ... A dim impression there was that it was the Lord's day, and that a furious snowstorm was debarring outdoor religious exercises.

"About noon, when the storm was at its height, we were all startled by a heavy cannonade, which commenced upon our left and soon extended far along [our] lines. It seemed as though a great battle were opening. The rebels must have taken advantage of the storm suddenly to cross the river. What greatly strengthened this impression was that presently a brisk cannonade also commenced along the rebel lines.

"Our suspense and excitement were, however, ere long quieted by an undisturbed soldier who ... shouted, 'Washington's Birthday!'

"Ah, yes, how stupid not to have remembered. ... Federals and Confederates, both shooting at the memory of Washington!

"Fortunate, no doubt, that the old gentleman is dead. If living, he might be exposed to both fires."

In Lee's army, the winter found the men in their usual state of want. "The rations," says South Carolinian J. F. J. Caldwell, "were reduced from one and one-eighth pounds of flour to a pound, from three-quarters of a pound of bacon to half, one-third, and finally one-quarter of a pound. Beef was rarely issued in any quantity. Sugar was liberally furnished for two or three months, but no coffee, of course. We fell into more fashionable habits, breakfasting late and dining at four or five. There was not often a third meal. We were only too happy to get two full ones."

Work-wise, it was not a hard winter. D. Augustus Dickert explains: "We had little picketing to do. . . . Guard duty around camp was abolished for the winter; so was drilling, only on nice, warm days; the latter, however, was rarely seen during that season.

"The troops abandoned themselves to baseball, snow fights, writing letters, and receiving as guests in their camps friends and relatives who never failed to bring with them great boxes of the good things from home, as well as clothing and shoes for the needy soldiers. Furloughs were granted in limited numbers. Recruits, and now the thoroughly healed of the wounded from the many engagements, flocked to our ranks, making all put on a cheerful face."

A vignette of the winter is given by Stonewall Jackson's aide, James Power Smith:

"One day there came a note from Lee asking Jackson to come to see him at his convenience. In the evening Jackson said he would ride up there the next morning, and directed me to be ready to accompany him.

"When the early morning came, the country lay under a heavy fall of snow and the cold was severe, with the snow still falling. I turned

Evening roll call in a Confederate camp.

over in my blanket and went to sleep again, thinking that the general would not go. But an orderly awoke me, saying that the general was ready to mount and waiting for me.

"I was soon in the saddle by his side, without my breakfast; and a worse ride than that one, in the face of the storm for twelve or fourteen miles, I never had.

"General Lee was surprised and quite indignant that General Jackson had come. Walking out into the snow without his hat, he reproached Jackson, saying, 'You know I did not wish you to come in such a storm. It was a matter of little importance. I am so sorry that you have had this ride.'

"Jackson blushed and smiled, and said, 'I received your note, General Lee!'"

At Jeb Stuart's headquarters, things were generally quiet that winter, and by mid-February Heros von Borcke was growing bored.

"The remnant of February and a part of March dragged slowly by, so dull and eventless that existence was scarcely tolerable, and we looked forward to the commencement of spring and the reopening of the campaign with intense longing.

"On the 15th of March Stuart left for Culpeper, where he had to appear as a witness at a court-martial; and Pelham [met him there]. . . . The general had placed me in charge over the pickets at the different fords up the Rappahannock from Fredericksburg. . . .

"On the morning of the 17th, which was one of those mild, hazy March days that betoken the approach of spring, we were suddenly stirred up, in the midst of our lazy, listless existence, by the sound of a cannonade which seemed to come from the direction of United States Ford . . . about ten miles above Fredericksburg.

"I was in my saddle in a moment, fancying that the enemy was attempting to force a passage at one of the points placed under my charge; but when I had galloped in hot haste up to the river, I found that the firing was much further off. . . . When I reached my pickets I received a report that a heavy fight was going on in the direction of Culpeper Courthouse, near Kelly's Ford, at least fifteen miles in a straight line higher up the river.

"The cannonade, which seemed growing louder and fiercer all through the morning, gradually slackened as the day advanced; and in the evening when I returned to camp was completely silenced. . . .

"It was a beautiful calm evening, the silence of which was broken only by the song of the thrush or the monotonous tapping of the

The cavalry fight at Kelly's Ford.

woodpecker—one of those evenings that seem made for a melancholy and sentimental mood. And, strange to say, by such a mood was I now completely overcome, my thoughts constantly reverting to my dear friend Pelham, with an obstinate foreboding that some dreadful fate must have befallen him. . . .

"Next morning, about an hour before daylight, I was roused from my slumbers by hearing someone riding up to my tent, and startled out of bed by the voice of one of the couriers Stuart had taken with him, who, with much agitation of manner, reported that the general had been engaged with Fitz Lee's brigade in a sanguinary battle against far superior numbers of the enemy, and had beaten them [the Confederates had actually been thrown back, then took control of the field as the Federals retired across the river], but at the cost of many lives, and among them that of Pelham, the gallant chief of our horse-artillery.

"Poor Pelham! He had . . . met his death in a comparatively small engagement after passing safely through so many great battles. Being on a visit of pleasure [in Culpeper], he . . . at the first sound of the cannon, hastened . . . on a horse [he had] borrowed . . . to the field of action. . . . He rushed forward into the thickest of the fight, cheering on our men and animating them by his example. . . . A fragment of a shell, which exploded close over his head, penetrated the back part of the skull and stretched the young hero insensible on the ground.

"He was carried at once to Culpeper, where the young ladies of Mr. S.'s family tended him with sisterly care; but he never again recovered his senses. . . .

"This sad intelligence spread through the whole camp in a few minutes, and the impression of melancholy sorrow it produced on all is beyond description, so liked and admired had Pelham been, and so proud were we of his gallantry. One after the other, comrades entered my tent to hear the confirmation of the dreadful news. . . .

"I was much touched by the behavior of Pelham's Negro servants, Willis and Newton, who, with tokens of the greatest distress, begged to be allowed at once to go and take charge of their master's body— a permission which I was, however, constrained to refuse. . . .

"I received a telegram from Stuart ordering me to proceed by the next train to Hanover Junction, there to receive Pelham's body and bring it to Richmond, and then to make all the arrangements necessary to have it conveyed to Alabama, his native state. I started at once and reached the Junction in time to receive the corpse, which, along with several others, was enclosed in a simple wooden case and under the charge of one of our artillerymen, who, with tears in his eyes, gave me the particulars of his gallant commander's death.

"I did not reach Richmond until late at night, and, not finding the hearse, which I had telegraphed to be in readiness at the station, was obliged to remove the body into the town in a common one-horse wagon. Immediately on arriving I went to Governor Letcher . . . who kindly afforded all the assistance in his power, and placed a room at my disposal in the Capitol, where the Confederate Congress held its sessions. The coffin was placed in it, covered with the large flag of the State of Virginia, and a guard of honor was placed over it.

"The next day I procured a handsome iron coffin, and with my own hands assisted in transferring the body to its new receptacle. I was overcome with grief as I touched the lifeless hand that had so often pressed mine in the grasp of friendship. His manly features even in death expressed that fortitude and pride which distinguished him. By special request I had a small glass window let into the coffin-lid just over the face, that his friends and admirers might take a last look at the young hero, and they came in troops, the

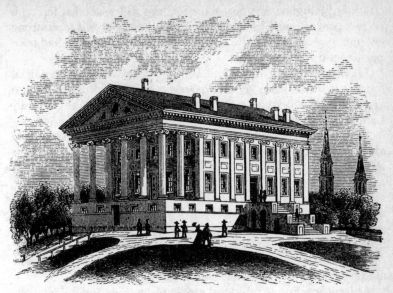

Confederate capitol

majority being ladies, who brought garlands and magnificent bouquets to lay upon the coffin.

"Meantime I had communicated with several members of Congress from Alabama, friends of Pelham's father, and it had been decided that his remains should be conveyed to Alabama in charge of a young soldier, a connection of the family who had just been released from one of the Richmond hospitals.

"The afternoon of the following day was appointed for the departure, and at five o'clock we carried the coffin to the station, the Richmond battalion of infantry doing the military honors, and a large number of dignitaries of the Confederate States, friends, and comrades following.

"Alabama paid as solemn a tribute of respect to her gallant son as he deserved to have shown him. As soon as the frontier of the state was reached, a guard of honor escorted the coffin, and at every station on the road ladies were waiting to adorn it with flowers."

Toward the end of March General Lee came down with a heavy cold, and he was also stricken with a series of pains in his chest, back, and arms that were diagnosed as being related to "an inflammation of the heart-sac." He had probably suffered a mild heart attack. Although it was necessary for him to forsake his tent and enter a private house for warmth and bed rest, Lee was soon strong enough to resume his regular duties. His health, however, had been permanently diminished.

The first days in April found Union General Hooker preparing for a visit to the army by the President and Mrs. Lincoln, due to arrive on the fourth. A grand review was ordered. As related by Lieutenant Jesse Bowman Young:

"Many miles of marching were necessary in order that all the army should be marshaled at one point, as their camps were scattered over a large extent of country.... From far and wide they came, their bands of music mingling in patriotic strains in the glowing, buoyant air, the generals in splendid uniforms and showily mounted on prancing horses, the artillery ... at a gallop, the cavalry dashing across the plains, the staff officers gayly loping their horses hither and thither with their orders and messages; and, in brief, the whole mechanism of an army, handled with skill, ease, grace, and military pomp, amid intense enthusiasm and ardor.

"At last the whole army stood in line of battle—General Hooker, with the President and other noted visitors from Washington, in the midst of a brilliantly dressed body of officers, posted in front of the center of the line. When the troops had presented arms and the banners had drooped, and the bands had united in a piercing blast of music, the commanding general and troops passed in review, proud, hopeful, exultant, confident in their leader, and believing in their beloved President, 'Father Abraham.' "

At one time during the proceedings, General Darius Couch joined the President's party. "Mr. Lincoln, sitting there with his hat off, head bent, and seemingly meditating, suddenly turned to me and said, 'General Couch, what do you suppose will become of all these men when the war is over?' And it struck me as very pleasant that somebody had an idea that the war would sometime end."

Returning to Jesse Bowman Young: "During that visit the President made a hasty visit to many of the camps of the soldiers, galloping from one encampment to another, greeted with hearty cheers, showing his long, ungainly, awkward figure to poor advantage on horseback, making a very brief address now and then to 'the boys,' and leaving his image—the picture of patience, fidelity, political shrewdness, and indomitable gentleness and human kindness—indelibly printed in their hearts."

Lincoln returned to Washington encouraged by the look of the

Lincoln visiting the camps.

troops but with the troubling awareness that their commander's self-assurance had risen to a dangerous level. Hooker had begun claiming that he'd created "the finest army on the planet." The Confederates, he said, had better be ready to run, for he planned to drive straight for Richmond. He capped his boasting with: "My plans are perfect, and when I start to carry them out, may God have mercy on General Lee, for I will have none."

New misgivings beset the harried President, and he voiced his classic line: "The hen is the wisest of all the animal creation, because she never cackles until the egg is laid."

28

The Onset of Chancellorsville

DOWN IN Charlotte, North Carolina, Stonewall Jackson's wife, Mary Anna, had been following events at Fredericksburg by means of letters from her husband. She relates:

"As the spring advanced and the season for campaigning drew nearer, General Jackson grew more and more anxious to have a visit from his wife and child [the new baby he had not yet seen]. His solicitous consideration for the health and safety of the little one had led him to advise their not traveling until the winter was over; and now he showed great eagerness to have a visit before the campaign should open. . . .

"Little Julia was nearly five months old now, and was plump, rosy, and good. And with her nurse, Hetty, we set out upon this visit, so full of interest and anticipated joys. We made the journey safely, stopping in Richmond to spend Sunday, and arrived at Guiney's Station [south of Fredericksburg] at noon on Monday, the 20th of April. Hetty and I were all anxiety to have our baby present her best appearance for her father's first sight of her, and she could not have better realized our wishes. She awoke from a long, refreshing sleep just before the train stopped, and never looked more bright and charming.

"When he entered the coach to receive us, his rubber overcoat was dripping from the rain which was falling, but his face was all sunshine and gladness; and, after greeting his wife, it was a picture, indeed, to see his look of perfect delight and admiration as his eyes fell upon that baby. . . . He was afraid to take her in his arms, with his wet overcoat; but as we drove in a carriage to Mr. Yerby's [a house near Hamilton's Crossing], his face reflected all the happiness and delight that were in his heart. . . . Upon our arrival at the house he speedily divested himself of his overcoat, and, taking his baby in his arms, he caressed her with the tenderest affection. . . .

"During the whole of this short visit, when he was with us, he rarely had her out of his arms. . . . When she slept in the day, he would often kneel over her cradle and gaze upon her little face with the most rapt admiration. . . . And yet with all his fondness and devotion to the little lady, he had no idea of spoiling her. . . . One day she began to cry to be taken from the bed on which she was lying, and as soon as her wish was gratified she ceased to cry. He laid her back upon the bed, and the crying was renewed with increased violence.

"Of course, the mother-heart wished to stop this by taking her up again, but he exclaimed, 'This will never do!' and commanded 'all hands off' until that little will of her own should be conquered. So there she lay, kicking and screaming, while he stood over her with as much coolness and determination as if he were directing a battle. . . . When she stopped crying he would take her up, and if she began to cry again he would lay her down again; and this he kept up until finally she was completely conquered, and became perfectly quiet in his hands.

"On the 23rd of April—the day she was five months old— General Jackson had little Julia baptized. . . . The next Sabbath was a most memorable one to me, being the last upon which I was privileged to attend divine service with my husband on earth, and to worship in camp with such a company of soldiers as I had never seen together in a religious congregation. . . . I remember how reverent and impressive was General Lee's bearing, and how handsome he looked, with his splendid figure and faultless military attire. . . . My husband . . . never appeared to be in better health than at this time, and I never saw him look so handsome and noble. . . .

"General Jackson did not permit the presence of his family to interfere in any way with his military duties. The greater part of each day he spent at his headquarters. . . .

"Our military leaders had diligently employed the winter months in preparing their troops for the greatest efficiency in the approaching campaign. . . . General Lee found himself at the head of an army unsurpassed in discipline and all the hardy virtues of the soldier. . . . The splendid morale of this army did not need improve-

ment. . . . Insufficient clothing and scanty rations produced no effect upon it. . . .

"But as the campaign drew on apace, my delightful visit was
destined to come to an end. . . . [It] had lasted only nine days, when,
early on the morning of the 29th of April we were aroused by a
messenger at our door saying, 'General Early's adjutant wishes to
see General Jackson.' As he arose he said, 'That looks as if Hooker
were crossing.' He hurried downstairs, and soon returning, he told
me that his surmise was correct—Hooker was crossing the river,
and . . . he must go immediately to the scene of action. . . .

"He thought a battle was imminent, and under the circumstances
he was unwilling for us to remain in so exposed a situation as Mr.
Yerby's. He therefore directed me to prepare to start for Richmond
at a moment's notice. . . . After a tender and hasty good-bye,
he hurried off without breakfast. Scarcely had he gone when the
roar of cannons began—volley after volley following in quick
succession—the house shaking and windows rattling from the rever-
berations, throwing the family into great panic. . . .

"My hasty preparations for leaving were hardly completed when
Mr. [Drury] Lacy, the chaplain, came with an ambulance, saying he
had been sent by General Jackson to convey his family to the railroad station as speedily as possible in order to catch the morning
train to Richmond. . . . He brought a cheerful note from my husband, explaining why he could not leave his post, and invoking
God's care and blessing upon us in our sudden departure. . . .

"A rapid and continuous rattle of musketry showed us that the
battle was now under way, and before we left Mr. Yerby's yard we saw
several wounded soldiers brought in and placed in the out-houses,
which the surgeons were arranging as temporary hospitals. This
was my nearest and only glimpse of the actual horrors of the battlefield. . . .

"How sad and harrowing was my drive to the station on that
terrible morning! The distance was several miles, and as we journeyed along over a newly cut road, filled with stumps and roots, we
could hear the sounds of battle, and my heart was heavy with
foreboding and dread.

"We were in good time for the train, and . . . in a few hours we
were in Richmond among kind friends."

Mary Anna did not know that what she believed to be a major
thrust on Hooker's part was really only a demonstration against
Lee's right, a cover for more serious work elsewhere. Hooker, com-

Sedgwick's corps crossing the Rappahannock.

manding about 135,000 men, had devised a superb plan to employ against Lee's sixty thousand. (Lee was particularly short of troops at this time because Longstreet, with two divisions, was on detached duty to the south, his principal mission to gather supplies.) Hooker's plan called for John Sedgwick, with some fifty thousand men, to demonstrate against the defenses below Fredericksburg, while a larger part of the army marched up the north bank of the Rappahannock for the purpose of circling southward to a position a distance west of Lee's left-rear. Although a hitch developed in that a cavalry force under General George Stoneman, ordered to make a raid around Lee to disrupt his communications, failed to get going in time and thus negated its value to the campaign, Hooker's infantry plan lost little of its promise.

The circling columns headed for Chancellorsville, south of the Rappahannock about ten miles west of Fredericksburg, and they achieved a concentration there on the evening of April 30.

"Chancellorsville," according to Henry Blake, the captain from New York, "consisted of a large brick building, built in the style of the last century [the 1700s]; and, with the exception of massive pillars in its front that extended from the basement to the roof, was very plain in its appearance. Negro cabins, cooking-houses, and other small outbuildings were upon the grounds near the dwelling, which was occupied by the Chancellor family [even as the Yankees made their intrusion]; and the garden contained a private cemetery which was planted with pines and savins, beneath the branches of which the kindred of the proprietors slept in their graves."

General Darius Couch, now second-in-command to Hooker, says that the movement to Chancellorsville had been "brilliantly conceived and executed. . . . All of the army lying there that night were in exuberant spirits at the success of their general in getting 'on the other side' without fighting for a position. As I rode into Chancel-

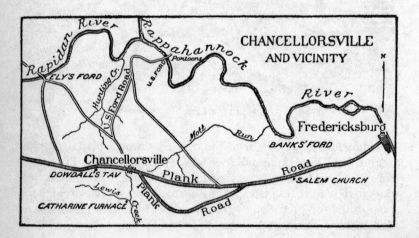

Hooker's march to Chancellorsville

lorsville that night the general hilarity pervading the camps was particularly noticeable. The soldiers, while chopping wood and lighting fires, were singing merry songs and indulging in peppery camp jokes.

"The position at Chancellorsville not only took in reverse the entire system of the enemy's river defenses, but there were roads leading from it directly to his line of communication."

Hooker was supremely pleased with his work, announcing to the army that "our enemy must either ingloriously fly or come out from behind his defenses and give us battle on our own ground, where certain destruction awaits him." To a group of officers the general said, "I have the rebellion in my breeches pocket, and God Almighty himself cannot take it away from me." Some of the listeners were chilled by this remark, one saying to a friend, "I do not like that sort of talk on the eve of battle. There is no sense in defying the Almighty when you are fighting General Lee."

Lee had hoped to avoid a showdown fight with Hooker until James Longstreet returned from the south, but he had no intention

Union troops at the Chancellor House

of "ingloriously flying." At first uncertain which of Hooker's wings
was the greater threat, he did nothing more than to send Richard
Anderson's division toward Chancellorsville to guard the roads to
his rear. Lee relates:

"The enemy in our front near Fredericksburg continued inactive,
and it was now apparent that the main attack would be made upon
our flank and rear. It was therefore determined to leave sufficient
troops to hold our lines, and with the main body of the army to give
battle to the approaching column. Early's division . . . and Barksdale's brigade . . . with part of the reserve artillery . . . were intrusted with the defense of our position at Fredericksburg; and at
midnight on the 30th General McLaws marched . . . toward Chancellorsville. General Jackson followed at dawn next morning."

This dawn of Friday, May 1, was a grim dawn for Hooker. His

exultation had faded. He was losing his nerve. To the surprise of his subordinate commanders, he kept the army inactive as the sun rose high.

"With such superiority of numbers on the Union side," says Francis Walker, the Second Corps staff officer, "there was no justification for an hour's delay. The cry should have been 'forward,' at least until the turning column . . . should be deployed before Lee's positions. Not only is this the sole policy of safety and success in movements like those which Hooker had undertaken, but two additional reasons, perfectly obvious at the time, existed to make such a policy in this instance peculiarly imperative.

"One was that the farther Hooker pushed forward from Chancellorsville toward Fredericksburg, the better was the opportunity afforded for the development of his superior infantry and artillery. The ground about Chancellorsville was low, much of it densely wooded. By moving promptly out toward Fredericksburg, Hooker would have placed his army on high ground, obtaining commanding positions for his artillery and comparatively clear ground for the movements and maneuvers of his infantry.

"The second reason, special to the situation, imperatively demanding an immediate advance, was that to gain four or five miles

Richard H. Anderson

toward Fredericksburg was to uncover Banks' Ford [see map, page 356]; and, by so doing, to shorten, by nearly one-half, [communications with the wing under Sedgwick].

"So plain was this dictate of the situation that General Hooker— though after a hesitation most ominous of evil—gave the order for an advance.

"There were three roads leading toward Fredericksburg. The first was the river road.... The two other roads ... [were] the turnpike and plank road.... Thus three columns, within easy connecting distance, took up the march together....

"These columns proceeded, against all the opposition the enemy was able to offer, until they gained a ridge which sweeps across the three roads mentioned, crossing the turnpike somewhat more than two miles from Chancellorsville. [Here the fighting intensified, but Hooker kept the advantage.]

"The position reached was one in every way easy to hold. It afforded room and range for a powerful artillery, and could readily have been crowned before night by ninety guns. The ground in front was largely open; the roads behind sufficiently numerous for a rapid reinforcement of the line or for a safe retreat. The field was exactly such a one as the men of the Army of the Potomac had always been crying out for—one on which they could see the enemy they were called to fight.

"Yet this position General Hooker, in an evil hour, determined to abandon—not for one farther advanced, but for the low and wooded ground about Chancellorsville, relinquishing the very *form and show* of aggression, retreating before the enemy and taking up a line which was completely commanded by the [abandoned] high ground.... The act was little short of suicide....

"The Army of the Potomac, which at noon [had been] in full advance on Fredericksburg, with high hopes elate, had now, under the evil inspirations which had withered the courage of its commander, abandoned the initiative [and] surrendered the main benefits of the splendid success achieved at the outset of the campaign, retreating [under vigorous harassment] before the enemy and taking up a defensive position.

"And such a defensive position! The new line was drawn through low and largely wooded ground, commanded here [and] enfiladed there by the batteries which the advancing enemy were already establishing on the high ground which had been abandoned....

"As Generals Couch, Meade, Sykes, and Hancock sat on their

horses in a group, close behind the division of the last-named officer, General Meade, looking up the road, exclaimed with great emphasis, 'My God! If we can't hold the top of a hill, we certainly cannot hold the bottom of it!'

"General Hooker, however, did not share the regret . . . at the abandonment of the advanced position. To Couch, on reporting at headquarters, he said confidently, 'It is all right, Couch. I have got Lee just where I want him. He must fight me on my own ground.' "

Adds Couch himself: "To hear from his own lips that the advantages gained by the successful marches of his lieutenants were to culminate in fighting a defensive battle in that nest of thickets was too much, and I retired from his presence with the belief that my commanding general was a whipped man."

Couch noted a change in the mood of the men in the ranks. "The high expectations which had animated them only a few hours ago had given place to disappointment."

29

Jackson's Flanking Maneuver

THE LATTER part of May 1 found Hooker busy with his defensive preparations, while Lee engaged in assessing their nature by means of scouts and probes. By nightfall the Confederate commander had learned that "the enemy had assumed a position of great natural strength, surrounded on all sides by a dense forest filled with a tangled undergrowth, in the midst of which breastworks of logs had been constructed, with trees felled in front so as to form an almost impenetrable abatis. . . . It was evident that a direct attack . . . would be attended with great difficulty and loss, in view of the strength of his position and his superiority of numbers. It was therefore resolved to endeavor to turn his right flank [which lay, of course, to the Confederate left] and gain his rear, leaving a force in front to hold him in check and conceal the movement."

Stonewall Jackson's aide, James Power Smith, says that the plan was matured in the dead of the night, while the Confederate troops were asleep on the ground.

"Sometime after midnight I was awakened by the chill of the early morning hours, and, turning over, caught a glimpse of a little flame on the slope above me; and, sitting up to see what it meant, I saw, bending over a scant fire of twigs, two men seated on old cracker boxes and warming their hands over the little fire. I had but to rub my eyes and collect my wits to recognize the figures of Robert E. Lee and Stonewall Jackson."

Returning to Lee's account: "The execution of this plan was intrusted to Lieutenant General Jackson with his three divisions [about 28,000 men]. The commands of General McLaws and Anderson [hardly 20,000 men in total] . . . remained in front of the enemy. Early on the morning of [Saturday] the 2d, General Jackson marched by the Furnace and Brock roads [see map, page 364], his movement being effectually covered by Fitzhugh Lee's cavalry, under General Stuart in person."

Switching to the Union side and to newsman-historian William Swinton:

"This movement, skilfully masked as it was, was not made with such secrecy but that those who held the front of the Union line saw that *something* was going on. And, more especially, in passing over a hill near the Furnace the column plainly disclosed itself to General Sickles, who held a position within sight of that point.

"Now, it happened that the road along which Jackson's column was filing there bends somewhat southward, so that, though the movement was discovered, it was misinterpreted as a *retreat* towards

Last council of Lee and Jackson

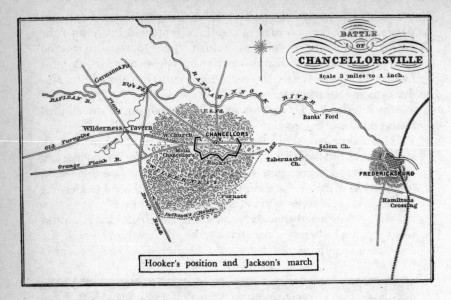

Hooker's position and Jackson's march

Richmond on the part of Lee. . . . If the idea suggested itself that it might be a movement to turn the right, it was still judged [in final analysis] . . . to be a retreat.

"With the view of determining this, but yet more under the conviction that Lee was withdrawing, Sickles was sent out with two divisions to reconnoiter and attack him. At about three o'clock in the afternoon he advanced through the Wilderness for a mile and a half or two miles, reached the road on which Jackson had moved, struck the rear of his column, and began to take prisoners. Elated by his success, the result of which he communicated to Hooker, General Sickles asked for reinforcements; and . . . Pleasonton's cavalry and two brigades of infantry were sent him."

In the end, the chief effect of Sickles's work was to hasten Jackson's march. Hooker continued to delude himself that Lee was in full retreat. Even earlier, however, the Federal commander had instructed his right to prepare for the *possibility* of a flank attack. Unfortunately, the key figures there remained unconcerned. It seemed highly unlikely that Lee, after leaving a part of his army at Fredericksburg, would divide it a second time. Moreover, the woods on the Federal right seemed to be too thick to host a successful approach.

Among the Confederates riding at the head of Jackson's column was Heros von Borcke:

"By about four o'clock we had completed our movement without encountering any material obstacle, and reached a patch of wood in rear of the enemy's right wing, formed by the 11th Corps, Howard's, which was encamped in a large, open field not more than half a mile distant. Halting here, the cavalry threw forward a body of skirmishers to occupy the enemy's attention, while the divisions of Jackson's corps . . . moved into line of battle as fast as they arrived.

"Ordered to reconnoiter the position of the Federals, I rode cautiously forward through the forest, and reached a point whence I obtained a capital view of the greater part of their troops, whose attitude betokened how totally remote was any suspicion that a numerous host was so near at hand. It was evident that [our presence] . . . was regarded as merely an unimportant cavalry raid, for only a few squadrons were drawn up in line to oppose us, and a battery of four guns was placed in a position to command the plank road . . . over which we had been marching. . . .

"The main body of the troops were listlessly reposing, while some regiments were looking on, drawn up on dress parade. Artillery

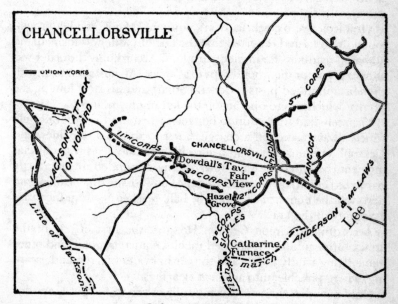

Jackson's evening attack

horses were quietly grazing at some distance from their guns, and the whole scene presented a picture of the most perfect heedlessness and nonchalance, compatible only with utter unconsciousness of impending danger.

"While complacently gazing on this extraordinary spectacle, somewhat touched myself . . . with the spell of listless incaution in which our antagonists were locked, I was startled by the sound of closely approaching footsteps, and, turning in their direction, beheld a patrol of six or eight of the enemy's infantry just breaking through the bushes and gazing at me with most unmistakable astonishment. I had no time to lose here, that was quite certain; so, quickly tugging my horse's head round in the direction of my line of retreat and digging my spurs into his sides, I dashed off before the bewildered Yankees, and was out of sight ere they had time to take steady aim, the bullets that came whizzing after me flying far wide of the mark.

"On my return to the spot where I had left Stuart, I found him, with Jackson and the officers of their respective staffs, stretched out along the grass beneath a gigantic oak and tranquilly discussing their plans for the impending battle, which both seemed confidently to regard as likely to end in a great and important victory for our arms.

"Towards five o'clock Jackson's adjutant, Major Pendleton, galloped up to us and reported that the line of battle was formed and all was in readiness for immediate attack. Accordingly the order was at once given for the whole corps to advance. All hastened forthwith to their appointed posts—General Stuart and his staff joining the cavalry, which was to operate on the left of our infantry.

"Scarcely had we got up to our men when the Confederate yell, which always preceded a charge, burst forth along our lines, and Jackson's veterans, who had been with difficulty held back till that moment, bounded forward towards the astounded and perfectly paralyzed enemy, while the thunder of our horse artillery, on whom devolved the honor of opening the ball, reached us from the other extremity of the line."

According to Union General Howard, the first effects of the attack "appeared in the startled rabbits, squirrels, quail, and other game flying wildly hither and thither in evident terror, and escaping, where possible, into adjacent clearings."

Only now did Howard become fully aware of his peril, and his feverish efforts to ward off disaster came to nothing.

Howard trying to rally his men.

Returning to the Confederate side and to Heros von Borcke, who, along with many other men on horseback, was having trouble advancing:

"The more hotly we sought to hasten to the front, the more obstinately did we get entangled in the undergrowth, while our infantry moved on so rapidly that the Federals were already completely routed by the time we had got thoroughly quit of the forest.

"It was a strange spectacle that now greeted us. The whole of the 11th Corps had broken at the first shock of the attack. Entire regiments had thrown down their arms, which were lying in regular lines on the ground, as if for inspection. Suppers just prepared had been abandoned. Tents, baggage, wagons, cannons, half-slaughtered oxen covered the foreground in chaotic confusion, while in the background a host of many thousand Yankees were discerned scampering for their lives as fast as their limbs could carry them, closely followed by our men, who were taking prisoners by the hundreds."

The few regiments that tried to stand were soon swept away. Stonewall Jackson, riding at the front, urged his units to "Press on! Press on!" Leaning forward on his horse, he extended the heel of his right palm at arm's length as though literally trying to push the attack.

An aide riding with the general, Captain R. E. Wilbourn, says that "frequently . . . he would stop, raise his hand and turn his eyes toward heaven, as if praying for a blessing on our arms. . . . Our troops made repeated charges, driving the enemy before them every time, which caused loud and long-continued cheering along our entire line, which was ever the signal for victory—and General Jackson would invariably raise his hand and give thanks to Him who

Confederates sweeping through Howard's lines.

gave the victory. I have never seen him so well pleased with the progress and results of a fight as on that occasion."

Confederate Private John Casler takes up: "We had a nice chance to plunder their camps and search the dead; but the men were afraid to stop, as they . . . were near a good many officers who might whack them over the head with their swords if they saw them plundering. But the temptation was too great, and sometimes they would run their hands in some dead men's pockets as they hurried along, but seldom procured anything of value.

"I saw a wounded man lying beside the road and had got past him; but, noticing he was an officer, I ran back to him to get his sword and pistol. . . . He was shot through the foot. . . . I took off his belt and sword, which was a very fine one, but found no pistol in the scabbard. . . . He said he supposed he must have lost it in the fight . . . but I thought he had it in his bosom, so I unbuttoned his coat and searched him for it, but could not find it. . . . He had a fine gold watch and chain. I was looking at it when he told me to take it along. But I would not do it. I told him that, as he was wounded and a prisoner, I would let him keep it."

It was now about 7 P.M. and daylight was beginning to fade. Jackson's front was only about half a mile west of Hooker's headquarters at the Chancellor House.

"The situation at this moment," explains Northerner William Swinton, "was extremely critical, for, the Eleventh Corps having been brushed away, it was absolutely necessary to form a new line, and it was difficult to see whence the troops were to be drawn; for just at that moment Lee [having responded to the sound of Jackson's assault] was making a vigorous front attack on Hooker's left and center, formed by Couch's and Slocum's corps. Hancock's front, especially, was assailed with great impetuosity; but the attacking column was held in check in the most intrepid manner by Hancock's skirmish line under Colonel [Nelson] Miles.

"The open plain around Chancellorsville now presented such a spectacle as a simoom sweeping over the desert might make. Through the dusk of nightfall, a rushing whirlwind of men and artillery and wagons swept down the road, and past headquarters, and on towards the fords of the Rappahannock; and it was in vain that the staff opposed their persons and drawn sabers to the panic-stricken fugitives.

"But it chanced that at this moment General Pleasonton, who had gone out with his cavalry to reinforce Sickles [in his attack on the rear of Jackson's marching column], was returning; and, on learning the giving way of the right wing, he moved forward rapidly, sent his horsemen on the charge into the woods, and, bringing into position his own battery of horse artillery, and such guns—twenty-two in all—as he could collect, he poured double charges of canister into the advancing line.

"Hooker, too, flaming out with the old fire of battle, called for his own old division, the darling child of his creation, now under General [Hiram] Berry, and shouted to its commander, 'Throw your men into the breech. Receive the enemy on your bayonets....' Berry's division, unaffected by the flying crowd streaming past it, hastened forward at the double-quick in the most perfect order, with fixed bayonets, and took position on a crest at the western end of the clearing around Chancellorsville.

"Here ... Berry's men and the artillery of the Twelfth Corps ... and [William] Hays' brigade of the Second Corps formed a line to check the enemy in front, while Pleasonton and Sickles assailed his right flank; and fifty pieces of artillery, vomiting their missiles in wild curves of fire athwart the night sky, poured swift destruction into the Confederate ranks."

A bright moon was shining, so the darkness was not absolute. As recalled by Southerner J. F. J. Caldwell:

"Volley after volley of musketry was poured by the Confederate line ... upon the enemy; the enemy replied with equal rapidity; cheers, wild and fierce, rang over the whole woods; officers shouted at the top of their voices to make themselves heard; cannon roared and shells burst continuously. ...

"Night engagements are always dreadful, but this was the worst I ever knew. To see your danger is bad enough; but to hear shell whizzing and bursting over you, to hear shrapnel and iron fragments slapping the trees and cracking off limbs, and not know from whence death comes to you, is trying beyond all things. And here it looked so incongruous—*below*, rage, thunder, shout, shriek, slaughter; *above*, soft, silent, smiling moonlight and peace!"

Stonewall Jackson was at this time with the troops on the left of his attack. In spite of the resistance he had begun to encounter, he intended to persist, his aim to swing farther behind Hooker's right and cut him off from the Rappahannock.

"It was impossible, however," says Southerner John Esten Cooke, "to execute so important a movement until his troops were well in hand, and the two divisions which had made the attack had become

Opposing Jackson with artillery fire

mixed up in a very confused manner. They were accordingly directed to halt, and General A. P. Hill, whose division had not been engaged, was sent for and ordered to advance to the front, thus affording the disordered divisions an opportunity to reform their broken lines.

"Soon after dispatching this order, Jackson [accompanied by two or three of his staff and a number of couriers and signal sergeants] rode out in front of his line, on the Chancellorsville road, in order to reconnoiter in person, and ascertain, if possible, the position and movements of the enemy, then within a few hundred yards of him. . . . The fighting had temporarily ceased, and the moon, half-seen through misty clouds, lit up the dreary thickets, in which no sound was heard but the incessant and melancholy cries of the whippoorwills."

As continued by Jackson's aide, James Power Smith:

"He . . . began the ascent of the hill toward Chancellorsville, when he came upon a line of the Federal infantry lying on their arms. Fired at by one or two muskets . . . he turned and came back toward his line, upon the side of the road to his left. As he rode near to the Confederate troops, just placed in position and ignorant that he was in the front, the left company began firing . . . and two of his party fell from their saddles dead. . . .

"Spurring his horse across the road to his right, he was met by a second volley from the right company of Pender's [actually James Lane's] North Carolina brigade. Under this volley . . . the general received three balls at the same instant. One penetrated the palm of his right hand. . . . A second passed around the wrist of the left arm and out through the left hand. A third ball passed through the left arm halfway from shoulder to elbow. The large bone of the upper arm was splintered to the elbow-joint, and the wound bled freely.

"His horse turned quickly from the fire, through the thick bushes which swept the cap from the general's head and scratched his forehead, leaving drops of blood to stain his face. As he lost his hold upon the bridle-rein, he reeled from the saddle and was caught by the arms of Captain Wilbourn [who was riding beside him]. . . . Laid upon the ground, there came at once to his succor General A. P. Hill and members of his staff.

"[I] reached his side a minute after, to find General Hill holding the head and shoulders of the wounded chief. Cutting open the coat-sleeve from wrist to shoulder, I found the wound in the upper arm, and with my handkerchief I bound the arm above the wound to stem the flow of blood. Couriers were sent for Dr. Hunter McGuire, the surgeon of the corps and the general's trusted friend, and for an ambulance.

"Being outside of our lines, it was urgent that he should be moved at once. With difficulty, litter-bearers were brought from the line nearby, and the general was placed upon the litter and carefully raised to the shoulder, I myself bearing one corner. A moment after, artillery from the Federal side was opened upon us. Great broadsides thundered over the woods. Hissing shells searched the dark thickets through, and shrapnel swept the road along which we moved.

"Two or three steps farther, and the litter-bearer at my side was struck and fell; but, as the litter turned, Major Watkins Leigh, of Hill's staff, happily caught it. But the fright of the men was so great that we were obliged to lay the litter and its burden down upon the road. As the litter-bearers ran to the cover of the trees, I threw myself by the general's side and held him firmly to the ground as he attempted to rise. Over us swept the rapid fire of shot and shell, grapeshot striking fire upon the flinty rock of the road all around us, and sweeping from their feet horses and men of the artillery just moved to the front.

"Soon the firing veered to the other side of the road, and I sprang to my feet, assisted the general to rise, passed my arm around him, and, with the wounded man's weight thrown heavily upon me, we forsook the road. Entering the woods, he sank to the ground from exhaustion; but the litter was soon brought, and, again rallying a few men, we essayed to carry him farther, when a second bearer fell at my side. This time, with none to assist, the litter careened, and the general fell to the ground with a groan of deep pain. Greatly alarmed, I sprang to his head, and, lifting his head as a stray beam of moonlight came through the clouds and leaves, he opened his eyes and wearily said, 'Never mind me, Captain; never mind me.'

"Raising him again to his feet, he was accosted by Brigadier General Pender: 'Oh, General, I hope you are not seriously wounded. I will have to retire my troops to reform them, they are so much broken by this fire.'

"But Jackson, rallying his strength, with firm voice said, 'You must hold your ground, General Pender. You must hold your ground, sir!' and so uttered his last command on the field.

"Again we resorted to the litter, and with difficulty bore it through the bush, and then under a hot fire along the road. Soon an ambulance was reached; and, stopping to seek some stimulant at ... Dowdall's Tavern [Melzi Chancellor's], we were found by Dr. McGuire, who at once took charge of the wounded man. Passing back over the battlefield of the afternoon, we reached the Wilderness [Tavern], and then, in a field on the north, the field-hospital of our corps under Dr. Harvey Black. Here we found a tent prepared, and after midnight the left arm was amputated near the shoulder, and a ball taken from the right hand."

Jackson came through the operation well, and it was believed he would make a good recovery. When General Lee received the news of what had happened, he exclaimed, "Thank God it is no worse!"

On the battlefield, the wounding of Jackson had been quickly followed by the disabling of his senior subordinate, A. P. Hill, whose shins were painfully bruised by a shell fragment. This devastating damage to the corps' command structure ended the effort to sever Hooker's communications with the Rappahannock, and the various units turned to reorganizing and to constructing defenses.

On the Union side, says William Swinton, "the operation of Jackson, resulting in the doubling up of Hooker's right, made important changes in the line indispensable: so during the night a new front was formed on that flank. . . . The Eleventh Corps was for a time out of the fight; but Reynolds' corps, which had up to this time been operating with Sedgwick on the left, below Fredericksburg, arrived that evening, and, with its firm metal, more than supplied the temporary loss. No idea was [as yet] entertained of retreating; and if Lee did not retire, it was evident that the morrow must bring with it a terrible struggle."

The night itself saw another struggle as Union General Sickles initiated a movement to improve his corps' position on Hooker's right. As narrated by Union soldier Warren Goss:

"Peering into the darkness, halting here and there to catch the faintest sound, the advancing line suddenly encountered the enemy. . . . A blinding flash illumined the darkness, and the terrible discharge of musketry resounded through the woods. The foes charged each other with mutual yells, cheers, and shouts. . . . The deep tones of the cannon marked time to the incessant roll of musketry. . . .

"The impossibility of giving orders in the darkness, among the tangled thickets, soon produced its effects. Brigades were broken into regiments, regiments into companies, and these into smaller groups, while friend and foe seemed confusedly playing a sanguinary game of hide-and-seek. . . . Friends encountered each other as enemies, and each mistook foes for friends."

Relates an unidentified Union private: "About a dozen of us got broken off as short as a pipe-stem from our regiment. . . . Matt Jenkins, a little corporal with a big voice, was the ranking man. . . . We were cautiously groping through the brushwood, where the occasional flash of musketry only made us all the blinder, when a blaze and the roar of a volley in our front showed us that we had encountered an enemy. Their shot, however, had pattered all around without injuring any of us.

"Our little corporal, with his big voice, which sounded all the world like a major-general's, shouted out, 'Reserve your fire, men!' and then gave orders to Captain *this* and Major *that* and Colonel *someone else*, as if he was in command of a brigade.

" 'Thunder!' said someone in the party we had encountered, 'you needn't make all that fuss. We'll surrender!' And then . . . about twenty of *our own company*, including the captain, came in and surrendered to Matt Jenkins!"

The chaotic operations continued for about an hour. In the end, surprisingly enough, Sickles found his position at least partially improved. Returning to narrator Warren Goss:

"The battle gradually died away, only blazing out here and there fitfully as little squads encountered each other in the tangled wilderness. . . . The moon now shone brightly, and the woods were strewn with dead and wounded, and the wearied contestants needed rest. Silence succeeded the dismal uproar and lurid lights of midnight battle."

The silence was not absolute. The whippoorwills could be heard again, and their sharp, doleful calls made an eerie mix with the anguished laments of the wounded. "Multitudes," says Union Lieutenant Jesse Bowman Young, "lay bleeding and dying between the lines where no help could be afforded them."

30

A Turbulent Sunday Morning

THE CAMPAIGN'S overall situation was now a curious one. Hooker had spent the past two days making serious mistakes, but they were still redeemable. Lee had acted with boldness and skill, but his situation was more precarious now than at the start. His gravely outnumbered army was in three segments. Early's division was facing Sedgwick at Fredericksburg. Jackson's corps was facing Hooker's right. (This corps was now under Jeb Stuart, the ranking general in the unit's zone of action.) The remainder of the army, under Lee himself, was facing Hooker's left. The two wings opposing Hooker were not in contact, a condition that could not be allowed to continue. Lee's next move (since he wasn't thinking in terms of retreating) must be to advance both wings and try to push Hooker back so that the wings could join flanks. Unknown to Lee, another problem was looming. Hooker had sent word for Sedgwick to carry Marye's Heights and march toward the rear of the wing under Lee's personal control.

The total number of troops under Lee and Stuart at Chancellorsville at dawn on Sunday, May 3, was probably less than 48,000, whereas Hooker had about 90,000. "The situation," says Northern soldier Warren Goss, "was by no means discouraging. . . . We still held the point where the roads converged at Chancellorsville . . . and from these converging roads as a pivot we could have directed a terrible blow upon either one or the other of [Lee's] severed wings . . . before they could be united."

The trouble was that Hooker felt he must keep three of his six

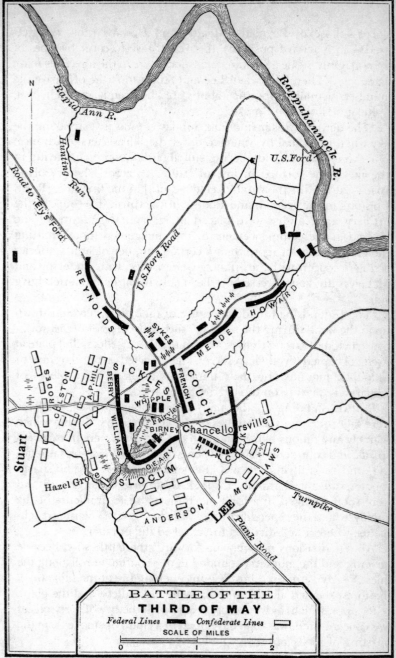

BATTLE OF THE
THIRD OF MAY
Federal Lines ▬▬ *Confederate Lines* ▭
SCALE OF MILES
0   1   2

RUSSELL & STRUTHERS, ENG'S, N.Y.

377

corps—those of Reynolds, Meade, and Howard (now reorganized)—in rearward positions, their chief task to cover his lines of retreat. Only Sickles, Slocum, and Couch were in the fore. (See map, page 377.) Therefore, when Lee and Stuart took the offensive the numbers actually opposing them were about equal to their own.

Relates Heros von Borcke:

"The dawn of this memorable Sunday . . . was just streaking the sky when I was sent by Stuart to order the skirmishers to advance, our three divisions, numbering still about 28,000 men, having in the meantime formed in line of battle . . . across the . . . plank road—A. P. Hill's [now under Henry Heth] in the first line, [R. E.] Colston's in the second, and Rodes's in the third. The bulk of the artillery and cavalry were placed in reserve, the nature of the ground at the commencement of the engagement not admitting the employment of more than a certain number of light batteries acting in concert with the infantry. General Lee, with Anderson and McLaws's divisions, pressed on the enemy from the Fredericksburg side. . . .

"The Federals had made good use of their time, having thrown up in the wood during the night . . . successive lines of breastworks, constructed of strong timber, and on the [Chancellorsville] plateau itself, occupied by their reserves, had erected a regular line of redoubts, mounted by their numerous artillery, forty pieces of which were playing on the narrow plank road. . . .

"Notwithstanding . . . the many disadvantages under which we were laboring, and the fatigues of the last few days, during which scarcely any rations had been given out, our men were in excellent spirits, and confident of success. [They all knew of Jackson's wounding, and the rallying cry was "Remember Jackson!"] The sharpshooters advanced rapidly through the dense undergrowth and were soon engaged in a lively skirmish with the tirailleurs of the enemy, whom they speedily drove to the first line of their entrenchments, where a well-directed fire checked the pursuers.

"All our divisions now moving forward, the battle soon became general, and the musketry sounded in one continued roll along the lines. Nearly a hundred hostile guns opening fire at the same time, the forest seemed alive with shot, shell, and bullets, and the plank road, upon which, as was before mentioned, the fire of forty pieces was concentrated, was soon enveloped in a cloud of smoke from the bursting of shells and the explosion of caissons.

"This road being our principal line of communication, and

crowded therefore with ambulances, ammunition-trains, and artillery, the loss of life soon became fearful, and dead and dying men and animals were strewing every part of it. How General Stuart and those few staff officers with him who had to gallop to and fro so frequently through this *feu infernal* escaped unhurt seems to me quite miraculous. Several of our couriers were wounded. One had a leg torn from his body by a cannon-ball while I was in the act of giving him some directions, and died soon afterwards. General Stuart had a horse killed under him in the first half-hour of the fight, and my own was twice wounded, first in the back by a musket-ball, and next in the chest by a piece of shell. . . . It was fortunately able to carry me through the day [but was actually fatally hurt].

"Stuart was all activity, and wherever the danger was greatest there was he to be found, urging the men forward and animating them by the force of his example. The shower of missiles that hissed through the air passed round him unheeded; and in the midst of the hottest fire I heard him, to an old melody, hum the words, 'Old Joe Hooker get out of the Wilderness.' "

At one time Stuart's left was hit by a counterattack made by

Hooker on the defensive

French's division of Couch's corps. One of the members of a brigade headquarters group stationed behind the attack was New England's Captain Samuel Fiske ("Dunn Browne").

"Our boys charged in splendid style through a thicket of tangled wood for half a mile or more, driving the enemy before them like chaff, slaying many, taking some prisoners, and fairly running over some and leaving them in our rear. Indeed, they [the bluecoats] charged with too much impetuosity and advanced so far that they were not properly supported on the flanks and were exposed to an enfilading fire of artillery as well as musketry.

"To halt our line and form it anew a little farther to the rear in the woods, I was sent forward by the general, together with a fine young friend, one of his aides—both on foot, as our horses were left behind as utterly impracticable in that thicket of undergrowth. We had separated, he to the right and I to the left; delivered our order to the colonels and assisted in executing it in the midst of a fire . . . from front and rear (our own artillery . . . occasionally dropped a shell among us) and both flanks. . . .

"I hastened to retrace my steps to report progress to the general. I was hindered some little time in picking up prisoners whom I didn't

Prisoners taken by Hooker's army.

like to leave with arms in their hands in the rear of our line. I would disarm and put them in squads of three or four, in charge of some one of our slightly wounded men . . . and then on again, till I had picked up some twenty or more of the 'Butternuts.'

"[I] had a couple of the fellows on my hands, and none of my own men in sight, and was hurrying them forward by the persuasion of a cocked revolver, expecting every moment to come upon our general—when all at once, pressing through a terribly dense portion of the undergrowth, I found myself face-to-face, at not twelve feet distance, with at least a whole regiment of the brownest and most ill-looking vagabonds that I ever set eyes on, every one of them with a gun in his hand. . . .

"Here was a big mouthful to swallow for a belligerent patriot, intent on squelching the rebellion, who had just gotten his blood up. . . . Here was a capital chance for a man, who had just gotten his hand in at the business of capturing prisoners, to put a thousand or fifteen hundred more in his bag—if they would only let him. . . .

"One of the impudent wretches he had captured a few minutes before turned round with a grin and says, 'Cap'en, I reckon things is different from the way they was; and you'll hev to 'low you're our prisoner now.'

"A very sensible remark of the young man, and timely, though he hadn't a shirt on his back, and only a part of a pair of pantaloons.

"Things *was* different from the way they were—with a vengeance. I gracefully lowered my pistol to an officer who stepped out from the ranks, and presented it to him . . . [with] the remark that 'doubtless it would be more disagreeable for a whole regiment to surrender to one man than for one man to surrender to a whole regiment.'

"The hard-hearted fellows didn't seem to care at all for my misfortune, and only laughed. . . . I was courteously treated, and sent at once to the rear. . . .

"We soon came upon other portions of the bloody field, and had to pick our steps among mangled corpses of friend and foe; past men without limbs, and limbs without men; now seeing a group of [Confederate] surgeons and assistants operating on the wounded under a tree, and now passing a group of ambulance-men carrying on a stretcher some groaning sufferer. Occasionally a wounded horse, struggling in his death agony, would kick at us; and occasionally a wounded secesh would mutter a curse as he saw the 'damned Yankee' pass. And in a little time we were far in the rear, and I was turned over to the care of the provost-marshal."

(Samuel Fiske was on his way to Libby Prison in Richmond. Exchanged in a short time, he returned to the army. A year later, during Grant's Wilderness Campaign, the contemplative, literate, and engaging captain was mortally wounded near the same spot where his capture had occurred.)

French's counterattack had been stalled for good, and, after what Von Borcke calls "a raging conflict, protracted for several hours, during which the tide of battle ebbed and flowed on either side," Stuart's men reached Hooker's advanced works.

W. L. Goldsmith, a junior officer in A. P. Hill's division, was one of the first to go over.

"Here I first saw hand-to-hand fighting. A young Federal soldier came at me with fixed bayonet. With sword in my right hand, I knocked up his musket and grabbed it with my left hand. The tussle was a fearful one; but George Kelly, a sergeant of Company D, shot and broke the Federal's thigh. The poor fellow fell, but continued to fight game. I could have cleaved his head with my sword, and Kelly started to brain him with his clubbed musket; but I forbade it, and called on my brave enemy to surrender . . . which he did."

According to Von Borcke, the taking of the outer works was only a partial success, for the enemy simply retired to a stronger set of works. Even the partial success "was only gained with a sad sacrifice of life, while countless numbers were seen limping and crawling to the rear.

"The woods had caught fire in several places from the explosion of shells—the flames spreading principally . . . over a space of several acres . . . where the ground was thickly covered with dry leaves; and here the conflagration progressed with the rapidity of a prairie fire, and a large number of Confederate and Federal wounded thickly scattered in the vicinity, and too badly hurt to crawl away, met a terrible death."

Shrill cries for help issued from the sea of flames and smoke, and a number of rescues were achieved by groups of Federals and Confederates, some of them working together. An unidentified Union private who, though wounded himself, formed a team with two Confederates, tells of an effort that failed:

"We were trying to rescue a young fellow in gray. The fire was all around him. The last I saw of that fellow was his face. It was a handsome face. His eyes were big and blue, and his hair, like raw silk, [was] surrounded by a wreath of fire; and then I heard him scream, 'O, Mother! O, God!'

Rescuing the wounded from the flames.

"It left me trembling all over like a leaf."

(Southerner John Casler was one of the men who, a few days later, was detailed to bury the victims of incineration. "We could see where they had tried to keep the fire from them by scratching the leaves away as far as they could reach. But it availed not; they were burnt to a crisp. The only way we could tell to which army they belonged was by turning them over and examining their clothing where they lay close to the ground. . . . We buried them all alike by covering them up with dirt where they lay. It was the most sickening sight I saw during the war, and I wondered whether the American people were civilized or not, to butcher one another in that manner; and I came to the conclusion that we were barbarians, North and South alike.")

The morning fight continued hottest in Jeb Stuart's zone of attack. Heros von Borcke says that the Federals, firmly settled in their stronger entrenchments, "now poured forth . . . a fire so terrible upon our advancing troops that the first two divisions staggered, and, after several unsuccessful efforts to press onward, fell back in considerable confusion. In vain was it that our officers used every effort to bring them forward once more. In vain even was it that Stuart, snatching the battle-flag of one of our brigades from the hands of the color-bearer and waving it over his head, called on them, as he rode forward, to follow him.

"Nothing could induce them again to face that tempest of bullets and that devastating hurricane of grape and canister vomited at close range from more than sixty pieces of artillery, and the advantages so dearly gained seemed about to be lost.

"At this critical moment we suddenly heard the yell of Rodes's division behind us, and saw these gallant troops ... charge over [our] front lines and fall upon the enemy. ... Their works were taken and they were driven ... from the woods to their redoubts on the [knolls] of Chancellorsville.

"A slight pause now intervened in the conflict, both sides, after the terrible work of the last few hours, being equally willing to draw breath awhile; and this gave us an opportunity to re-form our lines and close up our decimated ranks. The contest, meanwhile, was sustained by the artillery alone, which kept up a heavy cannonade; and, the nature of the ground being now more favorable, most of our batteries had been brought into action, while from a hill on our extreme right [Hazel Grove], which had ... been abandoned by the enemy ... twenty 12-pounder Napoleons played with a well-directed fire upon the enemy's works, producing a terrible effect upon their dense masses."

It may have been at this time that a notably freakish experience fell to one of the Union staff officers. Says an unidentified observer: "It was the funniest thing I saw. The concussion of a shell tore all his clothes off him, but didn't seem to hurt him any. He was running around almost stark naked trying to find his pocketbook."

General Hooker, headquartered at the Chancellor House, had spent the hours of battle on the porch facing southward toward the field, doing little but listen to the uproar and frown with anxiety. "I doubt," says second-in-command Darius Couch, "if any orders were given by him to the commanders ... unless, perhaps, 'to retire when out of ammunition.' None were received by me [on the left], nor were there any inquiries as to how the battle was going along my front. On the right flank, where the fighting was desperate, the engaged troops were governed by the corps and division leaders."

Requests came to Hooker for reinforcements and ammunition. To one solicitor, he replied, "I can't *make* men and ammunition." All the while, many thousands of troops, all well-armed, lay idle in the rear, their commanders fretful over not being called forward. Hooker's reasoning was that his lines of retreat had to be kept absolutely secure because his first responsibility was the protection of the Northern capital.

At about 9 A.M. Hooker was leaning against a pillar at the porch steps when he became a casualty. "Cannonballs [were] reaching me from both the east and the west, when a solid shot struck the pillar near me, splitting it in two and throwing one-half longitudinally against me, striking my whole right side, which soon turned livid. For a few moments I was senseless, and the report spread that I had been killed. But I soon revived, and, to correct the misapprehension, I insisted on being lifted upon my horse."

Hooker rode around to the back of the house just as General Couch, who'd heard the rumor that Hooker was dead, arrived in front. "The shattered pillar was there, but I could not find him or anyone else. Hurrying through the house, finding no one, my search was continued through the back yard. All the time I was thinking, 'If he is killed, what shall I do with this disjointed army?'

"Passing through the yard, I came upon him, to my great joy, mounted, and with his staff also in their saddles. Briefly congratulating him on his escape . . . I went about my own business. This was the last I saw of my commanding general in front. . . . He probably left the field soon after his hurt, but he neither notified me of his going nor did he give any orders to me whatever. . . . It was not then too late to save the day. . . . But it is a waste of words to write what might have been done."

There were still substantial numbers of Federal troops at the front holding firmly to their defenses, though virtually abandoned and continuing to suffer heavily from the enemy's artillery fire.

Confederate narrator Heros von Borcke resumes:

"About half-past ten we had news from General Lee informing us that, having been pressing steadily forward the entire morning, he had now, with Anderson's and McLaws's divisions, reached our right wing. I was at once dispatched by Stuart to the commander-in-chief to report the state of affairs and obtain his orders for further proceedings. I found him with our twenty-gun battery [on the Hazel Grove hill], looking as calm and dignified as ever, and perfectly regardless of the shells bursting round him, and the solid shot ploughing up the ground in all directions.

"General Lee expressed himself much satisfied with our operations, and entrusted me with orders for Stuart directing a general attack with his whole force, which was to be supported by a charge of Anderson's division on the left flank of the enemy."

It was only now that the female occupants of the Chancellor House, who had been cringing in the cellar, were evacuated. "One of the ladies fainted," says a Union officer. "It was a forlorn sight to see that troupe passing through our lines at such a time. Soon after they left, the house . . . took fire [the result of Confederate shell-bursts]."

Returning to the Confederate side and the seemingly omnipres-ent Von Borcke:

"With renewed courage and confidence our three divisions [Stuart's] now moved forward upon the enemy's strong position . . . encountering, as we emerged from the forest into the open opposite the plateau of Chancellorsville, such a storm of canister and bullets that for a while it seemed an impossibility to take the . . . [defenses] in the face of [the fire]. Suddenly we heard to our right, piercing the roar and tumult of the battle, the yell of Anderson's men, whom we presently beheld being hurled forward."

Elements of McLaws's division also took part in this assault. As narrated by D. Augustus Dickert of Kershaw's brigade:

"Here one of the bravest men in our regiment was killed, Private John Davis, of the 'Quitman Rifles.' He was reckless beyond all reason. He loved danger for danger's sake. Stepping behind a tree to load—he was on the skirmish line—he would pass out from this cover in plain view, take deliberate aim, and fire. Again and again he was entreated and urged by his comrades to shield himself, but in vain. A bullet from the enemy's sharpshooters killed him in-stantly. . . .

"The [Union] batteries in our front were now raking the matted brush all around and overhead, and their infantry . . . began pour-ing volleys into our advancing columns. . . . When near the turnpike road, General Kershaw gave the command to charge. . . .

"A perfect sea of fire was in our faces from the many cannon parked around the Chancellor House and graping in all directions but the rear. . . . Some of the pieces of the enemy's artillery were not more than fifty yards in our front, and the discharges seemed to blaze fire in our very ranks. Infantry, too, were massed all over the yard. And in rear of this one vast, mingling, moving body of hu-manity, dead horses lay in all directions, while the [enemy's] dead and wounded soldiers lay heaped and strewn with the living.

"But a few volleys from our troops in the road soon silenced all opposition from the infantry, while cannoneers were hitching up their horses to fly away. Some were trying to drag away their caissons and light pieces by hand, while thousands of bluecoats, with and without arms, were running for cover to the rear."

Again in Von Borcke's words:

"A more magnificent spectacle can hardly be imagined than that which greeted me when I reached the crest of the plateau and beheld, on this side, the long lines of our swiftly advancing troops stretching [right and left] as far as the eye could reach, their red flags fluttering in the breeze and their arms glittering in the morning sun; and, farther on, dense and huddled masses of the Federals flying in utter rout."

General Lee, according to his military secretary, Charles Marshall, "accompanied the troops in person. . . . The white smoke of musketry fringed the front of the line of battle, while the artillery on the hills in the rear of the infantry shook the earth with its thunder and filled the air with the wild shrieks of the shells that plunged into the masses of the retreating foe. To add greater horror and sublimity to the scene, the Chancellorsville House and the woods surrounding it were wrapped in flames.

"In the midst of this awful scene General Lee . . . rode to the front of his advancing battalions. His presence was the signal for one of those uncontrollable outbursts of enthusiasm which none can appreciate who have not witnessed them. The fierce soldiers, with their faces blackened with the smoke of battle, the wounded crawling with feeble limbs from the fury of the devouring flames, all seemed possessed with a common impulse. One long, unbroken cheer, in which the feeble cry of those who lay helpless on the earth blended with the strong voices of those who still fought, rose high above the roar of battle and hailed the presence of the victorious chief.

"He sat in the full realization of all that soldiers dream of . . . and as I looked upon him in the complete fruition of the success which his genius, courage, and confidence in his army had won, I thought that it must have been from some such scene that men in ancient days ascended to the dignity of gods.

"His first care was for the wounded of both armies, and he was among the foremost at the burning mansion where some of them lay.

"But at that moment, when the transports of his victorious troops were drowning the roar of battle with acclamations, a note was brought to him from General Jackson [who, lying in his hospital tent to the west, had been assessing the progress of the battle by its sounds]. It was brought to General Lee as he sat on his horse near the Chancellorsville House, and, unable to open it with his gauntleted hands, he passed it to me with directions to read it to him.

"The note . . . congratulated General Lee upon the great victory.

"I shall never forget the look of pain and anguish that passed over his face as he listened. With a voice broken with emotion he bade me say to General Jackson that the victory was his and that the congratulations were due to him. . . .

"I forgot the genius that won the day in my reverence for the generosity that refused the glory."

Von Borcke says that "the flight and pursuit took the direction of United States Ford, as far as about a mile beyond Chancellorsville, where another strong line of entrenchments offered their protection to the fugitives, and heavy reserves of fresh troops opposed our further advance."

But Lee was not ready to quit. John Esten Cooke explains that he "hastened to bring the Southern troops into order again, and succeeded in promptly reforming his line of battle. . . . His design was to press General Hooker and reap those rich rewards of victory to

Lee at Chancellorsville

which the hard fighting of the men had entitled them. Of the demoralized condition of the Federal forces there can be no doubt, and the obvious course now was to follow up their retreat and endeavor to drive them in disorder beyond the Rappahannock.

"The order to advance upon the enemy was about to be given when a messenger from Fredericksburg arrived at full gallop and communicated intelligence which arrested the order just as it was on Lee's lips."

31

Lee Clinches His Greatest Victory

I T WAS about eleven o'clock the previous night (Saturday, May 2) that Union General Sedgwick received Hooker's orders to carry Marye's Heights and advance upon Lee's rear at Chancellorsville. Sedgwick's command now numbered about 25,000. (It will be recalled that Hooker had summoned Reynolds' corps from Sedgwick's wing to reinforce the main army.) To oppose Sedgwick, Jubal Early had only about nine thousand men, and he was further handicapped in that he had no way of knowing that Marye's Heights would be the point of attack. His units were spread down the river to Hamilton's Crossing. Sedgwick, indeed, was positioned down that way, having come over the river at the spot Franklin had used in December.

As the Union van began working its way up the river toward Fredericksburg in the darkness, it was lightly opposed by Confederate skirmishers. Meanwhile, the Confederates on Lee's Hill were fueling rows of extra bivouac fires in an effort to make Sedgwick believe that reinforcements were moving in.

Among the Confederates bivouacked on Lee's Hill was General William Barksdale, whose brigade had performed so well against Burnside. Around midnight one of Barksdale's regimental commanders, Colonel B. G. Humphreys, came to consult with him. In the colonel's words:

"I found him wrapped in his war blanket, lying at the root of a tree.

" 'Are you asleep, General?'

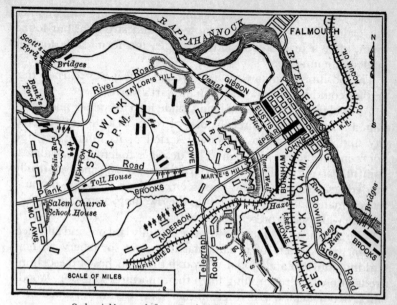

Sedgwick's attack from Fredericksburg to Salem Church.

" 'No, sir. Who could sleep with a million of armed Yankees all around him?' he answered gruffly.

"He then informed me that it was determined by General Early to hold Marye's Hill at all hazards; but that his brigade and a portion of the Washington Artillery had to do it."

Adds the Washington Artillery's adjutant, William Miller Owen:

"About 2 o'clock in the morning of May 3d Captain Miller, with the two guns of the third company, Washington Artillery, was ordered to take position on Marye's Hill. . . . Colonel Walton protested against this order, and told General Barksdale it was not right to send the guns to this exposed position when the supports were so meager—that on December 13 we were supported on Marye's Hill by the whole corps of Longstreet. The general insisted, and the guns were sent."

Switching to the Union side and to A. M. Stewart, the regimental chaplain from Pennsylvania:

"We found ourselves on Sabbath morning at dawn in the rear of that famous old city . . . Fredericksburg; and in the immediate front of those formidable rebel works from whence Burnside was so disastrously repulsed. . . . Our regiment, in company with another, was ordered forward to try their works and strength, but found them, after a brief and bloody struggle, too formidable for our inadequate numbers."

The position's flanks were also probed, but it was learned that neither could be turned. Again in Stewart's words:

"As final preparations were being made for a desperate and determined assault upon the rebel works, I rode back through the old city, and found it almost wholly deserted of its inhabitants; the doors and windows all open. The desolate quietness was almost painful. Passing on the lower skirts of the city, a long and beautifully shaded gravel carriage-way was seen, leading to a fine old and retired mansion. Riding along it to the dwelling, a strange, poetic, and fairy-like scene presented itself.

"The grounds and gardens were beautifully laid out and adorned with a great variety of ornamental trees and shrubbery, all now budding into leaf and bloom. Through the branches of these, hundreds of birds were carolling forth their morning songs. . . . Woodbines, honeysuckles, and roses, in their May freshness twined over the arbors, colonnades, and porticos; yet was there no sound of human voice or footsteps. Had superstition been a ruling feeling, it might have been taken for a place enchanted.

"The front door of the capacious old mansion stood open. I entered, and the sound of my footsteps and [hallooing] voice echoed strangely through the empty halls. The so late proud and luxuriant occupants all gone. . . .

"On the old stone steps I sat me down and tried to realize that it was the Sabbath—read a chapter, sang a psalm, and offered up a prayer for the speedy approach of peace founded upon righteousness."

While the chaplain tarried at the mansion, things were beginning to stir on the field between the opposing lines. As explained by Confederate narrator William Miller Owen:

"At 9:30 A.M. a flag of truce came out of the town and was met about one hundred yards in front of the stone wall by Captain Robert Brown of the Brown Rifles, and Sergeant-Major William Blake of Company K, 18th Mississippi Regiment. The enemy requested permission to take off their killed and wounded, but [were] . . . very properly refused. . . .

"It was noticed by Blake that the bearers of the flag peered intently at the foot of the hill where our infantry were, and our men would lift their heads above the stone wall, showing plainly how small their numbers were. This was just what the enemy wanted to discover, and, being satisfied, retired to their own lines. . . .

"At about ten o'clock, emboldened by the discovery of our weakness made under a flag of truce, the enemy suddenly appeared to spring out of the ground, in line of battle, from behind the ridge near the town. At the same time, thirty or forty guns opened upon our positions from the Stafford Heights. It was a beautiful sight, but a terrible one for us. On the columns charged with a rush, with loud shouts and yells."

One of the Union participants was Chaplain Stewart, who had rejoined his unit:

"Our regiment was on the left, and supporting the assaulting column. . . . In an instant the whole rebel works were in a blaze of fire, with a cloud of smoke, and from them a rain of leaden death was poured upon our advancing columns, and the earth strewn with the wounded and the dying, even as grass before the scythe of the mower. Yet on they pressed at a brisk run, with fixed bayonets, and none waiting to fire a gun. The flag of each regiment was proudly carried in front by its sturdy standard-bearer. When one of these fell, the emblem was snatched up by another, and still borne on.

"Still onward pressed the columns, each seemingly intent to be ahead and enter first the rebel works. Every yard of advance was strewn with the fallen. It was a moment of unutterable excitement. A lifetime seemed compressed into a few minutes. . . .

"The first line of earthworks [the stone wall] was reached. Our soldiers now, without any special attention to military order—the stronger having gotten ahead—scrambled, as a flock of sheep, up and over the embankment and bounded into the ditch, bayoneting or capturing its rebel occupants.

"Then, with a shout, the second line above was similarly carried in triumph; and finally, accompanied with tremendous cheers from the whole corps, the upper tier of works, with their batteries which had made such havoc in our ranks, were taken at the point of the bayonet."

The Washington Artillery's William Miller Owen was a distance from the scene of action at this time, but it was within his view. "Looking towards Marye's Hill, I saw it was crowded with the enemy. They had evidently overrun our small force. . . . I turned my horse's head towards Marye's Hill. . . . I was in a very belligerent state of mind. . . . For the first time we had lost guns in action."

Owen soon turned back, for there was nothing he could do. Chaplain Stewart goes on to say that "as soon as the old Stars and Stripes were seen to wave over the highest rampart, both officers and privates seemed wrought up to the highest possible human excitement. The feelings of many seemed too deep and strong even for cheers. . . . Scarcely an eye was dry. . . .

"I rode on horseback with our regiment till the last works were stormed and the firing ceased. Then, giving my horse in charge of a wounded soldier, I turned back over the field of mutilation and death. What a price at which to purchase a few earthen ditches!

". . . I busied myself in bringing into a right position this arm broken and bent under the fallen body; straightening that mangled leg; binding up the fractured head; tying a handkerchief or canteen cord above some jetting artery; turning into a more easy position this poor fellow, whose fountain of life was fast oozing out from a fatal wound; and all the while speaking such words of comfort, direction, and encouragement as the occasion and case suggested.

"During the morning I had obtained two bottles of wine from . . . the Lacy House, across the river. Having these in my pockets, a few spoonfuls were poured into the mouths of those seeming most faint. . . .

Stone wall after the assault

Capture of a Confederate gun on Marye's Heights

"So calmly did many of our dear young men lie in their last sleep that not a few were taken hold of, in order to arouse and assist, before becoming convinced that they were dead."

The greater part of Sedgwick's corps, with Jubal Early's forces pushed out of the way, was already on the march toward Lee's rear at Chancellorsville. As it happened, Lee's new enemy was a one-time friend. The two had served together in the United States Army, Lee then a colonel and Sedgwick a major. Lee still thought of his old friend as "Major Sedgwick."

Among the several Confederate horsemen from Fredericksburg who came looking for Lee to tell him what had happened was a young Mississippian known as "Brother William," who, operating unofficially, had the mistaken idea that he was riding ahead of all, that his mission was critical. A depiction of his arrival is given by artilleryman Robert Stiles, who was in Lee's immediate vicinity at the time:

"I was standing in the shade of a tree, near our guns, which had been ordered to draw out on the road, head of column to the rear, that is, toward Fredericksburg . . . when my attention was called to a

John Sedgwick

horseman coming at full speed from the direction in which we were [facing], and as he drew near I saw it was 'Brother William,' and that he was greatly excited.... His horse was reeking with sweat and panting from exertion.

"When his eye fell upon General Lee he made directly for him, and I followed as fast as I could. He dashed to the very feet of the commanding general ... and, gasping for breath, his eyes starting from their sockets, began to tell of dire disaster at Fredericksburg. Sedgwick had smashed Early and was rapidly coming on in our rear.

"I have never seen anything more majestically calm than General Lee was. I felt painfully the contrast between him and dear little Brother William. Something very like a grave, sweet smile began to express itself on the General's face; but he checked it, and, raising his left hand gently ... he interrupted the excited speaker ... at the same time saying very quietly, 'I thank you very much, but both you and your horse are fatigued and overheated. Take him to that shady tree yonder, and you and he blow and rest a little. I'm talking to General McLaws just now. I'll call you as soon as we are through.'

"... Brother William ... began a mild protest ... but he did not persist in it—he simply could not. He had already dismounted, and he started back with me to the tree, leading his horse.

"Unfortunately, I had none of General Lee's power over him, and he began to pour out to me his recital of disaster and prediction of ruin. All was lost below. Sedgwick had stormed the heights. . . . Early had been beaten and pushed roughly aside, and at least thirty thousand victorious troops were rapidly pressing on in our rear. . . . If not already too late, it very soon would be, to do anything even to *moderate* the calamity.

"In vain I suggested that General Lee could not be ignorant of all this; that his scouts had doubtless given him information; that General Early certainly would have found means to communicate with him; that Lee had beaten Hooker, and his calm and self-reliant bearing clearly indicated that he felt himself to be master of the entire situation.

"But Brother William would not be comforted or reassured. General Lee had not been upon the spot and could not know; *he* had been, and *did* know. The very calmness of the General showed he did not appreciate the gravity of the situation.

"While we were thus debating the matter, General Lee finished with McLaws, who at once started his division on the back-track to reinforce Early. . . . And, true to his promise, Marse Robert now called for Brother William, and, as he approached, greeted him with a smile, saying, 'Now what were you telling us about Major Sedgwick?'

"Brother William again told his tale of woe. . . . When he had finished, the General thanked him, saying again, 'I am very much obliged to you. The major is a nice gentleman. I don't think he would hurt us very badly. But we are going to see about him at once. I have just sent General McLaws to make a special call upon him.'"

Confederate narrator John Esten Cooke takes up:

"There was little to be feared now from General Hooker, large as the force still was under that officer. He was paralyzed for the time, and would not probably venture upon any attempt to regain possession of Chancellorsville. With General Sedgwick it was different. His column was comparatively fresh, was flushed with victory, and numbered . . . more than twenty thousand men. . . . It was thus necessary to defer the final blow at the main Federal army . . . to meet General Sedgwick. . . .

"[McLaws] moved speedily down the turnpike to check the enemy, and encountered the head of his column about halfway [to Fredericksburg], near Salem Church. General Wilcox, who [earlier] had been sent by Lee to watch Banks's Ford, had already moved to bar the Federal advance. When [McLaws] joined him, the whole force formed line of battle, a brisk action ensued, continuing from about four in the afternoon until nightfall, when the fighting ceased. . . . General Sedgwick made no further attempt to advance that day."

The long, violent Sunday was finally over. Sedgwick ended the day surprised and chagrined that Hooker, with numbers in abundance, had not come to his aid. At the same time, Hooker was angry with Sedgwick, whom he had expected to take Marye's Heights at earliest dawn so as to arrive behind Lee during the morning fighting at Chancellorsville. (Incredibly enough, Hooker later blamed Sedgwick for the campaign's failure.)

John Esten Cooke continues:

"On Monday morning, May 4, the theater of action on the southern bank of the Rappahannock presented a very remarkable complication. General Early had been driven from the ridge at Fredericksburg; but no sooner had General Sedgwick marched toward Chancellorsville than Early returned and seized upon Marye's Heights again. He was thus in General Sedgwick's rear, and ready to prevent him from recrossing the Rappahannock at Fredericksburg. Sedgwick meanwhile was moving to assail Lee's flank and rear, and Lee was ready to attack General Hooker in front.

"Such was the singular entanglement of the Northern and Southern forces on Monday morning after the Battle of Chancellorsville. What the result was to be the hours of that day were now to decide.

"Lee resolved first, if possible, to crush General Sedgwick, when it was his design to return and make a decisive assault upon General Hooker. In accordance with this plan, he on Monday morning went in personal command of three brigades of Anderson's division, reached the vicinity of Salem Church, and proceeded to form line of battle with the whole force there. [Jeb Stuart, with Jackson's corps and the cavalry, had been left facing Hooker.]

"Owing to unforeseen delays, the attack was not begun until late in the afternoon, when the whole line advanced upon General Sedgwick, Lee's aim being to cut him off from the river. In this he failed, the stubborn resistance of the Federal forces enabling them to hold their ground until night. At that time, however, they seemed to waver and lose heart. . . . They were now pressed by the Southern troops, and finally gave way."

As detailed by Pennsylvania's Chaplain Stewart:

"A retrograde movement—*retreat*—commenced, in order, if possible, to recross the river. The road to Fredericksburg, along which we had advanced, as well as the heights which had been taken with such bloodshed, were now effectually reoccupied by the rebels. But one way of escape was left, and that across a rough country, to Banks' Ford, five miles above Fredericksburg. . . .

"When the order to fall back was given, our regiment was in the extreme front, next the enemy. By some oversight of drunken generals, cowardly aides, or ignorant orderlies, we received no notice of the fact, nor any orders to fall back, and of course still maintained our position against the enemy.

"All the rest of the corps fell back at 9 P.M., while our regiment, at 11 P.M., was closely beset in the front, on the left, and in the rear by large masses of the rebels. . . . An impromptu council of war was at once held. . . .

"Our council . . . was terminated in a summary manner by the rapid approach of an overwhelming rebel force, whose long lines . . . seemed like dim rows of specters. When within easy range, a heavy volley of musketry was poured upon us, and, at the same time, a general shout, cheer, scream, or yell went up from the rebel ranks.

"This strange, curious, unearthly sound seems peculiar to Johnny Reb. The nearest transfer into print may be by 'Ki-*yi*—ki-*yi*—ki-*yi*,' with a vigorous screech on the '*yi*.' This, uttered in the darkness of night, amid the crash of firearms, and by a flushed and determined enemy, who, at the time, must have been thirty to our one, had, it must be confessed, somewhat of terror connected therewith. . . .

"A retreat was determined on. The rebels being in strong force in front, in our rear, and upon our left, but one possible way of escape was left, and that seemingly almost hopeless, through a cedar swamp, woods, and underbrush, over logs, fences and ditches— across fields, hills, and valleys, several miles to the Rappahannock, where a pontoon bridge was said to be constructed, but just where, none of us knew.

"Off we started, keeping as well together, and in as good order as the darkness and numerous obstructions, together with the shouts and volleys of a fast-pursuing enemy, would admit. Being myself mounted, it seemed a matter of special doubt whether a horse could, by any possibility, get through the way we were forced to go. As we struggled through the cedar swamp, several of my young friends, who were floundering along on foot, assured me that, if I expected to get away, I must dismount and abandon the horse. To this the generous animal seemed to have a decided objection. Getting into the spirit of the affair, she leaped over logs, fences, and ditches in a manner which would have done credit to a fox hunter.

"After a retreat worthy of Xenophon's descriptive pen, we rejoined our corps ere it crossed the river, [a movement effected] sometime between midnight and dawn."

This ended Sedgwick's part in the campaign. Again in the words of Southerner John Esten Cooke:

"On Tuesday morning Lee returned with his men toward Chancellorsville, and during the whole day was busily engaged in preparation for a decisive attack upon Hooker on the next morning."

But Hooker had determined to follow Sedgwick in retreat. The harried commander's final problem was not posed by Lee but by nature. As explained by Northern Lieutenant Jesse Bowman Young:

"On Tuesday night, May 5, a rainstorm set in which caused the river in the rear of the Union army to rise suddenly and threateningly. That night, one by one, the regiments . . . were withdrawn. Nobody was allowed to sleep. It was intimated in all directions: 'Boys, we are going to retreat again to our old camps at Falmouth. Keep wide awake, or you will be left behind.'

"Drenched to the skin, sinking into the mud at every step, the way barricaded by wagon trains and artillery and ambulances, the roads chock full of troops retreating step by step through the darkness and tempest, the weary army made its way through the woods . . . back toward the United States Ford. Here the pontoons had been broken by the rising river, and delays occurred in order to repair damages.

"The strain on the nerves of the boys under such circumstances can perhaps be imagined. No one wanted to awaken the suspicions or even draw the attention of the rebels. . . . The horrors of a night engagement and the danger of a panic must be avoided.

"Keeping their eyes turned toward the rear, watching lest the advancing [Confederate] skirmishers might suddenly open fire from the woods, grieved with unutterable sorrow that so many lives had been thrown away and an opportunity wasted that promised a great victory, and wondering when this cruel war would be over, the troops went through the mud and rain toward their old winter quarters."

Adds Union Private Warren Goss:

"They left behind their dead and [many of their] wounded, twenty thousand muskets, fourteen pieces of artillery, and their confidence in Hooker. Their loss in killed, wounded, and prisoners was 17,197 men [as opposed to Confederate losses of about thirteen thousand]. . . .

"Thus ended the campaign which Hooker opened as with a thunderbolt from the hand of Mars, and ended as impotently as an infant who has not learned to grasp his rattle."

32

The Stage Is Set for Gettysburg

FOR THE first few days after his arm was removed, Stonewall Jackson progressed nicely. He became strong enough to be transferred to a house near Guiney's Station, south of Fredericksburg. A gratified General Lee sent him cheerful messages, once informing a courier: "Give him my affectionate regards, and tell him to make haste and get well and come back to me as soon as he can. He has lost his left arm, but I have lost my right."

According to John Esten Cooke: "When the wound of the great soldier took a bad turn [he had contracted pneumonia] and it began to be whispered about that the hurt might prove fatal, Lee was strongly moved, and said with deep feeling, 'Surely General Jackson must recover! God will not take him from us, now that we need him so much. Surely he will be spared to us, in answer to the many prayers which are offered for him.' "

Mary Anna Jackson arrived at her husband's bedside on Thursday, May 7.

"Oh, the fearful change since I had last seen him! It required the strongest effort of which I was capable to maintain my self-control. When he left me on the morning of the 29th [only eight days earlier], going forth so cheerfully and bravely to the call of duty, he was in the full flush of vigorous manhood. . . . *Now*, his fearful wounds, his mutilated arm, the scratches upon his face, and, above all, the desperate pneumonia which was flushing his cheeks, oppressing his breathing, and benumbing his senses, wrung my soul. . . .

"From the time I reached him he was too ill to notice or talk much, and he lay most of the time in a semi-conscious state; but when aroused he recognized those about him, and consciousness would return. . . .

"Thinking it would cheer him more than anything else to see the baby in whom he had so delighted, I proposed several times to bring her to his bedside, but he always said, 'Not yet; wait till I feel better.'

". . . Friday and Saturday passed . . . bringing no favorable change to the dear sufferer; indeed, his fever and restlessness increased, and . . . he was growing perceptibly weaker. . . .

"Early on Sunday morning, the 10th of May, I was . . . told . . . that the doctors, having done everything that human skill could devise to stay the hand of death, had lost all hope. . . . The inevitable event . . . was now a question of only a few short hours. . . .

"I well knew that death to him was but the opening of the gates of pearl into the ineffable glories of heaven; but I had heard him say that, although he was willing and ready to die at any moment that God might call him, still he would prefer to have a few hours' preparation. . . . I therefore felt it to be my duty to gratify his desire. . . . I told him that before the day was over he would be with the blessed Saviour in His glory. With perfect distinctness and intelligence, he said, 'I will be an infinite gainer to be translated.'

". . . He said he had many things to say to me, but he was then too weak. Preferring to know his own desire as to the place of his burial, I asked him the question, but his mind was now growing clouded again. . . . I then asked him if he did not wish to be buried in Lexington, and he answered at once, 'Yes, Lexington, and in *my own plot*.' He had bought this plot himself when our first child died."

Mary Anna now had little Julia brought into the room. "He looked up, his countenance brightened with delight, and he never smiled more sweetly as he exclaimed, 'Little darling! Sweet one!' She was seated on the bed by his side; and, after watching her intently with radiant smiles for a few moments, he closed his eyes, as if in prayer. . . .

"Tears were shed over that dying bed by strong men who were unused to weep, and it was touching to see the genuine grief of his servant, Jim."

Dr. Hunter McGuire takes up:

"About half-past one he was told that he had but two hours to live, and he answered . . . feebly but firmly, 'Very good; it is all right.'

*Stonewall Jackson's daughter
as a bride. After bearing two
children, she died at age
twenty-seven.*

"A few moments before he died he cried out in his delirium, 'Order A. P. Hill to prepare for action! Pass the infantry to the front rapidly! Tell Major Hawks—' then stopped, leaving the sentence unfinished.

"Presently a smile . . . spread itself over his pale face, and he said quietly, and with an expression as if of relief, 'Let us cross over the river and rest under the shade of the trees.' "

Jackson's death stunned the entire Confederacy, and there was deep mourning even among people who knew him only through what they'd read and heard about him. Many Southerners wondered anxiously about the intentions of the Almighty in allowing this terrible thing to happen.

Even in the North, Jackson had his mourners; but, as stated candidly by General Oliver Howard: "Providentially for us, [Chancellorsville] was the last battle that he waged against the American Union. For, in bold planning, in energy of execution, which he had the power to diffuse, in indefatigable activity and moral ascendancy,

Jackson stood head and shoulders above his confreres, and after his death General Lee could not replace him."

The death of Jackson, then, was a plus for the Union in an otherwise fruitless campaign.

General Hooker, it must be noted, did not admit that the campaign was fruitless. Quite the contrary. As soon as his troops were safely back in their old camps, he sat down and composed a most remarkable address.

"The major-general commanding tenders to this army his congratulations on its achievements of the last seven days. If it has not accomplished all that was expected, the reasons . . . were of a character not to be foreseen or prevented by human sagacity or resource.

"In withdrawing from the south bank of the Rappahannock before delivering a general battle to our adversaries, the army has given renewed evidence of its confidence in itself. . . . On fighting at a disadvantage, we would have been recreant to our trust, to ourselves, our cause, and our country. . . . The Army of the Potomac will give or decline battle whenever its interest or honor may demand. . . .

"By your celerity and secrecy of movement, our advance . . . was undisputed; and, on our withdrawal, not a rebel ventured to follow.

"The events of last week may swell with pride the heart of every officer and soldier of this army. We have added new luster to its former renown. We have made long marches, crossed rivers, surprised the enemy in his entrenchments; and, wherever we have fought, have inflicted heavier blows than we have received. . . .

"We have no other regret than that caused by the loss of our brave companions, and in this we are consoled by the conviction that they have fallen in the holiest cause ever submitted to the arbitrament of battle."

Few of the soldiers were deceived by this address—and Washington certainly wasn't. When President Lincoln got the news of Hooker's retreat, he exclaimed, "My God, my God, what will the country say?"

Actually, the lamentations were less pronounced than they might have been. At least part of this was due to the fact that Hooker received a generally tolerant treatment among the war correspondents, who believed his reports that Lee had been fearfully hurt.

"Another such success to the rebels," wrote the *Boston Journal's* Charles Carleton Coffin, "would be a terrible disaster. They cannot long stand such an expenditure of blood. When the history of the war is written, it would not be strange if the Battle of Chancellorsville was reckoned about the most damaging blow thus far given the Confederacy."

More in keeping with the reality of the situation was Coffin's further assessment: "The country is not lost—or endangered, even—by this failure. There is no reason why men should lose heart or allow their hopes to go down. The struggle will not probably be decided by a great single victory—one grand triumph of arms, the annihilation of an army—but by powers of endurance. The party which can stand the pounding longest will win."

There were Southerners who shared this point of view, and it disturbed them, since they knew that a prolonged war would exhaust the South's resources.

(The concerns of thoughtful Southerners were compounded at this time by the news from the war's western theater. General Grant had begun to encircle fortress Vicksburg, key to control of the Mississippi River.)

Lee's triumph at Chancellorsville was a military masterpiece, yet it had really achieved nothing but to keep eastern affairs as they were—even as the Fredericksburg victory had done in December. The two armies continued to face each other across the Rappahannock. It was realized by Confederate leaders, both military and civil, that defensive victories, however spectacular, hadn't the capacity to speed the South toward independence; and it was now decided, with Lee in vigorous affirmation, that the time was right for another invasion of the North.

Such a move, it was understood, would be a gamble similar to that of the first invasion, the disappointments of which were well remembered. But Lee felt that this time he had a special edge. He had come to believe that his army, despite its numerical limitations and its problems with supply, was superior to any combination of troops the Union could place in its way. As for the primary concern of keeping the army in rations and fodder on the march: this was the time of year when the fertile farmlands of Maryland and Pennsylvania were nearing their days of bounty.

Other propitious considerations were that a move northward would draw the Army of the Potomac out of Virginia, that the Union might be startled into easing its pressure on Vicksburg, that the Peace Democrats would be given a new issue to use against Lincoln, and that England and France might yet be persuaded—

particularly if Lee achieved a victory on Northern soil—that the Confederacy deserved their recognition.

All in all, the risks of a new invasion seemed well worth taking, and Lee turned at once to forming his plans.

Events were now gravitating toward the fateful Battle of Gettysburg.

Quotation Sources

Abbott, John S. C. *The History of the Civil War in America*. 2 vols. Springfield, Mass.: 1863–1865.

Annals of the War. Philadelphia: The Times Publishing Company, 1879.

Battles and Leaders of the Civil War. 4 vols. Robert Underwood Johnson and Clarence Clough Buel (eds.). New York: The Century Co., 1884–1888.

Blake, Henry N. *Three Years in the Army of the Potomac*. Boston: Lee and Shepard, 1865.

Buell, Augustus. *The Cannoneer: Recollections of Service in the Army of the Potomac*. Washington, D.C.: The National Tribune, 1890.

Caldwell, J. F. J. *The History of a Brigade of South Carolinians*. Philadelphia: King & Baird. 1866. Facsimile edition by Morningside Bookshop, Dayton, Ohio, 1974.

Carpenter, F. B. *The Inner Life of Abraham Lincoln*. New York: Hurd and Houghton, 1868.

Casler, John O. *Four Years in the Stonewall Brigade*. James I. Robertson, Jr. (ed.). Dayton, Ohio: Morningside Bookshop, 1971. Facsimile of 1906 edition.

Coffin, Charles Carleton. *The Boys of '61*. Boston: Estes and Lauriat, 1884.

————. *Drum-Beat of the Nation*. New York: Harper & Brothers, 1888.

————. *Following the Flag*. Boston: Estes and Lauriat, 1865.

————. *Marching to Victory*. New York: Harper & Brothers, 1889.

————. *Stories of Our Soldiers*. Boston: The Journal Newspaper Company, 1893.

Cooke, John Esten. *The Life of Stonewall Jackson*. Freeport, N.Y.: Books for Libraries Press, 1971. First published in 1863.

————. *Stonewall Jackson: A Military Biography*. New York: D. Appleton and Company, 1866.

————. *Robert E. Lee*. New York: G. W. Dillingham Co., 1899.

————. *Wearing of the Gray*. New York: E. B. Treat & Co., 1867.

Crotty, D. G. *Four Years Campaigning in the Army of the Potomac*. Grand Rapids, Mich.: Dygert Bros. & Co., 1874.

Curtis, Newton Martin. *From Bull Run to Chancellorsville*. New York: G. P. Putnam's Sons, 1906.

Dabney, R. L. *Life and Campaigns of Lieut.-Gen. Thomas J. Jackson*. New York: Blelock & Co., 1866.

Davis, Varina Howell. *Jefferson Davis: A Memoir by His Wife*. 2 vols. New York: Belford Company, Publishers, 1890.

De Trobriand, P. Regis. *Four Years with the Army of the Potomac*. Boston: Ticknor and Company, 1889.

Dickert, D. Augustus. *History of Kershaw's Brigade*. Dayton, Ohio: Morningside Bookshop, 1976. Facsimile of 1899 edition.

Doubleday, Abner. *Chancellorsville and Gettysburg, Campaigns of the Civil War*, vol. 6. New York: Charles Scribner's Sons, 1882.

Draper, William F. *Recollections of a Varied Career*. Boston: Little, Brown, and Company, 1908.

Duyckinck, Evert A. *National History of the War for the Union*. 3 vols. New York: Johnson, Fry and Company, 1868.

Ellis, Thomas T. *Leaves from the Diary of an Army Surgeon*. New York: John Bradburn, 1863.

[Fiske, Samuel]. *Mr. Dunn Browne's Experiences in the Army*. Boston: Nichols and Noyes, 1866.

Gates, Theodore B. *The War of the Rebellion*. New York: P. F. McBreen, Printer, 1884.

Gerrish, Theodore. *Army Life: A Private's Reminiscences of the Civil War*. Portland, Me.: Hoyt, Fogg & Donham, 1882.

————— and Hutchinson, John S. *The Blue and the Gray*. Portland, Me.: Hoyt, Fogg & Donham, 1883.

Gordon, John B. *Reminiscences of the Civil War*. New York: Charles Scribner's Sons, 1904.

Goss, Warren Lee. *Recollections of a Private*. New York: Thomas Y. Crowell & Co., 1890.

Greeley, Horace. *The American Conflict*. 2 vols. Hartford: O. D. Case & Company, 1864, 1867.

Hill, A. F. *Our Boys: The Personal Experiences of a Soldier in the Army of the Potomac*. Philadelphia: The Keystone Publishing Co., 1890.

Jackson, Mary Anna. *Memoirs of Stonewall Jackson*. Louisville, Ky.: The Prentice Press, 1895.

Johnston, Joseph E. *Narrative of Military Operations*. New York: D. Appleton and Company, 1874.

Jones, J. William. *Personal Reminiscences, Anecdotes, and Letters of Gen. Robert E. Lee*. New York: D. Appleton and Company, 1874.

King, W. C., and Derby, W. P. *Campfire Sketches and Battlefield Echoes*. Springfield, Mass.: W. C. King & Co., 1887.

Lee, Captain Robert E. *Recollections and Letters of General Robert E. Lee*. New York: Doubleday, Page & Company, 1904.

Lee, Fitzhugh. *General Lee of the Confederate Army*. London: Chapman and Hall, Ltd., 1895.

Livermore, Mary A. *My Story of the War*. Hartford: A. D. Worthington and Company, 1889.

Loehr, Charles T. *War History of the Old First Virginia Infantry Regiment*. Dayton, Ohio: Morningside Bookshop, 1970. First published in 1884.

Lusk, William Thompson. *War Letters*. New York: Privately printed, 1911.

McClellan, George B. *McClellan's Own Story*. New York: Charles L. Webster & Company, 1887.

McClellan, H. B. *The Life and Campaigns of Major-General J. E. B. Stuart*. Boston: Houghton, Mifflin & Company, 1885.

McClure, A. K. *Abraham Lincoln and Men of War Times*. Philadelphia: The Times Publishing Company, 1892.

————. *Recollections of Half a Century*. Salem, Mass.: The Salem Press Company, 1902.

[McGuire, Judith W.]. *Diary of a Southern Refugee During the War*. New York: E. J. Hale & Son, 1867.

Moore, Frank (ed.). *The Civil War in Song and Story*. New York: P. F. Collier, 1889.

————. *The Rebellion Record*, vols. 2, 5, and 6. New York: G. P. Putnam, 1862 and 1863.

Neese, George M. *Three Years in the Confederate Horse Artillery*. New York and Washington: The Neale Publishing Co., 1911.

Oates, William C. *The War Between the Union and the Confederacy*. New York: The Neale Publishing Co., 1905.

Opie, John N. *A Rebel Cavalryman with Lee, Stuart, and Jackson*. Dayton, Ohio: Morningside Bookshop, 1972. Facsimile of 1899 edition.

Our Women in the War. Charleston, S.C.: News and Courier Book Presses, 1885.

Owen, William Miller. *In Camp and Battle with the Washington Artillery*. Boston: Ticknor and Company, 1885. Second edition by Pelican Publishing Company, New Orleans, 1964.

Palfrey, Francis Winthrop. *Antietam and Fredericksburg, Campaigns of the Civil War*, vol. 5. New York: Charles Scribner's Sons, 1882.

Pollard, Edward A. *The Early Life, Campaigns, and Public Services of Robert E. Lee; with a Record of the Campaigns and Heroic Deeds of His Companions in Arms*. New York: E. B. Treat & Co., 1871.

————. *The Lost Cause*. New York: E. B. Treat & Co., 1866.

————. *The Second Year of the War*. New York: Charles B. Richardson, 1864.

Pryor, Mrs. Roger A. *Reminiscences of Peace and War*. New York: The Macmillan Company, 1904.

[Putnam, Sarah A.]. *Richmond During the War*. New York: G. W. Carleton & Co., 1867.

Smith, James Power. *With Stonewall Jackson in the Army of Northern Virginia.* (Southern Historical Society Papers.) Richmond, Va.: B. F. Johnson, 1920.

Stevens, George T. *Three Years in the Sixth Corps.* New York: D. Van Nostrand, 1870.

Stewart, A. M. *Camp, March and Battle-Field.* Philadelphia: Jas. B. Rodgers, 1865.

Stiles, Robert. *Four Years Under Marse Robert.* New York and Washington: The Neale Publishing Company, 1903.

Stine, J. H. *History of the Army of the Potomac.* Philadelphia: J. B. Rodgers Printing Co., 1892.

Swinton, William. *Campaigns of the Army of the Potomac.* New York: Charles Scribner's Sons, 1882.

————. *The Twelve Decisive Battles of the War.* New York: Dick & Fitzgerald, 1867.

Tarbell, Ida M. *The Life of Abraham Lincoln.* 2 vols. New York: McClure, Phillips & Co., 1902.

Taylor, Walter H. *Four Years with General Lee.* New York: D. Appleton and Company, 1878.

Tenney, W. J. *The Military and Naval History of the Rebellion.* New York: D. Appleton & Company, 1865.

The War of the Rebellion: A Compilation of the Official Records of the Union and Confederate Armies. Washington, D.C.: U.S. Government Printing Office, 1880–1901.

Tomes, Robert. *The Great Civil War.* 3 vols. New York: Virtue and Yorston, 1862.

Under Both Flags: A Panorama of the Great Civil War. Chicago: W. S. Reeve Publishing Co., 1896.

Von Borcke, Heros. *Memoirs of the Confederate War for Independence.* 2 vols. New York: Peter Smith, 1938. Reprint of 1866 edition.

Walker, Francis A. *History of the Second Army Corps in the Army of the Potomac.* New York: Charles Scribner's Sons, 1886.

Wallace, Francis B. *Memorial of the Patriotism of Schuylkill County in the American Slaveholder's Rebellion.* Pottsville, Pa.: Benjamin Bannan, 1865.

Wheeler, Richard. *Sword Over Richmond.* New York: Harper & Row, 1986.

————. *Voices of the Civil War.* New York: Thomas Y. Crowell Company, 1977.

————. *We Knew Stonewall Jackson.* New York: Thomas Y. Crowell Company, 1977.

Young, Jesse Bowman. *What a Boy Saw in the Army.* New York: Hunt & Eaton, 1894.

Supplementary References

Angle, Paul M., and Miers, Earl Schenck. *Tragic Years, 1860–1865*. 2 vols. New York: Simon and Schuster, 1960.

Billings, John D. *Hardtack and Coffee*. Boston: George M. Smith & Co., 1889.

Blackford, W. W. *War Years with Jeb Stuart*. New York: Charles Scribner's Sons, 1945.

Catton, Bruce. *The Army of the Potomac: Glory Road*. Garden City, N.Y.: Doubleday & Company, Inc., 1962.

————. *The Army of the Potomac: Mr. Lincoln's Army*. Garden City, N.Y.: Doubleday & Company, Inc., 1962.

————. *Never Call Retreat*. Garden City, N.Y.: Doubleday & Company, Inc., 1965.

————. *Terrible Swift Sword*. Garden City, N.Y.: Doubleday & Company, Inc., 1963.

Commager, Henry Steele. *The Blue and the Gray*. Indianapolis and New York: The Bobbs-Merrill Company, Inc., 1950.

Cullen, Joseph P. *Where a Hundred Thousand Fell*; Historical Handbook No. 39. Washington, D.C.: U.S. Government Printing Office, 1966.

Davis, Burke. *Jeb Stuart the Last Cavalier*. New York: Rinehart & Company, Inc., 1957.

Davis, Jefferson. *The Rise and Fall of the Confederate Government*, vol. 2. South Brunswick, N.J.: Thomas Yoseloff, 1958. Reprint of edition by D. Appleton and Company, 1881.

Douglas, Henry Kyd. *I Rode with Stonewall*. Chapel Hill, N.C.: University of North Carolina Press, 1940.

Early, Jubal Anderson. *War Memoirs*. Edited by Frank E. Vandiver. Bloomington, Indiana: Indiana University Press, 1960. First published in 1912.

Edmonds, S. Emma E. *Nurse and Spy in the Union Army*. Hartford: W. S. Williams & Co., 1865.

Eggleston, George Cary. *A Rebel's Recollections*. New York: Kraus Reprint Co., 1969. Reprint of 1905 edition.

English, William H. *Life and Military Career of Winfield Scott Hancock*. Philadelphia: J. C. McCurdy & Co., 1880.

Evans, Clement A., ed. *Confederate Military History*. 12 vols. New York, London, Toronto: Thomas Yoseloff, 1962. Facsimile publication of 1899 edition by the Confederate Publishing Company of Atlanta.

Freeman, Douglas Southall. *Lee's Lieutenants*, vols. 2 and 3. New York: Charles Scribner's Sons, 1943–44.

Glazier, Willard. *Battles for the Union*. Hartford, Conn.: Dustin, Gilman & Co., 1875.

————. *Three Years in the Federal Cavalry*. New York: R. H. Ferguson & Company, 1874.

Gragg, Rod. *The Illustrated Confederate Reader*. New York: Harper & Row, 1989.

Guernsey, Alfred H., and Alden, Henry M. *Harper's Pictorial History of the Great Rebellion*. 2 vols. Chicago: McDonnell Bros., 1866, 1868.

Hancock, Ada. *Reminiscences of Winfield Scott Hancock*. New York: Charles L. Webster & Company, 1887.

Hansen, Harry. *The Civil War*. New York: Bonanza Books, 1962.

Harper's Encyclopaedia of United States History. 10 vols. New York: Harper & Brothers, 1915.

Hart, Albert Bushnell, ed. *American History Told by Contemporaries*, vol. 4. New York: The Macmillan Company, 1910.

Headley, J. T. *The Great Rebellion*. 2 vols. Hartford: Hurlbut, Williams & Company, 1863, 1866.

Henderson, G. F. R. *The Campaign of Fredericksburg*. Falls Church, Va.: Confederate Printers, 1984.

————. *Stonewall Jackson and the American Civil War*. 2 vols. London: Longman's, Green, and Co., 1913.

Holland, J. G. *The Life of Abraham Lincoln*. Springfield, Mass.: Gurdon Bill, 1866.

Holstein, Anna M. *Three Years in Field Hospitals of the Army of the Potomac*. Philadelphia: J. B. Lippincott & Co., 1867.

Johnson, Rossiter. *Campfires and Battlefields*. New York: The Civil War Press, 1967. First published in 1894.

Jones, John B. *A Rebel War Clerk's Diary*. Edition condensed, edited, and annotated by Earl Schenck Miers. New York: Sagamore Press, Inc., 1958. First published in 1866.

Jones, Katharine M. *Ladies of Richmond*. Indianapolis and New York: The Bobbs-Merrill Company, Inc., 1962.

Logan, John A. *The Great Conspiracy*. New York: A. R. Hart & Co., 1886.

Long, E. B. (With Barbara Long). *The Civil War Day by Day*. Garden City, N.Y.: Doubleday & Company, Inc., 1971.

Longstreet, James. *From Manassas to Appomattox*. Millwood, N.Y.: Kraus Reprint Co., 1976. First published in 1896.

Lossing, Benson J. *Pictorial Field Book of the Civil War*. 3 vols. New York: T. Belknap & Company, 1868.

Luvaas, Jay, and Nelson, Harold W. *The U.S. Army War College Guide to the Battle of Antietam*. New York: Harper & Row, 1988.

————. *The U.S. Army War College Guide to the Battles of Chancellorsville & Fredericksburg*. New York: Harper & Row, 1989.

McCarthy, Carlton. *Detailed Minutiae of Soldier Life in the Army of Northern Virginia 1861–1865*. Richmond: Carlton McCarthy and Company, 1884.

McGuire, Hunter. *Address Delivered on 23d Day of June, 1897, at the Virginia Military Institute*. Lynchburg, Va.: J. P. Bell Company, 1897.

Mitchell, Joseph B. *Decisive Battles of the Civil War*. New York: G. P. Putnam's Sons, 1955.

Morton, Joseph W., Jr., ed. *Sparks from the Camp Fire*. Philadelphia: Keystone Publishing Co., 1892.

Nichols, G. W. *A Soldier's Story of His Regiment*. Kennesaw, Ga.: Continental Book Company, 1961. Facsimile of 1898 edition.

Owens, John Algernon. *Sword and Pen*. Philadelphia: P. W. Ziegler & Company, 1883.

Page, Thomas Nelson. *Robert E. Lee, Man and Soldier*. New York: Charles Scribner's Sons, 1911.

Paris, the Comte de (L. P. d'Orleans). *History of the Civil War in America*. 4 vols. Philadelphia: Jos. H. Coates & Co., 1875–88.

Pennypacker, Isaac R. *General Meade*. New York: D. Appleton and Company, 1901.

Pickett, George E. *The Heart of a Soldier*. New York: Seth Moyle, Inc., 1913.

Pinkerton, Allan. *The Spy of the Rebellion*. New York: G. W. Carleton & Co., 1883.

Ropes, John Codman. *The Army Under Pope, Campaigns of the Civil War*, vol. 4. New York: Charles Scribner's Sons, 1881.

Sears, Stephen W. *Landscape Turned Red*. New Haven, CT: Ticknor & Fields, 1983.

Selby, John. *Stonewall Jackson as Military Commander*. Princeton, N. J.: D. Van Nostrand Company, Inc., 1968.

Smart, James G., ed. *A Radical View: The "Agate" Dispatches of Whitelaw Reid, 1861–1865*. 2 vols. Memphis, Tennessee: Memphis State University Press, 1976.

Stackpole, Edward J. *Chancellorsville: Lee's Greatest Battle*. Harrisburg, Pa.: The Stackpole Company, 1958.

Stephenson, Nathaniel W. *The Day of the Confederacy*. New Haven: Yale University Press, 1920.

Stern, Philip Van Doren. *Robert E. Lee, the Man and the Soldier*. New York: Bonanza Books, 1963.

Stowe, Harriet Beecher. *Men of Our Times*. Hartford: Hartford Publishing Co., 1868.

Symonds, Craig L. *A Battlefield Atlas of the Civil War*. Baltimore: The Nautical & Aviation Publishing Co. of America, 1983.

Tate, Allen. *Stonewall Jackson the Good Soldier*. New York: Minton, Balch & Company, 1928.

Thomas, Emory M. *Bold Dragoon: The Life of J. E. B. Stuart*. New York: Harper & Row, 1986.

Thomason, John W., Jr. *Jeb Stuart*. New York: Charles Scribner's Sons, 1930.

Tilberg, Frederick. *Antietam*, Historical Handbook No. 31. Washington, D.C.: U.S. Government Printing Office, 1961.

Truesdale, John, ed. *The Blue Coats*. Philadelphia: Jones Brothers & Co., 1867.

Webb, Willard, ed. *Crucial Moments of the Civil War*. New York: Bonanza Books, 1961.

Wilkes, George. *McClellan: From Ball's Bluff to Antietam*. New York: Sinclair Tousey, 1863.

Williams, T. Harry. *Lincoln and His Generals*. New York: Alfred A. Knopf, Inc., 1952.

Wilson, John Laird. *Pictorial History of the Great Civil War*. Philadelphia: National Publishing Company, 1881.

Wood, William. *Captains of the Civil War*. New Haven: Yale University Press, 1921.

Worsham, John H. *One of Jackson's Foot Cavalry*. Edited by James I. Robertson, Jr. Jackson, Tennessee: McCowat-Mercer Press, Inc., 1964.

Wright, Mrs. D. Giraud. *A Southern Girl in '61: The Wartime Memories of a Confederate Senator's Daughter*. New York: Doubleday, Page & Company, 1905.

Index

Abbott, Henry L. J., 255
Abbott, John S. C., 52
Acquia Creek, VA: Burnside's base at, 232, 233
Alexander, E. Porter, 236, 293, 295
Allen, Richard, 123
Ames, John W., 300–305, 306–7
Anderson, Richard H.
  at Antietam/Sharpsburg, 95
  and the Chancellorsville battle, 358, 363, 378, 385, 386, 398–99
  and the Fredericksburg battle, 241
Antietam, battle of
  aftermath of the, 155–70
  beginning of the, 102–15
  burying the dead at the, 142–43
  casualties at the, 145
  civilians at the, 110–11, 143–44
  and the Emancipation Proclamation, 153
  foraging during the, 198
  horrors of the, 145–49
  and intelligence reports, 141
  Lee's withdrawal from the, 140–54
  and Lincoln's tour of the battlefield, 160
  and the Lower Bridge fight, 131–39
  McClellan's views of the, 152–53, 204
  and morale, 141, 158
  Peninsula Campaign compared with the, 147

preparation for the, 89–92, 93–101
and the sunken road fight, 116–30, 146
Army of the Cumberland, 323–24
Army of the Potomac
  Burnside appointed commander of the, 201–5
  Burnside relieved of command of the, 336
  Confederate Army compared with the, 160–62
  desertions from the, 340
  and disease, 159
  Hooker appointed commander of the, 336
  Lincoln's visits to the, 153–54, 160, 350–51
  McClellan as commander of the, 4, 33
  McClellan relieved of command of the, 201–5
  morale of the, 90, 158–59, 339–44, 389
  pay for soldiers in the, 162–63
  recruiting for the, 162
  reorganizations of the, 1, 34–35, 207, 339–41
  at Rockville, 33–35
  and the winter camp of 1862–63, 313–16, 318, 319–20, 323–24, 337–44
Ashby's Gap, 192, 194, 195
Ashland, VA, 229

417